CLASS:
IMAGE AND REALITY

by the same author

THE EXPLOSION OF BRITISH SOCIETY 1914–1962 (Pan Books, London, 1963)
Revised and expanded edition: *The Explosion of British Society 1914–1970* (Macmillan, London, 1971)

CLIFFORD ALLEN: THE OPEN CONSPIRATOR (Oliver and Boyd, Edinburgh, 1964)

THE DELUGE: BRITISH SOCIETY AND THE FIRST WORLD WAR (Bodley Head, London, 1965; Little Brown, Boston, 1966; Penguin Books, London, 1967; Norton Library, New York, 1969; New Edition, Macmillan, London, 1973)

BRITAIN IN THE CENTURY OF TOTAL WAR: WAR, PEACE AND SOCIAL CHANGE 1900–1967 (Bodley Head, London and Little Brown, Boston, 1968; Penguin Books, London, 1970)

THE NATURE OF HISTORY (Macmillan, London, 1970; Knopff, New York, 1971; Delta Paperback (USA) 1973)

WAR AND SOCIAL CHANGE IN THE TWENTIETH CENTURY (Macmillan, London, 1974)

THE HOME FRONT: THE BRITISH AND THE SECOND WORLD WAR (Thames and Hudson, London, 1976; paperback reprint 1978)

WOMEN AT WAR 1914–1918 (Croom Helm and Fontana, London, 1977)

CLASS

IMAGE AND REALITY
IN BRITAIN, FRANCE AND
THE USA SINCE 1930

ARTHUR MARWICK

COLLINS
ST JAMES'S PLACE, LONDON
1980

William Collins Sons and Co Ltd
London · Glasgow · Sydney · Auckland
Toronto · Johannesburg

First published 1980
© Arthur Marwick 1980
ISBN 0 00 216199 0

Set in Monophoto Times
by MS Filmsetting Ltd, Frome, Somerset
Made and Printed in Great Britain by William Collins
Sons and Co Ltd, Glasgow

CONTENTS

PREFACE   9

INTRODUCTION   11
1 Class: Image and Reality   11

PART ONE *As it Was: the Thirties*   25
2 The Historical Context of Class   27
3 Academic Images of Class   44
4 Official Images of Class   59
5 Unofficial and Private Images in Britain   79
6 Unofficial and Private Images in the USA   98
7 Unofficial and Private Images in France   128
8 Hollywood Images of Class   143
9 BBC and Other Media Images of Class   157
10 The Realities of Class   172

PART TWO *As it Became: from the Second World
         War to the Present*   211
11 The Second World War and Class: the Case of Britain   213
12 The Second World War and Class in France and the
     USA   231
13 Image and Reality of Class in Post-war Society   256
14 The Cultural Revolution and the New Historical Context   290
15 Images of Class Today   305
16 Inequality, Distinctions and the Significance of Class   340

CONCLUSION   359
17 Convergence and 'National Character'   359

APPENDIX   365
BIBLIOGRAPHY   377
INDEX   401

'Now just one thing I beg of you, don't use that word proletariat in talking with me or of me. My gorge rises at it. I do not think in terms of socialism, in terms of class consciousness.'

(*Samuel Gompers*, American labour leader, 1919)

'The word "class" is fraught with unpleasing associations, so that to linger upon it is apt to be interpreted as the symptom of a perverted mind and a jaundiced spirit.'

(*R. H. Tawney*, British historian and educationist, 1931)

'Classes are not only a reality . . . they are also, to a certain extent, myths.'

(*Maurice Duverger*, French historian and political scientist, 1955)

'Revolution is inevitable, in France, in Western Europe, and even in the Soviet Union . . . because these societies are still class societies.'

(*Teng Hsiao-ping*, deputy Prime Minister of China, 1975)

PREFACE

My first and biggest debt must be to the archivists and librarians in the many archives, British, American and French, listed in my bibliography and at the end of Chapter 8, who were not only consistently courteous and helpful, but never failed to respond constructively to my surprising determination to pursue what I called 'images of class'. For valued advice, and help of many kinds, I would wish to thank Mr Jeremy Boulton, Miss Anne Fleming, Mr Ian Thomson, Mr Malcolm Terris, Mr Henry Cowper, Dr Stuart Samuels, Dr David Culbert, Professors Dan Leab, Marc Ferro, Francois Bédarida, Jean-Noel Jeanneney, Patrick Fridenson, Bentley B. Gilbert, Harold Perkin and Douglas Johnson, Mr David Reilly, Professor Dana F. White, Dr Darlene Roth-White, Lord Fraser of Kilmacorra, and Lord Morrison of Hampstead. Drafts of my book were read, and most helpfully commented on, by John Raynor, Clive Emsley, Tony Aldgate and Bernard Waites. Peggy Mackay typed the first draft and parts of later drafts; Karen Smith prepared the final complex version for publication: my deep thanks to both. The proofs were read by Maggie Smales and Caroline Harvey.

For granting access to, and permitting me to quote from, copyright materials acknowledgements are due to: the Keeper of the Public Records and the Controller of Her Majesty's Stationery Office for Crown Copyright material; the Archivist of the United States; the Director and Trustees of the Imperial War Museum, London; the Centre de Documentation Syndicale of the Sorbonne; the Institut Nationale d'Histoire Sociale of the National Archives, Paris; the British Library of Political and Economic Science; the British Broadcasting Corporation Written Archives Centre; the Centre for Military Archives, King's College, London, and Lady Liddell Hart; the Modern Records Centre archive repositories and the depositors of papers, University of Warwick; University of Birmingham; the Transport and General Workers Union; the Archivist of the Churchill College Archives Centre; the Mass Observation Archives; the Labour Party and the Transport House Library; Mr G. H. P. Buchanan (Viscount Margesson Papers); Messrs Allen and Overy and the Trustees of the late Viscount

Monckton of Brenchley; Mrs D. Brinton-Lee; Mr W. A. Haslam; Mr A. Mackay; Mrs F. Spragg; Captain A. V. S. Yates; Mrs J. Reid; the Tamiment Library, New York Universities Library; Archives of Labor and Urban Affairs, Wayne State University, Detroit; Archives Division, the State Historical Society of Wisconsin; the Immigration History Research Center, University of Minnesota Library, St Paul; the Social Welfare History Archives, University of Minnesota Library, Minneapolis; Atlanta University Library; and the Special Collections, Robert W. Woodruff Library, Emory University, Atlanta.

I am very grateful to the British Academy and the Research Committee of the Open University for grants which financed parts of the travel and research involved in this book.

This book tries to steer a new course through a much charted subject. If, after all the help I have received, it has still ended up on the rocks, that is my fault alone.

INTRODUCTION

1

Class: Image and Reality

Some years ago, after appearing on the BBC's *The Book Programme* with broadcaster Robert Robinson and historian A. J. P. Taylor, I received the following remonstrance from a viewer:

> Perhaps I am being a little niggling but I wonder whether, before you come into my sitting room again, you could make some effort to improve your unkempt appearance.
> It was clear from your accent and dress last night that you have risen, by dint of hard study, from the working classes. Your accent is completely acceptable, but your appearance is NOT.

Historians do not usually have invaluable pieces of primary source material delivered direct to their own front door. However, there is perhaps nothing very surprising in yet another piece of evidence that class categories remain uppermost in the minds of many British people. Indeed, many commentators have been only too ready to lavish the blame for Britain's economic and social crisis of the 1970s on the continuing grip of class distinctions. Britain is often contrasted with countries such as France where, it has been argued, the competitiveness of the French in tendering for, say, a North Sea oil platform, is due to the social unity between employers and employed in French industry; or the United States, said to be a country of opportunity, mobility and an absence of snobbery. Yet one does not have to look very hard at either America or France to see that in both countries there exist phenomena which do look suspiciously like class distinctions. The conservative newspaper *Figaro*, for instance, prints snide cartoons poking fun at working-class activism; the *New York Times* still publishes page upon page of old-style society gossip. Writers on the history or politics of the three countries in the period since 1930 are obliged to refer frequently to class. The broad failure of the left in France, from the time of the Popular

Front right through to Giscard d'Estaing, to achieve anything on
the scale of the British Labour Party is often attributed to the
'middle-class' composition of French society. Similar explanations
have been offered to account for the absence of a major Socialist or
Labour party in the United States. Two recent writers, Michael
Howard and Paul Addison, have suggested that Britain's achievements in the Second World War may have been due to the rigid
nature of her class structure.[1] Harry Truman has sometimes been
singled out as a President who achieved that office (by accident)
despite coming from a lower social class than his predecessors. The
provincial middle-class character of French parliaments has been
remarked upon, as has the upper-class character of British ones. It
is a commonplace of politicians and journalists that in recent years
'class distinctions' have been 'diminishing' or 'disappearing' –
whatever, exactly, these three terms may mean.

None of this proves that classes actually do exist. It does indicate,
though, that people *believe* that classes exist, and are influenced in
their behaviour by that belief. What people believe is true, so the
truism goes, is true. But truisms do not take us very far, since a more
important question might be 'how true?' or, rather, 'how significant?'
in relation to all the other social phenomena in which people believe
or by which they are affected. One can go further and say that a
pragmatic assessment of a range of evidence suggests that there is a
strong presumption that classes do indeed exist, though again the
question of how *important* they are must remain for later exploration.

From the very beginning of this book I shall be using phrases like
'upper class', 'middle class', and 'working class' though I shall not
have established the complete validity of such terms: the commonsense assumption, again, will be that readers, having grown up in
the societies being studied, or in other societies like them, will have
an idea of what is meant by such phrases, even if they are desperately
anxious to run ahead of me in refining, developing or even abolish-
ing some of them. If one wishes to assess the *boeuf Stroganoff* in a
particular restaurant, one has to assume, in ordering, that *boeuf
Stroganoff* does actually exist in that restaurant, even if, in the
upshot, one is presented with stewing steak doused in shaving
cream.

Some authorities will already have rushed in here. Why do I
pussyfoot around the topic of the existence and significance of class
when there are shelves groaning with books which demonstrate
conclusively the existence of gross inequalities in the distribution of,

let us say, political and economic power, of housing accommodation and of educational opportunity? The problem, and it is the problem which lies at the heart of the dialectic between the image and the reality of class, is that while the existence of *inequality* can be clearly demonstrated, it is not so clear that the demonstrable inequalities are related to *class* in any fully acceptable sense of that term. Statistical studies have to depend on the manner in which official bodies serve up the raw statistics. The national censuses do, in presenting their findings, offer a range of 'social classes', 'socio-economic groups' or 'occupational groupings', but none of these coincides with the notions of class actually found in everyday speech, in the newspapers or in historical studies of the period under review. The American census, for instance, has fifteen 'socio-economic groups': do Americans talk and behave as if they belong to fifteen different social classes? This point is elaborated when I discuss what I call 'official images' of class. Most studies of the inequalities of class are based on occupational statistics. But is occupation the same as class? How do we decide which occupations go into which classes? Is the foreman in the same social class as the other members of the factory work force? Is not a doctor who ministers to an aristocrat in a different social class from one employed by a trade union benefit scheme? How do small shopkeepers in deprived areas compare with the owners of multiple department stores? Isn't it the case that in speaking of class, most people have birth and social background and a person's associates in mind as well as occupation?

To some authorities these are tiresome questions. If one has a *theory* that fundamentally there are only two classes in society – the employed class, usually referred to as 'the working class', and the owners of capital, variously referred to as 'the upper class', 'the middle class', 'the upper middle class' or, occasionally, 'the capitalist class' or 'the bourgeoisie' – it is pretty easy to make a division between manual workers and the remainder of society, and to show that throughout the period we are studying manual workers have tended to suffer from major disadvantages as compared with the other part of society. The presumption of this book will be that we can in fact expect there to be more than two classes: *colloquially*, people speak of more than two classes; *historically*, the evolution of modern society suggests at least three classes. Once we introduce the possibility of a third, or more classes, it becomes much more difficult to draw the lines and much less easy to juggle with the figures.

The problem can be put in a number of ways. We can show that,

subjectively, classes exist, and we can prove, objectively, that inequalities exist; but it is not so easy to tie the two together. We can
recognize that people do perceive the existence of something they
call class, but we cannot be sure that this class has an objective
existence; we can perceive that inequality exists, but we cannot be
sure that this inequality is due to class. We cannot be sure, that is,
unless we equate class with occupation, or unless we have some
theory which, we believe, enables us, of itself, to allocate a person
or group to a particular class. For example, Marxist sociology
declares that a person's social class is determined by his relationship
to the mode of production. It is not here contended that Marxist
sociology or, indeed, any other theoretical approach to class, is
necessarily wrong; simply that, in complex modern societies, determining someone's relationship to the mode of production is not
an easy task, and that any such definition of class does not, at first
sight, coincide with what I am calling the *colloquial* and *historical*
interpretation of class.

This book seeks to explore the subjective aspects of class, to
clarify the images of class held by different groups in the different
societies, and then to integrate these images with the realities of
social inequality. What people write, say and think about class
provides the broad categories – 'upper class', 'working class' and so
on; once one has broad categories which actually seem to meet the
circumstances of a particular society at a particular point in time,
one can then organize the detailed quantitative evidence regarding
social inequality. It may be that some of the *a priori* theories about
the nature of class turn out to be supported by this line of inquiry;
but it very firmly starts from the evidence rather than from the
theory.

First, however, I should say something about the other approaches which have, very properly, held the field for so long. To
many sociologists, 'class' is an abstract concept, vital for the precise
analysis of contemporary society but not corresponding directly
with any exact social or historical reality. Over and over again,
sociologists writing about class, with all the laboured nullity of the
reaction shots in an American television soap opera, warn us against
the dangers of 'reification', that is, of taking for real something that
is only a theoretical construct.[2] I take an exactly opposite view:
I believe that class is real – though, of course, I have yet to demonstrate this – but also believe that, in keeping with historical reality,
it is messy and not amenable to the sort of precision to which so
many social scientists aspire. Disciples of the German sociologist

Max Weber insist that one should not confuse a person's class (relating only to his economic position in society), his status (or social prestige) and his 'party' (or position in regard to political power). W. G. Runciman tells us that:

> Much of the trouble is caused by the use of the term 'class' in ordinary language. 'Class' is apt to be used not only as a general term for social stratification but also in a context where it is in fact status which is meant. To talk about 'working-class' homes or 'middle-class' education or 'U' and 'non-U' speech is to talk about style of life, and therefore status, not about location in the economic hierarchy as such.[3]

I prefer the 'ordinary language'. I prefer 'class' to mean what people in everyday life mean by it, rather than what Runciman or Weber tell me I should mean by it. I have never yet heard anyone speak of 'working-status' homes, nor of 'middle-status' education. Sociologists, I fear, often preach in preference to practising. John Raynor, in his excellent book on *The Middle Class*, tells us that really he would prefer to speak of the 'middle stratum'[4] but then proceeds cheerfully to go on talking about the middle class throughout the rest of the book, apart altogether from the fact that he is no more prepared to call his book *The Middle Stratum*, than I am to call my book *Status: Image and Reality*, or *Strata: Image and Reality*. If the Weberians wish to put a very limited meaning on the term class, that, of course, is their business, and good luck to them. But for historians attempting to make a comparative study of different societies and their evolution through a period of time, it does not seem to make a great deal of sense to place the same person in one particular class for one purpose, a different status group for another purpose, and yet a different 'party' for still another purpose. Class, perhaps, is too serious a subject to leave to the social scientists.

Marxist sociologists do not make this division into what many sociologists, I fancy, would call the different *dimensions* of social stratification. Marxists have an overview of all historical development which envisages, in the early modern period, a bourgeois class struggling against a feudal class, and, following the victory of the bourgeoisie, a gathering struggle against it in the nineteenth and twentieth centuries by the proletariat or working class. In the feudal period the landed aristocracy monopolized the means of production; in the capitalist era the bourgeois class monopolizes the means of production: those who have only their labour to sell belong to the proletariat; in between, there may be a transitional class, the petty bourgeoisie, which will eventually be forced down into the proletariat. In its standard European sense, the word bourgeoisie means the town-based commercial groups who became increasingly influential from at least the seventeenth century onwards, but the word has never been admitted to any consistent, or indeed frequent usage in the ordinary English language; nor has the word proletariat ever become acclimatized.

It is no prerogative of mine to say that any of these usages is wrong; as long as one is clear that one is speaking in a Weberian sense, or in a Marxist sense, or in the various senses (usually conflicting: to one school of American social scientists class is taken to be exactly what Runciman says it should not be, as is made clear by the title of a book by one of the leaders in the field, W. Lloyd Warner's *Social Class in America: The Evaluation of Status*) which have been developed by a host of sociologists since then, no harm is done. For myself, to repeat, I prefer, *as a starting point*, colloquial usage to that of any one theory. It is interesting, therefore, to discover when people began to use such phrases as 'middle class' and 'working class'. Asa Briggs showed that they came into everyday usage in Britain at the beginning of the nineteenth century when society was feeling the effects of the early Industrial Revolution.[5] During this period Britain was transformed from a society in which people were spoken of as belonging to a particular 'estate', or 'rank', or 'order', or 'station' in life, into a rather more fluid society where the less hierarchical word 'class' came to be used.

Again we have some problems. Whatever the upheavals of the Industrial Revolution in Britain, the significant upheavals in France at that time were those of the French Revolution. Industrialization came later in America, and even later in France. Pre-industrial America, in the immediate aftermath of the American Revolution, was a rather different society from pre-industrial Britain. Certainly, both the American Revolution and the French Revolution upset the established orders of *ancien régime* European society. Indeed, in showing starkly that political equality did not result in economic and social equality, the French Revolution contributed to the establishment of the notion of class, whereby men were unequal, but the inequality was no longer formally underpinned by a series of laws defining the different ranks in society. Whatever the deeper economic realities, the American Revolution was in some of its intentions a revolution on behalf of common citizenship and against the grosser legal inequalities of unregenerate Europe. Yet as industrialization developed in America, so America seemed to acquire some of the contours of the social classes recognized at the beginning of the century in Britain. If, then, class is taken on the one hand, colloquially, to exist when people start actually talking about it, and on the other hand, historically, to exist when the older, legally defined estates and orders of society are replaced by different group-ings, related in some way to the development of industrial society, but not formally defined by law, then class, to repeat, must be related to the great complex of historical events that took place at the end of the eighteenth century and the beginning of the nineteenth century and include the American Revolution, the French Revolu-tion, and the whole process of industrialization.

But the precise historical development of each of the three coun-tries in this period was rather different. Thus my starting point in looking at class is the different historical and economic evolution of the three countries, not any one universal model upon which the varied developments of the three countries can be seen as minor variations. Insofar as industrialization is a common experience, there are, of course, substantial elements of the universal. I find myself very much in agreement with the British sociologist, Anthony Giddens (though his vocabulary is not mine), when he writes:

> the combination of the sources of mediate and proximate struc-turation distinguished here, creating a threefold class structure, is generic to capitalist society. But the mode in which these elements are merged to form a *specific class system*, in any given society, differs significantly according to variations in economic and political development.[6]

Now, quite clearly, the classes of which historians speak when describing modern industrial society were in formation long before the Industrial Revolution. Thus there need be no embargo upon speaking, for analytical purposes, of different social classes when, say, discussing the seventeenth century. But the social classes recog-nized in this book are those recognized by the people of the period themselves, shaped in the early nineteenth century, and developed in the twentieth in accordance with the individual histories and traditions of the three countries. Three fundamental principles are at stake. First, discussion of class must be fixed within a specific historical and social context. Second, the language used should as far as possible be the language of the people studied, not part of some abstract theoretical framework. Third, what is herein said about class must be firmly anchored in the immense range of evidence which historians have at their disposal: diaries, letters, government statistics, acts of parliament, films, social surveys, extant housing, oral interviews, novels, and much more besides. One recalls those bloody warriors in the arena of medieval parliamentary studies, H. G. Richardson and G. O. Sayles, whose elemental hunting call was one to which all historians must respond: 'It is to the sources . . . that we would direct the reader who would know the truth.'[7] *The* truth is beyond the grasp of this book. Here is only one small contribution to an immense topic. But if it be objected that this appeal to the traditional sources can result only in a subjective approach to class, then I would reply that at least this book is based on some evidence, whereas the 'objective approach' often turns out to be based on no evidence whatsoever. I have not, I should admit, spent years searching in the works of Marx, Weber, Ossowski, Parsons or Warner in the hope of coming up with further theoretical refinements.[8] I have instead worked in some of the major historical archives in Britain, France and the United States. These three countries make a sensible choice for a comparative study; but my reason for confining myself to them is that, frankly, my knowledge of the evidence extends no further.

Class is not fixed and unchanging. This book is not, as some with whom I have shared my earlier thoughts have surmised, about changing images of the unchanging reality of class. The nature and significance of class changes as society changes. When that excellent historian Peter Clarke studies the changing influence of class on political behaviour, he seems too readily to assume that while political behaviour changes, class remains a constant; with him, however, I speak of the 'colloquial' meaning of class,[9] though, unlike him I do not find this an inferior usage.

To inch a little closer to what in the colloquial and historical usage of this book is meant by class and class society, it is worth considering what is not meant. A class society is not the same as a caste society, nor is it the same as a pre-industrial society of estates and orders (though some of the elements of modern class were already apparent in such societies). It is not the same as a status society (if such a society has ever actually existed) in which there is a continuous gradation of strata rather than a relatively small number of fairly discrete social classes. It is, obviously, not the same as a classless society, in which either there are no inequalities at all, or in which any inequalities are totally based on variations in natural talent, or in assessable variations in contributions made to the well-being of the community. In modern societies there are manifest inequalities based on sex, race, and age; but class is different in kind from these sources of inequality since they are biologically determined, which class is not. In certain societies the inhabitants of particular regions, or the members of particular religious faiths, have been at a disadvantage; these are not class distinctions. By looking closely at what classes are not, we come closer to seeing what classes are: classes are groupings across society, broadly recognized by members of that society, involving inequalities, or, certainly, *differences*, in such areas as power, authority, wealth, income, prestige, working conditions, lifestyles and culture; people of any one class, it is assumed, associate much more with one another than they do with members of other classes.

Two broad theories have been presented to explain what has been happening to class in the modern period. Conservative sociologists have presented a model of *disintegration*. Organization into social classes, having reached a peak at the end of the nineteenth century or the beginning of the twentieth century, then began to break down into a status society of continuous gradations. Against that is the Marxist view of the *polarization* of social classes, with, eventually, only a capitalist class on one side, and a working class on the other. In Marxist theory, the intensified development of social classes leading towards polarization also enhances the probability of conflict between social classes. In fact, it will be argued in this book, historical trends seldom proceed entirely in the same direction. One phrase of special ambiguity is *class consciousness*. This concept is now so closely associated with Marxist theory that it is probably unwise to attempt to use it divorced from that theory. In Marxist writings, whose subtlety, of course, I traduce here, growing class consciousness means growing political awareness, growing willingness and determination to fight for the interests of one's class against the opposing class. Yet growing consciousness of one's own class might be quite compatible with accepting the place of that class in a stable society. Thus, throughout this book I have chosen to use the phrase *class awareness* to signify the definite sense of belonging, culturally, to a distinctive class, without necessarily believing in any form of political activism on behalf of that class.

Earlier, I mentioned some of the other sources of inequality in modern society, including sex. Generally, and on the whole quite rightly, studies of class regard the question of allocation to a particular class as, so to speak, a family matter. Women and children, it is held, belong to the social class of the husband and father. This remained true for most of the period studied in this book, and therefore the question of women and social class is not given special treatment. It is, however, appropriate to make a number of fundamental points in this introductory chapter. Two assumptions, which have gone unchallenged until recently, have held the field. The first is that, through their innate conservatism and ingrained respect for due form and ceremony, women have tended, much more than men, to bolster any existing social hierarchy; and have deliberately operated the institution of marriage to make sure that their offspring do not risk moving down in the social scale. The second assumption has been that for women marriage has offered the best opportunity for upward social mobility.

On the first point, I would be inclined to agree that in the period under review women, for the most part, have tended to support, rather than oppose, the existing class structure, though as women have fought harder for their own rights, arguably, so too have they become more critical of the existing social hierarchy. On the second point, however, it becomes more and more apparent that existing orthodoxy is very suspect. There is now survey material, albeit of a rather limited nature, to support the view that younger women were (and are) quite as likely to marry for love, and therefore risk social descent, as for social advancement.[10] A moment's thought brings to mind the very characteristic case of the female school teacher married to the manual worker. Looking to the future, this family background can often be a strong impetus to social advancement for the offspring. In the British context one thinks of D. H. Lawrence, son of a miner and a school teacher, and of the Labour and European politician, Roy Jenkins, product of a similar marriage. One source of inequality not often discussed in serious works is that of physical beauty. I have no theories to offer about the relationship between social class position and looks, but the relationship is one which will, intriguingly, flit in and out of the coming pages.

What, then, is this book trying to do? It seeks, by employing the traditional methods of historical study, to add something to the general understanding of the nature of class; it also seeks to assess the distinctions and the similarities between British, French and American societies. In comparing three such countries one might well, in a different book, compare their physical geography, their economic achievements, their political institutions. It would also, if my opening paragraphs have not been totally wide of the mark, seem important to compare their social structures and their respective perceptions of social class. But the material for such comparisons scarcely yet exists in print. As one develops the comparative approach, the question of class begins to seem analogous to that of periodization. No historical writing would be possible without such broad concepts as 'the Renaissance', 'the seventeenth century', 'the period of the first Industrial Revolution', or 'the Thirties'. These are blunt concepts, and much fruitful historical debate takes place over, for example, when the Renaissance began, or when it ended. But if blunt, these concepts do have a reality: we ourselves in everyday life speak of 'the thirties', 'the sixties', 'the post-war era', and so on. Similarly, I am arguing, there is reality, though much imprecision around the edges, in speaking broadly of 'the working class', 'the peasantry', 'the upper class', and so on.

This book poses a number of questions (whether it answers them is a different matter). First, what evidence is there that class (as distinct from inequality) exists? Second, what makes class take the forms it does? Third, what is the significance of class? In dealing with the first question, I speak of different 'images of class', and this discussion forms a central part of the more original elements in this book; in dealing with the second (which actually begins the inquiry), I speak of the 'historical context' of class; in dealing with the third question, drawing particularly heavily on the work of others, I speak of such concepts as 'the realities of class' and 'the geography of class'. I hope to prove wrong those who say that in our present society classes no longer exist; and then to go beyond that to assess how far, in comparison, say, with race, religion, or sex, class is still an important source of inequality, or determinant of political events in contemporary society.

Chronology is an essential element in historical study, and the book is divided into two chronological periods. Part One attempts to validate my belief that by using certain approaches one can set up a reasonable comparative picture of social class as it was in the three countries in the 1930s. Part Two is largely concerned with some of the major historical developments which have altered the picture as it has been established for the 1930s: there are many longer-term processes apart from the Second World War and what, following a number of other writers, I term the 'Cultural Revolution' of the late 1950s and early 1960s, but I concentrate heavily on these particular congeries of events: too often, indeed almost invariably, class is treated in isolation from social and political events. At the end of Part Two, I attempt to assess class and its significance today, what has changed, and what has remained the same since the 1930s.

In all this, most attention has been given to what I call the 'images' of class. The four images studied I have labelled 'academic images', 'official images', 'unofficial and private images', and 'media images'. The first image is mainly to be found in the published writings of those who had a committed view about class and social structure, whether a scholarly or a polemical one. The second image is that presented by official sources, census returns, acts of parliament, and social policy documents. The third image is the most interesting, but the most fragmented: it is compiled from private papers, surveys and interviews. The final image is drawn largely, though not exclusively, from feature films. These may seem to be a particularly suspect source. Yet all historical sources are suspect; and my interest is in the 'unwitting' testimony, the hidden assumptions and attitudes, rather than the conscious, and often biased, message. The more one makes a comparative study of films, the more one becomes aware that, however exceptional within the context of its own country, every film is in fact a product of its own culture. No film maker, it becomes clear and clearer, can really go beyond certain assumptions accepted within his own country. Thus a comparison across countries of different films brings out very strikingly contrasts in basic perceptions about the nature of class in the three countries. Over and over again it has been pointed out to me at seminars and conferences that films are made by members of the upper and more prosperous segments of society. That I would never deny; but I am far more interested in the fact that almost all of the films discussed in this book were seen by large audiences. There *is* a law of the market; the bigger its commercial success the more a film is likely to tell us about the unvoiced assumptions of the people who watched it. It is the tedious documentary, or the film financed by political subscription, which tells us least.

Having traced out the four images, the idea is that they should, as it were, be superimposed on one another, so that a broad mapping for each country is achieved. Class, as a fully rounded historical reality is, I believe, a fusion of the historical context, the subjective imagery, and the objective inequalities. Not all of the pieces fit together as closely as I would wish. That's life; that's history.

Notes

1. Paul Addison, *The Road to 1945* (1976), pp. 76, 104, 129–32, 139, 221, 261–2 and 270–6; Michael Howard, 'Total War in the Twentieth Century: Participation and Consensus in the Second World War', in B. Bond and I. Roy, eds., *War and Society: A Yearbook of Military History* (1975), pp. 222–3.

2. See e.g., A. H. Halsey, *Change in British Society* (1978), pp. 5–6; Colin Crouch, *Class Conflict and the Industrial Relations Crisis* (1977), p. 3; E. Digby Baltzell, *Philadelphia Gentlemen: the Making of a National Upper Class* (1958), p. 6.

3. W. G. Runciman, *Social Science and Political Theory* (1960), p. 138.

4. John Raynor, *The Middle Class* (1969), p. 11.

5. Asa Briggs, 'The Language of Class in the Early Nineteenth Century', in A. Briggs and J. Saville, eds., *Essays in Labour History* (1960). See also Raymond Williams, *Culture and Society 1780–1950* (1958), pp. 14–15.

6. Anthony Giddens, *The Class Structure of the Advanced Societies* (1973), p. 110.

7. H. G. Richardson and G. O. Sayles, *The Governance of Medieval England* (1963), p. vii.

8. Karl Marx's rather fragmentary remarks on class have been brought together in *Karl Marx: Economy, Class and Social Revolution*, ed. Z. A. Jordan (1971).

   For Weber see the collection translated and edited by H. H. Gerth and C. Wright Mills, *From Max Weber: essays in sociology* (1970).

   See also Stanislaw Ossowski, *Class Structure in the Social Consciousness* (1963); R. Bendix and S. M. Lipset, eds., *Class, Status and Power: a reader in social stratification* (2nd edition, 1966); Talcott Parsons, 'Social Classes and Class Conflict in the Light of Recent Sociological Theory', in *Essays in Sociological Theory* (revised edition, 1964), pp. 323–35; and W. Lloyd Warner (with M. Meeker and K. Eells), *Social Class in America: a manual of procedure for the measurement of social status* (1960).

   The most recent overview is Leslie Benson, *Proletarians and Parties: Five Essays on Social Class* (1978).

9. Peter Clarke, 'Electoral Sociology of Modern Britain', *History* (February 1972).

10. R. Zick, 'Do American Women Marry Up?', *American Sociological Review*, vol. 33 (1968), pp. 750–9. Glen H. Elder, Jr, 'Appearance and Education in Marriage Mobility', *ibid*, vol. 34 (1969), pp. 519–32 and Norval D. Glenn, Adreain A. Ross and Judy Corder Tully, 'Patterns of Intergenerational Mobility through Marriage', *ibid*, vol. 39 (1974), pp. 683–99.

PART ONE

As it Was: the Thirties

2

The Historical Context of Class

Differences in geography, differences in history shaped the varying forms and perceptions of class in each of the three countries. The United States cover a vast and varied territory, with each one of the forty-nine inland states differing in some degree from even its nearest neighbour. The whole of Great Britain could be comfortably fitted inside, say, New York state, or California. While America in the 1930s had about three times the population of Britain, Britain and France were roughly equal in population size, though France occupies twice the geographical area. Like the simple nail which may support the most complex and potent painting by Picasso or Rembrandt, this point about America must be hammered home. We may well decide that we can speak of a French working class, or of a British upper class, but may we not have to make distinctions between an upper class in Texas and one in New England, between the mine workers of Oklahoma and the garment workers of New York, or between a middle class in Iowa and one in Washington D.C.? The importance of geographical sectionalism has long been stressed in historical writing about the United States; its significance is not least in the realm of social class.

Sheer distance counted for far more in the 1930s than it does today. To most inhabitants of the East Coast, California seemed very remote and it conjured up few of the glories it was to acquire from the 1940s onwards: true, Hollywood had a status and prestige of its own, but both Stanford and the University of California were minor seats of local learning offering little challenge to the Ivy League schools or even to some of the mid-western state universities. Travel was usually by long-distance train, rarely by unreliable small prop-driven aircraft. Movies and radio were a standardizing influence, but on the whole America was characterized by the vigour and independence of its local newspapers and, in some degree, of its local radio stations. The divide which Americans were most aware of was that between north and south. Industrialization in the south had been slow and patchy; in some parts the hegemony of the old

27

planter class stood undiminished; large numbers of poor whites as
well as blacks scratched a miserable existence from the land even in
the best of times; the whole social system was grounded in the
legally ratified inferiority of the blacks.

America had no undisputed metropolitan centre. Towns, and the
growth of the urban bourgeoisie are integral to the development of
class in the era of industrialization. In France and Britain, Paris and
London respectively occupied unique positions related in several
ways to the social hierarchies of the two countries. In America, New
York was undoubtedly the commercial and cultural capital; but
Washington was the political capital with a special social round of
its own; Boston stood at the centre of traditional New England
society and Philadelphia was another great social and cultural
capital; many in the south looked to New Orleans as the pace-setter
for high culture and fashion.

History and geography meet together in demography. Britain had
the most homogeneous population of the three societies, despite the
existence of the four separate nationalities, English, Welsh, Scottish
and Irish. Religion was of real social and political importance only
in that small part of 'John Bull's Other Island' remaining under
British rule, Northern Ireland, which, however, is excluded from
the scope of this book. In France, Protestants and Jews formed
distinctive groupings within the Catholic majority; and anticlericalism was a political issue which could sometimes divert attention from matters more obviously related to class. Already, because
of France's low birth-rate, some of the lowest unskilled jobs were
being performed by immigrant aliens from southern Europe and
North Africa. It was 'a bad thing to be French', if you were looking
for work on the roads, wrote the roving workman, Georges Navel,
in his invaluable autobiography: 'illiterate Piedmontese are handier,
for contracts at rates cut by forty per cent.'[1]

But it was in America that questions of race and ethnicity were of
such turbulence as to come near to submerging those of class. The
American census had a separate enumeration for blacks (around
ten per cent of the population in the 1930s) and it also listed the most
important ethnic groups as English, Irish, Scottish, Polish, Italian,
Russian and German. Bureaucratic tact averted the separate
enumeration of Jews but the Jewish communities in practice had a
special significance in American society, which cut across and
complicated lines of class. Religious differences often reinforced
ethnic differences, as in the case, say, of Catholic Irish or Italians
against German or Anglo-Saxon Protestants. Many factory workers

brought to home and workplace the attitudes of the East European peasantry or of the Central European petty bourgeoisie. Aliens of all descriptions – Japanese, Hindus, Filipinos, Arabs, Mexican 'wetbacks' (so called from having, whether in myth or reality, swum the Colorado River) and *braceros* (contract workers) – flooded both the orchards and the gold mines of California. There were Cuban and Spanish workers in Florida. Over them all brooded a great fear of America's rigorous immigration legislation. Fear of expulsion from the country kept most immigrants well away from any form of labour organization, although, by a very American paradox, recent European immigrants were often conspicuous among the handful of active and ideologically committed labour activists.[2] Either way, these developments all ran counter to the emergence of a coherent working class and a working-class awareness: the few activists were cut off at the top; the majority were divided off by fear, language and cultural differences at the bottom.

Immigration and immigration legislation shaped the American social structure and perceptions of it; but the still more potent force was that emanating from the historic institution of slavery and its continuing legacy. It could well be argued that in America in the 1930s the fundamental social distinction was between the ten per cent of the population who were black, and the rest. Largely, though, this distinction was still mainly relevant in the south. Although the First World War had touched off a wave of migration to the industrial north, there were still parts of America in which no black faces had ever been seen.

Alongside the divisiveness of racial and ethnic background as a force militating against the formation of coherent social classes must be placed the very strong sense of national pride among established citizens in America as a force making for unity across social classes. Such phrases as 'all American', 'native-born American' or 'A-1 citizen' are not just those of propaganda, but are to be found again and again in letters written by private individuals.[3] Here the excluded groups are inside American society itself, and the phrases 'un-American' and 'anti-American' were already embedded in the American vocabulary by the 1930s. In France, the strong attachment to 'La Patrie' could often overcome sectional distinctions, as, most famously, it appeared to do in August 1914. A well-known British newsreel of the 1930s was titled 'Premier takes stock, finds Britain best'. Complacency is a notable characteristic in the Britain of the 1930s, but on the whole nationalism is understated in comparison with both France and America. Crown and Empire are focal points, the latter giving rise to a continuing contempt for non-British races overseas, and, perhaps, to an instinct for hierarchy at home.

If we look back over the political history of the three countries we find France and the United States marked out by their very different revolutionary traditions. Britain stood alone as the country with an aristocracy in continuous existence since the Middle Ages. By the early twentieth century this aristocracy, which had always recruited from below, was providing the frame for what, for the moment, I shall term an upper-class 'box' into which the most successful products of commerce, industry, government and the professions could continue to be absorbed, often without benefit of title. This particular historical legacy cannot be stressed too much. Whereas titles were non-existent in the United States and nearly always slightly suspect in France, in Britain those born into aristocracy not only had no need to be on the defensive, but conferred a kind of legitimacy on those who associated with them. On the other hand, the French ballerina Cléo de Mérode was at some pains to insist that her aristocratic-sounding name was no pseudonym. When doubts were expressed by 'one of my friends, the Duke of N' she produced papers to demonstrate not only her authentic connection with the house of Mérode but also that her title was rather better than the Duke's.[4] This story has its setting earlier in the century, but, for very different reasons, it is difficult to imagine it referring at any time to either a British or an American context. One rather special sort of surrogate peerage had come into existence in France as a result of an Act of 1806 whereby Napoleon created the two hundred share-holders of the Bank of France. By the 1930s, 'The Two Hundred Families' had become a popular synonym to embrace France's richest and most powerful families (such as Rothschild, Schneider and de Wendel).

The old adage about the French is that they wear their hearts on the left but their pocket books on the right. The considerable truth in this is a direct corollary of the nature of the French revolutionary tradition. Political parties deliberately sought left-sounding labels though their politics were very far from left-wing: the major centre grouping of the 1930s, which participated in all the shifting governments of the period was always known as the Radical Party, though actually the full and technically correct title was Radical and Radical Socialist Party. Republicanism, citizenship, patriotism, were all rallying cries for small businessmen, shopkeepers, peasant proprietors and even industrial workers, and could at times overlay any sense of class. At the same time elements of the orders and estates of the *ancien régime* were refurbished and perpetuated in the Napoleonic codes. French citizens in the 1930s were defined as industrial workers (*ouvriers*), white-collar workers (*employées*), *artisans* (meaning, unlike the English or American homonym, employers of up to five workers), small, medium or large merchants (*commerçants*) or industrialists (*industriels*), small, medium or high civil servants (*fonctionnaires*), and so on. Precise labelling of relatively small occupational groupings in this way can be anti-thetical to the formation of all-inclusive classes.

The anti-aristocratic tradition was strongest of all in the United States, whatever the practical realities in regard to wealth and power. President Roosevelt and his associates were often pilloried by Republicans as members of the East Coast aristocratic establish-ment. The sentiment went deep in American society. It can be seen in some of the Hollywood social comedies of the thirties (*The Lady Eve* is a good example) where self-made businessmen quietly rebel against their aristocratic wives with the defiantly popular gesture of knotting their napkins round their necks whenever they sit down to a meal. When a former associate of John L. Lewis, the miners' leader who in 1935 formed the Committee (later Congress) of Industrial Organizations (CIO) as a rival to the craft-orientated American Federation of Labor, wished to express the strength of his feelings against Lewis, he twice, in a letter to William Green, president of the American Federation of Labor, referred with bitter contempt to Lewis as a 'Lord'.[5]

The differing political and social traditions of the three countries were reflected in, and reinforced by, their respective educational systems. Education in France was controlled from top to bottom by the state. In theory, and on occasions in practice, this provided elements of democracy: children from modest backgrounds could make their way up through the secondary schools, the *lycées* (run by the central government) and *collèges* (run by the local authorities) to the *grandes écoles* at the top, providing post-graduate and pro-fessional training and careers in industry and the professions (in-cluding that of *professeur* in the secondary schools). But the system was also highly stratified. Children from the primary schools aiming to become primary school teachers (*instituteurs*) went off on an entirely separate route through special primary school teacher training colleges. In the main, poorer families did not aspire to push their children up the educational ladder. Even after secondary education became free in 1933 there were many other costs associated with education in the *lycées*. On the other hand there were private schools, so that rich or devoted parents whose children had failed to get on to the competitive ladder could buy an education which would enable them to join the ladder higher up. Outside the state system, also, stood the private, and very expensive, School of Political Sciences, offering a training for higher civil servants.

In theory, then, though much less so in practice, the French system was concerned with merit rather than social background and social ethos. In Britain there were fewer pretensions on this score. The main institutions for maintaining the ethos of the upper class and for marking off the assimilated from the unassimilated were the most prestigious of the privately run public schools: the nine schools investigated by the Clarendon Commission of 1861–64 (and hence termed the Clarendon schools) – Eton, Winchester, Westminster, Charterhouse, St Paul's, Merchant Taylor's, Harrow, Rugby and Shrewsbury – plus about the same number again of such schools as Glenalmond, Haileybury, Repton and Rossall. The two ancient universities of Oxford and Cambridge were both effectively private (and again very expensive) institutions. For most, though not all, public schools products they topped off the upper-class education; they could also socialize into the upper-class style students of lower social origins who, often through scholarships, had arrived at Oxbridge from other types of secondary school. Such schools were in varying degrees fee-paying, with scholarships and a limited number of free places. State-sponsored free education did not in general extend beyond a rather crude elementary education to the age of fourteen.

Nineteenth-century America appeared to have avoided both the excesses of meritocracy and of social grading in establishing a general progression from common school, to high school, to state university. The fundamentally democratic and, up to a point, 'classless' nature of this system, in comparison with those of France and Britain, must be stressed, but with three qualifications. First, there were always social groups too poor to be able to profit from the system. Second, in the south it was racially segregated. Third, side-by-side with the system there existed high prestige, expensive private schools, such as Groton, Philips Exeter, Philips Andover, St Paul's, St Mark's, Choate, Hotchkiss, St George's, Deerfield and Pomfret in New England; Buckley in New York; Hill in Pennsylvania; Episcopal High and Woodberry Forest in Virginia; Asheville in North Carolina; and Cranbrook, Lake Forest and Shattuck in the mid-west; and the prestigious 'Ivy League' universities and colleges. These, together, were just as dedicated as were their counterparts in Britain to the inculcation of a special upper-class ethos.

INDUSTRIALIZATION AND INDUSTRIAL RELATIONS

Geographical size, urban distribution, racial and ethnic composition, religion, political history and traditions, and educational institutions are all important; but still more basic to the forms of class are the extent to which industrialization has progressed and the manner in which occupations have evolved. The striking thing about France in the 1930s is the high proportion of the population engaged in agriculture (37.4 per cent of the total population); in England and Wales only 5.3 per cent of the population were so occupied (7.6 per cent in Scotland). America comes in between with a fifth (21.2 per cent) of her much larger and more variegated population engaged in agriculture. France, then, had a very important social group of *paysans*, small proprietors producing, it might be, wine or cereals or butter, whose significance is not well described by the English word 'peasant'. Compared with Britain, France and America had large numbers of small enterprises: they, rather than Britain, were nations of shopkeepers (and, in the French case especially, of inn-keepers). The proprietors of such enterprises tend to form a particular type of middle grouping in the social structure. The obverse of all this is that Britain was distinguished by the high proportion of her total population (about 46 per cent) engaged in industry as against 37.1 per cent in France and 32.7 per cent in America.[6] France, though, had changed most in the previous generation, the demands of the First World War having been largely responsible for the creation of a new Parisian industrial class of metal workers. British industrial workers were, nonetheless, consolidated and organized in a manner which was just not true of America or France. The evolution of British trade unions indicated a high level of working-class awareness, if not consciousness. The much smaller and poorer French trade union movement was, among other problems, split between the socialist-led General Confederation of Labour (CGT), and the communist-led General Confederation of United Labour (CGTU); there was also the Catholic French Confederation of Christian Labour (CFTC). In America, the American Federation of Labor was almost exclusively a craft organization. When attempts at establishing industrial unions within the old framework finally proved unsuccessful, an angry division emerged between the AFL and the new CIO. Many sectors of American labour remained unamenable to any form of union organization.

With her great wealth and her primacy in technology and mass production techniques, America had every appearance of being the most advanced capitalist economy. Yet we would miss much of vital significance in comprehending the image and reality of class in America in the 1930s if we failed to note how very primitive and indeed barbarous economic relationships were in many parts of the United States. In the Labor Department files relating to coal mining, and in the private papers of Secretary of Labor Frances Perkins, eviction, victimization and a brutality and callousness which would have seemed out of place in nineteenth-century Britain, are constant themes.[7]

President Hoover's organization for unemployment relief (POUR), the forerunner of the New Deal agencies, depended heavily on such private bodies as the American Red Cross and the American Legion. A Red Cross report in the POUR files conveys the archaic quality of mining life in Arkansas in April 1932:

> At Jenny Lind it is estimated that there are seventy-five miners needing relief immediately. The mine, after working one day a week for two years closed permanently four months ago. The miners, many of whom did some farming, have sold off their stock gradually, and are now completely without resources. They have applied to the Red Cross Chapter for assistance and in addition made a solicitation of funds in the business streets of Ft. Smith. A canvass of the rural territory around Jenny Lind has resulted in contributions of enough food and supplies to last them for several days. The miners have had three or four meetings, not of protest, but to consider ways and means of getting along.

Another Red Cross report, this time on Monongalia County, West Virginia, noted that there was not one miners' union in the whole county, and that in Kanawha County, about twenty-five families were living in tents as a result of evictions. On 1 November 1931, the Rock Island Railroad Company in Oklahoma closed down all the mines in the vicinity of the town of Hartshorne because it had replaced its coal-burning engines with oil burners. A 'top committee called the Citizens Committee on Unemployment Relief' with a banker as chairman, a lumber merchant as vice-chairman, and also containing one contractor and two attorneys, was formed. On Wednesday 17 February, reports reached the Committee that plans were afoot to stage a demonstration and take food from the stores at Hartshorne. The Sheriff, the Mayor of Hartshorne and the City Attorney visited several groups of men in the villages of the area and persuaded them not to carry out the alleged intention of marching in one big group to Hartshorne and there breaking up into small groups of 20 or 25, sending a group to each store to take food; however, they were not successful in getting the men not to march.

On Thursday, February 18th, the group of unemployed miners number [sic] 75 marched into Hartshorne in a quiet orderly fashion led by one A. A. Snider, a schoolteacher, who is reported to 'have been a Socialist once'. As the march progressed the group became larger till the crowd numbered five hundred when they arrived at the Hartshorne Court house. A meeting was held in the court house at which assurance and [sic] were given the men that everything possible would be done to relieve the situation. $175 were collected and distributed AT ONCE to the most needy. At 3 p.m. that same afternoon a meeting of about 75 business and professional men of Hartshorne was held sponsored by the Committee at which approximately $2,500 was pledged of which amount about $1,000 was paid in cash. To this amount there was added today $500 from Governor Murray as a personal donation, thus giving the Committee about $3,000 to carry on with. It is estimated that this will last three to four weeks.[8]

After President Roosevelt took office, shoals of letters poured into Washington giving very vivid and moving descriptions of the sort of conditions being endured by large sections of the American people. The shadow of Dickensian England lies across a heart-rending pencilled (and illiterate) letter addressed to Mrs Roosevelt from a girl in Denver, Colorado, saying that she is seventeen years old, but has been working as a domestic servant since the age of twelve. Kept up till eleven or twelve at night, or to one or two in the morning if her employers hold a party, she has to rise at five in the morning. She is lucky, she says, to get one half day off in a week, and all this for wages of twelve dollars a month: 'i am so tired i cant hardly do my work the next day.'[9]

In many ways the automobile industry provides the paradigm of twentieth-century economic and social development in the United States. Yet in Detroit and its immediate environs in the 1930s industrial relations were scarred by a primitivism which was only exceeded in the remoter mining areas of West Virginia, Oklahoma,

and California. It was a world in which foremen seemed to have
absolute power. Female employees at one factory, it was said, were
frequently raped by the foreman, who 'went around bragging about
copping a cherry' while the other men took matters much in the
spirit of a spaghetti western: 'In fact, the guys laughed. Today they
would probably kill the foreman or do him some great bodily harm
instead of just laughing it off and saying, "The babe got took, that
is all".'[10]

The primitivism of some areas of American society certainly
generated much violence which often seemed like class conflict
according to classic Marxist theory, but it also inhibited clear perceptions of class roles. Labour leaders, indeed, were often drawn
from outside the ranks of labour in a manner almost unheard of in
the European countries. Among the automobile workers' leaders
were both a Reverend and a Ph.D. (Homer Martin and Carl
Haessler). Curiouser and curiouser: two leading union organizers
among the southern sharecroppers were Harry L. Mitchell, owner
of a dry-cleaning establishment, and Henry Clay East, owner of gas
station *and* local sheriff who, when out organizing, 'prominently
displayed his star and pistol'.[11] Perhaps we come near to an important truth here. In archaic, advanced, sprawling, pluralistic
America, rich in natural wealth, the stakes were high, while loyalties
to large, static, and perhaps slightly mythic classes of the type described by European socialists were low: union organization could
so easily become another means towards making a fast buck. Along
with complaints about the brutality of employers, Department of
Labor files are also full of the protests of poorer workers excluded
from unions by the high dues charged.[12] Can we perhaps detect the
lack of cultural focus for workers' loyalty in the attendances of
70,000 reported at *college* football games (the French workers had
their cycle races, the British their professional football)?[13]

Industrial relations were very far from happy in Britain in the
1930s. They were much worse in France. As the industrial relations
charter achieved by France's Popular Front government in 1936,
the Matignon Agreement, brings out, victimization of strikers was
still very much the rule, collective bargaining the exception. No
lives were lost in industrial disputes in Britain in the inter-war years
(though there was one death in Northern Ireland). On separate
occasions demonstrations in France resulted in workers being killed,
and police violence against left-wing trade unionists reached a peak
in 1938. But on the whole, purely industrial confrontations were
carried through without anything approaching the violence, intimi-

dation, trigger-happy reactions of the police, and employment of professional 'goon squads' which turned several American disputes into infamous battle fields: at Republic Steel in Chicago more than one hundred people were shot, many in the back, and ten were killed.

There is a striking appraisal of British conditions, and revelation of American assumptions, in a report of an American Federation of Labor delegate who visited Britain in 1937. Credit for the basic harmony in British industrial relations was not due to 'the labor unions themselves alone', though, as he put it in true American style, the British trade unions had 'created the basis for respect when they proved their metal on the picket lines'. They showed, he said, that 'they would and could fight for their principles and objectives'. But the British employer deserved credit too: 'Time after time I asked the same questions – "How do you try to settle disputes?" I would ask. "Do you have strike breakers, bring in thugs with guns and gas, use stool pigeons or stooges?" And every time I got the same answer. That answer was "No".' His conclusion was pure John Wayne: 'We can operate in peace when our strength has shown employers the wisdom of living in peace with us.'[14] This attitude is central to class relationships in America: slug it out first, then shake hands and settle down with the powers-that-be.

IDEOLOGY AND MODES OF EXPRESSION

Industrial organization and industrial relations are one context within which class is shaped. The economic and social ideologies prevailing in the particular society provide another. Once again we have to single out America: this time for the faith in America's bounteous natural wealth, boomed out, despite all the evidences of the depression, in films and from political platforms, and voiced privately in letters. Formally, all three countries adhered to the principles of private enterprise and the classical political economy. But in Britain and France this was largely from fear that in a world of scarcity any other system would be worse. The two countries sought what comfort they could from contemplation of their over-seas Empires of inferior peoples. The British and French were enveloped in a spirit of retrenchment, low aspirations, and a due and established order of things. Any gains could only be made at the expense of someone else. American individualist theory, on the contrary, was positive and expansionist. Capitalism was presented as an integrated, interdependent system, in which merit attached to all who contributed to its success, in however small a way; and an individual dignity belonged to all who participated in this success.

The whole thrust of New Deal economic policies was towards raising purchasing power. But the diagnosis which held that the central problem of the depression was that of under-consumption was not confined to members of Roosevelt's entourage or of his political persuasion: theorizing about under-consumption can be found in all levels of society from the very early 1930s. The official New Deal version of this economic philosophy was put by Roosevelt's Secretary of Labor, Frances Perkins, in a speech to the American Federation of Labor convention at San Francisco on 5 October 1934: 'As profits increase employers are bound to recognise that workers must receive increased wages and have shorter hours of work in fair proportion to the increase in earnings of the industry if we are to maintain the balance between purchasing power and productive power now so obviously necessary to maintain an internal market.'[15] The mass media publicized this doctrine. A Social Security Board documentary of 1937 explained that unemployment compensation 'helps maintain purchasing power and so keeps the wheels of industry turning.' Pathe News in a Social Security Board trailer used the same metaphors: unemployed compensation to the unemployed man 'means not needing charity or going on relief', whereas 'to the community it means a continuation of buying power'; not only does it keep 'the wheels turning', it 'puts a brake on depression'.[16] But long before these films had reached the cinema screens many employers were announcing their belief in the magic of maintaining purchasing power. In announcing their cooperation with the New Deal the National Retail Dry Goods Association contrasted the potential for an expanding harmonious society in America with the restrictive, bitter societies of old Europe:

> The United States has sufficient resources, productive capacity, human energy and skill, to provide at least a fair minimum standard of life continuously for all the people. Relations of the United States with the rest of the world are tranquil. It is not torn by internal political or class strife. There is no natural basis for the present disorganised state of economic affairs. All conditions exist for renewed prosperity and progress.[17]

No doubt it was in the cynical interests of rich employers and powerful politicians to advocate such theories. A correspondent from New York City urged Mrs Roosevelt to give 'a straight talk' to the rich married women of New York who provided their daily domestic servants with only one dollar for a day lasting from 8.00 a.m. to 6.00 p.m., a wage, he said, which it was utterly impossible for any 'respectable woman' to live on. His own economic interest was not unconcealed, for he wrote 'as manager of a few apartment houses situated in the colored section of New York City'.[18] The economic interest of the lady from Minneapolis who owned a ladies' dress shop is also apparent; but for all that the language in which she chose to write to Frances Perkins is very significant: 'The army of girls that do housework are naturally good spenders. They are mostly young girls, and it is only natural that they should crave the things that money buys. At the present rate of salary, not only is their purchasing power reduced but the morall [sic] broken.' Undoubtedly these theories did penetrate deep into American society. In the course of an address to the Association of Southern Women to Prevent Lynching the speaker found time to remark that 'when businessmen take more out of society than they put back, we lost our greatest economic asset, purchasing power'. One domestic servant (admittedly a well-educated one) writes: 'buying is such an important economic factor now more than ever', while another, an uneducated one, laments: 'I can not see were [sic] there is any chance to increase buying power.'[19]

In Britain the theory of under-consumption had been pioneered by J. A. Hobson at the end of the previous century. In the 1920s the concept had been taken up by the Independent Labour Party, at that time still the most important intellectual component of the British Labour Party. Operating along a different track, J. M. Keynes, one or two other leading thinkers in the Liberal Party, and various other political and non-political figures in the 'middle opinion' movement of the 1930s advocated maintenance of purchasing power. But most British economic thinking was unadventurous and restrictionist, in the Labour Party as much as in the Conservative Party. The prevailing ideology was of struggle for essentially limited resources, rather than of expanding the totality of resources, though both Ramsay MacDonald and Stanley Baldwin and their associates hoped to secure reductions in living standards by co-operation rather than confrontation. In France the prevailing orthodoxy was equally that of rigid restrictionism, and, if necessary, brutal deflation. The French Socialists, with their doctrine that they could not participate in the government of a capitalist country, refused to take office in France till the formation of the Popular

Front government in 1936. As part of his compromise with capitalist society, Léon Blum, the Socialist Prime Minister of the Popular Front government, did now advocate policies explicitly directed at under-consumption. But the substantial wage rises of his first summer were followed by a 'pause' and, eventually, by the old deflationary policies.

Side by side with often appallingly inhumane conditions of work, went the professed American assumption that every job had its own individual dignity and professional skill. This came through most strongly in such service trades as barbering or bar tending. The chances were that the man who served you your drink in a bar in France was the proprietor himself; in Britain he might quite possibly be a transient employee with no skill, no stake, no status, and no future; in America he would quite probably have had some kind of professional training, enabling him, among other skills, to produce the variety of mixed drinks which were a special feature of American drinking habits. The point is made most strongly by the prolonged discussion of the problem of domestic service which assumed the dimensions of a major social question in the United States, as it did not in either France or Britain. 'The term "servant"', Mary V. Robinson of the Department of Labor Women's Bureau declared in a radio broadcast of May 1938, 'has been discarded as a relic of a bygone era. Today we talk about the problem of domestic workers or household employees.' Characteristically, it was argued that while being a servant required professional skill, employing a servant required *managerial skill*. In April 1931 a conference of the National Committee on Employer–Employee Relationships in the Home produced these conclusions:

> That there is urgent need of education among the employers of labor in the home, and that until they themselves have mastered their jobs as home administrators there can be no satisfactory solution of the problems of employer–employee relationships . . .
> That it is possible, where the home-maker is trained, cooperative and interested, to organise the work of the home on a business basis, with hours, duties, wages and responsibilities clearly defined, and to encourage and preserve the self-respect and personality growth of the worker.
> That where such conditions are maintained, a superior type of employee can be secured for household work and a satisfactory work relationship can be maintained. . . .

Six years later, to the question: Can household employment 'be made socially acceptable'?, the reply was that this would involve the lady of the house earning 'her social and economic status by meeting her responsibilities as administrator and manager'.[20] Whereas the French and British, in their different ways, continued to attach clear distinctions of status and prestige to different occupations, Americans believed, or affected to believe, not just in the dignity of labour, but also in the dignity of management. Primitive conditions and lofty aspirations could make a deadly combination from the point of view of class formation.

Many different circumstances come together to shape the particular forms of class and perceptions of class obtaining in different societies. Perceptions of class, especially, are naturally affected by the vocabularies and modes of expression available. French is a more precise, less flexible language than English. American English has been subject to influences and inflections unknown in Britain, and has incorporated some styles of expression which are more European than British. Without any doubt the whole style of economic, political and social thinking associated with Marx and with political sociology in general took much deeper root in France than it did in the two Anglo-Saxon countries. The pragmatic traditions of British thought were much less compatible with Marxist categories than were French traditions of intellectual conceptualization, and the faith in economic individualism of the British, and, above all, of the Americans, was hostile to Marxism. Of course, the French were individualists too, but given also to seeking a large ideological identity, clerical or anti-clerical, Catholic or Marxist. Almost all explicit French comment on class is coloured either by Marxism or by the categories of nineteenth- and early twentieth-century political sociology which itself absorbed so much of Marxist thought. In Britain, and even more so in America, there is a strong tendency either for Marx to be ignored (the ignorance was often genuine!) or for a deliberately anti-Marxist line to be taken. Here, I am not exclusively thinking of professional sociologists and political commentators: the jargon of the top has a way of filtering down. In America this particular point is made most clearly in connection with one unique aspect of American styles of expression on the subject of class. While French academic sociology of the 1930s is expressed in a lucid sweeping style, American sociology, together with the official publications and pronouncements affected by it, was already becoming morassed in jargon. We find the ordinary letter-writer speaking of the 'data' in a manner impossible to imagine among most British or French correspondents.

With regard specifically to vocabulary, a few basic comments may be made. 'Bourgeois' and 'bourgeoisie' are, of course, both French words. In normal French usage they are deployed in a variety of slightly indistinct ways, while English usage is so confused as to make both terms well worth avoiding: a British film critic in the thirties, for example, said of Gaumont Graphic newsreels that they suggested 'a bourgeois atmosphere redolent of public houses'.[21] A *cru bourgeois* in the language of French wine is a good, but middle-level wine, rather than the very best. But bourgeoisie, in the particular language of class, is widely recognized as meaning the uppermost class which has derived its position from commercial and industrial wealth. Sometimes to be absolutely clear the phrase *haute bourgeoisie* is used. A clearer term, but more used in books than elsewhere, is *classe dirigeante* ('directing class'). French has two words for worker – *travailleur* and *ouvrier*: the former carries the implication of work of any sort (by hand or by brain) whereas *ouvrier* quite precisely means 'manual worker'. In keeping with the revolutionary tradition, the French sometimes speak of *les classes populaires* or simply of *le peuple*. This is not the place to dwell on such semantic questions. They will be taken up again when they occur in the real usage of real people as revealed in the primary sources. But they do form an important part of that historical context which forms the first dimension of social class as that term is understood in this book.

Notes

1. Georges Navel, *Travaux* (1945), p. 128.
2. Detail from National Archives [NA], Washington, RG 176:167/2806, and RG 86:6; and from Archives of Labor and Urban Affairs [ALUA], Wayne State University, Detroit, AWOC, box 20, files 20–9, and Oral Histories by Nowak and by Pagano.
3. Letters in NA, RG 86:926 and RG 47:25, 67; and in Social Welfare History Archives, University of Minnesota Libraries, Minneapolis, Family Service of St Paul Correspondence.
4. Cléo de Mérode, *Le Ballet de ma vie* (1955), p. 15.
5. Archives Division, The State Historical Society of Wisconsin, Madison, American Federation of Labor Papers, U.S. Mss., 117A/11C, box 3.

6. Statistique générale de la France, *Résultats statistiques du recensement général de la population effectué le 8 Mars 1931,* tome 1, IIIe partie (1935), p. 187; League of Nations, *World Economic Survey* (1939), p. 84; United States Bureau of Census, *Historical Statistics of the United States* (1960), p. 163; *Encyclopedia of the Social Sciences* (1933), p. 206.
7. NA, RG 174:167; Columbia University Library, Frances Perkins Papers, box 83.
8. NA, RG 73:371–3.
9. NA, RG 86:926 (undated letter of July 1933).
10. ALUA, Oral History by Dan Gallagher.
11. Jerold S. Auerbach, 'Southern Tenant Farmers: Socialist Critics of the New Deal', *Labor History* (Winter 1966), p. 8.
12. NA, RG 174:167/2351, 2355, 2358, 2360.
13. See, for example, Pathe News item, NA, RG 47:4.
14. Robert J. Watt, 'Labor Relations in Britain and Sweden', *American Federationist* (February 1939), pp. 162–4.
15. NA, RG 47:39.
16. NA, RG 47:7 and 47:25.
17. NA, RG 86:54.
18. NA, RG 86:926.
19. *Ibid*; and Atlanta University Library, ASWPL, box 3: address by Arthur Raper, 14 January 1937.
20. NA, RG 86:75 and 86:927.
21. Donald Fraser, 'Newsreel: Reality or Entertainment?', *Sight and Sound* (Autumn 1933), p. 89.

3

Academic Images of Class

In the previous chapter I addressed myself to the question, 'What makes class take the forms it does in the different individual countries?' I move on in this and the following half-dozen chapters to ask, 'What evidence is there that class (as distinct from inequality) exists?' I approach this question through study of the four images which arise naturally from the different kinds of available source material. I begin with 'academic images', embracing those both of detached scholars and engaged polemicists.

As far as the systematic study of social class is concerned, academic sociology in the 1930s was much more advanced in France than in Britain or America. Despite the work of Thorstein Veblen at the turn of the century, most American sociologists paid little attention to class, a concept which orthodox academics considered irrelevant in a country of enterprise and opportunity like the United States; Selig Perlman's *A Theory of the Labor Movement* (1928) argued that American workers were 'job conscious' not 'class conscious'. Only towards the end of the 1920s did the Lynds publish their pioneering work, the detailed anthropological study of a single community.[1] In Britain, even though the occupational structure and the prevailing social ideologies were well suited to the articulation of clear notions of class, academic sociologists also showed great reluctance to bring social class within their domain. But France had a tradition of what is now usually termed 'political sociology' in which the conceptual work of Marx, and of Weber and Durkheim, were thoroughly digested into large-scale systematic attempts to confront the social world as it really was.

One of the most cited authorities on class in France was François Simiand, professor at the Conservatoire National des Arts et Métiers and director of studies at the École Pratique des Hautes Études. His course of lectures on political economy, given at the Sorbonne at the end of the 1920s, included an extended discussion of 'social classes', which was essentially historical in nature.[2] In the Middle Ages, and then more significantly in the sixteenth and seventeenth centuries, he declared, there arose the 'bourgeoisie of the towns' – the Third Estate in French society, which, already very important under the *ancien régime*, became dominant after the French Revolution. In the nineteenth century there emerged a 'Fourth Estate' of manual workers, though the Revolution itself had abolished the legal and statutory recognition of classes (Simiand did not explore the question of whether the word 'class' was used, or is appropriate to the pre-Revolutionary era). But even in the 'very democratized' society of his own day, there existed distinct groups of people who, in everyday life, have much closer relationships with each other than with people in other groups. In amplification of this indication of the contemporary existence of class, Professor Simiand permitted himself a mild joke, pedantically signalled in advance and carefully distanced by being told at second hand. 'A distinguished economist, not lacking in humour, once said at a conference: "Two men belong to the same class when their wives associate with each other." ' After that frivolity, Simiand retreated almost at once into a rather formalistic, economist's view of classes: they 'are defined on the one hand by the category of income and wealth, and on the other by the manner in which these resources are disposed of'.

Simiand now addressed himself to the language of class, declaring the most frequently used labels to be 'working class' (*classe ouvrière*) or 'wage-earning class' (*classe salariée*). Closely related to these is the category of 'white-collar workers' (*employés*): 'On the other side we usually postulate one single opposing class; but the fact that we use various labels such as "employing class", "bourgeois class", "capitalist class", "property-owning class" seems to suggest that this notion needs closer scrutiny.' So, working his way now through the social classes, Simiand begins with 'the two obvious ones': first, 'the peasant class' (*classe paysanne* – it is simpler to use the English homonym even though the translation is far from exact), and, second, 'the working class'. Third, people speak of 'the middle classes', although, he remarks in an interesting aside, this is 'a title often used more in wish-fulfilment than reality'. The main categories making up the middle classes are the 'high artisans' (*haut artisanat* – but once again the English homonym does not provide an exact translation), 'small and medium merchants and industrialists' and 'medium functionaries', and possibly also the small share-holders (*la petite fortune mobilière*). Together these categories have the cultural characteristics of a class, seen in their lifestyles and marriage patterns. But they are not, Simiand points out in one of his neatest perceptions, 'an initiatory or dominant class' for they are 'dominated by economic forces'.

Fourth, there is the *classe bourgeoise*, who are not, Professor Simiand insists, mere *rentiers* – they work! Into this bourgeoisie the aristocracy has merged and the class as a whole can be separated out by the distinctively high amount spent on housing, suggesting, according to Simiand's calculations, a bourgeois class of five per cent of the population. However, there should probably be a sub-division into a number of 'degrees': the petty bourgeoisie, who come close to being *the* middle class (as distinct from his third, lesser, category of 'middle classes'); the medium bourgeoisie; and the grand bourgeoisie; and, finally, above these, 'a category of magnates (*magnats*)', who have special traits of their own but also share common bourgeois characteristics. Simiand, then, distinguishes 'peasants', 'workers', 'middle classes', and a 'bourgeois class', ranging from '*the* middle class' through four 'degrees' to the 'mag-nates' at the top.

The most thorough study of class in France in the 1930s was the doctoral thesis, presented in 1934 by Louise-Marie Ferré, entitled *Social Classes in Contemporary France*,[3] which has been unjustly neglected by historians and sociologists. Mlle Ferré's approach was historical in that she worked logically through all the possible docu-mentary sources relating to class, rather than beginning with any given theory about how classes *ought* to be. She was, inevitably, strongly influenced by the French tradition of codification of occupational groups; and she was one of the first academic writers to make a detailed study of social legislation with a view to bringing out the references to class concealed therein. For example, she contrasted the Law on Working-Class Pensions of 5 April 1910 with the Law on Social Insurance of 5 April 1928. The first, she noticed, purported to be concerned only with workers and peasants, though, as she pointed out, certain categories of white-collar workers were also brought in; the second was concerned with all employees and could even be extended, on an optional basis, to certain small employers and members of the liberal professions. These changes in terminology she took as indicating changes in psychological and social perceptions of class and class relationships.

The rather complicated list of five social classes arrived at by Ferré repays close attention. It was as follows:

1. The clerical class.

2. The nobility.
3. The bourgeois class, including what she termed 'the economic bourgeoisie', as well as the liberal professions, the judges and magistrates, and officers and high civil servants.
4. The intermediate classes (white-collar workers in commerce, industry, banks, and medium functionaries).
5. The popular classes – in this revealing category she included workers, peasants, small employers, small and medium merchants, artisans, small industrialists, and small functionaries.

To these five classes she added a sixth grouping of the rootless and unfortunate who lay outside the class structure.

A number of points leap out immediately. The overtones of *ancien régime* and the Estates General are resonant. It would be highly unusual in Britain for the clerical class to be singled out for separate consideration, though not totally unknown in America. The noble class, of course, was another of the historic classes of the Estates General. Her remaining three classes suggest a mixture of Marxist sociology and the politics of French popular radicalism: her bourgeois and intermediate classes sat happily with the former, her popular class is very much part of the latter. This fifth class is not the proletariat but, in a very French sense, 'the people', containing many elements which in other countries would be regarded as belonging to the lower-middle class, and which were such a bastion of the Radical Party. The final grouping, that of the down-and-outs, derelicts and unclassifiables, though it has echoes of the Marxist *lumpenproletariat*, is one not often encountered among European commentators on class in the inter-war period. Indeed it was more usually in the United States that the existence of some such grouping as this was perceived.

In practice, few French authorities followed Ferré in recognizing the sacerdotal interest as a separate class. Most did, however, recognize the continuing independent existence of the nobility, though they do not attribute great significance to it. Almost all writers feel bound to spend some time on the ambiguities, even in French, of the words 'bourgeois' and 'bourgeoisie': 'for the *clubman*', wrote Jean Lhomme, the bourgeois 'is the man of an inferior class'; he is, said Maurice Halbwachs, 'a man without distinction'.[4] Yet there was almost universal recognition of the bourgeoise as the real upper class of France. On the meaning of the phrase 'popular classes' there was far less unanimity. When used, it is often with reference to all elements outside the grand bourgeoise, *except* the working class; in other words, it means Ferré's class 5 with the industrial workers thrown out but with her entire class 4 brought in. Indeed, while radical politicians might wish to court a vast popular class bearing the emblem of democratic citizenship, what comes through most strongly in the literature is a sense of the isolation within French society of the industrial working class.[5] When Ferré declared that the processes of social levelling were assimilating the working class into the general culture of the popular classes,[6] her standpoint was that of a left-wing radical. The more usual view was that put by Henri Simon of the University of Bordeaux to one of the annual conferences of the Catholic social and educational organization, Commission Générale des Semaines Sociales de France, which chose, at Bordeaux in 1939, to discuss 'The Problem of Classes in the National Community and in the Human Order'.

> Without doubt there exists in France a proletariat . . . and there exists equally a purely capitalist class, which controls the economic power of the nation and which employs a very large number of workers (*travailleurs*). But these are the two extreme categories of society, and if the first is large (perhaps a third or a half of the productive population), the other only includes a few hundred individuals. Between the two, is situated the social grouping which is probably the largest, and the most active; and also the most diverse, the one which includes skilled workers, artisans, peasants, engineers, functionaries, merchants, entrepreneurs, who cannot be classified among the proletariat since they have capital, or at least the means of hoping to acquire a little capital, nor among the capitalist class, since the most substantial part of their incomes is derived from their work or their personal capacities.[7]

In a special collection of essays devoted to the 'Middle Classes', issued in the same year by the École Normale Supérieure, Professor Maurice Halbwachs made the astonishing, but obviously deeply felt, judgement that the inferior and separate status of the working class arose in part from the fact that in their work they operated only on 'inert material', whereas the middle classes operated on 'living people' and therefore had to be blessed with special psychological perceptions.[8]

The existence of social classes, then, was not in doubt among French academics. And despite a sociological tradition which allowed for the use of such labels as 'proletariat' and 'bourgeoisie', most studies recognized the untidiness of the real social world. Discussions of class, said Raymond Aron, must include much of the unscientific resonance of popular language.[9] The Catholic *Semaines Sociales* accepted that 'the existence of social classes is an observable fact to which history has attested the reality'.[10] That reality, in the 1930s, was perceived by those with an academic or political interest in the subject to be as follows: at the top, what was variously termed the 'high bourgeoisie', and 'grand bourgeoisie', or the 'directing class'; a separate nobility was recognized, but seen as little more than an appendage to this class. At the bottom, and rather apart from the rest of society, was the working class, though some commentators sought to integrate it within the 'popular class'. It was not usual in French to speak of a 'lower class'. Most writers, including Marxist ones, recognized the special significance in French society of the 'middle classes' as well as of the peasantry; the plural usage, however, did not imply several distinct classes, but simply the variousness within one class.

Professors Simiand, Halbwachs and Simon all rejoiced in the apparent resilience and significance within the economy of the middle class. Yet an important phenomenon of the 1930s, in France as elsewhere, was the discovery of (or rather rediscovery of, and new emphasis on, since the plight of the middle class is always with us) the need for middle-class unity and identity in the face of the ravages of a hostile world. The middle classes, that mass of Frenchmen 'who are simultaneously both workers and owners, who carry the skills, the responsibilities and the risks', are caught 'between the anvil of plutocracy and the hammer of the proletariat', declared the economist and politician Henri Clerc.[11] But, as with 'the popular classes', the conception here is clearly political rather than social. In fact the history since the end of the previous century of the forming and reforming of middle-class protection organizations, such as the International Institute of the Middle Classes, suggests that the academic commentators are correct in stressing both the significance of the middle classes in France and their heterogeneity, which made any unified political action almost an impossibility.

AMERICAN IMAGES

Simiand and other French academics, charting the broad lands of political economy or political sociology, also commented on social class in both Britain and America, and I shall return briefly to these 'external images' at the end of this chapter. American academics preferred to contemplate their own navels, and rather microscopic portions of their navels at that. The study of *Middletown* (actually Muncie, Indiana), published in 1928 by Robert and Helen Lynd, was very different from contemporary French works on class. The approach was anthropological, based on interviews, and confined to one small community. As a preliminary model of the social structure, within which to cast their interviews, the Lynds chose the trichotomous one of 'upper class', 'middle class' and 'lower class'. But once embarked upon their researches they felt bound to reject this for the simpler dichotomous model of 'business class' and 'working class'.[12] 'Working class' really meant all employees, and included a range of occupations falling far outside the mere industrial working class; the very use of the word is most untypical of American academic thought of the time, where 'lower class', the original first choice, was much more common. For their second study, *Middletown in Transition*, published in 1937, the Lynds basically held to their dichotomous model, though they did move cautiously towards sketching a six-fold structure, defined as: upper class; upper-middle class; lower-middle class; an 'aristocracy of local labour'; the working class; and 'the ragged bottom margin'. This last category is really only a poetic description for the non-class of unfortunates identified in France by Louise-Marie Ferré, and which in later American usage came to be termed the 'under class'. The functional dichotomous model (employers and employees), and the inclination towards a longer continuous gradation into six classes were both characteristic of the way in which American sociological thought was crystallizing at this time. The Lynds reported that they discovered no real working-class consciousness and that traditional American values associated with free mobility and an open society were still strongly held to.[13]

The passion of American academics for highly detailed studies of populations small enough for heads to be counted and responses quantified, employing complex methods and clotted jargon upon which to frame large claims, reached its first full flowering in the articles, and then in 1941, in the first of the 'Yankee City' series of W. Lloyd Warner. Warner settled for two crucial indicators of class, as he saw it: 'participation' and 'status'. Put crudely, a person shows his social class by participating in most activities with other members of the same class; and that class is determined by the status allotted to it by the other members of society. Warner therefore got to work with 'Evaluated Participation (EP)' and the 'Index of Status Characteristics (ISC)'. Confining himself, as did the Lynds, to the study of one small community, and, like them, giving it a cover name ('Yankee City' for Newburyport in New England), he developed a model of the American class structure which certainly has a clear and simple ring to it: upper-upper; lower-upper; upper-middle; lower-middle; upper-lower; and lower-lower.[14] The range is longer than in comparable European studies, and the lower-lower class at the bottom has some of the implications of an 'under class'. As an alternative, Warner used the categories 'level above the common man', 'the common-man level' and 'level below the common man'. This simple trichotomous model strikingly brings out a central assumption among Americans; most Europeans took it for granted that 'the common-man level' was the bottom of the social scale. Warner was immensely influential, and a number of his disciples undertook important studies around this time – *Deep South* (1941), for example, by Davis, Gardner and Gardner, which postulated, side-by-side with a separate black social structure, a white upper class, middle class and lower class.[15]

While most academic research in America concentrated on anthropological investigations of small communities, the Great Depression and the controversies and policies of the New Deal gave a special impetus to the airing of all types of social issue, including those of social class. An early pamphlet on *Labor and the New Deal*, published by the Public Affairs Committee, a private group of academics, publicists and businessmen, favoured strong unions and the universal adoption of collective bargaining, but its view of social class was very much that of received American opinion:

In Europe, until the advent of the totalitarian state in some countries, labor was a closely-knit class aware not only of its strength and of its group interest but it has organised into political parties, fraternal and educational organisations, all of which have functioned as part of the labor movement. In the United States, however, the worker has never felt himself as different from his 'boss', except in the matter of income. In the United States also, the employee identified himself largely with the middle and property-owning class. This lack of labor consciousness resulted naturally enough from the peculiar progress of the United States, founded on democratic principles, whereas European countries were stratified into class groupings.[16]

Those who actually worked among the unemployed were more sensitive to the subtleties of American social distinctions, though

perhaps in a slightly idiosyncratic way. Helen Hall of the National
Federation of Settlements said of a rather unfashionable area of
Philadelphia that the clergy and the politicians 'are our gentry';
park guards and policemen 'give style to our middle classes, and
their steady income is the envy of the icemen, truckmen, and construction workers who, with seasonal employment [sic] always
around the corner, are so often our poor.'[17] The Roosevelt government's deliberate sponsorship, through the National Labor Relations Act, of collective bargaining, and, more important, the expansion of unionism through the activities of the Congress of Industrial
Organizations led to a more careful interest in class. At the end of
the decade, E. Wight Bakke (a 'government man' of a special
American sort, administrator and Yale professor) published two
books, *The Unemployed Worker* and *Citizens Without Work*. Both
are somewhat patronizing in tone and clearly recognize the 'working
class' as being quite different in culture and aspirations from people
like Bakke himself.[18] The second work is noteworthy for having an
entire chapter of face-to-face interviews entitled 'The Working
Class'. Against the rather trite views of *Labor and the New Deal*
Bakke argued that a genuine, fully formed working class was now
emerging in the United States, though the conclusions to which this
led him were at the opposite pole to those of orthodox Marxism.
Full implementation of New Deal policies, he maintained, would
persuade the workers to seek complete fulfilment within the working
class rather than through striving after upward mobility or identification with the boss. His interviews with workers revealed a deep
sense of class awareness. This awareness could become, as Bakke
believed was already the case in other nations, 'the very foundation
stone for social stability'.[19]

Discovery of the working class was accompanied by a new interest, paralleling that in France, in the middle class. Lewis Corey,
a leading American Marxist, in a very sympathetic study of the
problems and preoccupations of the American professional classes
and white-collar workers, distinguished between the petty bourgeoisie and the bourgeois capitalists, and called on the former to
join in the workers' struggle against the latter.[20] While Corey spoke
of *The Crisis of the Middle Class*, in the same year (1935) a right-
wing populist, Alfred M. Bingham, published his *Insurgent America:
Revolt of the Middle Classes*, a rallying cry for the establishment of
an American middle-class party. The proposal had more than a
smack of fascism to it, but Bingham produced a neat summary of
certain important aspects of American class imagery:

One can argue, with Marxian logic, that . . . in reality there are only two classes of people, those who live by their labor, and those who live by owning property, that is by capitalism. But the fact that there is such wide currency to the idea of a 'public', between and more important than 'capital' and 'labor' is significant, for we are governed by ideas. We are what we think we are. And if the bulk of people, in a modern capitalistic country like the United States, think of themselves as being of the middle class, having interests between those of 'capital' and 'labor', then there is such a middle class or middle group of classes.[21]

Unlike Clerc in France, Bingham was not motivated by fear of the working class, which he said was weak and lacking in class consciousness; to him the middle class was *the* important class. The middle class and, in particular, its role in American politics also received the attention of a Harvard professor of government, Arthur N. Holcombe. Above all, however, his study corroborated those of Bakke in suggesting that class was now becoming a force in American life, even assuming the place once held by geographical sectionalism:

The urban middle class, like the upper and lower classes in the urban population, has become increasingly conscious of its special interests at the same time that it has become increasingly aware of the great opportunities in national politics offered to it by the changing circumstances of the present age. Class-consciousness waxes as sectionalism wanes among the underlying forces in American politics, and the struggle of classes in some form threatens to become as important in the years ahead as the intersectional struggles in the years behind.[22]

But the fact that sectional rivalry produced civil war in the nineteenth century, says Holcombe, does not necessarily mean that there will be class war in the twentieth century. Although, then, an inclination towards speaking the language of class can be detected, particularly at the end of the decade, American intellectuals and polemicists presented a considerably less clear view of class than did their counterparts in France. There is talk of an upper class, but the relationship, if any, of the detailed anthropological studies' local upper class to the kind of national upper class referred to by Holcombe is nowhere made clear. The 'middleness' of much of American society is widely stressed; to describe those below the 'middle', 'lower class' is a term more used than 'working class'.

BRITISH IMAGES

The received, though paradoxical, academic view in Great Britain as to the non-existence or non-importance of class, was well expressed in the first edition (1927) of the standard *Survey of the Social Structure of England and Wales* by A. M. Carr-Saunders and B. Caradog Jones. Roundly they declared that 'belief in the existence of social classes . . . is a result of studying social theory of doubtful value and of neglecting social facts'.[23] The 'social theory of doubtful value' was, of course, Marxism. But it was not only dislike of Marxism which pointed refined minds away from class; sometimes it was simply a matter of obedience to the dictates of good taste. As R. H. Tawney, a social historian and socialist policy-maker rather than an academic sociologist, noted in his classic study, *Equality*, 'the word "class" is fraught with unpleasing associations, so that to linger upon it is apt to be interpreted as the symptom of a perverted mind and a jaundiced spirit'. Tawney took a very commonsense view of class, recognizing that it 'relates, not to this or that specific characteristic of a group, but a totality of conditions by which several sides of life are affected'.[24] But such public avowals were rare in an intellectual world in which sociology had yet to establish its respectability as an academic discipline, though certain social facts of the 1930s did push Carr-Saunders and Caradog Jones towards a marginal revision of their earlier judgement: 'is it not a mis-reading of the social structure of this country', they demanded in the second edition of their *Survey*, 'to dwell on class divisions, when in respect of dress, speech, and use of leisure, all members of the community are obviously coming to resemble one another?'[25] The writers need only have looked around them to see how minimally members of the community were coming to resemble one another, just as we need only glance back at the newsreels of the thirties to see obvious differences in dress and to hear clear distinctions of speech. There was a peculiar perversity in formal academic views on class since the topic inevitably found its way into general works on economics, wages and income, notably those of A. L. Bowley or Josiah Stamp,[26] or particular studies of *Life and Labour*.[27]

It is true that J. R. Hicks, author of what was once a standard text-book on elementary economics, did not get round to mentioning class until his last chapter, on 'The Inequality of Income', but his statement there sums up well British academics' assumptions which in the 1930s lay behind the more bland denials of the existence of social class.

In Britain, as in most other countries, the great majority of the population have incomes rather below the average for the community as a whole. The number of people with incomes above the average is relatively small; but some of these people have incomes very much above the average. It is customary, in ordinary speech for political purposes, to refer to this last group (small in numbers but with large incomes) as 'the wealthy'; the larger group, whose incomes are above the average, but less markedly above it, as the 'middle class'; and the largest group, most of whose incomes are below the average, as the 'working class'. It should, however, be noticed that *class* differences are not by any means wholly due to differences in incomes; for social purposes a person belongs to the middle class if he lives in a middle class way and associates with middle class people. The distinction between working class and middle class is as much a matter of the way income is earned as of the size of the income; . . . It is not possible to divide the population into clearly marked classes, each consisting of people with lower incomes than people in the classes above them, and higher incomes than people in the classes below them.[28]

Hicks, one cannot help noticing, speaks of 'the wealthy', not of 'the upper class'. There was indeed much shyness over speaking *in public* about an upper class, though one could, without violating good taste speak of an 'upper-middle class'.

The British social context made it very difficult for academic writers on social and economic topics to avoid the language of class, despite the fundamental instinct of the class to which so many academics belonged that class was not something that should be talked about, or, at least, not too much. Still, I must mince my jibes, for many British academics of progressive views genuinely believed, like Louise-Marie Ferré in France, that class distinctions, so notorious a feature of the Victorian age, were indeed withering away. The perception of class structure which surfaces from all the discreet shilly-shallying is of a well-defined working class, a rather less well-defined middle class (with many writers from time to time referring to a 'lower-middle class'), and some sort of other class above that, often given some such polite (or fairly polite!) epithet as 'the wealthy' or 'the upper-middle class'. In the academic literature, such had been the impact of the First World War, the progress of social welfare and the effect of trade union organization, the concept of a 'submerged class' or 'under class' had almost totally disappeared.

EXTERNAL IMAGES

Broadly (to turn finally to external images), the American view of Europe (Britain and France not usually being distinguished from each other) was of a continent upon which the course of history had so deeply imprinted the contours of class that there was a segregated, embattled working class, and a self-perpetuating, haughty upper class. Almost all French commentators were agreed in seeing France as the most tradition-bound and static of the three societies, with America as the most mobile and least class-conscious, and Britain coming somewhere in between. The British had no view of either America or France.[29] As would be expected, the French perceptions of their fellow Western democracies repay attention. French scholars had little difficulty in perceiving a distinct British upper class, with its effortless sense of superiority.[30] They made almost an obsession of the ethics of 'the gentleman' which they believed dominated the upper class and provided a basis for emulation on the part of the middle class, whose considerable wealth compared with their French counterparts was also stressed.[31] French academics recognized the special coherence of the British working class, and, naturally, the absence of any significant rural element. Most French observers felt that there was a small upper class in the United States. but in the main they saw America as a thoroughly middle-class society to a degree which was true neither of Britain nor France. Unlike the European middle classes, the American middle class, as Paul Vaucher put it, was not a 'residue' (left behind in the formation of the grand bourgeoisie) but a 'new creation'. This middle class was free to forge its own system of values since it had to compete neither with aristocracy nor with proletariat.[32] Of such are the visions of intellectuals; now let us test them against some other images of class.

Notes

1. Helen and Robert Lynd, *Middletown: a Study in Contemporary American Culture* (1928).
2. *Cours d'économie politique, professé en 1928–1929 par M. François Simiand* (1929), pp. 440–85.
3. Louise-Marie Ferré, *Les Classes sociales dans la France contemporaine* (1934).
4. Jean Lhomme, *Le Problème des classes* (1938), p. 262. Maurice Halbwachs, *Les Classes sociales* (Les Cours de Sorbonne, 1942), p. 102.
5. See especially Maurice Halbwachs, *ibid*, p. 89ff.
6. Ferré, *op. cit.*, p. 102.
7. *Semaines Sociales de France XXXI, Bordeaux 1939: le problème des classes dans la communauté sociale et dans l'ordre humain* (1942), p. 172.
8. Maurice Halbwachs, 'Les Caractéristiques des classes moyennes', *Inventaires III: classes moyennes* (1939), p. 41.
9. Raymond Aron, 'Le Concept de classe', in *ibid*, p. 7.
10. *Semaines Sociales XXXI, op cit.*, p. 499.
11. Henri Clerc, *Pour sauver les classes moyennes* (1939), p. 33.
12. Lynd, *op. cit.*, pp. 22–3.
13. Helen and Robert Lynd, *Middletown in Transition: a Study in Cultural Conflicts* (1937), pp. 41–73, 458–60.
14. W. Lloyd Warner and Paul S. Lunt, *The Social Life of a Modern Community* (1941), *The Status System of a Modern Community* (1942).
15. Alison Davis, Burleigh B. Gardner and Mary R. Gardner, *Deep South: a Social Anthropological Study of Class and Caste* (1941).
16. Public Affairs Committee, *Labor and the New Deal* (1936), p. 2.
17. Helen Hall, introduction to *Case Studies of the Unemployed: Compiled by the Unemployment Committee of the National Federation of Settlements* (1931), p. xxv.
18. E. Wight Bakke, *The Unemployed Worker* (1940), *Citizens Without Work* (1940).
19. Bakke, *Citizens Without Work*, pp. 85–105.
20. Lewis Corey, *The Crisis of the Middle Class* (1935).
21. Alfred M. Bingham, *Insurgent America: Revolt of the Middle Classes* (1935), p. 47.
22. Arthur N. Holcombe, *The Middle Classes in American Politics* (1940), p. 57.
23. A. M. Carr-Saunders and D. Caradog Jones, *A Survey of the Social Structure of England and Wales* (1927), p. 71.
24. R. H. Tawney, *Equality* (1931), pp. 65, 69.
25. Carr-Saunders and Caradog Jones, *A Survey of the Social Structure of England and Wales* (1937), p. 66.

26. A. L. Bowley, *Wages and Income in the United Kingdom Since 1860* (1937); A. L. Bowley and J. Stamp, *The National Income 1924* (1927).
27. H. Llewellyn Smith, ed., *New Survey of London Life and Labour*, 9 vols. (1930–5).
28. J. R. Hicks, *The Social Framework: an Introduction to Economics* (1942), p. 179.
29. Here I am speaking solely of academic or polemical writers addressing themselves directly or indirectly to problems of class.
30. J. Lhomme, *Le Problème des classes* (1938), p. 264.
31. G. Lecarpentier, 'Revenus et fortunes privés en France et en Grande-Bretagne', *Revue Politique et Parlementaire* (October 1937), pp. 73–81.
32. Paul Vaucher, 'Les Classes moyennes aux États-Unis', in *Inventaires III* (1939), pp. 155–6.

4

Official Images of Class

The most obvious place to look for official images of class is in the national census, which each country has been carrying out at ten-yearly (in Britain and America) or five-yearly (in France) intervals since the early nineteenth century. Census statistics are served up in a variety of ways, none of them, unfortunately, directly usable by the historian looking for straightforward answers to questions such as 'How many people belonged to the working class?' or 'What proportion of the people were middle class?' All three countries classify major occupational groupings, such as 'agriculture and fisheries', 'manufacturing industry', 'extractive industry', 'transport and communications' or 'commerce and banking', not to mention those 'not gainfully employed'. Hidden within each of these categories might be owners, top executives, white-collar workers and manual labourers. In France, the 'not gainfully employed' included, in the 1930s, not only those who were living off private investments and who were therefore 'bourgeois' in some degree, but also the retired, who belonged to all social classes, and vagabonds, who belonged to none. Category 8A – 'personal services' – included shoe-blacks, also on the margins of the social structure, as well as proprietors of baths, who must have been solid lower or middle bourgeois. However, the French census also reported on 'individual occupational status'. Here the classification was into P for owner or head of establishment (*patron* or *chef d'établissment*), I for self-employed (with that touch of false romance engendered in British ears by the French language, *isolé*), E for white-collar worker (*employé*), and O for manual worker (*ouvrier*), with the unemployed being treated as a separate category. The weakness of this classification as a representation of the real class-structure of France is made evident by the way in which the *paysans* are included among the owners, as are wives who assist their husbands in running a business, be it factory, farm, shop or inn. There was official recognition of differences in social status; and certain assumptions about the nature of different occupations are apparent. For example, the

59

category 'liberal professions' was applied only to those working on their own account, such as doctors, dentists, solicitors, barristers or architects.[1] But as far as the French census was concerned there was no such thing as an upper class or a bourgeoisie, or any structure of classes after the fashion in which that term was popularly used, and is used in this book.

Fundamental to social relationships in all three countries was the legal concept of contract of service. Qualified in a variety of ways by industrial legislation, especially in Britain, this concept nonetheless had the effect of placing employer and employee in a master-servant relationship. French law recognized the distinction between, on the one side, the employer, and, on the other side, the white-collar worker and the manual worker. The *Code of Work* (*Code de Travail*), whose seven closely worded volumes came stumbling out between 1910 and 1936, drew a distinction between the intellectual and non-intellectual qualities of the white-collar and manual workers respectively. A law of 23 April 1924 laid down that manual workers in commerce or industry were to be paid at least twice a month and at intervals no greater than a fortnight, whereas white-collar workers were to be paid at least once a month. The *Code* itself explained the reason for making the distinction: manual workers were less inclined towards thrift than white-collar workers! The superior status of the white-collar worker was embodied in a law of 8 August 1935 concerning workers' rights to wages and salaries when a firm went bankrupt: while manual workers were guaranteed wages only for the last fortnight of employment, white-collar workers were covered for a whole month.[2]

Laws of 18 March 1919, 26 June 1920 and 1 June 1923 governed the position of the merchant. He had to be enrolled on the official register of commerce, he had to publicise his official number, and he had to keep certain official account books which were open to government inspection. Other laws were passed specifically to protect the interests of the merchants, particularly in such matters as safeguarding them against the risks involved in borrowing money to run their businesses. Legislation of an even more favourable nature was enacted in the interest of the artisans. By the law of 17 March 1934 all artisans were, like the merchants, required to enrol on an official register.[3]

AMERICAN CENSUSES AND CONTRACTS

Predictably, the American census did not recognize social classes, though as far back as the 1890s a number of census officials had argued in favour of classifying gainful workers into social-economic groups. In an article published in 1897, William C. Hunt, for many years chief statistician for population in the Bureau of Census, grouped the gainful workers into four groups (and indeed, in three cases, termed them classes): A, the proprietor class; B, the clerical class (i.e. clerks, not clerics); C, skilled workers; D, the labouring class. Ever since the First World War, Alba M. Edwards of the Bureau of Census had taken up the cry of the 1890s for classification into social-economic groups, and in the 1930s this became official Bureau of Census policy.[4] The six social-economic groups officially adopted were described as follows: 1. Professional persons; 2. Proprietors, managers and officials, comprising farmers (owners and tenants), wholesale and retail dealers, and other proprietors, managers and officials; 3. Clerks and kindred workers; 4. Skilled workers and foremen; 5. Semi-skilled workers; 6. Unskilled workers, including farm labourers, factory and building construction labourers, other labourers, and the servant classes.

The full detail of this taxonomy may be studied in all its glory in the Appendix on pages 366–75. In a discussion of it Edwards remarked that the composition of groups 1 and 2 was probably sufficiently clear. Group 3 he glossed as 'the so-called white-collar workers', the clerical assistants to executives, officials, and business and professional men, comprising office assistants, sales people, telegraph and telephone operators, and all others doing various types of clerical and kindred work. The remainder of his explanation was stronger on tautology than illumination:

Skilled workers and foremen – group 4 – comprise foremen and the followers of skilled trades, such as blacksmiths, carpenters, machinists, etc. Semi-skilled workers – group 5 – include apprentices, machine tenders, workers in the needle trades, etc. They are manual workers who have a moderate degree of skill and of manual dexterity. Unskilled workers – group 6 – include the laborers and the different servant classes. Most of them have no special training.

Clearly a social hierarchy is implied, though the term class is scrupulously avoided, save for the 'servant classes' right at the bottom of the heap. The placing of the professions at the top suggests that prestige rather than power is the criterion here. Group 2 contains a startling range, and in its lowest sub-section (see Appendix) would seem to contain under such headings as 'manufacturers', 'owners and managers' and 'bankers' some of the most powerful men in the whole of American society. The weakness of this hierarchy as a guide to social relationships in the America of the thirties is brought out by the remarkably high proportion of black females shown by other studies using this classification to be in group 1 (they happened to be schoolteachers) and by the number of blacks who show up in group 2-a. Having no wish to see his system of social-economic groups blown up on the sensitive trip-wire of American white racism, Edwards hastened to appease: 'The relatively large proportion of the Negro workers classed as "proprietors, managers, officials" is explained', he wrote, 'by the fact that 15.9 per cent of the Negroes, as compared with 13.1 per cent of the native whites and 6.3 per cent of foreign-born whites, were farmers (owners or tenants).'[6]

While America did not have the formal codifications of commerce and labour to be found in France, great stress was placed on the notion of contract of labour. In law, indeed, America was a supremely Marxist country, recognizing two economic classes, employers and employees. To this dichotomous structure some states still added to the underside a 'pauper class', marked off by definite legal disabilities.[7]

CENSUS AND SOCIAL LEGISLATION IN BRITAIN

Britain had been the first country, in 1801, to institute a national census, and was the first to introduce an explicit class hierarchy as one of the forms in which census data could be presented. The five-class schema was introduced in 1911, although only for the specific purpose of enabling the Registrar General to make a comparative study of infant mortality. It certainly served its turn in bringing out the dreadful infant death rate at the bottom of the social scale, but it did not necessarily come much closer than the French or American formulations to an exact description of class as an historical or popularly understood phenomenon. The hierarchy was given as: Class I, Professional etc. occupations; Class II, Intermediate occupations; Class III, Skilled occupations; Class IV, Partly skilled occupations; Class V, Unskilled occupations. The British scheme had anticipated one of the basic imperfections of the American one: the rather vague 'Intermediate' Class II included proprietors of businesses, managers and bankers, as well as certain professions not considered good enough for Class I – school and university teachers among them.

The literature of the decision-making process as coders and supervisors agonized over how to allocate people to these different classes makes choice reading. In 1931, for example, certain unskilled workers were transferred from Class IV to Class V, and some clerks from Class II to Class III.

Detailed sub-division of proprietors and managers of businesses and of salesmen and shop assistants according to the type of business in which they are engaged, and classification of drivers of self-propelled vehicles according to whether they were engaged in conveyance of passengers or goods are also new features of the 1931 classification. New groups have also been distinguished for die-casters, insulated cable and wire machine workers, wheel-wrights, paint-sprayers, restaurant counterhands, oilers and greasers of machinery, slingers and riggers, and Fire Brigade officers and men. Certain transfers such as those of painters of pottery, japanners of metal and french polishers to the order of 'painters and decorators' also affect comparisons with 1921.

There also took place in 1931, 'the transfer of railway porters from Class IV, locomotive engine firemen and cleaners, ticket collectors and examiners from III to IV, haulage and carriage contractors, cleaners and restaurant keepers from III to IV, warehouse and storekeepers' assistants from IV to V, agriculture machine attendants and dynamo and switchboard attendants from IV to III, and farm bailiffs from III to II.' Special headaches were apparently caused by 'females returned as following occupations believed to be invariably or almost invariably followed by males only, and vice versa'. Such cases were always to be referred by the coder to his supervisor.[8] But for all the detail, evoking faint echoes of the French codes, the five-fold classification of the British census was occupational rather than social and most useful for providing broad contrasts in medical and mortality statistics: general practitioners still sometimes use it today in classifying their own patients.

A much more rewarding area of study for official images of class is to be found in social welfare legislation. Until the Second World War almost all British legislation on such topics as housing, industrial injuries, unemployment insurance, health insurance and medical provision, old age and widows' pensions, and holidays with pay, concerned only the problems of one social group, which stands out quite starkly as a statutory working class (the phrase most often used is 'working classes' – the plural recognizing the wide range of occupations and incomes – but as with the French 'middle classes', it is clear that one single class is envisaged). Much the same was true of government discussion of household budgets and the cost of living. Education has already been discussed as contributing to the context within which class develops: inevitably legislation in this sphere reverberates with official assumptions about class.

Housing legislation provides the clearest evidence of official recognition of a working class. The Housing Acts of the late Victorian period, which permitted the building of housing subsidized by the rates (but not by national taxation), were explicitly concerned with the working or 'labouring' class. A report from a Select Committee of both Houses of Parliament on the Housing of the Working Classes in 1902 explained that

> the expression 'labouring class' means mechanics, artisans, labourers and others working for wages, hawkers, costermongers, persons not working for wages but working at some trade or handicraft without employing others except members of their own family, and persons other than domestic servants, whose income does not exceed the average of thirty shillings a week, and the family of any such persons who may be residing with them.

At the end of the First World War housing became a matter of much greater concern to central government when, in the Addison Act of 1919, central funds paid for out of national taxation were for the first time made available for the building of houses at subsidized rents. One of the background papers to the act, in stressing the requirement that the houses built must be 'for the occupation of the working classes', noted that a stricter definition of this term was now required, and proposed an upper income limit of £200 per year, a figure arrived at by taking the £160 per annum which was then the upper income limit for those covered by workmens' compensation and national health insurance, and making an allowance for wartime inflation.[9] Legislators, however, recognized that class was not to be defined by income alone. Before enacting each housing act of the inter-war period parliament discussed how a sharper definition might be drawn up, and each time it concluded that the phrase 'housing for the working classes' was sufficient in itself. This was the position maintained by the Labour Minister of Health, Arthur Greenwood, when presenting his housing bill to the House of Commons in April 1930, despite the vigorous questioning of the

Independent MP, Eleanor Rathbone, and the eccentric support of the Liberal MP, Lieutenant-Commander Kenworthy:

MISS RATHBONE asked the Minister of Health what interpretation is placed by the Ministry upon the term working classes in administering the Housing Act of 1890, 1909, 1923, 1923 (2), 1924, 1925, and in the Bill now before the House?

MR GREENWOOD: The term 'working classes' is generally well understood, and I am not aware of any practical difficulty in its interpretation. The term has not been defined for the general purposes of any of the Acts mentioned in the question, and I do not propose to attempt the definition which Parliament and previous Ministers of Health have refrained from using.

MISS RATHBONE: Can the right hon. Gentleman tell us how he expects local authorities to know what classes of person should be admitted to the houses subsidised by the State if the Ministry have no accepted definition, and whether he is aware that large numbers of persons are taking advantage of subsidised houses and asking leave to build a motor garage?

MR GREENWOOD: The local authorities have never found any practical difficulties in defining it for themselves.

LIEUT-COMMANDER KENWORTHY: Is there any reason why a working man should not have a motor car and a motor garage?[10]

Nor were the courts anxious to rush in where parliament feared to tread. In the case of *White v. St Marylebone Borough Council* in 1915 it was held that 'a chauffeur in the employment of a private individual' was 'a member of the working classes'; but in *Arledge v. Tottenham Urban District Council* in 1922 it was simply held that the words 'working classes ... must receive their ordinary and natural construction. ...'[11] There was indeed no problem: those who applied for 'council' houses knew themselves to be working-class, or knew that they were bidding to live in segregated estates of a profoundly working-class character, a perishing thought for clerical workers and above, who, in any case, were amply catered for by the low mortgages and private building boom of the 1930s. Slum clearance was a slightly different matter: here property rights and guarantees of rehousing were at stake. Thus the fifth schedule of the Housing Act of 1925 – 'an act to consolidate the enactments relating to the Housing of the Working Classes in England and Wales' – repeated as the eleventh schedule to the 1936 Housing Act, gave statutory force to the suggested definition of the 1902 Select

Committee, though only, it must be stressed, in matters of slum clearance and rehousing. For the purposes of the schedule, a house was to be considered a 'working man's dwelling . . . if wholly or partially occupied by a person belonging to the working classes'. So far so good. Then the definition:

> the expression 'working class' includes mechanics, artisans, labourers and others working for wages, hawkers, costermongers, persons not working for wages, but working at some trade or handicraft without employing others except members of their own family, and persons other than domestic servants, whose income does not exceed an average of three pounds a week, and the families of such persons who may be residing with them.

All that had changed since 1902, apparently, was that wage levels had doubled. With this definition to guide them, local authorities were required, before embarking upon slum clearance schemes, to conduct 'a certified count of the working-class persons' in 'any "grey" properties proposed to be purchased'.[12]

The fear that subsidized housing might be going to non-working-class families shivered more timbers in Scotland than in England. In 1932 the Department of Health in Scotland called for a special investigation 'in regard to the steps necessary to secure that state-aided houses will in future be let only to persons of the working classes'. As in England, the single legislative definition to be found in the fifth schedule of the Housing (Scotland) Act of 1925 related only to slum clearance. The department's consultative council, in investigating the problem, seemed to suggest that, belonging to a poor country with a large industrial working class and a relatively small middle class, the Scots recognized fewer clear distinctions between the two. It recommended the imposition of a family income test supported by an attestation form declaring the income recorded to be the true one. Describing those who would not pass the income test as the 'well-to-do', the consultative council reckoned them as amounting to only five to ten per cent of the total population of Scotland. As to formulating an 'all-embracing and reasonably water-tight' definition of the term 'working classes', that task, the council confessed, was beyond them. In any case it was the council's opinion that 'the term "working classes" in the Acts' was 'an unsatisfactory and an unfortunate one'. Apart from the absence of any definition for general application, the apparent impossibility of arriving at such a definition, and the differences of opinion that existed as to who were to be included in the term, there were, said the council, 'many families who, according to the general acceptation of the term, will be considered as coming within it and who are better off financially than many others who are not generally considered to be persons of the working classes'.[13]

The concept of a working class and its housing was not confined to the local council estates. The Central Housing Advisory Committee (CHAC) of the Ministry of Health held a watching brief over problems relating to working-class housing in private ownership, particularly in regard to health and hygiene and infestation by rats, mice and bugs of all descriptions; infestation, together with undue consumption of tinned food, being, in the bureaucratic mind, persistent characteristics of working-class life in the older urban areas. It was in keeping with the general tone of commitment and social concern in the 1930s, as well as of the ethic which treated the working class as an object, fit for analysis and for patronage, that the Board of Trade should have commissioned the Council for Art and Industry to prepare a report on *The Working Class Home: its Furnishing and Equipment.* In this case it was assumed that a family with an income of £5 a week or less could be regarded as working-class, though it was recognized that 'custom may regard some of the families within this limit as belonging to the so-called lower middle class'.[14]

The first piece of industrial injuries legislation, the Workmen's Compensation Act of 1897, was restricted to those employed 'by way of manual labour'. Shortly before the First World War came the first legislation on national health insurance and unemployment insurance. At that time no one earning less than £160 per year paid income tax, the token, as it were, of middle-class respectability, financial solidity, and support and sustenance for the community. In any case, a very clear distinction was indeed felt to exist between an annual salary, which could readily be taxed, and weekly wages which in those days long before Pay As You Earn could not. The £160 figure, the frontier, as it were, of the feckless working class, was also used as the upper income limit for those covered by the Workmen's Compensation and National Insurance Acts. Those who thought of themselves as middle class were believed, correctly, to have no wish for any truck with provision so clearly intended for the working classes. However, as in so many other areas, the Great Depression of the inter-war years was to modify both image and reality. Amidst the muddy morass of mass unemployment there proliferated a rich undergrowth of law and regulation concerning exactly who was, and who was not, entitled to the protection of unemployment insurance. The basic principle remained that the qualification was that of doing manual labour, with doubtful cases being settled by the income limit, which by the 1930s had risen to £250 a year. Occasionally the courts were asked to rule on the question of what constituted manual labour. On one occasion the High Court ruled that manual labour and manual work meant the same thing! On another occasion it reversed a Ministry of Labour decision by declaring that acrobats and professional footballers were not manual labourers but public performers.[15]

Quite the most revealing document on the state of law and opinion in the thirties on the distinction between a wage-earning working class, as a fit object for state-sponsored social security, and a salary-earning middle class, expected to make provision for hard times through its own thrift and higher earning power, is the 1936 Report of the Unemployment Insurance Statutory Committee on Remuneration Limits for Insurance of Non-Manual Workers, which was chaired by Sir William Beveridge, than whom none was better fitted to transmit the views of the more progressive elements in British officialdom. The committee noted that the Ministry of Labour's letter of 27 February 1935, which had placed the matter before them, had spoken of raising the 'salary' limit for those covered by unemployment insurance and that the term 'salary' had been used by many of the witnesses testifying before the committee. But, and one can detect the stern precision of Sir William Beveridge, 'the term used in the Unemployment Insurance Act is neither "salary" nor "income" but "remuneration".' The essence of the problem, the committee explicitly recognized, was that the remuneration limit applied to 'persons who would normally describe their remuneration as wages, rather than salary, and are practically indistinguishable from other wage-earners'.[16] At a time of economic hardship, when many salaried occupations were afflicted by unemployment, much of the evidence from employees supported raising the income (or 'remuneration' as Beveridge insisted) limit, and employee associations in favour included those representing journalists, architects, correctors of the press and others connected with the printing trades, textile managers, coke-oven managers, colliery under-managers, navigating officers, marine engineers, chemists, shop assistants, actors, musicians, theatrical employees, and life assurance workers. The banking and insurance associations were divided, while the chartered accountants and solicitors' clerks, rock solid in their sense of middle-class respectability, were firmly against. Most teachers, along with municipal employees and civil servants, were excluded from the provisions of unemployment insurance in any case, but it is worth noting that the great bulk of teachers expressed strong hostility to any raising of the income limit.[17]

The majority of the committee recognized that in strict logic there were great difficulties in making the distinction between manual and non-manual occupations, but in discussing the distinctions between, say, a dairyman's foreman and a chief dental mechanic, a butcher's manager in a small shop and a butcher's manager in a large shop, or a linotype compositor and a typist, the committee implicitly recognized that guidance was always to be found in the accepted conventions of British society (the first in each pair being treated as manual, the second as non-manual). Most of the witnesses who favoured increasing the income limit had argued for a doubling of the existing figure of £250 a year, although a Royal Commission in 1932 had suggested the figure of £350. So, perhaps with greater respect for the principle of splitting the difference than for sociological accuracy in defining wage-earning occupations, the committee recommended a limit of £400. However, the crux of the issue is contained in the minority report signed by two out of the seven members of the committee: their argument for a figure of £300 was that the main Unemployment Insurance Act of 1920 had clearly intended the inclusion of only 'that body of non-manual workers which corresponded in the matter of income to the general body of manual workers'.[18]

The same principles governed national health insurance legislation and the widows, orphans and old age contributory pensions, introduced at the end of the 1920s. Non-manual workers earning more than £250 could voluntarily contribute to the health insurance scheme and gain an entitlement to sick pay, though not to free medical attention, widely viewed as yet another mark of working-class status. The detail of medical care and, more significantly, of institutional provision – where the crude but potent divisions were between those who used private nursing homes, those who used voluntary or local authority hospitals, and paid, and those who used voluntary or local authority hospitals and did not pay – brings us into a realm where, as in education, official attitudes are submerged under those of an influential private body, in this case the medical profession; they will be dealt with in another chapter as part of the unofficial images of class. Since the contributory pensions scheme contained fewer exemptions than any of the other social security programmes of the thirties, it provides probably the best indicator of the composition of the legislatively recognized working class of the period. In December 1936, 17,750,000 people were included in this scheme: if allowance is made for the exemptions, and a few other additions are made (for example to allow for persons over the age of sixty five) this gives a figure of 18,250,000, eighty-five per cent of the total gainfully employed population.

The calculations which produced this figure of eighty-five per cent were made by Lord Amulree's Committee on Holidays with Pay, which saw itself as being concerned with 'workpeople coming within the employment field, including the unemployed, who are either manual workers, or non-manual workers in receipt of not more than £250 a year'.[19] While no criticism can legitimately be made of Lord Amulree, nor of the committee, which included such important trade-union leaders as Ernest Bevin and George Hicks, the careful marshalling of the evidence in the committee's report makes it a key document not only in revealing the definition and size of the statutory working class, but also for showing the paternalistic, and even patronizing, attitudes of the state towards that class, as well as the meanness of the master–servant mentality of many British employers. It also brought out the explicit distinction between 'salaried employees' who for eighty years or more had had an entitlement to holidays with pay, and 'wage-earning employees' who usually had no such entitlement. The terms of reference of the Amulree committee were: 'to investigate the extent to which holidays with pay are given to employed work people and the possibility of extending the provision of such holidays by statutory enactment or otherwise; and to make recommendations'. Among the problems which exercized the committee were that paid holidays might discourage work people from saving up money for themselves and that if they did get paid holidays they might simply take other jobs; even so, among such other jobs, fruit-picking was thought to be acceptable. More positively, the committee, reflecting on 'the current widespread desire to improve the nation's physique', agreed that an annual holiday 'contributes in a considerable measure to work people's happiness, health and efficiency'. Nonetheless, it remained 'incumbent on the employee to save the extra money' so that 'the wife or mother may receive the benefit of a change and, if practicable, of a rest, as well as the actual employee'.[20]

Just as Lord Amulree's committee was concerned solely with the question of holidays for the working class, and just as the housing advisory committee within the Ministry of Health was really concerned with working-class housing standards, equally the food council of the Board of Trade was concerned with the diet and living standards of the working class. So widely recognized was this (among those who had actually heard of the food council of the Board of Trade, that is to say!) that in February 1939 the Trade Union Congress asked that a trade union representative should be added to the council; coming at the end of the long inter-war deflation, 1939 was a year of rising prices. The official view of the president of the Board of Trade was that the price rises which had occurred 'did not mean . . . a deterioration in the living standards of the working class'. On the question of the appointment of a TUC representative to the council, the reaction of Geoffrey Peto, chairman of the council, was both suspicious and patronizing: such a representative, he feared, might use or abuse his position 'for purpose of party politics', though, he had to add, he had 'not so far met a representative of the Labour Party on a non-party body who was not a satisfactory colleague'.[21]

Educational legislation, insofar as it defines class, like medical care and hospital provision, takes us into the border realm where attitudes are determined by private institutions as well as by official policy. Suffice it to say that in England and Wales, and in large degree in Scotland, there was a tripartite educational structure, based on the famous public schools and the private preparatory schools associated with them, the various forms of direct grant secondary and primary schools, and the public elementary schools (PES in the bureaucratic code). The spirit of class solidarity fostered by the previous war had helped to build a path, albeit a narrow one, across the lower reaches of this divided world: direct grant secondary schools were instructed to provide at least twenty-five per cent of their places free to pupils from the public elementary schools who had passed the special scholarship exam. Board of Education circular number 1421 of October 1932 sought to obstruct even this narrow path by replacing the free places with 'special places' with a scale of fees based on means. Undoubtedly, the prime motive was one of economy, and in practice the Board of Education did not stop any local authorities from continuing to honour the old system rather than the new, but pupils who did make it to the secondary schools, by whatever route, continued to find themselves officially categorized by their social origins in the form of the labels 'ex-PES' or 'non ex-PES'.[22]

SOCIAL LEGISLATION IN FRANCE AND AMERICA

In keeping with her complex social structure of occupation groups

and estates, France's social security provision was much more fragmented than that in Britain. Such laws as were enforced had often
been achieved only against great resistance, sometimes even from
those whom they were intended to benefit. Broadly, in the 1930s,
social insurance was obligatory for all employees, male and female,
earning up to 18,000 francs per annum in cities with a population
over 200,000 and up to 15,000 francs in other localities; the income
limit was extended upwards to 25,000 francs for those with more
than two children.[23] But in contrast with the labour and industrial
codes, and with social security legislation in Britain, the images of
class which emerge are not very distinct. Clearly, the grand bourgeoisie, the professions, and much of the medium and petty bourgeoisie are excluded, but the main force behind this legislation was
not a clear perception of a working class and its distinctive needs,
but rather sporadic responses to specific need and a wish to encourage a rise in the birth rate. French social security legislation, it might
be said, was concerned more with the family than with class.

Compared with France, and indeed with Britain, America under
the presidency of Roosevelt after 1932, underwent a great flurry of
social legislation. But, predictably, the images of class which can
fitfully be glimpsed are very blurred compared with those intrinsic
to British social policy. Roosevelt's administration acted with great
éclat and vigour, but policies were not always very different in conception from those of Herbert Hoover. Hoover had established the
President's Organisation for the Unemployed (POUR), a main
function of which was to provide loans for those out of work. The
underlying assumption of this plan, an assumption which persisted
throughout the decade, was that 'the great mass of unemployed are
people like ourselves, the only difference being their unfortunate
economic position at the present time'. There was a hierarchy, but
it was presented as a hierarchy of continuous gradations rather than
of classes: these 'people like ourselves' ranged 'from the unskilled
workers at the bottom of the scale up through the skilled mechanics,
miners, machine operators, and minor "bosses", to book-keepers,
stenographers, typists, accountants and junior executives'.[24]

Roosevelt himself, whatever perception he had of the status of
his own family and close associates in society, had no very developed
view of the class structure. In his speeches he tended to speak of 'the
people of the nation' or 'the citizen and his family'. The preamble
to the National Recovery Act of June 1933 suggests that at this stage
he and his administration still held firmly to the integrationist model
of American capitalist society. The purpose of the act was:

To remove obstructions to the free flow of interstate and foreign commerce which tend to diminish the amount thereof; and to provide for the general welfare by promoting the organisation of industry for the purpose of co-operative action among trade groups, to induce and maintain united action of labor and management under adequate governmental sanction and supervision, to eliminate unfair competitive practices, to promote the fullest possible utilisation of the present productive capacity of industries, to avoid undue restriction of production (except as may be temporarily required), to increase the consumption of industrial and agricultural products by increasing purchasing power, to reduce and relieve unemployment, to improve standards of labor, and otherwise to rehabilitate industry and to conserve natural resources.

As he signed the act on 16 June 1933, the President declared that his goal was 'the assurance of a reasonable profit to industry and living wages for labor with the elimination of the tyrannical methods and practices which have not only harassed honest business but also contributed to the ills of labor'. The basic function of the act was to prepare codes by which industry was henceforth to be conducted. The codes would not be approved by the President unless they contained conditions 'for the protection of consumers, competitors, employees, and others, and in the furtherance of the public interest'.[25] The National Recovery Administration organization included separate advisory boards for labour, for industry, and for the consumers, but it did not extend to the professions nor to agricultural and domestic workers. Already some key themes have been announced: the functional economic model of employers, employees, and consumers – not a class model at all since presumably consumers are drawn from both of the other two groups – and the exclusion, at a high level, of the professions, and at a lower, of agricultural and domestic workers.

By the time of the congressional elections of 1934, Roosevelt was beginning to lose some of his faith in the possibilities of co-operation with business leaders. The National Labor Relations Act of 1935 was certainly the first powerful recognition by the American government of the special needs and position of labour. But the language was scarcely the language of class. The National Labor Relations Board addressed itself to the problems of 'employers and employees', or of 'employers and labor', but not of 'the working class'. In fact, the term 'employees', or indeed 'labor', embraced social groups which in Britain would have been separated out as middle-class. Where, then, there was anything like an official model of class, it was, as noted at the beginning of this chapter, a dichotomous one.

In preparation for America's first social security legislation, the President set up the Economic Security Committee, demanding of it that it draft a short and simple bill. However, as Frances Perkins, the Secretary of Labor, remarked, in a pluralist, federal nation like America, no bill dealing with the raising of funds for social security could be a simple one.[26] Three kinds of provision were envisaged: unemployment insurance, old age pensions, and pensions for blindness and other disabilities. In its deliberations the Economic Security Committee[27] gave much thought to defining which sections of the population should be covered by the social security legislation: the British system, which, as we saw, implied that there was one distinct and coherent working class for whom alone social security was intended, was rejected partly because of the great regional variations in earnings and living standards across the states, and partly because the greater social mobility of American society would take people in and out across any line defined by income, occupation or class. Instead, the Social Security Act of August 1935 applied to all employees, with certain specified exceptions; but only the first 3000 dollars of the earnings of those included in this scheme would count for social security purposes. To be an employee, as the act made clear, was simply to perform 'any service, of whatever nature, . . . for [one's employer]', to be, in fact, 'a servant' in the master–servant relationship recognized by Common Law; in practice, rulings were made by the Board of Inland Revenue, or by the courts. The Social Security Board was itself aware of the inadequacies of this manner of determining social security status, and was anxious to have ruled in those who were neither clearly servants, nor masters, such as insurance and real estate agents, and travelling salesmen.[28] But there was no hope for employees of bawdy houses, since they were in 'illegal employment'.[29]

In seeking out the official images of class betrayed in this legislation, three sections of the population deliberately excluded from it need closer scrutiny. Among those who were bluntly described as 'workers' (the American term is closer to the French *travailleur* than to the British 'worker'; British refinement would require 'employee'), teachers, government employees and workers in branches of national banks were excluded, as were all workers for non-profit-making organizations (because of a fear that their tax-exempted status might be infringed), and workers for religious organizations (so as not to infringe the principle of the separation of church and state). On a totally different basis, such professional groups as lawyers, physicians, dentists, osteopaths, christian science practitioners, veterinarians, professional engineers, architects, funeral directors, and certified, registered, licensed or full-time practising public accountants were excluded as not being employees within the Common Law concept of master and servant.

The third excluded group consisted of agricultural workers and domestic servants. The official line was that this was entirely in keeping with established practice in regard to all laws regulating employment conditions, a practice related to the irregularities of employment in these two sectors and the difficulties of collecting pay-roll taxes. Washington was deluged with protests, many of them voicing the suspicion that the exclusions were not unrelated to the fact that a large proportion of both agricultural and domestic workers were black. These suspicions seemed to be confirmed by the violent hostility to sections of the bill expressed by many southern senators who, as the prime spirit in the drafting of the bill, Edwin E. Witte, noted, 'feared that this measure might serve as an entering wedge for federal interference in the handling of the Negro question in the South'.[30]

If the class images which lie behind all this seem indistinct or non-existent, the films which the government sponsored to put over to the nation the meaning of social security legislation help to sharpen the focus. The visual image that constantly recurs is of a blue-collar industrial worker; the word most used in describing those who are covered by social security is 'workers', though one of the films, made on behalf of the government by Pathé News, made the point that 'whether an office boy or a salaried executive you come under the Social Security Act'. When the excluded occupations are being listed, the image shown is that of a black maid.[31] The professions are never mentioned.

Officially, then, the American government took a functional view of society as being made up of basic economic interests, employers, employees, consumers, or, sometimes, 'the public', rather than of social classes. James P. Buchanan, the Texan Democrat who was chairman of the House Committee on Appropriations, was undoubtedly in a minority when, in writing to A. J. Altmeyer, chairman of the Social Security Board, he articulated the question in regard to the Social Security Act: 'Does it not appear as class legislation, pure and simple?'[32] But if we look at the implications of the legislation rather than at the overt intentions, then Buchanan does seem to have a point. The legislation implies: first, a class of employers who are excluded from its coverage; second, a professional middle class who are also excluded; third, a large included class of employees or 'workers' which extends much further up the social scale than the working class as defined for social security purposes in Britain, but has many gaps and omissions; and, fourth, an excluded 'under class' of casual workers in agriculture and domestic service, containing a large number of blacks.

A similar picture emerges from a study of federal housing policy. The Federal Housing Administration spoke not of social classes, but of 'middle income groups' and 'lower income groups'.[33] The objective of the Wagner Housing Act of 1937 was 'to remedy the unsafe and insanitary housing conditions and the acute shortage of decent, safe, and sanitary dwellings for families of low income, in rural or urban communities, that are injurious to the health, safety, and the morals of the citizens of the Nation'. The tenancy of public authority housing was to be restricted to families whose net income did not exceed five times the rental, or six times in the case of families with three or more minor dependants. So far, so classless. But Senator Wagner himself remarked during the congressional debates, 'there are some people whom we cannot possibly reach: I mean those who have no means to pay the rent'.[34] Once again an 'under class' is marked off from the decent working poor at whom social policy is aimed.

Notes

1. Statistique générale de la France, *Recensement des industries et professions: nomenclature des industries et professions* (April 1934); *Annuaire statistique de la France* (1934), p. 16; INSEE, *Résultats statistiques du recensement générale de la population effectué le 10 Mars 1946*, vol. III (1952), 'Nomenclature 1896 à 1936', pp. 11–33.
2. Dalloz, *Précis de législation industrielle*, 4th edition (1936), pp. 149–50, 225–6; André Rouast and Paul Durand, *Précis de législation industrielle* (1934), pp. 92–3; Dalloz, *Précis de droit civil*, 6th edition (1939), p. 916; Georges Ripert, *La Régime democratique et le droit civil moderne* (1936), p. 382.

3. Paul Pic, *Traité élémentaire de législation industrielle: les lois ouvrières*, 1937; Dalloz, *Précis de droit commercial*, 6th edition (1936), pp. 55–68; Jacques Etienne et Jean Beyl, *Manual-guide pratique de l'artisan* (1941); Ripert, *op. cit.*, pp. 369–75.
4. USA Bureau of the Census, *A Social-Economic Grouping of the Gainful Workers of the United States* (1933), pp. 1–7.
5. *Ibid*, p. 2.
6. USA Bureau of the Census, 'A Social-Economic Grouping of Gainful Workers in Cities of 500,000 or More: 1930', typescript (1938); Alba M. Edwards, 'A Social-Economic Grouping of Gainful Workers', in *Journal of the American Statistical Association* (1933), p. 387.
7. National Archives [NA], Washington, RG 47:26.
8. Registrar-General, *Decennial Supplement*, part IIA (1931), p. 7; *Classification of Occupations 1950*, pp. iii–ix.
9. Ministry of Reconstruction, *Housing in England and Wales: Memorandum by the Advisory Housing Panel on the Emergency Problem* (1918), p. 7.
10. House of Commons, *Debates*, vol. 237, col. 3079 (17 April 1930).
11. H. A. Hill, *The Complete Law of Housing* (1938), p. 57; W. Ivor Jennings, *The Law of Housing* (1936), p. 75.
12. Public Record Office [PRO], HLG 31/6.
13. Department of Health for Scotland: Consultative Council on Local Health Administration and General Health Questions, *Report of the Consultative Council in regard to the steps necessary to secure that state-aided houses will in future be let only to persons of the working classes* (1932), pp. 4, 6, 8.
14. PRO, HLG 37/4 (CHAC minutes); Board of Trade, *Report by the Council for Art and Industry: the Working Class Home: its Furnishing and Equipment* (1937), p. 8.
15. Ministry of Labour, *Report of the Unemployment Insurance Statutory Committee on Remuneration Limit for Insurance of Non-manual Workers* (1936), pp. 7–8.
16. *Ibid*, p. 4.
17. *Ibid*, pp. 8–14.
18. *Ibid*, p. 15.
19. *Report of the Committee on Holidays with Pay* (1937–8), Cmd 5724, pp. 48, 65.
20. *Ibid*, pp. 7–9, 47–56.
21. PRO, MAF 69/11.
22. PRO, ED 12/261.
23. See Henri Hatzfeld, *Du paupérisme à la sécurité sociale, 1850–1940* (1971).
24. NA, RG 73:377.
25. John D. Hogan and Francis A. J. Ianni, *American Social Legislation* (1956), p. 326.
26. Edwin E. Witte, *The Development of the Social Security Act: A Memorandum on the History of the Committee on Economic Security*

and drafting and legislative history of the Social Security Act, etc. (1962), p. 101.

27. The files containing the deliberations of the Economic Security Committee are in NA, RG 47.

28. These issues can be pursued through the files of the Social Security Board's *Social Security Bulletin*.

29. NA, RG 47:236 (6).

30. E. E. Witte, *op. cit.*, p. 143.

31. Films catalogued in NA as RG 47.27, 47.22, 47.19, 47.1 and 47.3.

32. Letter of 22 February 1937, NA, RG 47:237.

33. Federal Housing Administration, *Third Annual Report* (1936), p. 5.

34. Laurence M. Friedman, *Government and Slum Housing* (1968), p. 109.

5

Unofficial and Private Images in Britain

Academics and polemicists do not invent their images: within the
constraints of their intellectual or political persuasion, they attempt
to present a distillation of what is really happening in society.
Official images, both where they are stark and where they are, by
design, opaque, will have some influence upon the images held by
various groups and individuals throughout society. But much the
most interesting, if most difficult, activity, is to go in direct pursuit
of these 'unofficial' and 'private' images. The source material is rich
and varied, so I have devoted a chapter to each of the three countries.
The aim is to see how far people believe that classes exist, what they
think these classes are, and how people react to these perceptions.
Thus I shall be accumulating further evidence on how far classes, as
distinct from the objective realities of inequality, do exist. This additional set of images can then be placed together with the academic
and official, so that we have a broad frame, corresponding with
what people actually think and the language they actually use, into
which to integrate the objective evidence of inequalities and distinctions.

IMAGES AT THE BOTTOM OF SOCIETY

Britain's economic development since the Industrial Revolution had
created a large, and relatively homogeneous, class of industrial
workers. In the official mind there existed a quasi-legal working
class. Did the British working man have as clear an image of himself
and of his place in society? In general, the sources suggest a very
strong awareness of class, a ready and widely understood use of the
label 'working-class' but no specially strong political consciousness
or sense of class conflict. The overall image of society, where it can
be detected, was almost always a dichotomous one – workers on one
side, 'gaffers' on the other – but talk of the proletariat, the bourgeoisie, the capitalists, and of class struggle, was as rare as a bottle
of good claret in a miner's cottage; sometimes the image encom-
passed a local, friendly small employer, suffering many of the same

economic tribulations as the worker, with a class of 'rich', or 'gentry' away in the distance; sometimes there was an awareness, and resentment of, a local shopkeeping or petty professional class, but the phrase 'middle class' was not widely used.

That the British archives do not contain the wealth of popular writing on social issues to be found in America tells much about the closed and undemocratic nature of British political culture compared with American, and about the greater gulf between rulers and ruled. It also means that the voices of the majority – the less activist and less articulate – must be sought mainly in the social surveys and reports which were the special fruit of British upper- and middle-class concern with the social issues of the 1930s. Often there was little direct speech from those being studied, yet since the ostensible issues were always the standard of living or unemployment, never class, there is much valuable, unwitting testimony to be gathered. In 1933 two academics, H. L. Beales and R. S. Lambert, enlisted the help of certain social workers throughout the country in collecting 'memoirs' from the unemployed, which were then published in the weekly organ of the British Broadcasting Corporation, *The Listener*.[1] They offer a nice contrast with the testimony of the unemployed in St Paul, Minnesota, to be discussed in the next chapter. These memoirs have been much used by economic and social historians: I concentrate on them here because of their essentially unwitting, and even random nature as far as questions of class are concerned.

Of the twenty-five memorialists, all but four were, when employed, in manual occupations. Of these twenty-one, three openly described themselves or their environments as 'working-class': a skilled engineer, while disgusted with his former 'political and trade union associates', said he had met with sympathy and friendliness 'amongst the working class'; a skilled wood-carver explained how he could no longer afford butter, dripping and lard, which he called 'the elementary ingredients of a working class diet', and argued that education as well as organization would be needed to bring 'the working classes to the freedom they claimed'; and a house-painter referred to himself as 'a working-class parent' dealing with the 'usual small grocery store of a poor working-class district'. Most of the others, in some way or another, showed awareness of belonging to a specific working-class culture, without at any time directly using the language of class. A South Wales miner, who declared that he had 'always stood for independence', attributed his first spell of unemployment to a refusal 'to sell my principles'. A woman, while employed in an artificial-silk factory, 'had a lot to do with the weavers' trade union'. An unskilled labourer said of himself: 'I am good for hard work, but I like to leave it at that,' and 'our wants are not very many, but only by finding work shall I be able to satisfy them'. A Rhondda miner described reactions to labour exchange investigations into income, family circumstances etc.:

> To men who had worked in the only industry they had known (mining) for anything from fifteen to fifty years, this was a new experience, of the most humiliating and degrading kind. After being out of work for some time, investigation officers called at our houses to confirm information given at the Exchange – about birth of children, income, etc., and it seemed to creep into the minds of the men that they were being spied upon, and that if they were caught in the house, or street corner, or carrying coal, they were in for it. The officers were always very courteous and civil when making enquiries, or when interviewing at the Exchange. If a clerk or official had the misfortune to have a cruel-looking face, it sent shivers down many a man's spine, and stirred all sorts of thoughts as to what would happen if interviewed by such a person. When waiting in queues for interviews you could see men twitching nervously, thinking out their line of answers as to where they had been looking for work.

The tragedy of long-term unemployment was that it could destroy a man's confidence in himself. Quiet pride, steady self-respect and unambitious awareness are recurrent elements in the working-class self-image. A colliery banksman, who had 'never worked anywhere but the pit' spoke of 'the enduring fight to keep respectability'. The skilled engineer already quoted on the friendliness of the working class, described his life before he became unemployed as that of 'an ordinarily respectable artisan', with his activities 'divided between home, garden and public affairs', meaning by the last point that he had held 'every office possible' in his trade-union branch. A millwright described his work at a foundry in Derby: 'it was skilled work and I flatter myself that I was a good worker and quick'. Expressing his own lack of personal ambition, a letterpress printer declared that all he asked for was 'a fair-minded employer who will give me regular work at a living wage, letting me escape from the spectre of poverty, hunger and ill-health,' when he would 'give loyal and conscientious service'. An engineer's turner saw cycles of unemployment as the only prospect for the 'general run of artisans' like himself.

No very elaborate image of classes other than the one to which most of these unemployed men and women seemed to feel themselves to belong, nor of class structure as a whole, emerges from these memoirs. A rulleyman (or carter) noted the lifestyle of the boss, the privileges of an owner of an off-licence who took in lodgers (who nonetheless sounds, to an outsider, like a pretty working-class sort of character), and expressed a whole, if simple, social philosophy:

> Our loads were mainly gravel, sand and bricks, and we nearly always worked 3 or 4 on a job together. For a time I was taking coal to the waterworks. That was heavy work with long hours. The boss used to come down to the yard about 7 o'clock and give us our orders for the day. Then he'd go back to breakfast. Whilst we were sweating away in the afternoon he'd be playing golf . . . One chap who had an off-licence in N——— Street came and offered to work for £2.5s (£2.12s was the standard wage). He was an oldish man and couldn't stand his turn, but as we worked in gangs the rest of us carried him. What narked us, though, was that he didn't need the money as badly as some chaps. His family was grown up. He reckoned the beer-off only kept his wife, but I know for a fact that they had two lodgers as well. It's things like that that give the gaffers the whip hand.

A carpenter from an East Anglian village spoke highly of his employer: 'He is one of the best, has been the leading craftsman and employer in our village for many years (born and bred in the place), and has always charged a fair price.' This employer had kept the carpenter and another mate 'on long after lack of trade had made things difficult for himself'. But there was another class:

> If there is anything that makes me 'see red' it is the pictures and descriptions of such things as society weddings, court functions, and so on.
>
> However bad the times may be for us, these rich people seem to have thousands to spend on dresses and banquets and every other form of self-aggrandisement. There is something wrong somewhere and someone is just feeding us on lies. Short of money indeed! It comes to my mind the three days' beating I did last autumn for Lord —— shooting party. Do you think that's the sort of work I want? It wasn't so much that I got drenched to the skin right away and had to stick being drenched through for three days on end, for I only had the one suit and it would not dry in the night. I walked, or stumbled, miles and miles like it. I had no

skin left on my feet and it is a wonder I did not get double pneu-
monia. But it was the way we were badgered about and sworn at
and treated generally like dogs. I see no reason why our helpless
condition should merely be imposed upon by the gentry for the
benefit of their sport.

Curiously it was an ex-miner, ex-builder's labourer, ex-farmhand
who 'when a miner . . . never worried much about politics' who,
perhaps a little casually, spoke of 'the employing class' as having
'given the miners a very dirty deal'.
  Overall, given the indignities and suffering being inflicted on the
unemployed, it is perhaps surprising that they did not express
clearer hostility towards a 'ruling class' or a 'middle class'. Often
such specific animosity as emerges is directed towards trade-union
and labour leaders: 'the trade unions have never been any good
since the General Strike'; 'when it comes to a real test they are
hopeless'; 'these people do not care a brass farthing for the bottom
dog'. Though letters and articles in trade-union papers might insist
on the existence in society of two distinct classes, 'the employers of
labour on the one side and you, as a wage worker, on the other side',
continually at war with one another, or advocate the development
of class consciousness and a knowledge of class struggle, they would
often go on to admit that such notions were not at all entertained by
the vast majority.[2] Of the twenty-one unemployed working men and
women in the Beales and Lambert survey only one, a former fitter
in a London aircraft factory, described himself as 'a keen socialist',
identifying the evils of 'this system of capitalism' and of 'the control
of the capitalist class'; but, he lamented of his fellow unemployed,
'their main thoughts seemed to be only on sport. They would come
into the public library and their first thoughts were to inquire the
last score in a big cricket match or the results of the cup ties.' The
skilled engineer I have already quoted twice had thrown himself
'into revolutionary movements from time to time', but he added,
'it all seems so futile'. The aircraft-fitter's spirit of revolution was
perhaps mainly in the mind:

I would let my thoughts stray to the present order of society, and
the failure of the unemployed to unite together to do something
to smash the present order of things, to demand the right to work
and to live in decent conditions. These thoughts grew to such
dimensions that I should have been more than ready to revolt
against the present order of society.

It would seem, then, that there was a working-class awareness of its self and its own community, together with a more sporadic and unorganized awareness of other groupings into which it came into contact. Working-class self-respect often appears far more important than working-class sensitivity to the powers and privileges of other social classes. A skilled wire-drawer from Ambergate in the Beales and Lambert survey actually declared himself in favour of the principle of the means test, believing it to be 'a necessary safeguard'. Here he was well in tune with George Lansbury, leader of the Labour Party in the early 1930s. 'My own view is very simple,' Lansbury wrote to a colleague: 'if a person having exhausted statutory benefit applies for transitional benefit and is found to be in the possession of means sufficient for his own maintenance and comfort and that of those dependent upon him, I am not in favour of giving such a person public money.'[3]

Choice insights into the use and meaning of the phrase 'working class' are to be found in the little-studied but sadly touching letters of Charles Fisk.[4] In the later 1920s Fisk, who was then approaching his fiftieth year, was living in rooms in Chiswick, in south-west London, where he earned a precarious living as a nightwatchman. He was separated from his wife, described by the cataloguer of the collection as 'a prostitute', though this seems a narrow and technically inaccurate judgement – during the General Strike she was having an affair with a trade unionist who was clearly more concerned about the problems of getting a bus to his mistress than about the solidarity of the strike. Fisk wrote frequently to his wife, and at times commented on his landlady, her family, and their social status and what that implied:

> When I come home in the mornings I light my fire have a wash and Breakfast and then bed it is then $\frac{1}{2}$ past 9 and I go to bed then up again at 2 work again at 5. I keep my own Place Clean and the old Lady has never been in my room since I have been here only to Change my Sheets and Pillow Slips and Towels very nice old Lady only working-Class but very nice and Homely of course I keep her well supplied with Oil and Wood and other things. I have given her 1 Gallon of oil this Week she has 4 Lamps besides Gas. . . .
>
> Nice old lady only working-class. . . .
>
> These are rough and ready people clean working-Class people that wouldn't see you without.

Rather different insights are provided by the autobiographical fragments published in 1937 by the Nottinghamshire coal-miner George Tomlinson.[5] *Coal-Miner* has a preface of fat condescension penned by Arthur Bryant, affluent historical writer and pillar of Conservatism, and Tomlinson declares himself a Conservative. But he also writes that he was proud to be a miner, the son of a miner, and that though he had hated the pit he was grateful for what the men of the pits had taught him. Much of his book, whatever his conscious purpose, turns out to be a magnificent, unwitting testimony to the class solidarity of the mining community. Miners, he declares, love their country as intensely as anyone else even though they have 'much less to love it for than some have'. To the average miner, he claimed, the difference between the Conservative Party and the Socialist Party was that 'the Conservative Party looks after those who have money, and the Socialist Party looks after the working-man.'

> All that the ordinary miner understands about Conservatism is that local jumped-up people, with a small car and an equally small mind, and who live in the residential part of the town, as they love to call it, are Conservatives (or pretend to be). They who have made their money by selling him bacon, pit boots, and insurance policies, are now able to sit back in comfort and write to the local Press pointing out how the miner is in the wrong on each and every occasion, but who never in their lives entered a miner's home in order to get a proper understanding of him and his problems.

This evident resentment of the local middle class breaks out again when he describes his own Conservative principles as being 'higher than the mere gaining of some end for a jumped-up subscription lawyer'.

IMAGES IN THE MIDDLE

Lines separating working class from middle class, though often not commented on, or only in a rather muddled way, were known to be there. The print workers of the Typographical Association came, in income and lifestyle, at the top end of the working class (in their union discussions fellow members were 'mister', not 'brother' – the usual form of address among British trade unionists and again expressive of the sense of a common culture). The Typographical Association had a definition of 'workpeople' as covering 'all employees (male and female of all ages)' but excluding 'travellers, clerical staff, shop assistants, foremen and forewomen',[6] who, obviously, are perceived as being on the far side of the middle-class line. Melvyn Bragg in his oral history compilation, *Speak for England*, records a beautiful study of the ebb and flow of class sensitivity when the boss, Mr Hindley, a local celebrity in Cumbria, came to dinner with the family of his stable-boy. The stable-boy's father was a carpenter, but then his boss had been a railway porter – 'he wasn't society-bred or anything like that, and I think he'd been a porter and then a chauffeur or something like this,' notes the stable-boy who is the narrator:

> He had a marvellous dinner with my mother and father and he says, This is marvellous. He says, You know this is my way of life, and that's when I first got the jist like that he wasn't what he sort of pretended to be, that he was of working-class. You could tell actually by the way he talked and that, he wasn't society. But I thought he'd been rather more than what he was. And he really enjoyed his dinner. We had a bit of roast beef and Yorkshire pudding and new potatoes, and the way she did it, it was out of this world, the way she cooked – and a bit of apple cake afterwards.
>
> Everybody in Wigton seemed very rough then. Crude, real crude. And of course you couldn't put everybody on that scale, the way in which I was mixing and living then I mean, I was still working-class but I'd never found it as rough anywhere else since – we'll put it that way – as it was in Wigton then. This is where the slang element comes in. And I found – I was sitting in the house with Mr. Hindley and our John ran in, and Mam says, Look who's here? Oh, it's him, how do? Are you all right, John? Yis, I'se alreet. And he whipped round and went out again, you see. And that was the first words that got me . . . where I was always, Yes sir, no sir. But John says Yis. I says, that's awful, to myself I didn't mention it. And it was just that one word – yis. Ee I says, that sounds awful. And then of course my father started talking and then there was one or two more of them in, and I was just sitting listening. I was rather dumbstruck. I daren't open my mouth in case I let myself down, or made an ass of myself the other way – the way I'd been talking which didn't apply at home.[7]

Often, though, it is those just above the line, or ambiguously placed on it, who show greatest sensitivity to it, and to the social structure as a whole. In the Beales and Lambert survey it was the two most ambivalently situated of the four non-manual workers, the son of a city clerical worker, and a Scottish hotel servant, possessed of 'an all-round knowledge of high-class catering', who, in different ways, expressed the strongest awareness of class distinctions. The clerical worker's son, who had had various low prestige jobs, such as packer or delivery boy, was the only interviewee in the entire survey to put the point positively: 'One of the only hopes for England is a vast cataclysm, sweeping away class distinctions and finally wiping out all class warfare.' The experience of the hotel worker was more mundane: unemployment took him, as he saw it, from one class environment to another: 'I shed my pride, or rather, what remained of it, and took share of a room in a working-class locality where existence upon the dole is not an uncommon experience.'[8]

Even those white-collar unions which believed most strongly in affiliation with the TUC, when describing their members as 'professional workers' or 'black-coated workers' categorized them quite explicitly as 'middle-class'. In 1933, for example, the Guild of Insurance Officials and the Bank Officers Guild sought to arrange 'a conference of middle-class workers'. It is evident from the publicity material put out by the Guild of Insurance Officials that in status they aspired towards the condition of the higher professions: one leaflet, which showed a young woman sitting at her typewriter, put the questions: 'Do you, like all high-grade employees, belong to an organization? If not, why not?' It then pointed out that: 'Doctors are organized, Lawyers are organized, Teachers are organized.'[9] A speech delivered by Liberal MP Major H. L. Nathan to the London branch annual meeting in March 1932 was so highly treasured that it was reprinted as a pamphlet.

Major Nathan's speech was really a discreet plug for the Liberal Party and in particular for the policies outlined in the famous *Liberal Yellow Book* of 1928 – 'a momentous piece of constructive work, a guiding line for future progress', he called it – but along the way he offered some images of the middle class which are not only illuminating in themselves but evidently overlapped with the perceptions of the insurance officials:

When I was informed that the managements of many of our Insurance firms still refused to recognise the Guild of Insurance Officials, I was appalled that they should take such an obsolete view of a typical modern professional association. . . . Employees, whether working-class or middle-class, have been forced to form themselves into trade unions and associations to protect and further their interests. This movement has obtained the consent, tacit or open, of the great capitalists. . . . The Trade Union Acts – they apply to middle-class associations as well as to ordinary Trade Unions – gave legal sanction to this principle of collective bargaining. . . .

British labour is now joined together in vast trade unions, with which employers, through their own associations, bargain as to wages, pensions, and so forth. The association of men and women carrying on a particular profession or trade to further their interests is not the monopoly of the working-classes. Professional men have formed their own associations – their own trade unions, if you like – to protect their common interests to keep the standards of their profession high. . . . Nor have the employers as a class been slow to combine. . . .

I would remind the insurance managements that we are living in a difficult period of transition. A period, I hasten to add, in which the continuation of amicable relations between themselves and their employees is an essential requirement if safety and solvency are to be ensured.[10]

The social images contained within this passage have a wide relevance; the political message was less acceptable. While most white-collar workers shared the sense of being middle-class and the aspiration towards the status of the professions, they were not enthusiastic about the idea of associating with the trade union movement; this was particularly true in the south of England, slightly less true in the north.[11]

Teachers in the public elementary schools were in a precarious lower-middle-class profession with close ties to the working class. 'Masters' (and 'mistresses') in the top public schools stood on the fringes of the upper class (as described in Chapter 2). Inclusion within the provisions of unemployment insurance, we have noted, implied statutory working-class status: the teachers' associations were strongly against any extension of the scheme to include themselves.[12] In the higher professions the general tone was of confidence combined, perhaps, with that prevailing feeling among the highly educated of the time that class was not something whose existence one acknowledged. Certainly, no sense of class invades the pioneering study of *The Professions* (1937) carried out by Carr-Saunders and Wilson: any implied hierarchy is strictly one of moral

worth, and stockbrokers, who in lifestyle and manners stood probably highest in the social scale, are relegated to the very end of the
book.[13] Smaller businessmen – managers, provincial industrialists –
could sometimes express a sense of their distance from the real upper
class: 'To the small capitalist with money invested in business', a
manufacturers' agent wrote to Sir William Beveridge, 'the so-called
National government is utterly sectional; it runs about the City at
the bidding of the gilt-edged crowd who are useless to commerce.'[14]
The newspaper of the Lancashire cotton industry, the *Cotton Factory
Times* (which closed down in the late thirties) spoke of factory
owners and workers in Lancashire as belonging to the 'same family'
and, by implication, contrasted the local upper-middle class, which
it called the 'master class', with the national upper class in the south,
whose 'amazing lack of knowledge' of Lancashire conditions was
personified by the president of the Board of Trade, Walter Runciman.[15]

The top members of the medical profession often occupied that
'upper-class box' of which I have already spoken; and they were the
people who ran the British Medical Association. Their report on
'Hospital Policy' in June 1939 expressed clearly the images of class
which prevailed in Britain in the 1930s but which were seldom described in such an unabashed manner: after remarking that hospitals
had originally been designed for the destitute poor, but that they
now catered for the 'class above', that is 'the lower-paid workers',
the report continued:

The Association recognises that there is, in many areas, a shortage of institutional provision for the person belonging to the so-
called middle class. Although his income is above that usually
accepted for hospital purposes, with the result that he cannot
properly be treated in the public ward of a voluntary hospital, it
is often insufficient to cover the cost of a privately established
nursing home. The Association welcomes the development of
pay-beds in association with hospitals at fees within the capacity
of the middle class patients. To deal with the purely professional
aspect of this problem the Association has taken a number of
steps including the encouragement of provident associations.
These associations enable the subscriber to insure against the
contingency of illness which requires specialist attention in an
institution. In the Association's view these schemes should be run
on a sound actuarial basis and independently of any particular
institution. They will have the effect of attracting subscribers to

moderately priced pay-beds, and will provide within reasonable limitations for the cost of institutional accommodation and of consultant and specialist services. Pay-beds should be available also to the wealthier classes, the institutional and professional charges varying with the economic status of the patients.[16]

The report argued that voluntary hospitals should take in both free patients and paying patients, with an income limit for paying patients, the magic figure of £250 being suggested for the London area.

Contributing Patients – Applicants for hospital benefit, not being free, patients, whose income does not exceed a specified local scale, should be provided with hospital service on terms appropriate to their financial position. Where such payments are in respect of both maintenance and treatment the visiting medical staff should receive from the hospital authorities remuneration for their professional services by salary, by payment for definite services and responsibility, by honorarium, or by agreed payment to a staff fund placed at their disposal.

Private Patients – Applicants for hospital benefit whose income is above a specified local scale may be given service where special accommodation is available in private rooms, wards, annexes, or homes associated with voluntary hospitals. When private patients are admitted in the ordinary wards of a hospital as a matter of urgency, they should, as soon as convenient be transferred to whatever special accommodation is available. Private patients should pay to the management the charges for maintenance and to the practioner responsible the appropriate medical fees, which may be on an agreed scale between the medical staff and the board of management or may be by private agreement between the medical attendant and the patient.

'It is undesirable', declared the BMA finally, in yet another choice selection from this alas all too credible document, 'that private patients should be seen or treated at the out-patients department of a hospital. . . .'[17]

IMAGES AT THE TOP

While manual workers showed an awareness of a common working-class culture and of the existence of persons belonging to another class, or other classes in society, and while many middle-class persons, particularly those in the less prestigious professions, definitely showed a sense of distinctive middle-classness, the public affectation of many of those at the top of society was that classes did not exist, or that if they did, they were a bad and unnatural thing; but private avowals (not to mention public *behaviour*) indicate the existence of a quite well defined group with a clear sense of its own upper-class identity, and, often, of the social hierarchy spreading out underneath it. 'Toryism', wrote Alfred Duff Cooper, who had given up the Foreign Office for a political career and marriage to Lady Diana Manners, daughter of a duke, 'hates the division of Englishmen into classes'.[18] This was in 1926, four years before he offered himself as official Conservative candidate in a famous by-election at St George's, Westminster. As H. Montgomery Hyde, biographer of Stanley Baldwin, has written: 'He was keen to get back to the house and with the aid of a handsome military bearing, a good speaking voice and a brilliant wife, he was the ideal official candidate for this largely upper-class constituency where the Press Lords had threatened to split the Conservative vote.'[19] But evidently Duff Cooper recognized the existence of 'the working classes', for whom, his argument ran, the Tories had done much. Twenty-seven years later Duff Cooper hit a truer note in his autobiography *Old Men Forget*: 'Class is an inevitable adjunct of human nature. . . . If a classless society were possible it would be as useless as a rankless army and as dull as a wine-list that gave neither the name of the vineyard nor the date of the vintages.'[20]

The notion of the wonderful curiousness of other classes in society and of the extreme bad taste of George Orwell in mixing with other classes and advocating the overthrow of the hierarchy (as well as the crass condescension already mentioned) comes over heavily in Arthur Bryant's preface to *Coal-Miner*:

> . . . I received his manuscript. Part of it was very good: part of it less so. His experience of writing was obviously negligible. Yet passage after passage, written in words of one syllable, bore the unmistakable impress of the born writer. . . .
> . . . I have recently been reading a very interesting example of the kind of publication to which Mr. Tomlinson's book is so refreshing a contrast. It was called *The Road to Wigan Pier* and was, I believe, one of the choices of the 'Left Book Club'. It was written by a young literary man of refined tastes who at some apparent inconvenience to himself had 'roughed it' for a few weeks at Wigan

and Sheffield. The impression left by the first part of his book is
that Wigan and Sheffield are Hell: the corollary, worked out with
great skill in the second part, that every decent-hearted man and
woman, sooner than allow such conditions to endure a day longer,
should at once enrol in the ranks of those who are seeking change
by revolutionary methods. . . .

. . . But there is an even more fatal weakness in the premises,
for though Wigan and Sheffield may perhaps genuinely seem Hell
to a super-sensitive novelist paying them a casual visit, they do
not seem Hell to the vast majority of people who live there.[21]

Tomlinson may not have described the Nottingham coal mines as
'Hell' – but he graphically described the physical deprivations of
the miners' lives, presumably seen by Bryant as merely picturesque.
Another perception of the working class as seen from the highest
political office in the land was revealed when Jimmy Thomas, the
former trade union and Labour leader, was forced to resign from
the National government in 1935 for leaking budget secrets. Privately the Prime Minister, Stanley Baldwin, offered the explanation that
Thomas had 'fallen a victim to the two weaknesses of his class': he
had been 'a terrific gambler' and, while he had not deliberately given
anything away, 'what he most likely did was to let his tongue wag
when he was in his cups'.[22]
That there was a definite and very confident upper-class self-
image emerges clearly, though often obliquely, from the sources.
Typical is the way in which Lord Butler begins his autobiography:

The honours examination in my University is described as the
Tripos. I have spent the whole forty years of public life that are
recalled by this book perched, whether in circumstances of ease
or discomfort, on just such a *tripos*. One of its legs has been planted
in academic groves, another in the arena of politics, the third in
what was once our great Raj and is still culturally a microcosm of
the world.

His family, he soon tells us, had maintained 'a consecutive tradition
at Cambridge as dons since 1794'.[23] Goronwy Rees, the son of a
Welsh Presbyterian minister, reached Oxford in 1928: his public
school contemporaries there had, he discovered, complete confidence in their futures:

The undergraduates were officer cadets in the great army required to rule the British Empire, which still covered a third of the world's land surface. Some intended to be artists, and some even revolutionaries, but they all expected that British society would take special care of them. They expected – and events justified them – that the rest of life would be *like* Oxford.[24]

Martin Green, biographer of these 'children of the sun' describes Rees, together with the Cornish clay-worker's son, A. L. Rowse, as 'working-class'[25] – a description that upper-class Oxford would undoubtedly have endorsed.

However inaccurate in locating the exact social origins of those who came from outside their class, upper-class personalities tended to be meticulous in recording every detail in the breeding of those with whom they had to associate closely. Captain Harry Crookshank, Eton and Oxford, Foreign Office, Conservative MP at the age of thirty-one, Secretary for Mines, 1935–9, noted in his diary that the chief inspector of factories was 'an Eton and Magdalen man',[26] while Hugh Dalton, the most high-born of all the well-heeled leaders of the Labour Party, made similar notes on his new private secretary: 'Winchester, Trinity Cambridge (double 1st History), FO. . .'. On flights to France soon after the outbreak of war Dalton made boisterous jokes about how he and the Conservative Robert Boothby were both Etonians, while all the others on the flight were Rugbyans.[27] Crookshank, who was always having 'bother with the servants' and finally decided to sack the lot, quoted favourably the homily of Lord Trenchard, formerly chief of the air staff and before that a cavalry officer, in which he described a gentleman as 'one who looks after his men first'.[28] Crookshank's social philosophy was simple: 'People can't all have the same chance: what we want is to see everybody has *a* chance. You can't train a carthorse to win the Derby.' The upper class, in their own image of themselves, were thoroughbreds.

But were they really one homogeneous class? On the whole, the documents suggest that they were. Political persuasion, certainly, was not a relevant issue. John Strachey, who described himself as an 'upper-class Socialist', was on close terms with the gilded young Conservative, Robert Boothby.[29] Hugh Dalton moved freely in and out of the foreign policy discussions held among dissident Conservative politicians and civil servants.[30] Sir Stafford Cripps became notorious in the press in the 1930s as 'the red squire'. J. T. Murphy, an engineering worker and former member of the Communist Party, found Cripps to be 'a very likeable person, though a trifle conscious

of his old school tie'.[31] Cripps was thought to be so far to the left
that by the late 1930s he had been expelled from the Labour Party.
Yet, when in the early days of the war he found himself in lonely
isolation as Britain's ambassador to Stalin's Moscow, it was not to
his socialist cronies he turned, but to his fellow barrister, the Conservative MP, Sir Walter Monckton: 'Does your mind ever play like
mine with the old days when we battled in the Courts? They seem
very remote but that [sic] are happy memories to me and a great
comfort and resource.'[32] The fascinating Cripps–Monkton correspondence will be returned to in a later chapter.

Yet, at times one can clearly detect the feeling within the upper
class of a distinction between aristocratic and upper-middle-class
elements. To Lord Londonderry, Neville Chamberlain was 'a Birmingham tradesman'.[33] Captain Margesson, the Conservative whip,
seeking an explanation for Chamberlain's political success despite
his many obvious failings, believed that it was due to the way in
which Chamberlain's fellow countrymen 'saw in him a reflection of
themselves'. A strange understanding of the lives of most of Chamberlain's fellow countrymen, perhaps, since Margesson also noted
that Chamberlain had been to the 'usual' preparatory school and
public school, then continued:

> The ordinary Englishman sees in him an ordinary Englishman
> like himself; one who has been in business in a small way and has
> made a little – but not much – money; one who has been happily
> married and brought up a family of which the world knows little;
> one who wears the same business-suit every day, the black coat
> and vest, the striped trousers, the laced boots, and carries the
> same umbrella whether he is walking on a cloudless morning in
> the Park with Mrs Chamberlain (which he does every day at the
> same hour) or whether he is flying across Europe to meet the
> dictator to settle the affairs of nations.[34]

Chamberlain very well represents the symbiosis of nineteenth-
century industrial wealth and political achievement with the older
upper-class tradition. His nostalgia for Rugby was very real: 'You
had much more initiative than I at Rugby and I remember visiting
your study, the only one that I ever saw in any other House than my
own,' he wrote to Leslie Scott, who a few years later wrote in an
obituary for a Rugby school magazine: 'Neville Chamberlain and
I were contemporaries at Rugby in the middle eighties... It was
through the "Bug", as all good Rugbeans called the Natural History

Society, then run under the kindly guidance of that great naturalist, Puff Cummings, the Science Master, that Neville and I became friends.'[35]

Some men in powerful positions fell, by their own reckoning, outside the aristocratic upper class. When, in 1939, Sir James Grigg became permanent under-secretary at the War Office he was well on the way to establishing himself in the upper class, yet in a series of fascinating letters to his father he makes it clear that he does not see himself as being fully ensconced there yet. He was, as he recognized in his autobiography, a slightly difficult figure to place.

> I had myself enjoyed a good secondary and University education, by means of a scholarship supplemented by my father becoming a capitalist; I had what used to be called 'got on in the world'; I had lived an interesting and I hope useful life; I had met with all sorts and conditions from, as the phrases went, the highest to the lowest, and I had never once met from any of them patronage or sneers because I was the son of a carpenter. Was I a privileged person? Had my privileges been gained at the expense of the workers from whom I had originated?[36]

After describing to his father a visit to Lord Lothian's country house, he added, 'and that I hope will end our moving in aristocratic circles for a bit.' His sense of being in a middle, not a top (or, of course, bottom) position, is apparent in his reference, after the outbreak of war, to 'some of the richer people . . . continually seeking new funk holes' and to 'the Trades Unions . . . continually taking advantage of their present favourable bargaining position to introduce bigger and bigger doses of socialism'.[37]

By the objective indicators, Mrs Diana Brinton-Lee occupied a high social status: she had a small private income and her husband, employed in the film industry, was a former First World War major. But her diary of 1940 reveals her recognition of the line separating her from the upper class as she perceived it. After joining the Women's Volunteer Drivers Corps, she reported, 'the Corps was not lacking in wealth and good looks. Glancing round the room, I could see shining sculptured heads, lambent eyes, and elegant figures in Savile Row tunics, which fell open to reveal khaki ties pinned to the shirt bosom with large regimental diamond brooches.' To this she added, 'of course there were some middle-aged, middle-class people like myself.'[38] The notion of the association between social class and physical beauty has already, and will continue to come up

from time to time in this book. Mrs Brinton-Lee's view, like Montgomery Hyde's description of Duff Cooper, is the direct obverse of
the equally widely held view about the upper class consisting almost
exclusively of 'chinless wonders'.

At times upper-class figures seem to have a dichotomous view of
society, lumping the whole of the rest of society somewhat vaguely
into 'the working classes'. At other times the existence of a middle
class, or indeed of the distinction between aristocracy and upper-
middle class, is recognized. From below, the existence of the upper
class is pretty clearly recognized, though the vision becomes more
opaque as one moves into the working class. If we integrate the
images which have emerged so far with the historical context, we
can say that, in the 1930s, the nineteenth-century upper class, formed
out of the pre-industrial aristocracy (which itself contained many
former commercial elements) and more recent commercial and
professional recruits, had continued to develop, with the balance
tilting towards new wealth but the ethos still determined by the more
exclusive public schools; that the white-collar elements emerging
at the beginning of the century now formed a firm bottom edge to
a middle class which extended right up to an important upper-
middle class of successful professionals and provincial businessmen; and that the industrial working class was more cohesive than
ever before, with fewer fringe and submerged elements.

Notes

1. Subsequently published in book form as H. L. Beales and R. S.
   Lambert, eds., *Memoirs of the Unemployed* (1934, reprinted 1973). My
   discussion and the quotations contained in it are drawn from pages
   64–254.
2. *Railway Review*, 28 December 1934, 26 February 1937.
3. British Library of Political and Economic Science [BLPES], Lansbury
   Papers, vol. 25, sec. III O, fol. 3, George Lansbury to William Tait.
4. BLPES, Fisk letters. The letters quoted are dated 20 March, 1 May and
   5 May 1925. See also W. Franklin to Bess Fisk, 4 May 1926.
5. George Tomlinson, *Coal-Miner* (1937). This and the next paragraph
   refer to pages 84–93, 174–85, 212–27.
6. Modern Records Centre [MRC], Warwick University, MSS 39C:
   Typographical Association duplicated circular.

7. Melvyn Bragg, *Speak for England* (1976), p. 203.
8. Beales and Lambert, *op. cit.*, pp. 255, 260.
9. MRC, MSS 79: Guild of Insurance Officials, general purposes committee minutes, 25 January 1930, 28 January to 1 December 1933.
10. MRC, MSS 79: Guild of Insurance Officials, speech delivered by Major H. L. Nathan, MP, at London Branch Annual Meeting, 15 March 1932.
11. MRC, MSS 56/1/4: National Union of Bank Employees, executive committee minutes, 22–3 February 1936.
12. Ministry of Labour, *Report of Unemployment Insurance Statutory Committee on Renumeration Limit for Insurance of Non-manual Workers* (1936), p. 13.
13. A. Carr-Saunders and P. A. Wilson, *The Professions* (1937).
14. BLPES, Beveridge Papers, II b. 32 (pt 1), 28 September 1932.
15. *Cotton Factory Times*, 28 February 1936.
16. British Medical Association, *Hospital Policy*, 24 June 1939.
17. *Ibid.*
18. A. Duff Cooper, *Why Workers Should be Tories* (1926).
19. H. Montgomery Hyde, *Baldwin* (1973), p. 323.
20. A. Duff Cooper, *Old Men Forget* (1953), pp. 65–6.
21. Arthur Bryant, preface to *Coal-Miner*, *op. cit.*, pp. 8, 10, 11.
22. T. Jones, *Whitehall Diary*, ed. Keith Middlemass (1969).
23. Lord Butler (R. A. Butler), *The Art of the Possible* (1971), p. 1.
24. Goronwy Rees, *Chapter of Accidents* (1972), p. 93.
25 Martin Green, *Children of the Sun* (1977), p. 230.
26. Bodleian Library [Bod. L], Oxford, MSS Eng hist, d. 359: Crookshank Diaries, 20 July 1934.
27. BLPES, Dalton Diaries, 20 May 1940.
28. Bod. L, Crookshank Diaries, 16 October 1934, 1 March, 6 October, 2 December 1935.
29. John Strachey to R. Boothby, n.d. 1928?, quoted in Hugh Thomas, *John Strachey* (1960), p. 65.
30. BLPES, Dalton Diaries, 1938–40, *passim*.
31. J. T. Murphy, *New Horizons* (1941), pp. 311–12.
32. Bod. L, Monckton Papers, Dep. MT 3: Cripps to Monckton, 28 December 1940.
33. University of Edinburgh Library, A. Berriedale Keith Collection, GEN 145/4: Lord Londonderry to A. Berriedale Keith, 24 October 1940.
34. Churchill College, Cambridge [CCC], Margesson Papers, 1/5.
35. MRC, Lord Justice Scott Papers, MSS 119/3/P/CH. By permission of the University of Birmingham.
36. P. J. Grigg, *Prejudice and Promise* (1948), p. 402.
37. CCC, P. J. Grigg Papers: P. J. Grigg to his father, 23 July 1939 and 15 July 1940.
38. Imperial War Museum, Brinton-Lee Diary: entry for 17–23 August 1940.

6

Unofficial and Private Images in the USA

The language of class in America of the 1930s is haphazard; the image is fragmented. However, the fragments can be pieced together. The sources relating to such families as the Roosevelts, the Lodges, the Adams, the Biddles, the Cabots, the Duponts, the Lees and the Achesons suggest that deep among them there was a shared perception of their own position set well apart from the rest of American society, even though labels such as 'aristocracy' or 'upper class', striking when they occur, are used very infrequently. This perception is enshrined in the aphorism, 'the Cabots speak only to the Lowells, and the Lowells speak only to God'.

Whereas in Britain the institutions of the upper class evolved as part of the national heritage, in America there was a conscious, if uneven, privately sponsored, drive towards the creation of special upper-class institutions. The upper-class prep schools and the Ivy League universities were discussed in Chapter 2. Clear insights into the self-image of the American upper class are to be found in the social registers established by private enterprise in the main American metropolitan centres. Two distinguished American authorities, E. Digby Baltzell and Professor William Domhoff, have made most effective use of the social registers in their own recent studies of the American upper class.[1] The first social register was founded in New York City in 1888; by the 1930s there were in addition social registers for Chicago, Cincinatti-Dayton, Buffalo, Boston, Baltimore, Philadelphia, St Louis, Pittsburgh, Cleveland, San Francisco and Washington DC. The heart of American high society was in the long established families of the great metropolitan areas of Boston, New York and Philadelphia, and in the 'aristocracy' of the south: President Roosevelt's black valet described the American ambassador to Brazil as 'indeed nice from a aristocratic old Virginia family'.[2] The big cities had a lore of their own, well captured in the three imaginary letters of introduction invented by Robert Douglas Bowden in his 1937 biography of Boies Penrose, and cited by Digby Baltzell:

The Bostonian: Permit me to introduce Mr Jones who graduated
with highest honors in the classics and political economy at Harvard, and later took a degree at Berlin. He speaks and writes
French and German, and if you employ him, I am sure his learning will make his services extremely valuable to you.

The New Yorker: The bearer, Mr Brown, is the young fellow who
took hold of Street & Company's Chicago branch a few years ago
and built it up to one hundred thousand a year. He also made a
great hit as Jackson & Company's representative in London. He's
a hustler all right and you'll make no mistake if you take him on.

The Philadelphian: Sir, allow me to introduce Mr Rittenhouse
Palmer Penn. His grandfather on his mother's side was a colonel
in the Revolution, and on his father's side he is connected with
two of the most exclusive families in our city. He is related by
marriage to the Philadelphia Lady who married Count Tauge-
nichts, and his family has always lived on Walnut Street. If you
should see fit to employ him, I feel certain that his very desirable
social connections will render him of great value to you.

Attempts to establish social registers in Providence RI, Minne-
apolis-St Paul, Seattle-Portland, Pasadena-Los Angeles, Detroit,
Richmond-Charleston-Savanna-Atlanta were unsuccessful. Such
magnates as Henry Ford II whose automobile empire was based in
Detroit, however, appeared in the New York *Social Register*. Being
privately owned and produced for profit, the social registers had to
attune themselves to the demand and the opinions of the market.
A new family desirous of getting on to one of the registers had to
obtain forms through friends who were already within the magic
circle: the forms were then filled in, 'usually by the wife', Baltzell
comments, together with the names of sponsors of suitable repute.
By 1940 the total number of families in the various social registers
amounted to 38,450.[3] Another great upper-class institution, whose
robust American forms had but shadowy counterparts in Europe,
was provided by the ladies' clubs such as the Daughters of the American Revolution, the Junior League, the Association of Southern
Women to Prevent Lynching or the National League of Women
Voters, so that the term 'clubwomen' became almost a class label.

Roosevelt's administration could as readily be described as 'upper-
class' as any formed by Stanley Baldwin or Neville Chamberlain;
he was indeed much happier working alongside progressive Republicans than alongside lower status Democratic party bosses. In May
1933, Dean Acheson, son of the Episcopal Bishop of Connecticut,

became under-secretary of the Treasury. Although in his memoirs he does not dwell at all on his school days at Groton – an astonishing self-denial by the standards of an equivalent English upper-class autobiography – the influences show through all the same. 'Relations with President began well. Ten years older than I, he had left our school before I got there, but he regarded my having gone to it as a recommendation . . .' But Acheson was not enthusiastic about Roosevelt's presidential breakfasts:

> Gay and informal as these meetings were, they nevertheless carried something of the relationship implied in a seventeenth-century levée at Versailles. We think of these as stiff and formal, yet Saint-Simon tells us how Madame de Bourgoyne won a bet that she could not sit on a chamberpot in the presence of Sun King himself. This she did with the aid of her lady-in-waiting and her own voluminous skirts. Louis XIV could and did forgive her, his daughter-in-law. But, while the relations between royalty and all the rest of humanity, however exalted, could be informal, they crossed a gulf measured by light-years.

The impression given to Acheson by President Roosevelt 'carried much of this attitude of European – not British – royalty'. British royalty, Acheson commented interestingly if not necessarily accurately, was 'comfortably respectable, dignified and *bourgeois* [my italics]'. The President clearly was not bourgeois: he 'could relax over his poker parties and enjoy Tom Corcoran's accordian, he could and did call everyone from his valet to the Secretary of State by his first name and often made up Damon Runyon nicknames for them, too – "Tommy, the Cork", "Henry the Morgue", and similar names; he could charm an individual or a nation.' But, Acheson claimed, 'he condescended'. While many 'revelled in apparent admission to an inner circle,' Acheson did not.

> To me it was patronising and humiliating. To accord the President the greatest betterance in respect should be a gratification to any citizen. It is not gratifying to receive the easy greeting which milord might give a promising stableboy and pull one's forelock in return.[4]

A great deal of this, of course, betrays Acheson as much as it comments on Roosevelt; much of what is left is peculiar to Roosevelt and to a concept of the presidency rather than to a whole class. In effect we have two contrasting images contained within a common consciousness: Acheson's churchy aspirations after the 'bourgeois' dignity of British royalty, and the deliberate, if circumscribed, un-buttoning of manner, within the presidential circle, of which one can find many instances.

When Harold L. Ickes, Roosevelt's Secretary of State for the Interior, had an interview in 1933 with Fenner Brockway, the vigorous British socialist who still carried some of the style of his Anglo-Indian ruling-class antecedents, he proudly noted in his diary that Brockway had said that no member of the government in Great Britain would hold a conference in such a free and open manner and 'he commented also on the fact that I was in my shirt sleeves. He said he liked it.' Ickes recorded with relish the pleasure he derived from a British embassy stag party held in September 1940:

> I was the ranking guest and sat on Lord Lothian's right. On my right sat Lord Melchett. Lord Stonehaven was another guest who had recently arrived from England. . . .
>
> I was tremendously impressed with the self-control of these Britishers. . . .
>
> I was greatly impressed with Lord Melchett personally . . . He is a widely read and cultured English Gentleman – the kind we don't often produce over here where we have a much more narrow range of historical and current events and where the chief con-sideration is the making of money. . . .[5]

Ruthless acquirers of wealth could grope their way towards the upper circles. Patrick Kennedy, saloon-keeper son of an Irish immigrant, was very much not a proper Bostonian. At the turn of the century he sent his son Joseph across town to an upper-class Protestant day school, the Boston Latin School. When Joseph Kennedy himself addressed the school's tercentenary dinner in 1935, he made all the appropriate noises:

> To strangers I could not possibly convey the reasons for the powerful and sweet hold which the School has upon my affections. It would be like trying to explain to strangers why I love my family. . . The Latin school as we know it was a shrine that some-how seemed to make us all feel that if we could stick it out at the Latin School, we were made of just a little better stuff than the rest of the fellows of our own age who were attending what we always thought were easier schools. . . .[6]

By this time Joseph Kennedy had progressed through Harvard where he roomed in Harvard yard. With the right connections, and elements of the right manner, Kennedy proceeded to make a great deal of money very fast. Acceptable within Roosevelt's upper-class circles, he was appointed chairman of the Securities and Exchange Commission, the body charged with the job of monitoring business deals. In his influential appeal for business support for the President in the election of 1936, *I'm For Roosevelt*, he placed himself with which in the following fashion: 'I am rated a man of wealth, as that term is generally understood. I am the father of nine children, a fact which admits of no misunderstanding.' Then, breathtakingly, he added 'I have no political ambitions for myself or for my children. . . . The upward movement was legitimated with his designation as American ambassador to London. Or almost legitimated: at the outbreak of war Kennedy still awaited the full acceptance which would come when the family ceased to be referred to as Irish American, but simply as American.[8]

In France, the prestige of higher civil servants was considerable in America, it was not. In the United States there developed a unique style of public servant, whose basic experience was often formed in one of the many privately sponsored bodies concerned with social economic or political affairs, and who moved in and out of business academia, or both, and Government. In Britain such men have become known (to editorial writers in the quality newspapers, at least as 'the great and the good'. One of the most important of them in the America of the 1930s, Edwin E. Witte, was to refer to himself as 'a Government man', and that is the label I have adopted. From 1922 to 1933 Witte was both professor in the department of economics at the University of Wisconsin, and chief of the Wisconsin Legislative Library. A phone call from Washington on 24 July 193 fixed Witte's appointment as executive director of the Technical Board of the Committee on Economic Security. Witte compiled record (not published till many years later)[9] of all the discussion and manoeuvres which went into the making of the Social Security Act. It is also quite a roll-call of the influential among government men, businessmen, foundation men, clubwomen and freemasons. In the President's final selection for his Advisory Council on Economic Security five labour leaders and one representative of the National Consumers League were balanced by six businessmen together with two clubwomen, two government men, two editors and two freemasons. The chairman was Frank P. Graham, president of the University of North Carolina.

The social group we are discussing tended to see society as consisting not of a range of classes but of 'us', the small minority, and 'you', the public. It has been well said of Roosevelt that:

He undoubtedly shared the conventional anti-union bias of his social class. As a New York law clerk, he certainly showed no interest in labor problems. The matter simply did not interest him. It is virtually impossible to find even a single stray remark or thought about labor as a group, about unions, or about labor-management problems which the young FDR may have committed to paper before he entered politics.

Roosevelt's first campaign all but ignored industrial working-men as a group. He did not think of them as being distinctive in a political sense. In fact, he did not think at all along social and economic class or group lines. His chief concern was clean Government. His enemies were the bosses.[10]

In a letter to Frances Perkins shortly after the election in 1932 Roosevelt expressed his hope as being to 'accomplish something worth while for the man at the foot of the ladder'.[11] Those whom he believed he served, and to whom he appealed, he referred to as 'the public as a whole' or 'the great mass of the people'. He saw his main enemies as 'a very powerful group among the extremely wealthy and the centralised industries'.[12] Big industrialists, more obviously, took the dichotomous view held by official America:

We, as manufacturers, and you, as workers, can formulate all the high-minded and high-principled plans in the world, but the old law of supply and demand still reigns and we cannot close our eyes or our minds to this fact. We, as manufacturers, must have the best stockings at the lowest possible price; and you, as workers, must supply us with the best possible labor at the best possible price.[13]

Government men sometimes had a more sophisticated view of society, recognizing a working and a middle class rather than just an undifferentiated public or vast mass of 'workers'.

There is a strange, but illuminating, little fable in a Public Affairs pamphlet, *The Homes the Public Builds*,[14] by two 'clubwomen' who were also 'government women'. It concerns two workers in a printing plant, Mike Grady and Bill Johnson, who hear about a new public authority building project. Because his income is low enough to qualify, Mike, who has three children, gets an apartment. Because he has four children to support, Bill's wife also works (in the local chocolate factory), and their joint income disqualifies them from being tenants of a public housing project. This apparent injustice is the subject for further discussion. The city housing authority representative admits that there are people who

> can't find good private houses at a rent they can pay. And yet they have to stand by and see their less prosperous neighbors get all the benefits of public housing while they themselves carry on in the slums, or at least in over-crowded houses. That's a very unjust situation, and it is quite understandable that it should cause some hard feelings.

The American people, says the representative, can be divided into three income groups: 'we can say pretty definitely that private enterprise can supply the top third with homes, and that housing subsidised by the government will be necessary for the bottom third for some time to come.' It was over the middle third that conflict raged:

> This middle third is made up of a great mass of self-respecting workers – skilled artisans, office and professional people. There is less than a thousand dollars difference between its lowest income and its highest. Even if we admit that, insofar as private enterprise can reduce the cost of housing to the consumer, this middle third will be the province of private construction, we haven't solved the problem. It may be ten or fifteen years before private builders can build enough decent houses for this middle group. Meanwhile, while other workers move into public housing, can we expect all these hard-working people to stay contentedly in their shabby houses, bringing up their children under poor conditions?

To that there was no answer. But the fable itself showed that in a context within which it would have been difficult in Britain to avoid speaking of 'working class' and 'middle class', as in the British Medical Association report quoted in the previous chapter, two American women of high social status preferred to view society as made up of 'income groups', and saw 'skilled artisans, office and professional people' as belonging to the same social group.

Undoubtedly it was a widely held view in the upper, and more prosperous middle sections of American society, that class had no real existence but for the exertions of agitators. Roosevelt's former Democratic associate, Al Smith, attacked him for trying, in a 1931 radio broadcast, to stir up class against class. The reverse of the coin was contained in a letter from a Santa Barbara doctor to Frances Perkins, in February 1935: 'Your vision will start the flow of a stream of a sense of responsibility of American people too long enmeshed in a pursuit of individual and class rights.'[15] In refusing to supply the committee on economic security with his payroll statistics, Joseph H. Hayes, assistant treasurer of the John A. Manning Paper Company, argued that 'it is a comparison of just such figures which is leading to class prejudice resulting in much injury to all classes of citizens', and that 'much information of this sort . . . given out to the public . . .' has resulted in 'the embitterment of one class of our citizens against another.'[16]

Mildred Woolley was born in 1889, the daughter of a southern businessman and lawyer, and as part of her education spent a year at the Sorbonne. She married a Belgian research chemist, Dr Seydel, who became the founder and president of the Seydel-Woolley (Chemical Dyes) Company of Atlanta. When the business foundered in the Depression, she became a columnist for the Hearst-owned paper the *Atlanta Georgian*, Americanizing her name slightly to Mildred Seydell. It was the very stuff of her column that class did not exist (and that colour should never be mentioned). She came on in full spate in March 1939 on the occasion of Eleanor Roosevelt's resignation from the Daughters of the American Revolution because of their refusal to rent a hall which was to be used for a black singer. A local Daughter of the American Revolution offered Mrs Seydell immediate congratulations: 'In these troublesome times when groups banned & individuals in high office with un-American ideas attempt to array class against class and race against race, an article such as yours in tonight's Georgian comes as a refreshing breeze, to drive the stench from the nostrils of the true American public.'[17]

IMAGES ACROSS SOCIETY

How, when prodded, Americans saw themselves in relation to class structure, was made moderately clear by the survey printed in the journal *Fortune* in February 1940. Asked, 'What word would you use to name the class in America you belong to?', those participating in the sample replied as shown below:

CLASS	%
Upper...	1.6
Other upper (best, highest etc.).......................	1.3
	2.9
Upper middle...	1.7
Other upper middle (above average etc.).............	0·8
Middle..	38.6
Other middle (in between, moderate etc.)............	5.5
Lower middle..	0.4
	47.0
Lower...	1.2
Other lower (poor, poorest etc.).......................	2.8
Working, laboring..	10.6
Unemployed, idle, unfortunate.........................	0.3
	14.9
Business, executive, white collar......................	2.0
Other miscellaneous answers...........................	5·7
Don't know...	27.5

Given the following ready-made labels, a different sample came up with a sharper, though not necessarily more accurate picture:

Upper class..	10.6
Middle class...	68.2
Lower class..	11.9
Don't know...	9.3

Fortune combined the two sets of results (how, mathematically, is not altogether clear) to come up with this mapping for America as a whole:

Upper class..	7.6
Middle class...	79.2
Lower class..	7.9
Don't know...	5.3

Fortune had no doubts about the significance of this:

> Thus confronted, every class and occupation, including even the unemployed and the lowly farm hand, decisively considers itself middle class. And the people who had previously described them-

selves as belonging to the 'working' or 'laboring' classes also mainly swing into the middle rather than identifying themselves with a lower class proletariat.

Only the blacks, apparently, did not participate in this upward swing.

The *Fortune* survey tells us many different truths about American society and perceptions of it at the end of the 1930s. We should not, however, wish away the term 'working class' quite so easily. The 38.6 per cent who plumped unprompted in the first survey for middle-class status is certainly the most significant figure; the next most significant figure is the 27.5 per cent who could not, without prompting, allocate themselves to any class at all. One other very significant point is that while *Fortune* magazine, in keeping with the well-established tradition that we have already noted, opted in its second survey for the label 'lower class', only 1.2 per cent, unprompted, allocated themselves to that category. What seems curious is that the miscellaneous 2 per cent allocated at the foot of the table to the category 'business, executive, white collar' could not be re-allocated among 'upper', 'upper-middle', 'middle' or 'lower middle'. But then we have already seen the tendency, rather in contrast to British practice, to run these occupations together (and even include skilled artisans as well).

A localized survey of a rural village in the middle west (Seneca, Illinois) found fair agreement on dividing the community into four classes:

CLASS	(*approx.*) %
Upper crust	4
Better class people	32
The working class	56
Bottom of the heap	8

These classes coincided with the lower four of Warner's classification – that is, from 'upper middle' downwards: there was no group 'equivalent to the upper class as found in a larger town or a great city'. There was 'fairly general agreement on the people who make up the "upper crust".' The firm use of the phrase '*the* working class' is striking; but in fact 'the dividing line between the "better-class people" and the "working class" . . . was the least visible of the social class lines,' and the figure selected to represent the class was no proletarian, but the village shoemaker.[18]

Those professions which were distinguished by taking their

earnings in fees, not salaries, clearly saw themselves as occupying a high status, an upper-class or an upper-middle-class position. They had, as we have seen, been set apart from employers and employed in the Social Security legislation. In American society, the legal profession above all provided a well trodden path upwards to the heights of power and influence. But upper-class status in the professions depends very heavily on providing a service to an upper-class clientele. The medical practitioner, or the lawyer, or the minister of religion, who provided his services in, say, a small mining community, was certainly no more than middle class in social status; and indeed, many of the letters written to the President or other members of his government, which are so articulate on the nature and problems of American society, originate from such people.

However, the core of middle-class America lay among the owners of the manifold small businesses and among the multifarious assemblage of executives and managers for the larger ones. No issue, save perhaps the general fecklessness of those lower in the social scale than they, touched the middle class more nearly than that of servants. 'I live in a middle-class neighborhood,' wrote one lady to Mrs Roosevelt. Some women there, she said, keep only one servant, more frequently there are none. She wrote that for most of her twenty-three years of married life 'mine has been a one-servant home'. Moving from Detroit to Washington in 1917, she found the servant problem easier there than in the north. But recently, the courtesy and old spirit of service had been lost. Above all, what most incensed the writer was that two maids had refused to call her two daughters in their late teens 'Miss Anne' and 'Miss Ruth'. Too many servants, she said in her parting shot, preferred 'relief' to 'work'.[19]

Frances Perkins's proposal of a universal minimum wage for servants brought a powerful response from the wife of a builder's merchant in Collins, Mississippi:

> You have brought the housewives of this community quite a laugh by advocating paying our servants a wage of 14 dollars per week. You see we would be delighted if we could possibly get that sum for our entire household expenses.
>
> For a family of five adults I have about 10 dollars a week to feed, clothe us and to pay a servant.
>
> My maid washes, irons and cleans the house working from 7 till about 1.30 for meals and the large sum of 1 dollar and 50 cents per week. She would gladly cook too, for two dollars. Some people pay less than I. And what can you do about it? They would starve or steal if we did our work alone.[20]

Then came the eternal cry of the southern provincial middle class against the cities of the East Coast: 'You people who have lived in cities make yourselves ridiculous when you try to set prices for the whole country. Frankly, if we were not suffering so much from the mistakes your administration is making we would get quite a laugh out of it. Never have we seen such foolishness in high places.' The letter concluded:

When we, who own small businesses make money enough to live decently we always advance our maid's wages, but please don't ask that we pay her more than our own income. This income is derived from what was once a flourishing lumber business and a large farm.

Mrs Roosevelt and Mrs Dall are also quite comical to us.[21]

Some small businessmen would have been only too happy to have been treated for social security purposes just like employees. This point was made to Arthur J. Altmeyer, secretary to the Technical Board of the Economic Security Committee, by the proprietor of the Morrison Fountain Supply Company of Oklahoma City, writing on headed notepaper garlanded by a recitation of all the fruits of middle-west civilization: coca cola, cones, dixi cups, Dr Pepper, fruits of syrups, glasses, Hersheys cocoa, liberty root beer, limes, liquid gas, malted milk, napkins, paper bags, pluto, sealrights, straws, welches, white rock. Why could not the Social Security Act, he asked, 'include the *small* businessman, for surely he gets old, and often without means, just like the men working for him'.

Economic insecurity sucked, and the positive policies of the New Deal, particularly the National Recovery Administration, pushed many of the lesser professional occupations towards organization and unionization. On the one hand 'organised labor' in the American context did not specifically connote 'working class'; on the other, many of those most jealous of their professional or white-collar status preferred to keep well clear of any form of union. The American Newspaper Guild was founded in Washington in December 1933, but encountered continuing 'difficulty in selling the Guild to the higher brackets'.[22] The American Federation of Teachers never numbered more than 33,000 members in this period: one president of the federation pointed out that a majority of teachers were against 'any form of organisation which tended to reduce the teaching profession to the laboring level'.[23] In Britain bank clerks had shown how zealously they wished to maintain their status by opposing moves that might have brought them within the limits of

National Insurance; in America, all the pressures were in the other direction. Indeed, it is quite clear that economic necessity and a realistic acceptance of the significance of employee status far outweighed any thoughts about social class. Many office workers saw themselves, in clear functional terms, as being worse off than manual workers. 'The laborer,' one office worker wrote to Mildred Seydell, 'gets the sympathy of the people, and provision has been made for thousands of them to eke out an existence, but there are any number of office workers out of work and unable to get re-located. . .'[24]

One major growth area in American society, the service trades, fell foul of the official model which divided all America into either employers or employees. In a time of depression, these 'in-between worker-employers'[25] – comprising tens of thousands of self-employed tailors, hairdressers, exterminators and shoe-repairers, or proprietors of laundries, cleaning-and-dying establishments, beauty parlors, garages, linen suppliers and parking lots – were placed in little doubt as to their economic dependence, particularly upon the suppliers of the machines they used. Small proprietors, as well as employees, in the service industries had to recognize that they too were 'labor'. But again, labour does not mean working class. As might be expected, the barbers were a particularly verbose, if not exactly literate group, and there were several letters from them in the Economic Security Committee files. 'We sure deal with the Public in Barbering,' wrote one, and 'in the suburban section we deal with the working class. . .'[26]

INDUSTRIAL WORKERS AND OTHER LOW-INCOME GROUPS

Much of the evidence emanating from individuals and groups within what in Britain would unhesitatingly be regarded as the working class does confirm the view that perceptions of class were not sharply defined in the United States. E. Wight Bakke, in his chapter on 'A Working Class', was endeavouring to demonstrate the formation of working-class consciousness in America in the late thirties: thus insofar as it demonstrates the opposite, the evidence collected in the interviews he conducted in Newhaven form rather sound testimony. The classic American position was put by an Irish welder:

I feel no particular unity with workers any more than with any other respectable citizen. Everybody has his work to do. Everybody can do his work better than anybody else, so what's the object in feeling that you belong to one group more than another? These people who agitate for a class struggle represent nobody. They represent nobody but themselves. The average American worker is a mighty sensible person and he knows that he is not the only pebble on the beach and that his own work is not the only work that needs to be done in society. He doesn't always understand how it is that the people who own bank accounts and bonds and industrial stock are useful, but he knows that they have some kind of relationship to his own job and he supposes that that relationship is an important one.[27]

Here is a notion of division of labour as cooperative venture at its highest.

Bakke found evidence of job consciousness rather than class consciousness. A carpenter began his interview with another classic statement:

Class lines? There ain't no class lines among American workers. There's only job lines; but believe me those are mighty strong. Why on one construction job you've got about five lines that are recognised by the men – from the laborer up to the general superintendent. Now let me tell you; you don't cross those lines either, when you think of the group you belong to. Why, you're closer to the boss if you happen to have the job that I did than you are to that fellow wheeling the cement in a wheelbarrow. You don't think of him as being a member of your class. That's one reason why the American labor movement ain't never going to get any place, because the big boys, the fellows who ought to be the leaders, don't think that they're in the same class with the fellows who use the pick and shovel. It's funny what makes you feel that way – the wages you get plus the responsibility that you have. You know right well there isn't any real barrier to you getting the boss's position except that there aren't very many such positions. But if you should be lucky and get it there ain't any real barrier to you having it, but when you get that way he's gonna associate with you just like he does with all his other associates right now, so you point yourself ahead instead of looking down at the rest of the men who might be thought of as belonging to the working class.

Another worker made some similar points:

The point is just this – you work with your own type of workers;
all you know about is trucking. You don't have any feeling that
you belong with the rest of the workers in the country. That's
what I understand there is in foreign countries, a feeling that men
belong to a working class; but here you don't particularly feel
that you are in one class or another. I suppose maybe its because
everyone thinks that some day you'll be a capitalist. Funny, you
know you never will, but at the same time you never think of
putting people in another class from yourself. So the only time
that you ever hear of there being classes in this country is when
you see an agitator up on the corner, and of course you don't have
time to listen to him. You're too busy doing your job.

But the last few words of that offer some hints. Even within the
vigorous assertion of the American myths, commonsense awareness of reality keeps breaking in. Bakke identified two 'status'
indicators involving differences between manual and intellectual
work, and between authority and control – though the first, at least,
again has perhaps more than a touch of the American myth, and
would seem nearer to a middle-class perception on the European
scale, rather than a working-class one. A mechanic put it this way:

You know it's hard to tell just what class divisions there are in
America, and I don't know just how to say it. It seems to me it's
something like this, that when you've a job where there's some call
for planning, some call for figuring out things – I think that's the
word, figuring out things – in your head, you feel that you're in a
different class from the fellow who handles things. Now that
fellow, I'll tell you right now, that fellow feels that he is just about
next to the top notch, even though he is paid a salary just like the
others are paid wages, but just the same, he feels that he is important, and he doesn't feel out of place when he's associating
with men like professors, lawyers, and doctors – and oh say –
bankers. He doesn't feel that he's out of place. He associates with
them and he's sure of himself. Now, sometimes, you know, a man
who's a real skilled artisan will be getting more money than that
fellow, but it isn't always the money that makes the difference;
it's the fact that you're figuring out things, or you ain't, and that's
a matter of your training. If you had a long experience of doing
that sort of thing, you get a confidence and assurance that just
naturally makes you feel a bit superior. Some men get that by
going to college. Sometimes it ain't so; sometimes they don't do

much figuring out in college, but at least they think that they've done it; but it isn't necessary to have gone to college if your training has been the figuring out of things. You feel pretty much the same way. Now, I think that's the big class division in America, a division that comes right in the experience of men, something that's real, something that they see every day. And it usually works out that the 'figuring-things-out' group is the same as the bosses and employers and the ones that tell you what to do. Now, of course, within the *figuring-out* group, and in the *handling-things* group, there's a lot of divisions too, but those aren't real class divisions.

'Of course there are classes in America,' said a toolmaker. 'But when you ask me to point out what makes that true, well, that's a tough one. Suppose you have what you need to make what *you* want to do mean something. Then you're in one class. Now, suppose you *don't* have enough, so that you have to give up trying to believe what *you* decided makes any difference. Then you're in another class.'

A man who called himself 'the best gun assembler in the whole damn country' remarked simply: 'It's funny how some guys feel they are working class and some don't. But I guess we all recognise it – all of us, when someone from the office waves to us. We feel sort of honored.' A machinist who declared that he had no class feeling could nonetheless pin down the obvious differences between himself and business and professional men:

> You can tell the difference when you meet them on the street. You can tell the difference by the way they look. Professional men, the businessmen have more confidence in their eyes; the workers' faces are drawn more, perhaps it's from worry, perhaps it's from working harder; I don't know, but at any rate you can tell the difference. Then when you come to the factory worker, you certainly can tell him every time. He doesn't have any hope in his eye at all or any spring in his step. His cheeks are all faded out because he works inside all the time and he doesn't look as if he hoped to ever be any better than he is right now.

A machine operator went a bit further:

> Hell, brother, you don't have to look far to know that there's a workin' class. We may not say so. But look at what we do. Work. Look at who we run around with and bull with. Workers. Look

at where we live. If you can find anyone but workers in my block, I'll eat 'em. Look at how we get along. Just like every other damned worker. Hells bells, of course there's a workin' class, and it's gettin' more so every day. What we need to do is work out ways to make bein' a worker amount to something.

Even a boilermaker who had risen to the position of general manager in a small firm was prepared to criticize the American dream. Guys like him, he admitted, had made the grade. But, he continued, 'how many of us did?'

That's the big point. How many of the gang I started with in Massachusetts? I'll bet not more than two or three. Now that's swell for us, and we are inclined to say, 'Ain't America grand? No class lines get in the way of a good man gettin' to the top, to hell with class lines.' Because you see we couldn't have got where we are if they had been too fixed. But that isn't the only place to get by a long shot. How about the rest of those birds? Haven't they got some rights? Don't they want somethin' out of life too? Course they do. But we've been so all-fired set on keepin' the ladder open that we've forgot the fellows who never even get one foot on it. Do you think my satisfaction balances out all that disappointment? I wonder. Sometimes I get disgusted with these damned union men I have to wrastle with, but then I think they are doin' more for the working men than I've done. I'm vain enough to think I've showed them what is possible in America. But those birds are actually workin' out means that all workers can use to get on. But how many can do what I've done? And, hell, even if they did work as hard and connived like I have, where would all of them find jobs like this?

Perhaps the words of the Irish-American with whom we began can be balanced out by these words from a mechanic who was an English immigrant:

Some day in this country, mate, just like in England where I come from, a man's going to be President because he stuck with the workers. Only in England you know we don't call him President. But the idea is the same. The working class in this country or any country is damned important and one of these days they're going to know it. I may not live to see it, but it will be a great day. And the reason is just this. You can't forever stir men up to big ambitions by holding out hopes that only a few can have. But if you get the workers together and give a man a chance to work right up to the top by being a worker – why that is something. And it'll be a damned sight more honorable than lickin' the boots of the gentry so as they'll let you be one of them. Workers for workers I says and before very long that'll mean that a man'll hold his head up and say, 'To hell with your black coats and white collars, I'm a workingman and proud of it.' Look at what we've done for ourselves. Can you show me anything else that's more important?

Evidence from private letters on the whole conforms to the stereotype of the absence of strong class sentiments in the United States. Consciousness of status seems a more obvious characteristic of many of the skilled workers. The moves towards organization of the unskilled workers led by the Committee for Industrial Organization brought angry responses from established rank-and-file-members of the American Federation of Labor. 'They seam [*sic*] to think that if they have a union card of any kind, they have a right to work any place they want to regardless of trade,' complained one of them. 'And a few of our weak kneed trade unionists (not too good mechanics) are wondering which way to fall,' he added.[28] The spirit of cooperative division of labour is to be found everywhere. Paternalistic firms, in particular, often found the appropriate deferential response. This is nowhere more strongly marked than among the female factory workers employed in the various industries controlled by Gerard Swope's General Electric Company, which on 1 January 1931 introduced its own private employment assurance scheme. One girl said that the scheme enabled the employees to realize 'the square dealings of the Concern in which they are employed'; another said that she was 'so fortunate to have a position with the Youngstown Mazda Lamp Company and then with such a wonderful guarantee of this kind to the employee'; a third concluded her eulogy by saying that she could go on writing for a long time but would 'close now and hope to have the pleasure of continuing my services with the Company as long as I am able'.[29]

Even those who bemoaned their lot often retained sufficient faith in the mobility of American society to blame themselves rather than any predetermined class position: 'I work in the mill because when I married I threw away my chance of ever being anything. . . . I work in a mill, I guess you'd say a lowly, common working boy, but my life once meant as much to me as yours do to you.'[30] The other side of mobility, as well as the strong strain of popular hatred for big corporations and monopolies, sometimes also showed through:

> Through no fault of mine I have become one of these unfortunate women. I had four hundred and eighty acres of land taken away from me because I could not pay the irrigation company the enormous water rate. For six years I have been slaving for my board and clothes, I am an elderly woman and a widow. There is thousands just like me in the United States of ours. We are reduced to serfdom and there seems to be nothing planned for our help. I sometimes wonder if we are considered human. Regardless of what people say and write there is no class of society in this country so miserable as the hired girls and women. I know women who have graduated from Business College and have done office work, who are now working as char-women. Not that I think they are any better than the ones who have no education, but they had the ambition to study for something better than meniel [*sic*] labor.[31]

Yet within the ambit of the organized trade union movement the language used had stronger resemblances to that current in France than in Britain. The preamble to the constitution of the American Federation of Labor declared:

> Whereas, A struggle is going on in all the nations of the civilised world between the oppressors and the oppressed of all countries, a struggle between the capitalist and the laborer, which grows in intensity from year to year, and will work disastrous results to the toiling millions if they are not combined for mutual protection and benefit.
>
> It therefore, behoves the representatives of the Trade and Labor Unions of America, in Convention assembled to adopt such measures and disseminate such principles among the mechanics and laborers of our country as will permanently unite them to secure the recognition of rights to which they are justly entitled.

Oddly enough, the constitution of the CIO was, if anything, less obviously expressive of a militant class model of society.

The brutality of the methods employed by the employers to resist organization in the motor industry inevitably produced stark images of warfare, even if the language used was nearly always that of employers and workers, rather than of class against class. The language of class is explicit in some of the circulars of the American Federation of Hosiery Workers, though in a neat American way it is combined with the philosophy of economic expansionism and emphasis on purchasing power:

> With wages of the working class reduced about 60% in the last ten years and the interest and dividends of capital increased more than 60% in the last ten years we find the whole purchasing power of the wage earner and the farmer reduced to a point that threatens the whole economic structure of the country. . . .[32]

Usually, however, and in rather marked contrast with Britain, language of class is most often found among various fringe groups less obviously co-members of the industrial working class. W. H. Sell of the Brotherhood of Painters, Decorators and Paper-Hangers, from Akron Ohio, complained to the Department of Labor that one Saturday morning as he was attempting to explain the benefits of the closed shop to a truck driver, an agent of the truck driver's company intervened to inform the driver that should he join a union he would be fired immediately. 'As to building up a buying power of the working classes,' Sell concluded, such an agent could do more harm in an hour than a union propagandist could repair in a month.[33] Complaining of tug-boatmen's exclusion from the New Deal Social Security provisions, one of them conjured up a graphic image: 'We are the same as a factory worker. Take a dinner pail go home each night.' But there was also praise for the New Deal: 'To the wor[r]king class it appears as the Santa Clause started his Xmas about August [1933]': the writer was in fact an employee of a dry goods firm.[34]

One particularly rich vein of working-class thinking is to be found in the correspondence conducted between the United Charities of St Paul, Minnesota, and unemployed men in the district.[35] 'Doles' are contemptuously rejected. One labouring worker, pondering the future of his four sons, asked, 'Will there be work for them so they can live like an American? Or will it be a dole system like England?' Generally, when the word 'worker' is used, it turns out to mean 'social worker'. A city salesman wrote, 'We had always had enough for poor people' – a recurrent phrase in American life and later taken up very forcefully by Jimmy Carter. A 'commin laberer', however, wrote: 'I think it is a shame and disgrace on the richest nation in the world to have widespread unemployment and to force all the working class on charity.' One extrovert who had had a colourful career as a salesman, a debt collector and a private detective, offered his services catching crooked applicants for United Charities benefits!

Of hardship and bitterness there is plenty. A blacksmith described himself as a 'forgotten common slave laborer'.[36] A disgruntled railway worker, after declaring that the American Federation of Labor and the Railway Union had no right to speak for anyone but themselves, delivered the following diatribe:

> The coming winter promises to be one of strikes and disturbances, in every industrial city of America. As the people see their hopes of escape from poverty and miseries of the past, being dashed to earth again, after the ringing declaration of our President on his acceptance to office. After all his energies of the past few months, to hope the downward course of the depression. It hurts, to see them all wasted by a hand-full of employers. It leaves us with a bitter taste in our mouth. A hardness in our heart. And more determined than ever, to wipe out the present system. If it can-not be readjusted to a more equitable, Christian and humane basis.[37]

The presenter of this stark, dichotomous image, it should be noted, gives his allegiance to Christ rather than to Marx. 'I am bursting with red hot revolt,' wrote a factory girl to Mildred Seydell. 'I am just a factory girl, working the long hours of the night, that others spend in refreshing sleep, earning barely enough to keep me alive, and hating every moment of my existence.'[38] But the tragic gem of the whole Seydell collection deserves to be quoted extensively.

> . . . Born, when the great war was and matured in a great depression with a so elementary education that I know about things a very little, there is only left for me to wonder about the world and mostly its people in a detached and futile sort of way. . . .
>
> I work in a factory doing dull and uninteresting sort of work for fourteen dollars a week.
>
> There are many of us young and futile, in factories here in Atlanta and elsewhere and we are the only people unmentioned in events. . . .
>
> . . . if I had money for means and psychology that would give me ambition to try – then I would be successful – a doctor, a lawyer or a great chemist, or yes, even an artist – I studied Art in night school.
>
> I know too, as well perhaps as you Mrs Reporter, that there have been ones who from the very bottoms have risen, but as

there have been such a few – I am unempressed [*sic*]. To college would have been wonderful but I could not go even to work it thru because I must stay to more than help on fourteen dollars a week to support my fathers family.

Yes, there are many of us who are no better than slaves of the factory time clock, male, female and young who know of no hope – and won't you please of kind charity try and find for us and give us some philosophy upon which to content ourselves and live?

We have our nights – our 'date' – we ride – go to shows and even get drunk. We have our morals and our lack of morals. Not many girls of our class level are looked down on because of her lack of morals. I know of love – and Lord! shes sweet – and I would marry and yet cannot – so all the more my futility.

I have read of communism garnered in American mills and factories and yet – I could not explain to you what manner of thing it is. I've read that my generation would not fight for stars and stripes, but most of whom I know would gladly fight, die and be cannon fodder, not so much for our government – which is to us just so much of grafting politicians but for the mere sake of doing something different. The spilling of blood is not offensive to us and we believe that death has been over press agented.

I would not have you to think tho that we do not believe our country the greatest in the world and because of what it has been and because of what it may be it is still ours – and in our hearts. The star spangled banner still creates with in us titanic emotions of pride. It is those perfidious gentlemen of governmental power who are using our country to further their own ambitions that are objects of our hatred. We pray for their ever lasting damnation. Why can't we have a simple and understandable democracy fearing god, instead of a complex and contradictory bureaucracy fearing only a possible unfixable investigation. . . .

I am not entirely hopeless tho because I have loved men like Will Rogers and Mark Twain.

Aye, tis interesting to wonder and to observe this world of ours and were I able to be a writer. I would not want for subjects to write on it. . . .[39]

But unlike the British miner, whom in some ways he recalls, this anonymous, but patriotic complainant does not seem to have had any further opportunity to develop and refine his talents.

It is when we finally descend into the realm of the domestic servant that we suddenly find the phrase 'working class' being bandied around. Partly, this is due to a skew in the evidence: the 'problem' of domestic service (though the nature of that problem was rather different depending upon which end of the breadline you were on) greatly exercised Mrs Roosevelt and Frances Perkins together with her colleagues in the Women's Branch of the Department of Labor, and letters, which form rich treasure trove for the social historian in the National Archives, were solicited from domestic servants. But domestic servants of the United States were, as a group, unquestionably among those most actively conscious of the brutal nature of inequality and dependency in the America of the 1930s. No doubt when one of them told Frances Perkins, 'I do not believe you know just what really is going on among the working class of girls,' her thoughts were more on the 'working' aspect of the phrase than on class in any sociological or historical sense. However, the wider sociological implication is clear in a letter from a Yonkers butler and chauffeur condemning the 'slavery' of domestic service and beginning, 'I am a great admirer of the wonderful work you have been doing for the working class, in general'; in a letter from a female domestic in West Lawn, Pennsylvania, beginning, 'since you are interested in the working class of people I am taking this opportunity to write you in the half of the domestic'; and in this punchline from another married woman working as a servant in Pennsylvania, 'people who have to hire help has no mercy for the working class'.[40]

Many of the writers clearly associate themselves with the factory workers and obviously have an image of a large, coherent working class distinguished by the degradation of its conditions of work. The point is reinforced by the woman, herself very much in a minority, who wrote, 'I went out working as a domestic worker as I did not care to go in a mill.' Others saw themselves as the true unfortunates of society, and some of the most rending letters come from girls who had been brought up in orphanages. Indeed, we begin to see among the domestic servants two of the other most potent sources of inequality in human societies, age and sex. All this comes through in a powerful letter which was simply signed 'one of the tired working women of Cinci':

> I want to add my letter along with the rest to the housewifes who are going to write to you. We all want to put in our plea about the hours that the working women who do house-work in the private homes have to work by. Most of us arise at 5.30 or 6.00 A.M. and work all day, cleaning, cooking and washing and ironing, putting

up fruit etc. etc., and if there is company for dinner in the evening
we usually finish up at 11.30 P.M. and sometimes 1.00 A.M. And
this goes on very often three or four nights a week. . . . Do you
think this is just or right for the same ladies who have worked all
day long to stay up until after midnight, just for the selfish
pleasure of some one else, who have no respect for the tired working girl or woman. . . . You people down at Washington are
planning for the *men* in factories and large mills to have the 40
hour week schedules or 8 hrs a day. Please, why not do something
for us women? There would not be so many nervous broken
down, worked to death women, if we had some kind of decent
hours to work by in these homes. God made women more frail,
and not nearly so strong as men, then why are men permitted to
work so many hours, then *they rest*, and us women because we
are poor unfortunately, and have to work for our living and earn
our daily bread besides we have to help others to, we have to keep
on and on over a long period of hours, and when we do get to bed
we are so tired and nervous we cannot go to sleep. And we cannot
all go to the factories to get work for, when we apply if we are
past 35 or 40 at the most we are told we are not wanted. Yet some
of us have better education, and are more efficient than the
dressed up and rouged dolls who make an attempt to work in the
factory. For us older women have our homes and other interests
at heart, and would do the work better, for we would not stay up
all nite like these young smarties, then they are not fit to work. . . .
There are fine women here who are working for $2.00 and $3.00
per week and it will hardly pay a working womens car fare and
life insurance, not to say anything about clothes for respectibility
– and if any of us say anything we are told they can get cheaper
women to replace us. . . .

The letter concludes with a clear presentation of that general identification of servant with factory worker mentioned earlier, when the
writer expresses her deep gratitude for what the administration has
already done for the 'working people' and most of all for the 'chief
problem' in the Pennsylvania mills.

   This identification of domestic servant with mill worker is one of
two powerful images which emerge from these letters by domestic
servants – though it was an image not fully shared by the mill workers
themselves, particularly the male ones. The other image, less explicit
but more pervasive, is of the domestic servants, who often call themselves 'the working class' being in effect a lower class or even an

under class, though the latter phrase is never, and the former, despite the sociologists, seldom used. But as the woman from West Lawn put it: 'to begin with it is about the most ignoble work one can do.' It was not, in most cases, that the servants saw their employers as necessarily 'superior'; it was rather that the employers, however contemptible in the eyes of the servants, at least had a foothold in society, from which many of the domestics felt themselves set apart. From a municipal home in Chicago came a letter 'composed by a group of women who have broken down in health and spirit from being undernourished at the shelter and the homes where we were employed' who simply signed themselves 'despairing':

> These unfortunate victims are forced to work 16 and 18 hours a day in private homes without wages (if her employers say she cannot afford to pay her) often in houses of low grade people who gloat over the fact that they can take advantage of these homeless women and make them sleep in basements where the sewer water is up to their ankles on rainy days. . . .

RACIAL AND ETHNIC MINORITIES

Sex, age, personal misfortune, these characteristics of deprivation cutting across class were not to get the same attention in Britain and France until the 1970s. Colour throughout was a fissure in American society. Though racism is still widespread in most societies changes in race relations have been so great in recent years that it is sometimes difficult to project oneself back into the rigid taboos which still governed American society in the 1930s, and into the mores of the south where much had remained unchanged since the Civil War. 'We hold these truths to be self-evident, that all men are created equal': this proud quotation from the Declaration of Independence was cited in a letter to President Roosevelt from a Chicago correspondent, whose main purpose was to protest against the exclusion of domestic servants and farm hands from old age security. The eulogy of the New Deal contains a slight shock for the British reader: 'The first time in the history of the USA that the administration did something for the under-dog, (most would say what's the matter with Abraham Lincoln? He did that for the Nigger but not a thing for the white man).'[41] Among blacks themselves, 'negro' and 'colored' were still accepted epithets. One black leader noted that many complaints had been forwarded to the various departments of Roosevelt's administration on the 'flagrant cases of heartless discrimination against Negroes with any kind of skill in the trades and crafts'. 'Negroes', he writes, would welcome admission into the local unions of the American Federation of Labor but are debarred by local traditions, thereby swelling the relief rolls and 'creating a dangerous frame of mind' among what he referred to as 'our masses'.[42]

However, the relationship of black to white was by no means a simple one. Just as white society was itself broken into classes, however jaggedly, so too was black society divided into different levels. The picture which emerges is not of a social structure in which all the upper floors are occupied by whites with the basement being crammed with blacks, but rather of two houses standing side-by-side: a tall one with a shallow basement, and a much lower one with a deep basement, the whites in the former, the blacks in the latter. In the north there was often a patronizing tolerance for the stalwart respectable black. The wife of an attorney in Belaire, Ohio, described 'the case of a colored family in my own town. The father of this family was a sturdy six-foot colored man, well educated as a minister in the colored church.' The man brought his wife and nine children to Belaire from Detroit when work failed there; although eventually given work under the Works Progress Administration he was now mortally ill in the county sanatorium with tuberculosis. 'Our Mothers Club has furnished the whole family with clothing. They are hard working respectable people and ask no help until in real distress.'[43]

In the south, a very delicate network of social relationships had developed. No black man could be addressed as 'Mr'. But in the case of John Hope, the pioneer black educationist who developed the all-black University of Atlanta, some embarrassment was spared by accepting that although he might not be 'Mr' he could be called 'Professor'. Detailed studies of Atlanta have shown how simplistic is the notion that southern cities were crudely divided into white city centre and suburbs, and black ghetto. In fact, there were three separate black communities in Atlanta, one inhabited by a highly educated group which shared many of the characteristics of the white upper-middle class.[44]

Well-established blacks were inevitably an important force in cities where the black population was itself very high. The point is well made by this letter from a local black leader to the mayor of Atlanta.

My Dear Mayor Key,

In view of the fact that your able administration has been so far reaching and effective in benefiting the entire population of the City of Atlanta, white and colored; we regretted the other day when we saw a new announcement of a Citizen Committee appointed to advise on the spending of funds to be secured for the city through the Works Progress Administration and a City Bond Issue, that there were no Negroes placed on your Committee to advise with and in regard to such spending that would be of a special benefit to the Negro population. We hope this was an unintentional oversight due to the many complex problems that face you daily.

Keeping in mind that the City of Atlanta is one third Negro, that the population of the first ward is 95% Negro and the population of the fourth ward is 61 % Negro, we regret that no representative for the Negro population of these wards is colored.

I believe we must keep in mind that the City of Atlanta is out to secure funds through the support of the entire city. To this end the colored population of the city will be expected to lend its support. Most certainly in the face of this support and cooperation in the securing of the money, we should have some recognition in advising on the spending, particularly as far as benefits to the Negro population are concerned. May we, therefore recommend that your committee be extended to include certain representative Negro citizens.

May we suggest that for the first ward A. T. Walden, President of the Citizens Trust Company and Mrs John Hope, the wife of Dr John Hope of Atlanta University and that for the fourth ward Bishop W. A. Fountain, Bishop of the Ame Church in Georgia, and Mrs H. R. Butler, Secretary of the Colored National Parent-Teachers Association, be considered to represent the Negro citizens on your committee.

Whether oversight or slight, that letter produced the desired result: the chairman of the Bond Campaign Committee reported to Mrs Hope that he was 'taking the liberty of appointing a number of the leading and outstanding citizens of your race to assist in this campaign'. He did not know, he added, 'of any class who will receive more benefit from the result of the passing of this bond issue than the colored people of Atlanta'.[45]

Ethnic middle America, the entity which was believed to bring together the various ethnic groups into one large class or pressure group, was a discovery of the 1960s. In the 1930s the various ethnic groups were very sharply divided from each other and from Anglo-Saxon America, and they tend to present two contrasting faces. Businessmen sought protection and trade advantage by binding closely together, the leading ethnic groups in various cities usually having their own chambers of commerce. When the Italian Chamber of Commerce of Boston was established it was agreed 'to have only one class of members, so as not to give the impression to create privileged classes by having two categories, as it had been previously proposed'.[46] Lower down the scale, the insecure immigrant masses preferred to keep a low profile, eschewing overt class action which might attract unfavourable attention, and seeking such security as they could find in the ethnic community. Patronage, collusion, corruption were often joined together in a relationship established between, in particular, Italian businessmen, Italian trade union bosses and Italian workers. The smaller face was that of those who brought with them European Socialist ideas. Even here, ethnic forces remained strong and Italian Marxists sought first of all to establish an Italian Labor Council of America, which would publish a weekly paper in Italian with only one or two papers in English; but in the wider American labour movement where the catch phrases and slogans and class concepts of European Marxism were to be heard, often their originators were European immigrants.

Private images of class in America reflect both the myths and reality of American life, the myths themselves having roots in real historical development. The very scale of the Great Depression, which swept away some bankers and executives as well as many clerks, many businessmen and a multitude of manual workers, a few professionals and masses of farmers, made it easier to think of the problems of that classless class, the unemployed, rather than those of a working class. Migrants could be pitied but also romanticized. The sentimental, moralizing, super-Christian *Tales of Americans on Trek* discussed the plight and the rehabilitation of a banker, a Mexican, a prosperous plumber, a European immigrant, and a black share-cropper.[47] All America was there, and all America shared adversity and regeneration. The administration excluded domestic servants from its social security legislation, yet it sought professionalization of that lowly occupation through such polite aliases as 'household employees' or 'domestic and personal service'. The dichotomy between myth and reality is well seen in a newspaper report of the administration's intentions. 'NEW DEAL FOR DOMESTIC WORKERS', said the headline in the *St Louis Despatch* for 20 November 1933; but then the article itself went on to discuss the conditions of 'servants'. Race was often more strongly felt than class, and sometimes confused with it. Yet in the peculiarly rich American sources there is ample evidence to refute the notion that ordinary Americans had no awareness of living in a society divided into social classes, and to demonstrate that many Americans spoke of 'an upper class' and of 'a working class', as well as of 'a middle class'.

Notes

1. E. Digby Baltzell, *Philadelphia Gentlemen: the Making of a National Upper Class* (1958); G. William Domhoff, *The Higher Circles: the Governing Class in America* (1970).
2. Atlanta University Library [AUL], McDuffie Collection, box 1.
3. Baltzell, *op. cit.*, pp. 6–29.
4. Dean Acheson, *Morning and Noon* (1965), pp. 164–5.
5. *The Secret Diary of Harold L. Ickes* (1955), vol. 1, p. 109; vol. 2, p. 503; vol. 3, pp. 318–19. Criticizing the Rockefellers for abstemiousness and religiosity, Ickes wrote of the head of that family, 'I suspect he is the only man of his generation *and class* who does this' (my italics).
6. Quoted by R. J. Whalen, *The Founding Father: The Story of Joseph P. Kennedy* (1965, paperback edition 1976), p. 32.
7. Joseph P. Kennedy, *I'm For Roosevelt* (1936), p. 2.
8. *Ibid*, p. 3.
9. Edwin E. Witte, *The Development of the Social Security Act* (1962).
10. Alfred B. Rawlins, Jr, 'Franklin Roosevelt's Introduction to Labor', in *Labor History*, vol. 3, no. 1 (1962).
11. Roosevelt to Perkins, 31 December 1932, *The Roosevelt Letters*, vol. 3 (1952), p. 95.
12. *Ibid*, pp. 95, 211.
13. Archives Division, the State Historical Society of Wisconsin [SHSW], Madison, Textile Workers Organizing Committee Papers: Albany Manufacturing Company, 'To Employees', 9 November 1940.
14. Edith Elmar Wood and Elizabeth Ogg, *The Homes the Public Builds* (1940).
15. National Archives [NA], Washington, RG 47, box 67.
16. NA, RG 47, box 25.
17. Robert W. Woodruff Library [RWWL], Emory University, Atlanta, Mildred Seydell Collection, box 12, folder 3.
18. Robert J. Havighurst and H. G. Morgan, *The Social History of a War-Boom Community* (1946), pp. 16–22.

19. NA, RG 86, box 926.
20. *Ibid.*
21. *Ibid.*
22. Archives of Labor and Urban Affairs [ALUA], Wayne State University, Detroit, American Newspaper Guild Records, boxes 7 and 36.
23. ALUA, American Federation of Teachers Records: *18th Convention* (1934).
24. RWWL, Mildred Seydell Collection, box 3, folder 1.
25. Tamiment Library, New York University Libraries, John Lyons Collection: John Lyons, 'The Service Industries' (September 1936).
26. NA, RG 174, 167/2283.
27. E. Wight Bakke, *Citizens without Work* (1940). The quotations which follow are from pp. 88–102.
28. SHSW, US MSS 117A 11C, box 1.
29. NA, RG 47, box 15.
30. RWWL, Mildred Seydell Collection, box 12, folder 3.
31. NA, RG 86, box 926.
32. SHSW, American Federation of Hosiery Workers Papers, series 6, box 1.
33. NA, RG 174, box 167/2283.
34. NA, RG 47, box 239/721.6.
35. Social Welfare History Archives, University of Minnesota Libraries, Minneapolis, Family Service of St Paul: Annual Reports 1932 folder.
36. NA, RG 86, box 923.
37. NA, RG 174, box 167/2283.*
38. RWWL, Mildred Seydell Collection, box 12, folder 3.
39. *Ibid*, box 7, folder 1: 19 January 1936.
40. The letters quoted here and in following paragraphs are in NA, RG 86, box 926.
41. NA, RG 47, box 237, 720.02.
42. *Ibid*, box 54.
43. *Ibid*, box 231, 622.2.
44. Dana F. White and Timothy J. Crimmins, 'Urban Structure, Atlanta', in *Journal of Urban History* (February 1976).
45. AUL, Neighborhood Union Collection, box 4.
46. Immigration History Research Center, University of Minnesota Libraries, St Paul, Donnaruma Collection: Istituenda Camera di Commercio Italiana, in Boston, Mass., 20 July 1927.
47. *Tales of Americans on Trek* (1940), compiled by Edith E. Lowry, Velma Shotwell, and Helen White.

7

Unofficial and Private Images in France

The Americans, in the large, are an extrovert lot. The French, notoriously, maintain restraint and reticence. In France the search for private images is a rather unrewarding one, especially since the main archives offer nothing like the wealth of documentation on the recent period to be found in the United States. Furthermore, when we turn to French images of class we are involved not just in another language, but in another vocabulary. While American English seemed scarcely to have enough words to provide adequate class descriptions of society, leaving us so often with the purely functional or economic terminology of 'employees', 'labor' or 'middle income group', French sometimes seems to have too many words. The various juridical labels, *artisan*, *industriel* etc., have already been discussed. To them one must add a particular favourite, which has no real equivalent in the popular usage of either Britain or America and which always sounds alien when imported into British or American academic usage, *intellectuel*. Ask a French university professor today what social class he belongs to, and he is still quite likely to say the 'intellectual class' (I speak from personal experience). While an *ouvrier* is an industrial manual worker (and *classe ouvrière* is the working class), a *travailleur* is any sort of worker, whether by hand or brain. Thus when René Garmy, a hard-line communist historian, was chucked out of the Communist Party in the 1930s he noted that along with himself as a *travailleur intellectuel*, there were also expelled two *ouvriers manuels*, which made things better somehow.[1] The words of political revolution, as distinct from those of social class, were in wide use: appeals are made to 'the people', to 'citizens', and to 'the masses'. Yet in colloquial usage the word *bourgeois*, even in France, has, we have seen, many meanings, running roughly from the Marxist sense of 'member of the propertied or ruling class', through the sense of 'ordinary respectable citizen', to being a term of familiarity implying affection, or possibly sometimes contempt; Professor Maurice Halbwachs, as we saw, offered the definition of 'man without distinction'. *Profession* in France comes near to meaning 'occupation' in English, though it is not without snobbish overtones: the *Confédération francaise des profes-*

sions in the 1930s was an association of medium and small business-men. Doctors, lawyers, artists – those of high formal education and usually charging a fee for their services – formed the '*liberal* profes-sions'.

For all that, the sense of class in the France of the 1930s was certainly a great deal stronger than that in the United States, even if it did not come through in the neat 'working-class', 'middle-class' labels of British usage. In his autobiography, published in 1930, the wealthy dress designer Paul Poiret established the milieu in which he, the son of a Paris draper, was born and brought up. The only precise phrase he uses in reference to his relatives is *petits bourgeois*, but in introducing a long story about a family funeral he remarks that 'a simple story will tell more than a long preamble about the social class to which I belong'.[2] When public opinion polls began in France at the end of the decade they presented their results by grouped occupational categories which clearly implied a sort of class hier-archy. At the top were the 'liberal professions' – sometimes desig-nated the 'intellectuals' – and the functionaries, then came the *commerçants* and *industriels*, then the peasants, and finally the workers (*ouvriers*). The French Institute of Public Opinion boasted that its surveys would have to be more subtle and more scholarly than the facile demonstrations Americans were used to. An immedi-ate revelation of this subtlety and scholarship was that pipe-smoking in France was commonest among peasants and functionaries, that ready-made cigarettes were smoked most by *commerçants*, that the rolling of one's own cigarette was most usual among the peasants and the *ouvriers*, and that the highest proportion of non-smokers was to be found among the functionaries and members of the liberal professions.[3]

Not only did the rest of French society see the peasants as a class apart, but so did the peasants. This comes out strongly in an investi-gation carried out in December 1934 and January 1935 by the left-wing Vigilance Committee of Anti-Fascist Intellectuals, whose findings are all the more authentic in that they run directly counter to the political views and interests of those conducting the survey. On the question of the peasants sharing common interests with the workers, it was discovered that such a feeling of solidarity existed practically nowhere: at best it assumed inchoate forms in the Haute-

Garonne, or existed in the most limited way in certain regions o
Creuse. There was mistrust of the workers (Nord), where there wa
not active hostility towards them (Calvados, Seine-et-Oise, le Cher)
The unemployed were thought simply to be lazy. There was jealous
of the workers' regular fixed wages and of the shortness of th
factory day compared with that worked in the fields. The one poin
on which the survey produced unequivocal unanimity was the tota
detestation in which civil servants were held by the peasants. Youn
bureaucrats, above all, were said to be unpunctual in their publi
service, and pedantic and contemptuous, as it was put in Seine
Inférieure, towards 'the people'. The assessment of the extent o
class-consciousness among the peasantry was a good deal less clear
cut. The correspondents were asked to give the percentage of class
conscious peasants in their department. The results ranged a
follows: one per cent in Calvados and Aisne, two per cent i
Charente-Inférieure and Nord, eight per cent in Alpes-Maritimes
ten per cent, 'with reservations', in le Gen and le Cher, ten per cent
apparently without reservations, in Saône-et-Loire, fifteen per cen
in Haute-Garonne, and the curious 'no reply' *and* twenty per cen
in Indre-et-Loire.[4]

Peasants might or might not be religious; without any doubt the
were opposed to any hint of collectivism or socialism; class war wa
something they simply didn't understand. Throughout France th
term 'peasant' covered a variety of occupations and many inter
mediate positions between the substantial landowner, the lease
holder and the property-less tenant. Yet there was a conscious self
image. Camille Peters, pioneer socialist propagandist among th
peasantry to whom he himself belonged, when addressing th
Socialist Party Congress at Bordeaux in 1930, could not resist pre
senting himself in the image of the stolid, shrewd, but unletterec
peasant. As the report makes clear, the audience, overwhelmingl
urban, savoured this image and found it good:

> Citizens, standing at this tribune, I have no need to tell you tha
> I am neither an intellectual nor an advocate. As we ourselves say
> nothing but my appearance shows you that I am a peasant. . .
> It will be significant . . . that on this platform the man we call th
> grandfather of Socialist doctrine as applied to peasant matters
> Compere-Morel, was followed by an authentic peasant, a vine
> grower who the day after tomorrow will take up his plough, hi
> *raclette*, and will go among his vines. Rest assured that it is muc
> less difficult to work his vineyards than to try to express befor
> you what he and his comrades are thinking (*loud applause*).

. . . I beg you to be indulgent towards me for certainly in my address there will be some mis-pronunciations; no doubt I do not handle the French language very well, but all the same in the course of several hundred public meetings which I have held among the peasants of my region they understood me and I believe that you also will be indulgent and that you will understand me (*very good! applause*).

The peasant, Peters continued, is a republican and a democrat: 'he knows, not that he would have studied much, but he knows all the same, what the French Revolution meant; he knows that the French Revolution has already given him a certain freedom, the enjoyment of his own property, illusory perhaps, but property which all the same gives him some reason for living and for working.'[5]

Camille Peters wanted to believe that, despite this, the peasants had an instinctive sympathy for socialism and for the working class. But Frenchmen of all political persuasions and of none were remarkably aware of the special distinctiveness within French society of middle-class groupings. 'In our country of small peasants and artisans,' said the left-wing socialist, Jean Zyromski, 'these intermediate categories' – the 'middle classes', as he called them in his next sentence – 'continue to play an important social role.' Another speaker at the same socialist congress spoke of 'the middle class' in the singular, and singled out 'the small artisan' and 'the small *commerçant*'.[6] These two speakers were concerned with the manner in which the interests of these middle classes diverged from those of the workers (while believing that they also diverged from those of the big industrialists[7]); yet the leaders of the CGT, conscious no doubt of the potential isolation of the small French working class, were keen to stress the value of cooperation with the middle classes. In its Reform Programme, put forward at the time of the Popular Front, the CGT addressed itself to the interests of 'the great mass of the nation', and sought a rallying of 'popular forces'. The concentration of industry and banking, the argument went, had brought a weakening in the position of the middle classes and a strengthening in the numbers of the industrial proletariat; but very far from disappearing, as socialist theory had previously argued, the middle classes remained numerically strong and politically active. In a country like France, the peasantry occupied a special position; there should be no divide between them and the urban proletariat. The Trade Union Movement could not conceive of a situation in which there would be a prosperous working class and an impoverished peasant class. In the towns there should be solidarity between the proletariat and the urban middle classes. Thousands of small bourgeois are becoming, not proletarianized, but impoverished. The peasant proprietor is often simply a labourer; the independence of the small merchant is becoming increasingly illusory; and among 'the new middle class', the technicians, the white collar workers, the liberal professions are also seriously affected.[8] This policy of unity with all the middle classes against the big industrialists and financiers was a product of a particular political situation in France, and above all of the threat of fascism; it was the opposite of the policy advocated by left-wingers like Jean Zyromski. But we are not here concerned with political programmes. The point is that, whatever the policies advocated, there is clear recognition of the existence of an independent middle class.

Middle-class self-awareness was also very strong, and not on the whole consonant with ideas of unity with the working class. The sharp divisions, right down at the bottom end of the middle class, between those who owned their own vehicles, and those who merely worked for some large firm, come out very strongly in the documents relating to various taxi-drivers' organizations preserved in the Trade Union History Centre of the Sorbonne.[9] On 23 January 1936, the Secretary General of the Union of Artisan Taxi-Drivers addressed a letter to his 'dear comrade', the Secretary General of the National Transport Federation, explaining why amalgamation of the small owners with the wage-earning drivers in one union would only cause friction. If the wage-earners gained a majority on the committee, which was almost certain, they would tend to neglect the special claims of the owners which they simply would not understand. The wage-earners at least had concrete, personified adversaries in their bosses; the small owners had to fight against the State, the city of Paris, the car dealers, the insurance companies, and many other amorphous entities.[10] The point was rather more acidulously expressed in a leading article on the front page of the issue of *L'Echo des Chauffeurs* for October and November 1937, in which the CGT was accused of seeking the 'extermination' of the artisan taxi-drivers through its campaign for limitations on hours worked. The article was entitled 'The artisan taxi-drivers must resist':

> ... without any valid reason, without any justification whatsoever, the C.G.T. has decided to exterminate the artisanry in all its forms.
> Of course, such a vicious doctrine is not officially published. No one says in statements and discussions that the artisanry must

disappear, but everything is done to bring about its disappearance. . . .

For the taxi-drivers who are the owners of their own vehicle,
the means found to make their living precarious and to set them
on the road to ruin, is very simple. . . .

We have said it often enough: to try to regulate the hours of
work of the artisans is to lead them to ruin, for it is thanks to their
independence and their freedom in hours of work that they are
able to stay in competition.

Our duty is to give whole-hearted support to these victims of
trade union tyranny, to encourage and assist them in their resistance to veritable laws of spoliation.

Evidently we are here confronted with a very lowly and insecure
fraction of the middle class, faced, as the article puts it, with the
hostile forces 'of the bosses and the trade unionists' (*du Patronat et
des Cégétistes*).[11]

There was a much more comfortable image to be found further
up the social scale. There is a wealth of printed material on those who
were usually happy to call themselves, and be called, 'bourgeois',
without further phrase or qualification. In the mid-1930s the conservative newspaper *Le Temps* ran a light-hearted column, 'In the
Margin', which frequently spoke of the 'bourgeois of Paris': what
he was reading in the newspapers, how he was reacting to current
events, and so on. On one occasion it was replaced by a chatty little
piece by a female columnist on the drought of August 1934, entitled
'Discourse of a *petite bourgeoise*'. The 'bourgeois' saw society in a
number of different ways. Some, as 'men of no distinction', recognized the existence of a ruling class above them; some saw themselves as forming the upper part of a two-class society; some sought
refuge in the verbal thickets of occupational, or professional, ticket-
ing which gave the impression of a common, classless, citizenship.
The *Confédération française des professions* frequently expressed its
fear of, and hostility to, the attempts it detected among trade
unionists and left-wing politicians, to replace 'a nation of professions', by 'a nation of classes'.[12] Edmond Goblot, a provincial
philosophy professor presented (in a famous book which is a personal testimony rather than a serious academic study[13]) the two-
class image: the bourgeoisie (in which he included himself) on the
one side and 'the people' or 'the popular class' (in which he included
the artisans) on the other. One recognizes 'a "bourgeois" from a
"man of the people" simply by seeing them pass in the street. One

never confuses a "monsieur" with a "man", still less a "lady" with a "woman".' 'What am I, who wrote these lines?' he asked:

> Owner? Capitalist? Certainly not! Rentier? Oh! on such a small scale! Profiteer? Not that I know of. I am surely a paid employee, because I live from my work. The university appears to me like a vast state industry which works in human material; I am not an owner, but a worker in that factory. Students are my primary material, graduates and postgraduates in philosophy. However I do not belong to the category of workers ('*travailleurs*') for I do not have eight hours of sleep and eight hours of leisure guaranteed by the Treaty of Versailles . . . in French society, whether I like it or not, I am a bourgeois, and I have no cause to take pride in that.[14]

Perhaps in the ejaculations 'Owner?', 'Capitalist?' there was a shadowy recognition in Goblot's mind of some powerful group elsewhere in society. In the newspaper articles of Emile Charpentier, the schoolmaster who, under the *nom-de-plume* of Alain, was the most widely read and respected of bourgeois writers on social and political topics, this recognition was rather more substantial and one derives a clear impression of the middleness of Charpentier and his reader, between unionized workers and powerful industrialists and financiers.[15] It was another schoolmaster, turned leader of the Radical Party, Edouard Daladier, who, in a speech of October 1934, publicized a famous phrase: 'Two hundred families are mistresses of the French economy and, in fact, of French politics.'[16] *Crapouillot*, which, with its urbane form of populist investigative journalism and plentiful illustrations, might well be termed the quintessential bourgeois magazine, devoted a special issue in March 1936 to 'the two hundred families', complete with a pull-out chart, placing the Bank of France in the centre and illustrating the radiation of power outwards through the great employers' and financial institutions and the major private and nationalized industries, naming such names as de Neuflizé, Tinardon, Duchemin, de Vogue, Mirabaud, Vernes, Holtingues and Rothschild, through the 'zone of the auxiliaries' (the universities, the press, the police, the churches etc.) till eventually, right on the fringes of the page, one comes to the poor, controlled and manipulated 'French people'. The tone of the second essay, 'Two Hundred and Something Families', is delicious:

Impeccable automobiles flash each day through the streets of Paris carrying groups of sedate gentlemen. They do not attract your profane attention, save by the very dignity of their occupants. Your curiosity had been all the more struck by the efflorence of their buttonholes. The faces are serious, lacking in any special peculiarities, yet identified by a certain common characteristic: viewed from a certain angle, they symbolise power (*rudesse*). That's all.

You have just been looking in on the members of the Holy Alliance, the unknown masters. They are called Dupont-Durand, or baron Durand, the name does not evoke in you anything completely precise. All the same, if an unknown prompt whispered to you: the big one with the bowler hat and the tooth-brush moustache is the president of your Electricity Company, his companion controls the banks X and Y, the one who is squeezed up on the flap seat represents the Z insurance group, certain precise images would then jump into your mind, good God, Yes! – the payment of your gas bill, the collection of your theft insurance. And your whisperer would have been able to complete your education by pointing out that the electricity gentleman is also the chemicals and oils gentleman, that he of the life insurances also holds railways, armaments and dress design, an astonishing and contradictory mixture.

These people have just come out of one of these Meetings in the course of which, without your knowing it, they have gauged your resources, decided what tribute you ought to disburse into their anonymous company [*anonyme*] in buying their light, their heat, their bread, their bleaching liquid, their wool, and in living out your destiny as a man. They have even discussed your lungs, poor dried up organs of the citizen that you are. . . .

These gentlemen are not wicked: they have insured their companies against every public calamity . . . they even dip into their own pocket if necessary.

They are intelligent, no doubt about that. Their youth was studious, they passed out from the great graduate schools. Some are your elected representatives, but yes, others come from ambassadorships, the army, the ministries: admire their ribbons of honour [*rosettes à socles*].

Much of the article was taken up with detailed individual biographies demonstrating, to the writer's satisfaction, that the three hundred or so names which cropped up again and again in the business annuals operated, not in an arena of free competition, but in private cartels, national or international, or in public utilities where the weaknesses of the state had left the monopoly of power in private hands. The writer was contemptuous of those (i.e. from the left and trade unionists) who spoke in facile fashion of 'the wall of money' or 'factory barons'. Nowhere in this special issue of *Crapouillot* is there any mention of the relationship of this oligarchy, this 'zone of the 200 families' (now revealed to be nearer to three hundred families), to the industrial workers; no suggestion is made that there is any exploitation of the working class, or that the cartels may have contributed to the creation of unemployment. It is to a middle-class readership that the discussion is being addressed: the menace offered by the two hundred and something families is to economic liberalism and to medium-sized and family businesses.[17] This is a middle-class image of the upper class.

BOURGEOISIE AND NOBILITY

In Britain the institutions of the upper class had evolved in a society in which there had always been an upper class; in America upper-class institutions had been deliberately created by private initiative; in France the evolutionary process had been much more deliberately associated with the might of the state than was the case in Britain. The prestigious lycées – particularly some of those in Paris – the *grands écoles*, certain sections of the higher civil service: these, along with the rituals of high society, the defined sequence of coming-out balls, the correct Paris address, together with the substantial country residence, inscription in the French equivalent of the *Social Register*, the *Bottin Mondaine*; these all contributed to the shaping of a special upper-class self-image. France had its own 'children of the sun' in the 1930s, not necessarily part of *Crapouillot*'s two-hundred-and-something families, but certainly sure that society would offer them a comfortable and prestigious living.[18] The special sense of destiny and dignity of French higher civil servants, way beyond anything to be found even in Britain, was much remarked upon.[19] The sense of class solidarity and the sense of a collective destiny comes through very clearly in the reactions of business leaders during and after the Popular Front government. In June 1936 the deputy Valette-Vialard declared openly that he was defending the owners' point of view: 'that is very natural, since I am an owner'. An employers' organization insisted in 1938 that 'the recovery of France will not be accomplished without vigorous action by the élites in favour of a nation internally more strong, that is to say economically more disciplined and socially more balanced'.[20]

Mondaine – belonging to the world of high society – is a key word. In Britain the aristocracy evinced security and confidence at the apex of a larger upper class, and set the style and tone for that class. In France the nobility, as nobility, was, in comparison, insecure and on the defensive, subject to much discussion and investigation, and was merely a part of the world of high society, absorbing rather than dominating the *mores* of that world. Its spokesman sought indeed to establish the concept of nobility as simply the ratification of success in business and government: 'the nobility', said M. le duc de Lévis Mirepoix, president of *l'Association d'Entraide de la Noblesse Française* (founded in 1932), 'was never a closed caste: it was a continuous creation'. In every civilized country, as M. le duc saw it, 'individuals sought to give their scattered achievements a permanent form,' and that was how the aristocracy came into being. The three aristocratic principles singled out by the Duke of Lévis Mirepoix would certainly have secured the lip-service too of almost all of the grand bourgeoisie: strong sense of independence, spirit of service, and deep feeling for the family and respect for and pride in the family name.[21] In introducing his study of *The Nobility 1938*, Jougla de Morenas declared that his aim had been to single out the 'excellent bourgeoisie', now barred by Republican principles from the legitimate pursuit of ennoblement, and the 'true nobility' which, however, sometimes pretended to titles beyond those to which it had any real claim, from 'unscrupulous adventurers, useless fops and the presumptuous newly enriched'.[22]

Some of those seized of a title, or of the noble particule 'de', did of course express contempt for the 'bourgeois'. Denis de Rougement in his *Journal of an Unemployed Intellectual* scoffed at the bourgeois who associated the idea of property with that of inheritance. Our unemployed intellectual was trying, not very convincingly, to demonstrate that just because he had inherited an island, a house and a few similar items, it did not follow that he actually owned anything;[23] an argument that does indeed take us well within the world of the intellectual. French 'intellectuals', I have already suggested, saw themselves as forming a separate 'fraction' within a class, if not an entire class, in part no doubt because this provided a good front for continuing to enjoy upper-bourgeois lifestyles while denying any association with the bourgeoisie. The perfect give-away is the tract *Manuels et intellectuels* by Gérard de Lacaze-Duthiers, in which he nobly attempted to bridge the gulf between the 'manual proletariat' and the 'intellectual proletariat'. All 'intelligent and sincere' workers must unite against the common enemy – 'capitalism'; at bottom, manual and intellectual workers 'not domesticated by the bourgeois class' had never ceased to fraternize. Their common fraternity, as explained by Gérard, might not, had they ever encountered it, have carried conviction with the 'manual proletariat' (certainly the copy in the *Bibliotèque Nationale* is punctuated with loud exclamation marks in the margin – though these are doubtless the work of an intellectual, rather than a manual, proletarian). After working on his books, says Gérard, the intellectual likes to perform some manual work, whereas, after a day's work, the manual worker likes to read. And anyway, writing is hard manual labour. 'False' manual workers flatter their bosses and want to be bosses themselves, but then there are 'false' intellectuals who consider themselves 'superior' (this is quite rich). Manuals provide intellectuals with their corporal needs, while intellectuals provide manuals with their spiritual needs. Intellectuals breathe the same air as manuals (what, one wonders, does the bourgeois breathe?). Nothing is vouchsafed about what the two sorts of worker eat or how they live, but two short passages clearly establish that the true ambience of Gérard de Lacaze-Duthiers is that of the upper class. Intellectuals who refuse to serve the bourgeoisie, he says, 'remain as poor as Job, till the day they commit suicide or starve to death in a slum. These intellectuals are as miserable as the most underprivileged proletarians. They go "to the office", instead of going "to the factory", and, just like a common manual worker, they take the metro.' That terrible indignity apart, it must be recognized that there are 'manuals and manuals' just as there are 'intellectuals and intellectuals'.

> Obviously, one could reproach certain representatives of these two categories of workers with more than one fault: the manual will be jealous of the gentleman (*le monsieur*) in a false collar who, for his part, believes himself the issue of the thighs of Jupiter. The worker (*ouvrier*) will reveal himself, in certain circumstances, to be gross and vulgar, will pretend to jostle or soil the clothes of the white-collar worker whom he regards as a bourgeois because he dresses differently, or because he unloads on him some hurtful or tasteless epithet. The intellectual will make a show of elegant manners, or what he assumes to be such, and display his ill directed knowledge to put down the poor buggers who can neither read nor write.[24]

I have spent so much space on Gérard de Lacaze-Duthiers because he was not only a distinguished figure in the French cultural scene of the 1930s but, more than that, his private papers do give a very good impression of the enclosed world, undoubtedly of high social status, inhabited by the intellectuals.[25]

MANUAL WORKERS

The *ouvriers* I have left to the last because that, it seems to me, is where French society in the 1930s left them. Much of the evidence (such as it is) for the working-class image of itself, and of society as a whole, derives from the *bouleversements* of the period of the Popular Front, particularly the great strikes of the summer of 1936 in which the strikers occupied their factories and workshops. At points of crisis, and at other times too, French labour leaders bandied around phrases like 'proletariat' and 'capitalist class' in a manner scarcely to be found in Britain, but at the same time the sense of confidence in the solidarity of the working class was considerably less – as seen, for example, in the CGT Reform Programme and its emphasis on the need for collaboration with the middle classes. For the views of ordinary workers, we have the actions and statements of those who participated in the mass strikes of June 1936. What is at once very clear is the lack of political or ideological motivation and direction in these strikes – strike activity was greatest where union organization and communist or socialist party influence was least.[26] About two million workers took part in the strikes which, in rather spectacular fashion, included one occupational group which in the British context would not automatically be included in the working class – though in the American it would definitely be included with 'labor' or 'the employees' – those employed in the big department stores. To call the strikes 'spontaneous' is to use a hackneyed and inexact adjective; yet it is the one that best meets the case. As the strikers themselves explained, they went on strike because 'everywhere people are going on strike'.[27] Far from there being a plan to overthrow the state, or to take over the factories, or even to make precise demands in regard to wages and conditions, most strikers had few ideas as to what exactly they were striking for. Employers were ignored, rather than in any way ill treated: 'That person we just passed was one of the directors. Everybody salutes him but without feeling, simply as a matter of routine.`...'[28] As observers noted, the strikes had the atmosphere of a fete, of a holiday. Strikers confided that shortly they expected to go back to much the same sort of life as before.[29]

What we have, then, is definite working-class *awareness*, but little working-class *consciousness*. The strikes were a gesture of working-class solidarity, a gesture of defiant, if rather baffled, pride, a gesture of recognition of the distinctiveness of *their* place of work, whose occupation they took over. Many strikers showed great ignorance of larger issues – 'they find it natural, alas, to know nothing,' commented Simone Weil.[30] There is less self-confidence than was to be found among British workers. There was, apart from the militant leaders (and the militant leaders were largely ignored in these strikes), no very clear impression of where the class enemy lay, or indeed of whether there was one, and certainly no image of the overall class structure of French society. The conclusion of Jean Lhomme (the academic we met in an earlier chapter) that the sit-in strikes of 1936 marked more a crisis *in* French society than a crisis *of* French society[31] may be borne in mind as one moves quickly to the abortive general strike of 1938. The contemporary imagery and language surrounding this event are very much those of the sharp polarization of classes. Certainly one can see a repressive right-of-centre government, strongly supported by members of the grand bourgeoisie, in confrontation with the militant leaders of the trade unions:[32] but that the social *awareness* of 1936, in the main body of the French workers, had become political *consciousness* by 1938 is doubtful.

Unofficial and private images in France, then, are a good deal less sharply focused than academic ones. There is fuzziness at the top: is there a line between nobility and grand bourgeoisie; where is the line between the grand bourgeoisie and the middle class; how do the 'intellectuals' fit in? There is fuzziness in the middle: are the peasants part of the middle classes, or a separate class? The working class does appear in quite sharp focus, though its view of the rest of society does not. Yet because individuals perceive only parts of classes or only one class, that does not mean that other classes do not exist; because the spectator at the back of the gods cannot see the chorus girl's cleavage, that does not mean that it does not exist.

If now we integrate all of the images collected so far with the historical context, we have a France which, partly because of the accelerated industrialization accompanying the First World War, has a class structure more clearly defined than in the late nineteenth century, yet a class structure still overlaid by the influence of political and religious traditions. The main components of that structure are: the grand bourgeoisie (including the nobility); a 'sub-class' of intellectuals somewhere on the fringes of the grand bourgeoisie (class, above all in its most subjective aspect, always being a matter of birth, background and who you associate with, as well as of 'occupation'); a sprawling middle class running from those in the liberal professions who did not get into the grand bourgeoisie (note the previous parenthesis) to the littlest artisans; a peasant class; and a working class.

Notes

1. René Garmy, *Pourquoi j'ai été exclu du Parti Communiste*, n.d., p. 3.
2. Paul Poiret, *En habillant l'époque* (1930), p. 19.
3. *Sondages*, August 1938, April 1939, June 1939.
4. Archives Nationales, Institut Francais d'Histoire Sociale [IFHS], 14 AS 261: Comité de Vigilance des Intellectuels Antifascistes, *Le Fascisme et les paysans* (1935), pp. 55 ff.
5. Camille Peters, *L'Action socialiste chez les ruraux: discours prononcé au congrès National du Parti Socialiste S.F.I.O.*, *Bordeaux 1930* (1931).
6. Parti socialiste, *XXXIVe Congrès National tenu a Marseilles, les 10, 11, 12 et 13 Juillet 1937* (1938), pp. 338, 372.
7. *Ibid*, p. 372.
8. *Le Plan de la CGT* (1936), pp. 174–6.
9. Centre d'Histoire du Syndicalism, Paris, Archives Syndicat FO des Taxis.
10. *Ibid*, file 36[1].
11. *Ibid*, file 37[2].
12. *La Confédération française des professions* (1936).
13. Edmond Goblot, *La Barrière et le niveau: étude sociologique sur la bourgeoisie française moderne* (1925).
14. *Ibid*, pp. 8–9, 12.
15. These writings can be studied in Alain, *Les Éléments d'une doctrine radicale* (1926).
16. Quoted by Jean Baumier, *Les grandes Affaires français: des 200 familles aux 200 managers* (1967), p. 25.
17. *Crapouillot*, March 1936, pp. 16–33.
18. See, e.g., Robert Brasillach, *Notre Avant Guerre* (1941).
19. These, and other examples, drawn from a range of private business archives, have been set in context by Patrick Fridenson in 'Le Patronat Français' in R. Rémond and J. Bourdin, eds., *La France et les Français en 1938–1939* (1978), pp. 139–58.
20. Halbwachs, *Les Classes sociales* pp. 38–9.
21. Association d'Entraide de la Noblesse Francaise, *Recueil des Personnes*

ayant fait leur preuves devant les Assemblées Générales, 1932–1949 (1950), preface by M. le duc de Lévis Mirepoix.

22. Jougla de Morenas, *Noblesse 38* (1938), p. 8.

23. Denis de Rougemont, *Journal d'un intellectuel en chômage* (1937), p. 13.

24. Gérard de Lacaze-Duthiers, *Manuels et intellectuels* (1932), pp. 9–10, 15–16, 20.

25. IFHS, 14 AS 212[2].

26. Antoine Prost, 'Les Grèves de juin 1936', in Cahiers de la Fondation Nationale des Sciences Politiques, *Léon Blum: chef de gouvernment* (1967), pp. 73–4. I have leaned heavily on this excellent article.

27. Georges Lefranc, *Histoire du front populaire* (1965), p. 148, n. 1.

28. Henri Prouteau, *Les Occupations d'usine en Italie et en France* (1938), p. 145.

29. The evidence on these two points is admirably summarized by Prost, *op. cit.*, pp. 81–2.

30. Quoted by Prost, *op. cit.*, p. 80, n. 34.

31. Jean Lhomme, 'Juin 1936', in André Siegfried, ed., *Aspects de la societé française* (1954), p. 92.

32. Jean Bruhat, 'La CGT', in Rémond and Bourdin, *op. cit.*, pp. 159–88.

8

Hollywood Images of Class

Finally, in studying images of class as they were in the 1930s, I turn to media images, or rather to a selection of some of the more significant media images. In this chapter I concentrate on Hollywood; in the next, I deal mainly with the British Broadcasting Corporation, appending briefer studies of British and French films. Media images, when examined across different societies, do bring out the differences in basic assumptions about such topics as class rooted in the different cultures. Film and radio offer us a fourth set of images to fit together with the other three images, and with the historical context, before we turn to the realities of inequality in power, authority, wealth, income, prestige, working conditions, lifestyles and culture.

If French and British films of the 1930s form little more than footnotes to the study of perceptions of class, Hollywood films, as in almost all other aspects of American imagery, have a central importance. Very many of the dramas and the comedies strongly reinforce the image of an East Coast upper class set firmly apart from the middle class below, though at the same time the central vision in almost all American films is, once confrontation had been faced and the conflicts resolved, of a harmonious, integrated social structure. The eponymous blonde of Frank Capra's *Platinum Blonde* (1931), Ann Schuyler, belongs to this upper class (impossible it may be noted, to imagine a play or film about an English lady being given such a title, or to imagine a member of the English upper class being played by such an actress as Jean Harlow, who is, however, magnificent in this part). A crack journalist, played by Robert Williams, is sent to investigate a salacious story linking the Schuyler family with a chorus girl. Setting out confidently, the journalist who has the pleasantly common name of Stuart Smith, declares that he knows these 'bluenoses'. His first encounters are with the Schuyler lawyer, who demonstrates his status by speaking with an anglified accent, and the Schuyler butler who, a most important point, demonstrates the status of the Schuyler family by being a genuine Englishman. (Much has been written on the role of blacks in American films; the overburdened book trade might still well support a study of the role of Englishmen in American films.)

The lawyer intimidates Smith by reminding him that he is a stock-holder in the newspaper, and that further he knows Smith's managing editor: 'Yale '21, I believe,' he says, carefully striking the bell of upper-class status. But Ann, the platinum blonde, decides that she wants to marry Smith. In an interesting twist on the Pygmalion theme – though it should be noted that Smith is not really very far down the social scale, being a successful and prosperous journalist – she decides also to turn him into a real upper-class gentleman. Is there any finishing school she could send him to, she muses? Yes, Sing-Sing, replies the lawyer. Smith expresses his own status by relating that he is white, male, over twenty-one, has never been in gaol, prefers Scotch to Bourbon, earns seventy-five dollars a week and has eight hundred and sixty-seven dollars in the bank. 'Schuyler Girl Elopes with Reporter,' say the headlines; a 'society gal', someone calls her; and someone else remarks that it is news 'when Ann Schuyler gets her nails manicured'; but it is Smith's Yale '21 editor who summarizes the class relationship: 'Ann Schuyler's in the blue book, you're not even in the phone book.'

Democratically, Smith wants to set up married life in his own small apartment, but the platinum blonde gently but firmly indicates that a whole wing of the family mansion is at their disposal. In keeping with the Hays code of morals, and as a part of the standard conjuring trick operated by Frank Capra and other directors in his genre, the marriage has actually taken place but is unconsummated. Smith wakes up, alone, in a posh bed, waited upon by a valet, again with an English accent. The valet gives him a pair of garters, another symbol of upper-class status. Smith says to him, 'you'd make a good wife'.

Smith's former colleague and close companion whom he somewhat charmlessly refers to as Gallagher (played by Loretta Young) turns up at the Schuylers' as a society columnist. 'We don't consider Gallagher a girl,' Smith explains to his wife. But when another former colleague arrives requesting Smith to write a piece under the by-line of 'Ann Schuyler's husband', Smith, in the inevitable reaction socks him on the jaw. 'Well bowled, sir, very neat,' comments the English butler. This piece of violence hits the headlines: 'Cinderella man grows hair on chest' (Cinderella man was to be a phrase used over and over again by Capra).

Smith and the butler get on well together, and the butler respectfully tells him that he is really quite out of place in this environment: 'You are an eagle in a cage,' he says. Meantime, Smith is also supposed to be writing a play, and it becomes very clear that most of it is in fact being written by Gallagher, though she appears happy to let him believe that all the ideas are really his. Smith finally realises his mistake in trying to cross the boundaries of class, while the platinum blonde decides that it would after all be better to be married to her upper-class lawyer. When the lawyer raises the matter of a divorce with Smith, he responds that he'll 'give her a divorce for her wedding present'. He then, naturally, socks the lawyer on the jaw, and the lawyer, as the effete hanger-on of the aristocracy, takes it without retaliation. Now sticking sensibly within his own social class Smith marries the faithful Gallagher.

The Smith-Gallagher combination of two journalists, very far from the breadline, but intimidated by an aristocratic Philadelphia family, appears again in George Cukor's *Philadelphia Story* (1940), based on the play by Philip Barrie. The aristocratic Philadelphia lady, played by Katherine Hepburn, has been divorced from another aristocrat, Cary Grant, and it is into this that James Stewart, as a journalist, blunders. When James Stewart remarks that the library contains a book written by him, Katherine Hepburn remarks that her grandfather had built the library. When he tells her that his father had taught English History at South Bend, Indiana, she comments that this sounds like a dance. Katherine Hepburn is now engaged to a former coalminer turned businessman – an admirable character and the epitome of the American success story, you might think, save that in the film he is portrayed as a narrow-minded bounder. 'You've got all the arrogance of your class,' he bursts out at one point against Cary Grant. Much of the plot centres on the night out which Katherine Hepburn and James Stewart have together. But, in the end, when the lower-class suitor is brushed aside, his place is taken, not by James Stewart, but, in a perfect re-matching of class backgrounds, by Cary Grant. James Stewart sticks strictly within his class and marries *his* faithful colleague and companion.

In *Holiday* (1938), a product of the same director, writer, and leading actors (though this time without James Stewart), Katherine Hepburn is the slightly rebellious Linda Seaton, the Seatons being described as one of America's top sixty families. Cary Grant, however, is the son of a grocer from Baltimore, who has worked his way through Harvard, and who has also worked in a laundry, a steel mill and on a garbage truck. His closest friends are an old couple; the husband is not exactly a horny-handed son of toil, but remarks that 'teaching at university doesn't pay me very much'. John Case (Cary Grant) has become engaged to Linda's sister Julia. On his first visit to the family home, he, of course, comes to the service entrance and is suitably overawed by the display of upper-class splendour. The repressive nature of upper-class society is expressed in the fact that Linda's brother has not been able to follow his chosen career as a musician (his concerto, when we hear it, is actually, but I suppose predictably, the most awful Hollywood kitsch). Julia's father questions Case about Baltimore's top families. Case in fact wins Seaton's admiration by making a lot of money in a clever business deal, but then rather loses it by refusing the proffered job in the Seaton family bank, declaring, in a rigorous rejection of the American work ethic, that he wants to drop everything and go on a journey of self-discovery – the 'holiday' of the title. The professor and his wife are planning to go to Europe so that the professor can do some research (not too many British university teachers were in a position to do this in the 1930s); Case wants to go, too, and is trying to persuade Julia to come with him.

There is a large and very formal party at the Seaton household. The professor and his wife arrive looking very shabby, and signify their lowly status by taking off both goloshes and shoes. The genetic origins of the rebelliousness of Linda and her brother are revealed when the latter remarks that 'Mother tried to be a Seaton and gave up and died.' Anxious now to bring Case into the family, the father suggests a honeymoon in London, together with a job in a British bank or a French firm, followed in due course by a house full of servants on 64th Street. Case refuses to be 'loaded down with possessions', says farewell to Julia, and joins the professor and his wife on the boat to Europe, where in turn he is joined by Linda. Love seems this time to have crossed class barriers; but Cary Grant has not joined the upper class, it is the rebellious Katherine Hepburn who has come down the social scale to join him.

In Preston Sturgess's film of 1941, *The Lady Eve*, Henry Fonda plays Charlie, the heir to the Pike's Ale fortune. An ocean liner stops specially to pick him up on his return from a snake-hunting expedition up the Amazon. On the liner he encounters a father-and-daughter team of card sharpers and confidence tricksters, the daughter being played by Barbara Stanwyck. Father and daughter set out to ensnare Henry Fonda but she in fact falls in love with him. He meantime has made the important status point that the family business is making ale, not beer – ale being the name that Americans give to imported British beer. A marriage is planned, but then ruined when Henry Fonda is shown a photograph of Barbara Stanwyck proving her to be a well known confidence trickster. 'Rotten likeness, isn't it?' is her deathless comment when faced with the photograph.

Later, long after the couple have parted, it is decided that yet another confidence trickster, passing himself off as the British aristocrat Sir Alfred McGlennan-Keith, will take Barbara Stanwyck on a visit to the Pikes, as his niece the Lady Eve. Mr Pike proves to be the epitome of the nouveau riche, fat, boisterous and vulgar, and one who, in an enduring piece of Hollywood symbolism, always tucks his napkin into his shirt collar when eating. Mrs Pike, however, really does come from an old-established aristocratic family, and, of course, they keep an English butler. Barbara Stanwyck does her upper-class English accent brilliantly, having great fun over the pronunciation of Connecticut, and only being let down when the script has her say 'apt to' in the American sense of 'likely to'. Without recognizing her, Henry Fonda falls in love with her all over again: when brought roses from him, she remarks offhandedly, 'Oh, the brewer's son.' They do get married, but she keeps the marriage from being consummated by embarking on an endless tale about all her former lovers. Still in his pyjamas he leaps out of the train, falling, naturally, into a heap of muck.

She refuses to accept money for a divorce; he refuses to meet her. Instead, he goes off on another expedition. They all meet again on the same ocean liner. She goes through the old routine. He recognizes her in her original character, but not as the Lady Eve, and embraces her. 'I'm married,' he says. 'So am I darling,' says she. In a rather complicated way, the class boundaries have indeed been broken; but the manners and style of the exclusive upper class, with their leanings towards British aristocratic pretensions, have been very carefully (not to say hilariously) delineated.

These perceptions and symbols echo through numerous films of the time. In Harry Beaumont's MGM film of 1932, *Faithless*, starring Tallula Bankhead, we see Bankhead first as a spoiled rich girl, whose holdings evaporate in the Great Crash; she is forced eventually to live with a wealthy nouveau riche who declares, 'if it wasn't for this Depression, I wouldn't have a chance with a swell like you.' In Capra's *You Can't Take It With You* (1938) the upper-class banking family identify the threat from the beautiful girl who is 'probably from some dull middle-class family'. By contrast, Capra's *Broadway Bill* (1934) is relatively lightweight as social comment. This story about a racehorse, with its stock, grinning, conniving, humoresque of a black stable boy, begins in Higginsville where the bank and all the main industries are controlled by J. L. Higgins, who has been steadily taking over the properties, such as the Acme Lunch Company, of the 'little people'. Dan Brookes is the son-in-law (played by Warner Baxter) who refuses to conform to the Higgins's tribal loyalties. He leaves his wife Margaret to race Broadway Bill and is given support by the rebel Higgins daughter, Alice (Myrna Loy). The shock of the dramatic victory and immediate death of Broadway Billy effect the necessary conversions all round. J. L. Higgins hands back the various properties to the little men who built them up. Having divorced Margaret, Dan marries Alice. J. L. Higgins shows himself to be an all-round good guy after all. With its populist, harmonious, personalized view of society, this film is just too sentimental to be really fully in tune with the great American myths.

American Madness (1932) had, however, taken a little further Capra's genteel criticism of the powers of big finance. A small banker, who has spent twenty-five years building up his business, and who has followed a very liberal policy in granting loans to all of his customers, is being pressed to agree to a merger with a big Trust. Rumour creates a panic run on the bank which completely cleans it out, and he is about to capitulate to the Trust on any terms, when his chief teller drums up the support of all the 'little men' in the community by telling them that 'the big guys have got the screws on him'; the 'little men' come in steadily to re-deposit their money and thus restore confidence. Everything ends cheerfully. The main message, insofar as there is one, is one we encountered frequently in studying the American ideological context; the need for expansionism and the maintainance of purchasing power. With regard to class structure, there is, as in *Broadway Bill*, the concept of enterprising middle America, the 'little men' or 'little people', with sufficient accumulation at least to need a bank. Beyond that, the big bankers, with their butterfly collars and bow ties, are very carefully contrasted with the ordinary workers in the bank. There is a fine rhythmic scene of the bank routine with safes being opened and shut almost as if they are the massive machinery of a factory: this is very much in keeping with an image we have already encountered, bank clerks seen as representatives of ordinary working men.

A major stage in Capra's development of the political parable of American society came with *Mr Deeds Goes to Town* (1936). Longfellow Deeds (Gary Cooper) is the small-town outsider figure from Mandrake Falls who unexpectedly inherits twenty million dollars; but, in a class pattern shared by all the films discussed so far, one in which truly lower-class people simply do not appear, he is in fact the son of the local doctor and himself follows a sort of professional (the French notion of 'intellectual' takes on horrendous implications) occupation by writing rhymes to order. His populist spirit of fun and freedom is demonstrated by the fact that he plays the tuba in the local brass band. But when, as a rich man, associating now with upper-class city types, he becomes chairman of the opera (perfect symbol of upper-class culture), his reaction on finding that the company has never paid its way is that of authentic middle-American philistinism: 'We must be giving the wrong kind of show.' Brought into a confrontation with the East Coast literati in a posh restaurant, his punch line (literally, since he delivers it before he socks his tormentors) is 'I guess I found out all great people aren't big people.'

A Washington journalist, played by Jean Arthur, is assigned to his story: she prints the phrase (for all the world as if it had never been heard of before in a Capra film) 'Cinderella man' to describe him. But in a heavily nostalgic scene it turns out that Jean Arthur is also from a (Middle American) small town just like Mandrake Falls. Deeds decides to give his money away to bankrupt farmers and others who need it. His slick Washington associates try to bring a court case against him, arguing that he is fomenting social unrest and rocking the foundations of the government system. After a long scene, the judge delivers the view on Deeds that he is 'not only sane, but the sanest man that ever walked into this courtroom'.

More explicitly political ground was occupied by *Mr Smith Goes to Washington* (1939). Mr Smith (James Stewart) is the son of the editor and publisher of a local newspaper, the champion of popular causes, though, once again, by no means a member of the manual working class. A senator dies, and the governor nominates Smith to take his place, along with Senator Paine (Claude Raines), who had once been a close associate of Smith's father in fighting the good fight. Of course, Mr Smith meets a journalist girl Friday, played once more by Jean Arthur. Her social status is nicely defined: her father had been a doctor, but she had had to go to earn her own living from the age of sixteen. Smith had had ambitions to use his new position to build a boys' camp in his home State which would be for 'all creeds, kinds and conditions'. But this innocent ambition runs foul of plans to build a dam developed by the Governor and Senator Paine, who turn out to be in crooked alliance, and who had chosen Smith to be their dupe. At last realizing what is going on, he refuses to have anything to do with them, and is therefore framed. In the final long, and magnificent climax, Smith endeavours to defend himself in a colossal Senate filibuster. Right to the end he appears to have lost; but Senator Paine finally repents and reveals all.

Now Capra was hymning the basic soundness of American institutions. He had moved away from the perceptions of class which informed *Platinum Blonde* and *American Madness*. The centre of gravity was in small-town America: the contrast was between local 'little men' on the one hand, and local bosses and Washington operators on the other, rather than between a middle class and an aristocratic class. However, the continuity in the make-up of his popular, or middle, class of 'little people' is striking: journalists, professors, small town bankers, and doctors, especially those whose daughters have to go out and earn a living (as journalists, naturally).

One or two films of a rather different character emanated from the studios of Warner Brothers, partly, perhaps, because of the close personal association between Jack Warner and Franklin D. Roosevelt. *Heroes for Sale* (directed by William Wellman, 1933) is a strange and gloomy film, which just about indicates the distinction between an upper-class banking family, who live in Winston Manor and whose son 'started way high up', and the misjudged and ill-treated bank clerk who 'started pretty low'. The film ends with a faintly hopeful reference to Roosevelt's inaugural address.

But it was another Warner Brothers movie (directed by Michael Curtiz) which turned out to be the only Hollywood film of the 1930s to deal satisfactorily with a genuine industrial working-class environment; and what a marvellous film it is. Andrew Bergman, in his otherwise excellent study, falls into the common error among intellectuals of a Marxist persuasion when he criticizes *Black Fury* (1934) for failing to present the sort of class structure and class relationships which Bergman *believes* exist,[1] when in fact, the film is arguably quite true to the rather different class structure and different perceptions of class which actually existed in America at the time.

The film is set in a Polish mining community in Pennsylvania. Joe Radek (played by Paul Muni) has no ambition beyond acquiring enough money to marry his girlfriend Anna, and set up as a pig farmer. This lack of overt working-class consciousness upsets Bergman; but in the objective world of America in the 1930s it was this very type of ethnic atavism which blanketed out the development of political consciousness. The immigrant mining community is carefully delineated in all its smoky squalor. Everywhere, company policemen are silently in evidence; the miners are contemptuously referred to as 'hunkeys'. Radek speaks very poor English and one of his friends is unable to read; yet Radek is able to drive the car which he borrows in order to take Anna out. But to escape from the squalor of the mining community and the almost inevitable fate of becoming a worn-out miner's wife, Anna goes off to Pittsburg with a company policeman.

It is through getting totally drunk in the aftermath of this devastating personal blow that Radek allows himself to be turned into an inflammatory strike leader by a sinister figure who is in fact a member of a professional strike-breaking agency. Through the manipulation of Radek this agency creates the crisis they are looking for: led by Radek, and against the advice of their own union leaders, the miners tear up their existing contract. In the lockout which follows, the agency bring in their own blacklegs and police thugs. Through starvation the miners are forced back to work under conditions much worse than those of the previous contract. Radek, an outcast among his former friends, at last becomes aware of what he has done. He barricades himself into the pit, placing explosives at strategic places. He announces that unless the owners concede proper terms to the men he will blow up the pit and himself with it.

Here we have the authentic representation of the real power of labour. Radek, the skilled workman, knows the pit, knows the handling of explosives, and the company cop who comes down to get him is simply no match for him. 'Dirty, tricky, underhanded hunkey,' mutters the cop. Once again in a Warner Brothers film there is one of these explicit political references to the Roosevelt government which, if we recognize Hollywood magnates as part of upper-class America, boosts my point about the upper-class nature of that particular Democratic regime. The Labor Relations Act is invoked to denounce and destroy the mischievous strike-breaking agency and to settle the strike on Radek's terms. Anna has come back to him, and he is restored to his former friendships. 'Now you can raise kids and pigs,' he is told. 'You betcha,' he replies in the final line of the film.

In *Black Fury* is contained almost the entire universe of the contexts, realities and imagery associated with one aspect of class in the United States in the 1930s. There is the primitivism, the violence and brutality, and the belief that conflict can be resolved into an integrated opportunity society. There is also the sense of the growing power and consciousness of the working class (though it is not overtly a political consciousness, which is where Bergman is thrown off the scent). Finally there are the factors of ethnicity and aspiration after mobility which always meant that working-class boundaries in the United States were much less tightly drawn than in a homogeneous, less mobile society like Britain.

Black Legion (1937) was another Warner Brothers film with strong elements of social conscience. It opened with a beautifully realistic re-creation of an industrial factory. We see the factory workers eating out of their lunch boxes (just as in *Black Fury* the miners are shown eating their lunch down at the coal face). The foreman has been promoted, and it is expected that the vacancy will go to Frank (played by Humphrey Bogart), but instead the promotion goes to a dedicated immigrant worker, Joe Dombrowsky, who does calculations on his slide rule throughout the lunch break and who goes to night school. Frank takes this very badly, and a workmate asks him: 'How does it feel like being pushed around by a Honjak?' Frank joins a racist, Ku Klux Klan style organization, the Black Legion, which carries out the most vicious floggings, burnings and shootings, directed against the Irish as well as against Central European immigrants. In a rather crude piece of motivational analysis, which so often figures as the American mirror-image of the crudest kind of Marxism, it is revealed that the Black Legion is actually run by some sleek, well-spoken rich men who do not themselves have any interest in racism, but who are making a vast income out of membership subscriptions. But the film has moved firmly away from any interest in the industrial working class as such: its concern is with violent racism, and, less directly, with the manipulations of the sinister rich who, however, are almost certainly not intended to represent the rich as a whole. Frank and his fellow members of the Legion are finally brought to trial, where the judge makes a long and powerful speech on behalf of the basic human rights of all citizens of whatever ethnic background. There is no miraculous resolution, and all of the prisoners, including Frank, are given life sentences. This film, which certainly does not shirk the tragedy of Depression America, ends with a slow lingering shot of the deeply suffering face of Frank's wife.

So much, then, for the attention paid by Hollywood to the American working class. We progress rapidly to the world of the social outcast, to the 'under class' that I have already mentioned. A recurrent image is that of the convict in his distinctive striped clothing. The evocative title of a most moving film is *I am a Fugitive from a Chain Gang* (Warner Brothers 1932). The principal character, played once more by Paul Muni, comes out of the First World War determined to succeed as a skilled professional engineer instead of returning to the clerical job in a shoe factory which he had before the war. But he cannot find employment anywhere and eventually, reduced to near-starvation, he teams up with another down-and-out

to intimidate a stall holder into handing over two free hamburgers.
But then the other down-and-out pulls a gun and forces Muni to
join him in robbing the stall-holder of all his takings. Both men are
immediately seized by the police and a harsh judge sentences Muni
to a chain-gang. The horrible brutality of this aspect of American
life is very fully detailed. Helped first by a black convict, and later
by the fraternity of the down-and-outs, Muni makes his escape. He
starts in 1924 as a labourer working for four dollars a day. In 1925
he has become a foreman earning nine dollars a day. By 1927 he is
a surveyor earning twelve dollars a day, and he is studying civil
engineering. In 1929 he is an assistant superintendent earning fourteen dollars a day. As his great American success story continues,
he escapes from the sluttish woman who has tried to ensnare him,
becomes general field superintendent, and is entertained to dinner
by his boss in a very consciously set upper-class environment with
dinner suits and the other trappings of fine society. Here he meets
another girl who delivers herself of a line which in various versions
echoes through a number of American films of the thirties in unwitting tribute to the potency of racism in American society. There
are no 'musts' in her mind, she explains, because 'I'm free, white
and twenty-one'. The other woman betrays him. Yet he is safe as
long as he remains in Chicago, where his respectable friends stand
by him. Given a promise that his criminal record will be purged by
a sentence of a mere ninety days of imprisonment, he voluntarily
returns to the State where he had been a convict. But instead he is
thrown back into the chain-gang and kept there on an indefinite
sentence. Once again he contrives an escape but this time there is no
opportunity to build himself up from, as his brother had put it, 'less
than nothing' to being a prominent citizen. The film ends with a
desperate shot of him as a permanent fugitive.

The main character in John Ford's famous film of John Steinbeck's equally famous novel *The Grapes of Wrath*, played by Henry
Fonda, begins as a member of the under-class, newly released from
penitentiary. The social world in which this story of migrant workers
trekking out to the California fruit farms is set, is one of fragmented,
violent, conflicting interests rather than of clearly defined social
classes. In the end, the film is a hymn to the American 'little people'
who prove able to absorb a man from the under-class: 'We are the
people' is the final phrase of the film.

Possibly the most wittily self-conscious portrayal of that vision
of the whole American society as embracing essentially an upper-
class and an under-class, which is at the same time rich in unintended

perceptions about basic American social assumptions, is the Para
mount film of 1941, *Sullivan's Travels*, written and directed by
Preston Sturgess as a deliberate tribute to the power of laughter in
an unhappy world. Joel McCrea plays John L. Sullivan, a Holly
wood film director who, in common with his two financial associates
shares those attributes which I have already suggested may legiti
mately be termed upper-class. Sullivan was educated in a private
boarding school, and is described by one of his associates as class I
the same associate also concludes a piece of dialogue with: 'You're
a gentleman to admit it – but then you are anyway.' Sullivan –
clinching symbol once again – has an English butler *and* an English
valet (played by Robert Greig and Eric Blore, respectively).

The opening discussion over the cutting copy of a film which
Sullivan has just made is highly polished. Sullivan is keen to put on
a film about the problems of capital and labour. He is reminded that
a previous venture in this vein 'died in Pittsburg' and that 'they
know what they like in Pittsburg'. 'If they knew what they liked,
Sullivan replies, with nice upper-class snobbishness, 'they wouldn't
live in Pittsburg.' His butler later tells him that only the morbid rich
are interested in the poor, and that social theorists are usually rich
people. However, Sullivan gets his own way to the extent of being
allowed to dress up in poor clothing and set out into the world
followed, however, by the whole monkey-load of film-makers and
their apparatus. He is then allowed to go off for two weeks on his
own to try to collect local colour. It is now that he meets Veronica
Lake. He tries to explain himself and his shabby clothes by saying
that he used to be a movie director: 'Ah, you poor kid!' is her response. Neither Sullivan, nor Sturgess, has much of a consistent
ideological line. When Sullivan gets slung in gaol, and then wants
to get out by explaining that he is a famous movie director, he is
asked by the cop, 'What are you doing in those clothes?'; his reply
is, 'I just paid my income tax.'

Sullivan sets off again, going the rounds of the doss houses
accompanied by Veronica Lake dressed up as a boy. After handing
out five-dollar bills to the other tramps, Sullivan has his boots and
the rest of the money stolen by one particularly villainous tramp. In
making his escape from Sullivan the tramp is run over and killed
by a train and, because of the boots, is subsequently mistaken for
Sullivan. Sullivan himself, still dressed as a tramp, tangles with a
railway cop, is knocked out, loses his memory, and is sentenced to
six years in a convict camp. The convict camp is portrayed with all
the usual total brutality. Even when Sullivan does remember his

name and sees a report of his own death in a newspaper, he gets nowhere with the intractable and sadistic camp boss. The convicts are
entertained in a church by a black preacher who describes them to
his black congregation as 'some neighbors less fortunate than ourselves' and instructs them not in any way to show any contempt for
or revulsion from the convicts, for 'we are all equal in the sight of
God'. The entertainment turns out to be a Mickey Mouse film. All
the convicts roar with laughter while Sullivan looks round in puzzle-
ment until finally he too joins in the laughter.

Sullivan tries to explain his predicament to a wise old convict,
protesting that 'they don't sentence picture directors to a place like
this for a little disagreement with a yard dick!' 'Don't they?' mutters
the old guy, continuing, 'I never seen a picture director – you look
like a soda jerk or plasterer maybe.' Then Sullivan has his brainwave.
He announces that he is the tramp who murdered John L. Sullivan.
Immediately he is put on trial, is recognized, and returns to his
former luxurious life. Now his financial associates want him to make
a serious film recounting his experiences. But Sullivan has learned
the realities of life amid the under class, and the power of laughter,
and he insists that henceforth he will make only comedies: 'Laughter
is all people have – it isn't much.' The film ends with a montage of
those striped emblems of the American under class, the convicts,
roaring with laughter.

Recognizable, then, in Hollywood films of the thirties are an
upper class, a middle America shading down from doctors, journalists and professors, to bank clerks, and an under class, usually
located on the far side of the law. There is not much of a showing for
a working class, though their existence is recognized in *Black Fury*
and *Black Legion*. Here there is an evident contrast with a whole
shoal of novels which hit America in the thirties and deal with industrial scenes, particularly strikes, in a quite overtly class-conscious
fashion.[2] Yet if our academic, official and private images are sound,
then probably the Hollywood movies do come closer than certain
self-conscious literary efforts to presenting American society with
basic assumptions about itself which were acceptable to most
Americans.[3]

Notes

1. Andrew Bergman, *We're in the Money: Depression America in the Movies* (1972), pp. 105–7.
2. This topic is fully discussed by F. M. Blake, *The Strike in the American Novel* (1972).
3. The films discussed in this chapter were viewed at: the Library of Congress, Washington DC; the State Historical Society of Wisconsin, Madison; the Pacific Film Archive, Berkeley, California; and the Museum of Modern Art, New York.

9

BBC and Other Media Images of Class

Hollywood, extravagant, romantic, propagator of myth, mirror of
basic assumptions, dominated by the rich and the powerful, was,
one might say, to American society as the BBC, tight-lipped, prissy,
propagator of basic assumptions, mirror of myths, dominated by
the upper-class, was to British society. The BBC had been set up as
a public Corporation with a monopoly of broadcasting in 1926.
When D. G. Bridson joined as a producer in 1933 he 'mentally
bracketed the BBC with Parliament, Monarchy, Church and the
Holy Ghost'. There were one or two individualists, such as the
Marxist, Archie Harding, whose 'father was a Colonel (retired) in
the Royal Marines' and whose 'background was impeccably Upper
Class', but who believed that the air should be open to the 'Working
Class no less than the Middle and Upper Classes'. Apart from these,
'the voice of the BBC remained the voice of the upper-middle class,
and almost the only accent heard on the air was standard southern
English. Out on the perimeter, in Scotland and Wales and Northern
Ireland, occasional purlings of the genteeler local Doric were permitted.'[1] The BBC, overtly, had no more to say about class than had
Hollywood, since it shared in the official and upper-class mythology
that classes in Britain scarcely existed, that to mention class distinctions was in extremely bad taste, and that to dwell on them was to
be guilty of dangerous subversion.

The notion that the BBC itself might actually put on a series of
talks on class originated from outside the Corporation. The Institute
of Sociology had managed in September 1937 to hold a discussion
of social stratification and class conflict without provoking distur-
bance and riot. From there the idea filtered through the little world,
dominated by the universities of Oxford and Cambridge, which was
BBC radio. Soon, the talks advisory committee of the BBC was
minuting 'CLASS: It was thought that this series would be most
interesting, though its controversial nature was realised.'[2] In a
memo of 17 March 1938, N. G. Luker of the talks department cited
that famous piece of Carr-Saunders-Caradog-Jonesery about the

insignificance of class distinctions, quoted in Chapter 3. In spite of that, he continued with commendable pragmatism, 'we do mean something by the familiar terms "upper", "middle" and "working" classes. Recognizable members of each of these could be in the studio. . .'[3] But having recognizable members of different classes together in the same studio was exactly what many directors of the BBC did not want. As the Director General, Sir John Reith, noted on 5 May 1938: 'Lady Bridgman' (one of the governors)

> . . . came in this morning most unhappy about this series. If it had to be done she hoped in particular the idea of having an aristocrat and a representative of the middle and working classes at the microphone together won't be carried out. I don't myself see that this would necessarily be unfortunate, but I see what she is afraid of. But, more important, she is generally apprehensive of stirring up strife. She agreed that there was a great deal of interest in this subject, but it could easily be harmful.
>
> It is of course vitally important to make certain that there is no political motive; and what about the speakers – London School of Economics as usual? Is this, in fact, as Lady Bridgman suspects, another attempt to get Left-Wing propaganda across?[4]

A few days later Reith was writing to H. A. L. Fisher, historian, former president of the Board of Education, and now head of an Oxford college: 'Lady Bridgman is very apprehensive about this series, and Millis does not care for it very much either, but I think they both realise that we should be in trouble with our Talks Advisory Committee and with the Discussion Group Committee if we were to forsake the idea altogether.'[5] A letter from Sir Ian Fraser, after a brief piece of upper-class political science, slid round to a perfect presentation of the upper-class self-image: the implication, worthy of the old Duke of Wellington himself, is that a social structure so perfect – spoiled only by an unfortunate handful of idle rich – is beyond discussion:

> . . . differentiation is inevitable, no matter what the political system. Whether leaders are born or elected, whether they rule by tyranny or by consent, they are a 'ruling class', they will meet together to discuss the art and method of ruling and will tend to separate out of the mass. The Communist Party in Russia, the Trades Union Leaders in England, are a 'ruling' or 'managing' class.

The idle rich class. There is little to be said for them but probably the only way which will not do more harm than good, to minimise their number is an adverse public opinion. But it is a mistake to suppose that all the rich are idle, or all the idle, rich.

England has gained much by having a class of people not compelled to earn their living, who have been able to devote their ability and time to developing our art of government, free institutions, etc. Our Parliamentary system, local Government, public work generally, has benefited enormously.

Many other countries, Sir Ian concluded in an imperial flourish, were beset by political instability because they did not have this 'reservoir of persons economically free and accustomed to responsibility from an early age'.[6] This splendid phrase seems to me as good a definition of an upper class as I have found in any work of sociology.

Meantime the Control Board had ruled that whether the proposed series ever went on the air or not, it should not be given the title 'Caste and Class'. The director of talks, Sir Richard Maconachie, canvassed some of the possible alternatives; they could choose something light and snappy to catch the attention, with, to explain what was really intended, some such subtitle as 'An enquiry into social distinctions'. Possible main titles would then, Maconachie thought, be: 'Sorts and Conditions of Men'; 'Our Proper Stations'; 'People of Our Sort'; 'The Likes of Us'; 'Both Sides of the Aitch'. Alternatively, Maconachie reflected, they could opt for 'something solid and informative, even if solemn, such as "Class Distinctions"'. But 'none of these seemed quite right'; Maconachie gritted his teeth and faced facts: 'it was urged that the right word was "class" and that it would be simply cowardice to avoid it.' However, steering clear of cowardice was all very well: it was 'at the same time . . . desirable to suggest that our approach would be impartial and scientific, not tendentious'. The answer, 'as good as we should get', was to go for *Class: An Enquiry*.[7] Once the Corporation had finally shot Niagara and actually broadcast the series (to which I shall return shortly), Maconachie committed his own true thoughts to paper: 'I was, as you know, opposed to the idea of doing this series at all, as I could not see how we could surmount the difficulties involved. As it turned out, those difficulties were apparently not even perceived!'[8]

Formally, then, the BBC tried to avoid any direct discussion of class. At the same time, its producers and managers, in varying ways, held quite strong stereotypes about the nature of class. These two primary characteristics, discretion and stereotype, come together in the famous incident of March 1934 involving the car worker, William Ferrie. A series of talks on 'Modern Industry and National Character' had been inaugurated on 26 February by a leading employer in the motor industry, Sir Herbert Austin, who had remarked that while the trade unions had no doubt done much to improve the conditions of the working class, it was time they adjusted their views to modern industrial developments. For the next broadcast it was decided to invite a genuine working man: hence William Ferrie. The unsophisticated technology of the thirties did not allow for the pre-recording of talks, which had instead to be very carefully edited and rehearsed, then read word-for-word from an approved script. However, when Ferrie reached the microphone, he said:

> Last week a big employer of labour, Sir Herbert Austin, gave a talk about the British working man, and I have been invited to say what I think about the British worker. I am a working man myself, but what I wanted to tell you has been so censored and altered and cut up by the BBC that I consider it impossible for me to give a talk without it being a travesty of the British working class. I therefore protest against the censorship of the BBC and will give the talk instead to the press.[9]

At this point Ferrie was cut off.

Each newspaper followed up the incident by giving its own selections from the talk as originally devised by Ferrie. All printed enough to convey its distinctive Marxist flavour, though only the complete authorized text of *The Banned Broadcast of William Ferrie* contained the central sentences: 'There has been a lot of talk about the Moscow Road. I have discussed it with my workmates. They feel that what is called the Moscow Road is the only working-class road and they know that they will have nothing to look forward to until they take that road.' The BBC's unwillingness to give air-time to belligerent working-class polemics is unsurprising, and far less significant than another of Ferrie's grievances: 'I also refused to drop my "aitches" and to speak as they imagine a worker does.'[10]

The acceptable face of proletarianism, as far as the BBC was concerned, was revealed in the broadcast hastily arranged for the following week, given by an anonymous 'working-class woman', said to be a caretaker, and described by the *Daily Express* as having a pleasant Cockney voice.

I asked my mother to help me with the talk by comparing experiences. I've not had an easy life, but when I compare it with hers it seems like a soft carpet. To begin with, she had eleven children. I have one and don't intend to have any more. My father's wages as a docker were about twenty four shillings a week, and once he went on strike and there was nothing. And yet I can't ever remember going hungry. But perhaps I've forgotten.

My mother made boxes at home. I can remember her getting up at half past six and making boxes practically all day, until six or seven in the evening. She used to sit at a bench working away and as soon as a dozen boxes were completed we children used to make them up into a bundle. I can remember seeing my mother's fingers nearly bleeding from making the boxes. She got tuppence-halfpenny a gross, and at the end of the week her earnings were about seven shillings. That doesn't sound much, but it was nearly a third of what my father earned, and it was a great addition to our family money.

One thing working women aren't is lazy. Buying tinned food may look rather lazy, but it's often cheaper. And it's the same about ready-made clothes. Ready-made clothes really are cheaper, and they fit better and they look nicer. And I think there are very good reasons for buying them. It's not laziness.

And then you often hear it said that working women today are always thinking about their appearance: they will have new clothes; they must have their hair waved; also they must wear silk stockings, instead of spending the money on something else they really need. But I think the fact that we want to look nice nowadays is a good sign. Women have got more time nowadays, and it seems to me quite alright that they should spend some of it on their personal appearance. I think it makes them better wives, too. A man likes you to look nice. There's more inducement for him to take you to the pictures.

Working in factories makes girls stand up more for themselves. When you work in a factory you get all your evenings off, and so you've time to go out and see things. I'm sure that's the real reason why so many girls would rather have factory life than service. In service you aren't sure of your leisure. And in any case you don't get every evening off. I know mistresses are said to be better than they were. But it seems to me that service will never really be popular unless the conditions about time off are very much changed. Women want time off nowadays.

It does not take a very sharp eye to see the hand of the producer in all this, particularly in the contrived responses to the stock accusations of the period about working-class housewives living out of tins, wearing silk stockings, or going frequently to the pictures. The conclusion was even more contrived: 'The thing that matters is not money and education, but character. The great thing is to be independent and capable of looking after yourself. Facing up to things – that's character.' Politics was alluded to briefly, but whether producer or speaker was responsible for the incredibly muddled views expressed is hard to say: 'I'm a Socialist, that's to say I always vote Labour, because I think that's the working-class party and that we ought to vote for them. . . It all seems the same whoever gets in. . . In any case my husband's a Conservative.'[11]

Stereotypes in regard to accent and the appropriately deferential manners to go with were certainly rampant in the BBC. One listener, commenting on the actor who played a law clerk in a programme entitled *Is That The Law?* remarked that 'it would be a change if somebody had been found who did not drop his aitches'. 'Perhaps I have been unlucky,' she continued, 'but I certainly do feel that a limited income is all too frequently associated in broadcast talks with lack of intelligence and the omission of aspirates. Surely all clerks and similar persons earning round about £4 a week do not necessarily possess these obvious indications of their inferiority?' After accent, deference: she could not help thinking that the very frequent use of 'sir' coupled 'with the awed tone employed in addressing the barrister was a trifle out of date.'[12] Prejudices and preconceptions about class come through in many ways. The programme *In Town Tonight*, which continued to run until well after the Second World War, consisted essentially of short interviews with celebrities or newsworthy persons visiting London. In reaction to a proposal to change this show, one regional director remarked that its appeal had been 'to that section of the community broadly covered by the term "lower middle class",' and went on to define this term as 'the class who just held a commission during the War, who just keep a maid, and who, not being Londoners themselves, refer quite affectedly and unnaturally to London as "Town".'[13]

In the sphere of culture and communications, the thirties were the era of that great British bore, the documentary, exemplified in the films of John Grierson, and Edgar Anstey and Arthur Elton, in the picture magazines *Picture Post* and *Illustrated*, and in such radio broadcasts as *Coal*, *Coronation Scot* and *Cotton People*. The British documentary meant educated upper-class people affecting to be sympathetic about uneducated lower-class people, while succeeding only in being resoundingly patronizing about them. *Cotton People* is a perfect paradigm. The 'Commère', in the word invented by the BBC and mercifully never rediscovered by the Women's Liberationists, was the young Joan Littlewood, best known in more recent times for her theatrical productions mounted in the working-class purlieus of the Theatre Royal, Stratford, in London's East End. There is sympathy indeed for the cotton workers, but their problems – the programme faces this fairly and squarely at the end – are really the fault of the nasty foreigners:

Joan:	You went into the mill the day after you left school, didn't you?
Vera:	Yes, that's right.
Joan:	And how old are you now?
Vera:	I was fourteen on 9th February.
Joan:	And wouldn't you sooner be back at school?
Vera:	Oh, I don't know. My legs still get very tired standing all day, and there's still a bit to learn. But I'm getting a proper wage now, – not just a learner's.
Joan:	I see. That makes a difference, doesn't it. . . . You looked scared to death, y'know, when I saw you the first day.
Vera:	Well, I was a bit scared of the machines, and the noise bothered me. I have to clean underneath the Frame every day, and I had to be careful where I put my fingers. But I've got used to it now.
Joan:	And you're beginning to like the work?
Vera:	Well, it's a bit monotonous, you know – but I like being with the other girls. *And you've got to work at something*. I'm learning dressmaking in the evening.
Joan:	Good for you! And the best of luck to you. And how long have *you* been in the mill?
Mr Barlow:	Fifty years come July 3rd.
Joan:	Well done! I should think you will want to celebrate, won't you? You know, when I was watching you working, I was thinking it must be nice to see something actually growing under your hands. It's not like being in an office, I mean, – just playing with figures.

Mr Barlow:	Nay, it's not! There's real variety i' *my* job! There's always something going off and going wrong.
Joan:	And what about Mr Fitton, the Managing Director?
Mrs Bolton:	Ah, I've known Robert since he was a little lad, and I knew his dad before him. He was a nice old gentleman, old Mr Fitton. . . .
Joan:	But what a terribly hard life you've had, Mrs Bolton. However did you keep going?
Mrs Bolton:	Ah, I've been happy and I've been sad. We've had our ups and downs, you know. Weaving's like married life, you never know what's going to happen next.
Joan:	But haven't you got away from it all for a bit? What sort of holidays have you had?
Mrs Bolton:	I went away to Blackpool for four days once.
Joan:	Four days? You mean you've only been out of Oldham four days in your life?
Mrs Bolton:	Aye, that's right.
Joan:	. . . I think you're the bravest old lady I've ever met!
Mrs Bolton:	God bless you, lass. I'm still happy.
Joan:	And God bless you.

> We have tried to show you the Cotton People as we in Lancashire know them, – a hard working, loyal, fair-minded race, – a Lancashire breed that has courage and beauty. Those people have had their struggles in the past and they will have them in the future, for there are still many wrongs that the past has handed on to the present. But Cotton cannot afford to give its people its due until Cotton can once more make its way in the world. And until a check is put on unfair foreign competition, Cotton and the Cotton People must suffer.[14]

Like it or not, the BBC was going to have its nose rubbed in some of the realities of the social structure through a development which ironically enough, the Corporation itself felt bound to initiate audience research. The first crude efforts in this direction were con ducted through a panel of voluntary log-keepers. The first result was a report on what was called the 'Listening Barometer'. Contained in an appendix was an item on 'Social Grade' which classified the log-keepers as forty-five-per-cent 'middle class', forty-nine-per-cent 'working-class', and six-per-cent 'unknown-class', and explained that 'middle class' meant 'persons in black-coated occupations', and that 'working class' meant 'manual workers'. A first investigation, by random sample, into winter listening habits gave the social distribution of listeners as forty-per-cent middle-class, and sixty-per-cent working-class.[15] In public, no upper class existed; even if it did, it was probably too small to be counted: or perhaps the BBC saw itself as representing the upper class, projecting its elevating materials upon an audience consisting exclusively of the middle and working classes. One fact of life that could not be ignored was that different classes in Britain ate different evening meals at different times, thus affecting listening patterns. More important, perhaps, the vast majority of the public had different eating habits from those practised by most members of the BBC. Up till the early evening, remarked a report entitled 'What Time do People Have Their Meals?'

rich and poor, with some minor differences, march fairly well in step, but at tea-time the ranks divide – a dichotomy which extends throughout the evening. For one section of the community high tea is the main evening meal, followed late in the evening by a light supper. For the rest there is an afternoon tea, followed by dinner which is the main evening meal. . . . the former section includes an overwhelming majority of the population, not only working class but lower middle class as well. It is probably no exaggeration to put the strength of this section at 95% of the families of urban England.[16]

At last, in the late autumn of 1938 the series on 'Class' which had caused so much heart searching, was broadcast. The introductory programme, *What do we mean by Class?* took the form of a discussion between the social anthropologist Tom Harrisson and the trade union leader George Isaacs. Harrisson began by saying that if asked to define what class was he would be forced to say that he didn't know. However, he offered his way of simplifying things. There were, he said, three main classes based on education: the people who leave school at fourteen; the people who leave school at about eighteen; the people who leave university at about twenty-two. Against this, Isaacs put the solid dichotomous view of 'the working class' on one side and 'the so-called leisure class' on the other. The working class, he said, included 'the oft-quoted "middle class", together with artisans, labourers, shopkeepers, housewives and all the professions'. To this soft Labourist, rather than hard Marxist formulation the chairman of the discussion, Professor T. H. Marshall, pioneer sociologist in the pragmatic British tradition, objected that it would result in putting 'all the bank directors, captains of industry, judges and Harley Street specialists into the working class'. Eventually, after programmes on *Does Education Create Barriers?*, *Jobs are Class Labelled*, *How Wealth Affects Class* and *How Class Affects Manners*, Marshall was again able to raise the voice of sanity: Britain did have, he said, an upper class, as well as a working class and a middle class.[17]

FRENCH FILM IMAGES

By the late 1930s there were almost nine million wireless-licence holders in the United Kingdom, which works out at very nearly one radio receiver to every family. Without doubt sound broadcasting was a popular medium, but what was broadcast by the BBC was very deliberately and consciously shaped, and thus talks on class or documentaries on cotton, tell us more about the broadcasters than about the society at which the broadcasts were aimed, which, in the mass, preferred in any case to listen to dance music. Hollywood films, on the other hand, were essentially the products of the famous studios – Warner Brothers, Metro-Goldwyn-Mayer and so on – and aimed above all at maximum popular success, and this success extended to both Britain and France. The French cinema usually associated with the thirties was self-conscious, arty, obsessed either by matters of form and style, or by questions of political ideology, though, as art, infinitely superior to the transient offerings of the BBC. (Through sheer cowardice, I have not, regrettably, studied French radio.) France, with small cinemas in Paris and the other big cities, catering to a clientele of intellectuals, could support (just about) 'serious' films, which were seen as the product of the individual genius, the *auteur* or 'author' of the film (Marcel Pagnol, Jean Renoir or Jean Grémillion, for example). These film-makers were just as upper-class as the makers of BBC radio programmes. Britain is the country of the social novel and the upper-class comedy of manners. British films, in comparison with French, tended to originate as novels or plays and to be 'films of the book' rather than the independent creative expression of their director (Marcel Pagnol's films were certainly this, but they, exceptionally, were often based upon the novels of small-town, or peasant society by Jean Giono). France had its 'commercial' films, but these were often costume dramas, and therefore shed even less light on contemporary attitudes to class than anything studied in these chapters.

The team of Pagnol and Giono produced those quintessential films of French peasant life, *Joffroi* (1933) and *Angèle* (1934). It also produced *La Femme du Boulanger* (1938), where the action centres on the tragic blow to a French village when, after his young wife runs away, the baker refuses to bake any more of his delicious bread. The rural hierarchy is carefully delineated: Monsieur le Marquis in the premier position, with the curé as his second in command, work together to restore the *status quo*. In an image to be repeated over and over again in French films (and quite alien to British films and British society) we see the Marquis and the baker quite unselfconsciously shaking hands as friends and fellow *citizens*. The Marseilles trilogy of films based on plays by Pagnol, *Marius* (1931 – directed by Alexander Korda), *Fanny* (1932 – directed by Marc Allégret), and *César* (1936 – directed by Pagnol himself), establishes a very French urban milieu of small independent proprietors: the café-owner and his son, the girl who has a fish stall on the quay, the ship's chandler and master sail-maker. A slight, but bridgeable distinction of status and wealth develops between the increasingly prosperous sail-maker and the café-owner, but at all times we remain in a small, provincial world where there is no discernible working class and no obvious upper class. The importance of hotels and cafes in French society, and of their habituées and employees in the French social structure is re-emphasized in the Marcel Carné film *Hotel du Nord* (1938). No social background is sketched in for the penniless lovers who attempt suicide, but the atmosphere is very strongly that of the *artisanat*. The sleazy elements contained in this film are more heavily stressed in the same director's *Le Quai des Brumes* (1938) and *Le Jour se lève* (1939), each starring Jean Gabin. In both, Gabin plays an outsider figure, dressed as an *ouvrier* but never related to any defined working-class occupational environment.

The film which is always mentioned as soon as one speaks of class in the French cinema of the 1930s is Jean Renoir's *La Règle du Jeu* (1938) (*The Rules of the Game*). Renoir's own affirmations on the subject of class have often been cited: 'I know that I constantly return to the same theme,' he once remarked: 'the differences of class.'[18]

René Prédal, in his standard work, *French Society 1914–1945 as seen through the Cinema*, has written that *The Rules of the Game* 'constitutes an exact and fundamentally pessimistic analysis of the social classes in pre-war France'.[19] An American historian, Charles William Brooks, after quoting Renoir on his preoccupation with 'the differences of class', goes on in a study of *The Rules of the Game* to insist:

> Renoir's story was the story of the times: it was in these years that the 'differences of class' became the critical factor in French politics and society. A few days before the right-wing press persecution finally succeeded in driving Roger Salengro, Léon Blum's Socialist minister of the interior, to take his own life, a well-known journalist of left-wing sympathies told Alexander Werth: 'In the past I used to lunch and dine with all sorts of people. Now I can be on friendly terms only with people who have more or less the same political convictions as I have. With the others, one is scarcely on speaking terms.

Actually the issue has been gently nudged along from class differences to political differences, not necessarily quite the same thing. Thus the statement that 'Renoir's films from 1932 to 1939, concerned with the "differences of class", became a running cinematic chronicle of the collapse of France in this decade,'[20] seems to me a trifle facile.

Despite the immediate hostility this film aroused among French audiences, because, apparently, it presented too undeceived a view of the decadence of French society, anyone looking for any clear message about the nature of the French social structure in the late thirties faces a number of puzzles. Accounts of the making of the film, in any case, suggest that Renoir allowed it to develop its own momentum and its own internal logic as he went along, so that the finished work would in any event be unlikely to present any simple image of contemporary France. The film is centred on an elegant aristocratic household, presided over by a *nouveau riche* aristocrat, complete with servants who play out a detailed hierarchical 'game' which echoes that of their social superiors. At the house-party there are two middle-class figures, Jurieu the aviator who has just completed a successful Atlantic solo flight at the beginning of the film, and the avuncular intellectual figure, Octave, played by Renoir himself, who fits quite easily into the aristocratic fun and games; what we most certainly do *not* have, is any member of the industrial working class – though we do have an *outsider* figure who is brought into the servants' establishment, Marceau, the poacher. Whatever comment Renoir was making, through his plot of infidelities, a shooting and a cover-up, one has come to recognize its milieu, right down to the very un-British detail of the Count shaking hands with Marceau, the poacher.

BRITISH FILM IMAGES

British films of the 1930s are a little more rewarding than might be suggested by the blanket of almost total critical silence in which they have been enveloped. They do not deal frontally with class any more than do the films of America or France. Frequently, their attempts at class description are no more than inept stereotypes. Many of the comedy and light entertainment films of the thirties, rooted as they were in working-class music hall or seaside entertainments, did bring in some quality of working-class life, though often such films suggest elements of patronage and contempt. They run the range through the films of Gracie Fields and George Formby, Albert Burdon, to the appalling *Spring Handicap* (1937) in which Will Fyffe submitted to the indignity of playing a characterless coal-miner turned unsuccessful bookie. Working-class environments and working-class characters often simply provided background for stories of crime or violence. *Broken Blossoms* (1936) is a weird, fascinating and almost operatic story of the daughter of a brutal East End boxer and her innocent relationship with a Chinaman (played by Emlyn Williams). *They Drive by Night* (1938) was the film of a novel about a released prisoner wrongly suspected of a murder which had in fact been committed by a multiple murderer who specialized in picking up women of loose morals. In the film a crude class note, absent in the novel, is introduced by making the killer a distinctly upper-class figure, referred to in a pub conversation as 'a real gentleman' and 'an educated gentleman'.

What the British cinema of the 1930s does have to offer is a handful of films in which a genuine attempt is made to recreate a working-class environment inhabited by real working-class people. First, chronologically, came the sound film version of the famous Edwardian play about Lancashire cotton workers, *Hindle Wakes* (1931) – there was an earlier silent version. Straight from Harold Brighouse's original play, the great dialogue between Alan, the factory owner's son, and Fanny, the factory girl, in which he finds that he has not been entirely the daring seducer after all, is repeated in the film:

Alan:	But didn't you ever really love me?
Fanny:	Love you? Good heavens, of course not. Why on earth should I love you? You were just someone to have a bit of fun with. You were an amusement – a lark.
Alan (*shocked*):	Fanny! Is that all you cared for me?
Fanny:	How much more did you care for me?
Alan:	But it's not the same. I'm a man.
Fanny:	You're a man and I was your little fancy. Well, I'm a woman and *you* are my little fancy. You wouldn't prevent a woman enjoying herself as well as a man, if she takes it into her head?
Alan:	But you mean to say that you didn't care anymore for me than a fellow cares for any girl he happens to pick up?

The film closes as Fanny selects for herself another beau from the factory production line: very refreshing after the insistent male chauvinism of the Capra comedies.

Then we have *Proud Valley* (1940), starring Paul Robeson, and giving a remarkably authentic portrait of a Welsh mining village. Here we have the truly heroic image of the working class, proud in song and ready in danger and self-sacrifice. The more standard, populist rendering can be found in the film of A. J. Cronin's *The Stars Look Down* (1939). Here workers are innocent dupes, and trade union leaders, villains. The war had actually broken out before the greatest of all working-class films was released, John Baxter's *Love on the Dole* (1941), based on Walter Greenwood's famous novel, was scarcely heroic: rather, it was totally sympathetic and comprehending in its understanding from the inside of working-class life in the Lancashire Depression.

But these films, of course, are exceptional. Most British films were transposed West End comedies in upper-class settings. It does, I think, say something about the equable acceptance of the class structure on the part of the population as a whole that such films were apparently quite popular. One of the greatest hits of the entire decade was that quite awful film, *A Yank at Oxford* (1938),[21] with, for the benefit of the American market, Robert Taylor as an obnoxious bumptious American student at Oxford. On the evidence of the success of this film it would appear that the British derived a special pleasure from the portrayal of upper-class fun and games carried out in the most childish and unpleasant manner.

Notes

1. D. G. Bridson, *Prospero and Ariel* (1971), p. 29.
2. BBC Written Archives [BBC A], Caversham, Talks: 'Class' Acc. no. 1420: talks advisory committee minutes, extract of 5 October 1937.
3. *Ibid*: N. G. Luker, memo of 17 March 1938.
4. *Ibid*: Reith, memo of 5 May 1938.
5. *Ibid*: Reith to Fisher, 9 May 1938.
6. *Ibid*: Sir Ian Fraser to Miss Stanley, 11 May 1938.
7. *Ibid*: Maconachie, memo of 27 May 1938.
8. *Ibid*: Maconachie, memo of 20 December 1938.
9. *The Times*, 6 March 1934.
10. Workers' Bookshop Ltd, *The Banned Broadcast of William Ferrie* (1934).
11. *The Times*, 13 March 1934.
12. BBC A, Talks policy file I, Acc. no. 1729/2: Miss M. P. Ussher to N. G. Luker, 8 August 1938.
13. *Ibid*: *In Town Tonight* file I, Acc. no. 9994: memo of 22 June 1937. (See Asa Briggs, *The History of Broadcasting in the United Kingdom: vol. II The Golden Age of Wireless* (1968), pp. 41–2.)
14. *Ibid*: North Region programme script, Cotton People, 23 March 1938.
15. *Ibid*: LR/65, 29 November 1938 and LR/67, 1 September 1938. R9/9/1–2.
16. *Ibid*: LR/68, 21 October 1938. R9/9/2.
17. The talks are reported in the *Listener*, 13 October 1938 to 1 December 1938.
18. *Cahiers du Cinéma*, 196 (1967), p. 66.
19. René Prédal, *La Société française (1914–1945) à travers le cinéma* (1972), p. 158.
20. Charles William Brooks, 'Jean Renoir's *The Rules of the Game*', *French Historical Studiés*, vol. VII (1972), p. 264.
21. Information in Denis Gifford, *The British Film Catalogue, 1895–1970* (1973), entries for 1938.

10

The Realities of Class

The different images revealed, if at times darkly, in the previous seven chapters make it possible to map out the main contours of the class structure of the three countries as understood by the people of these countries themselves, and to make broad contrasts between the three societies. Class, in the historical and popular usage of this book, suggests overlapping areas of inequality, particularly in power and authority, income and wealth, conditions of work, and lifestyles and culture. It remains to determine the extent of these inequalities in the 1930s, to separate inequalities due to class from inequalities attributable to other causes, to assess the significance of class in political behaviour and the part it played in the major political crises of the time. In short, even if we agree that classes existed, did they matter?

The subjective evidence, when fitted into the historical context, indicates, I have argued, that something which can be called an 'upper class' existed, though in different forms, in each of the three countries. A good definition of that class emerged in the previous chapter: a 'reservoir of persons economically free and accustomed to responsibility from an early age'. The latter phrase, perhaps, is loaded: I interpret it as meaning 'accustomed to being offered positions of power and authority at an early age' (since we are discussing a class or 'reservoir', the 'persons' may not necessarily accept the positions which are there for the taking). Is the existence of such a class borne out by the empirical evidence? Those authorities who, by different methods, have arrived at a view of the upper class similar to my own, see the British upper class of the 1930s as numbering about 1 per cent of the population, the American upper class about 0.5 per cent or a little more, with the French upper class coming somewhere in between, let us say about 0.8 per cent,[1] though these figures may be on the low side. Now, the ways in which power was exercised and the areas in which power was significant, differ in the three countries. With Britain, it is, I believe, proper to start with the traditional political institutions.

POWER IN GREAT BRITAIN

Let us plunge straight in by taking a look at the cabinet which was formed in 1935 by Stanley Baldwin, whose administration was still technically a 'National' government, though strongly Conservative in character. Baldwin, whose father had headed the family iron foundry, himself belonged to that successful element of the nineteenth-century industrial class which had merged itself into the upper class.[2] He had progressed through the appropriate educational channel from preparatory school to Harrow, to Trinity College Cambridge, where he took a third in history (upper-class figures often took firsts; it is part of upper-class lore that they seldom gain second-class degrees). Baldwin was forty-one before he entered Parliament, having inherited, on his father's death in 1908, the Bewdley seat in Worcestershire.

Next in the cabinet hierarchy was Ramsay MacDonald, the former Labour leader who had been responsible for forming the first National government in August 1931. As the illegitimate son of a Scottish servant lass and a ploughman, Ramsay MacDonald might well appear a glowing testimonial to the openness of the British power elite. His Scottish environment had provided him with educational opportunities which probably would not have been open to a similar figure in most parts of England. He rose through journalistic and political activity, not through the trade union movement. A year older than Baldwin, MacDonald arrived in Parliament two years earlier than the Conservative leader. He might well have become a successful Liberal leader (indeed many of his political attitudes were essentially Liberal) but the growing Labour Party provided an admirable vehicle for him: His intellectual qualities and his magnetism as a leader were considerable. Once persuaded to form his National government with Conservative support in 1931, MacDonald was rather easily absorbed into the Conservative political elite: he did not thereby become upper-class, but he certainly ceased to show any very strong signs of belonging to any other class.

Lord Privy Seal in the 1935 cabinet was the seventh Marquis of Londonderry, a direct descendant of Viscount Castlereagh, the famous statesman of the Napoleonic era; he was educated at Eton and Sandhurst, and entered the House of Commons at the age of twenty-eight. The Chancellor of the Exchequer was Neville Chamberlain, son of the famous Joseph Chamberlain by his second wife. Chamberlain's symbiotic relationship with Rugby has already been noted. It is true that as his elder half-brother, Austen, had been designated *the* politician in the family, Neville was sent to study commerce at the college that later became Birmingham University, and was then forced out into the business world, which perhaps puts a gloss on the Privy Seal's reference to him as 'a mere Birmingham tradesman', a remark which one cannot imagine anyone making about Austen Chamberlain, the politician, who, as Churchill said, 'always played the game, and always lost'. In any broad mapping of society, Neville Chamberlain belongs to the upper class: but his case does illustrate the subtle gradations existing within classes.

The Home Secretary, Sir John Simon, was a carefully assimilated first-generation member of the upper class. His grandfather had been a small farmer and mason at Stackpole Elidor in Pembrokeshire. His father was a Congregational minister and his mother the daughter of a farmer who had claimed descent from Cardinal Pole. An only son, Simon, in true aspiring middle-class fashion, was sent to Bath Grammar school. From there he won a scholarship to Fettes, one of the prestigious public schools which happened to be situated in Scotland (though born in Manchester, Simon in his later years revealed traces of a Scottish accent, which is doubly strange since the pupils of Fettes habitually spoke in an Anglified manner). According to the *Dictionary of National Biography*, Simon was 'a devoted upholder of the public school system', as was only proper in a first-generation recruit to the upper class. In 1892 he went up to Wadham College, Oxford, where he took a first in classics, was president of the Union in 1896, and in 1897 was elected a fellow of that most élitist of all colleges, All Souls. The traditional progression continued when in 1899 he was called to the Bar: although he earned only twenty-seven guineas in his first year as a barrister, Simon took Silk (that is to say, became a King's Counsel) after a mere nine years. The law, of course, was but a stepping stone to politics, and in 1906 he was elected Liberal member for Walthamstow. His appointment as Solicitor General in 1910 brought with it a knighthood at the age of thirty-seven. He twice refused peerages in order not to jeopardise his political career, which, however, was not especially distinguished. Speaking through a hole in the back of his head, he made himself notorious in 1926 when he declared the General Strike illegal: the *DNB* puts it quaintly, 'In May 1926 he achieved what had hitherto eluded him – a major Parliamentary success, when his speech on the illegality of the General Strike indubitably had some effect on bringing it to an end.' The biographer was on safer ground when he turned to that important, but elusive, matter of looks: 'In appearance Simon was a tall and well-built man with a fine head. He was not exactly handsome or distinguished, but his manner, and still more his conversation, at once displayed him as a person of consequence.' In his seventies, Simon, by then a sadly disregarded politician, took understandable pride in the fact that he could still read the London telephone directory without glasses.

With the Foreign Secretary, Sir Samuel Hoare, we return indisputably to established upper-class territory. The Hoares were an old Norfolk banking family, and Samuel's father, of Sidestrand Hall, Norfolk, the first baronet, had been Member of Parliament for Norwich; his mother was the daughter of the Commissioner of Audit. Educated at Harrow and New College, Oxford, Hoare took firsts in both classics and history, and entered Parliament as Conservative member for Chelsea in January 1910, the eleventh month of his twenty-ninth year. The Colonial Secretary was Ramsay MacDonald's son Malcolm; a new upper-class dynasty appeared to be in the making. The Dominions Secretary was J. H. Thomas, the Railwaymen's leader, who was one of the very few Labour Ministers to join MacDonald's National government in 1931. Thomas's liking for upper-class lifestyles was recognized in his nickname 'the Hon. stuffed shirt'; at the same time he religiously dropped his aitches in order to stress his working-class origins. We must put him down as a working-class member of this highly aristocratic cabinet (he was, incidentally, thirty-six when he entered Parliament).

Over the Secretary for War, the Viscount Halifax, son of the second Viscount and of the only daughter of the eleventh Earl of Devon, we need not hesitate. He was educated at Eton and Christ Church, Oxford, where he took a first in history, which in turn led on to a Fellowship of All Souls. Upbringing, personal courage and self-confidence helped him to surmount the affliction of an atrophied left arm. He married Lady Dorothy Evelyn Augusta Onslow, the younger daughter of the fourth Earl of Onslow. It is impossible to improve upon the comment (seriously intended) of his *DNB* biographer: 'the loyalty which at his wedding burdened him with a solid gold cup nearly two feet high as a tribute from the tenantry helped to ensure his election in January 1910 as Conservative member of parliament for Ripon.' (In January 1910 the future Viscount was not yet twenty-nine.) The Secretary of State for Air was Sir Philip Cunliffe-Lister, who commanded more than the normal ration of aristocratic aliases: born Philip Lloyd-Greame, he was on appointment elevated to the peerage as Viscount Swinton, taking the name from the Swinton estate which, complete with coal mine, had been inherited by his wife. Cunliffe-Lister was the son of a Yorkshire landowner and had been educated at Winchester and Oxford, where he took a second in law before being called to the Bar. In 1918, just into his thirties, he became Conservative MP for Hendon. His memoirs strike a familiar note: 'A new Member of the House of Commons feels rather like a new boy at school. At both the new boy is fortunate if he has seniors to take him under their wing. That was my good fortune; and some older Members who were old friends of mine, including Edward Wood [Lord Halifax], Walter Guinness [Lord Moyne], Sam Hoare [Lord Templewood], Judge Hills, Eddie Winterton and George Lane-Fox [Lord Bingley] invited me to join their small and rather independent group.'[3] Secretary of State for Scotland was Sir Godfrey Collins, eponymous head of the great Scottish publishing company, which more recently has shown its continuing greatness by publishing the British edition of this book. At the Admiralty, Sir B. Eyres-Monsell was the son of a Lieutenant-Colonel and grandson on his mother's side of Sir E. Ogle, the sixth baronet; he was now created Viscount Monsell.

With the President of the Board of Trade, Walter Runciman, we light upon a second-generation member of the upper class with a fascinating nineteenth-century background. His grandfather had been the master of a schooner, and his father had run away to sea, before building up a prosperous business as a shipowner and becoming the first Baron Runciman. The family were ardent Methodists in the oldest Methodist tradition. Walter Runciman was educated at South Shields High School (definitely middle-class, not upper-class) then privately (more usually a sign of an upper-class aspirant than of an established member of the upper class) and then at Trinity College Cambridge where he took a third in history. After joining his father's shipping business he became a Liberal MP in 1899. Runciman established himself as an important figure in the City of London and from 1920 to 1931 he was chairman of the United Kingdom Provident Institution. The Runciman family had not only arrived; they were securely established.

At the Ministry of Agriculture was a Scotsman whose background lay in that Scottish upper-middle-class whose products have often found it relatively easy to enter into the world of the English upper class. Walter Elliot's father was a livestock auctioneer and he was educated at Glasgow Academy (upper-middle-class, not upper-class) and Glasgow University, where he mixed with the assorted trio of James Maxton, the future left-wing socialist leader, Ronald Mavor, the future playwright, and John Boyd-Orr, the future nutritionist. Elliot took firsts in science and in medicine. He was essentially a man of the moderate middle, and when a cable reached him in the army in 1918 asking him to stand as a parliamentary candidate for Lanark, it is said that his reply was 'Yes, which side?' – the side, in fact, was that of the Conservatives.

The President of the Board of Education was Oliver Stanley, son of the seventeenth Earl of Derby, married to a daughter of Lord Londonderry; he had become an MP at the age of twenty-eight. But the Minister of Labour was altogether a humbler man: from a Torquay Baptist family, Ernest Brown had had neither public school nor university education. A not dissimilar background, but greater upward mobility was shown by the Minister of Health, Sir Kingsley Wood. He was born in Hull, the son of a Wesleyan Minister. Young Kingsley was educated at the Central Foundation Boys School off the City Road in London, where his father was for nine years Minister of Wesley's Chapel with which Kingsley Wood himself retained a life-long connection, serving for many years as a treasurer. Wood could not aspire to the Bar; he became a London solicitor. Nor could he aspire to immediate entry into Parliament; he was elected to the London County Council in 1911. The new social security legislation of that year created for Wood, as it was to do for others, opportunity for advancement. Wood became principal adviser to the Industrial Insurance companies in their negotiations with the government; subsequently as chairman of the London Insurance committee he played an even more important role in the discussions leading to the setting up of the Ministry of Health, and this was the immediate background to his knighthood in 1918. In December of that same year he became Conservative MP for West Woolwich. To a true member of the upper class Wood remained 'insignificantly dreary and bourgeois'.[4]

No such comment could be made about the First Commissioner of Works, W. Ormsby-Gore, whose father was the third baron Harlech and whose mother was a daughter of the tenth Marquis of Huntley. At various times, Ormsby-Gore was Lord Lieutenant of Merionethshire, Chairman of the Midland Bank, and a trustee of the National Gallery, of the British Museum and of the Tate Gallery. One bright young man in an otherwise elderly cabinet was Anthony Eden. This graceful and gracious epitome of the upper-class style ('the best-dressed fool he'd ever met', was Mussolini's verdict; Eden's memoirs of his youth are something of a lament for Edwardian aristocratic society[5]) was Minister without Portfolio responsible for League of Nations affairs. The cabinet list was completed by another Minister without portfolio, Lord Eustace Percy: father,

the seventh Duke of Northumberland; mother, daughter of the
eighth Duke of Argyle; education, Eton and Christ Church, Oxford,
where he took a first in history.

That lump of potted biography calls for little extra comment,
though it can be further shaped with the help of W. L. Guttsman's
statistical analysis of the British political elite.[6] In classifying
ministers and MPs, Guttsman speaks of 'the aristocracy', 'the middle
class' and 'the working class', putting in the middle-class category
many figures whom I would regard as belonging to the upper class.
However, his main conclusion is clear: 'the political élite has remained rather firmly wedded to the upper strata of British Society'.
In the 1930s the Conservative Party was in effect Britain's ruling
party. Of all Conservative MPs in the inter-war period, over twenty-
seven per cent had been educated at Eton, around ten per cent at
Harrow, and around forty-one per cent at the various other public
schools. The upper class is a tiny 'reservoir' in the whole population;
streams trickle in, and in swim the Runcimans, the Simons, and perhaps, with a struggle, the Woods. Not all of the denizens of this
reservoir necessarily aspire after political power: those that do, get
there smoothly and soon; relative to their numbers they exercised a
grossly disproportionate control over positions of political power.
That is one of the most obvious realities of class in the Britain of the
1930s. No need to go on at length about the disproportionate absence of working-class figures: for example, out of the 108 cabinet
ministers serving between 1916 and 1935 only 21 can unequivocally
be ranked as working-class. In parliament as a whole, working-class
representation was rather better (much better than in the American
House of Representatives or the French Assembly, though still way
short of correlating with working-class strength in the population
at large) and middle-class representation was much better still. But
simply appearing as an MP, for perhaps the lifetime of only one
parliament, was of rather small importance compared with being
one of the influential minority who floated back into parliament
election after election, joining governments, or forming influential
backbench cliques: this minority in the thirties was still predominantly upper-class.

Upper-class dominance of political power was confirmed by the
composition of the higher civil service. In the Britain of the thirties,
ministers ruled; but it helped to have the wholehearted cooperation
of civil servants: the failing minority Labour government of 1929–
31 found the civil servants, doing their duty as they saw it, yet
another obstacle, supposing one were needed, to the carrying

through of distinctive Labour policies. Entry to the higher civil service was most usually direct by 'open competition', only very rarely by promotion from below. As the 1931 Royal Commission on the Civil Service freely admitted, indeed boasted, great weight in the open competition was placed on the 'interview test', the perfect opportunity for the display of the gentlemanly qualities inculcated at the public schools and Oxbridge; with magnificent, but revealing, upper-class nonchalance the Commission itself airily dismissed the argument, in fact an overwhelmingly compelling one, that this inter- view 'offered scope for the display of class prejudice'.[7] In any case the broad picture is clear. In 1929 over a quarter of those entering the higher civil service by open competition came from the Claren- don Schools; by 1939 this figure had dropped slightly to about a fifth, with a third of all successful candidates coming from some type of public school. As Professor R. K. Kelsall has further pointed out: 'Amongst the most senior members of the 1939 and 1929 groups (Secretaries and Deputy Secretaries) the proportion of Clarendon School men in the open competitions entrants was as high as a third; and the percentage of such men amongst other types of entrant of this rank was similar.'[8]

In keeping with the traditions of the British Civil Service, the names of individual civil servants are not widely known either to contemporaries or to historians. However, it is worth giving atten- tion to one or two 'top' figures. As part of the (modest) reorganiza- tion of the Civil Service that took place at the end of the First World War, it was decided that the formal position of Permanent Head of the Civil Service should rest with the Permanent Secretary of the Treasury. This, from October 1919, was a brilliant career civil servant, Sir Warren Fisher, whose upper class education, as well as his handsome good looks, are stressed by his *DNB* biographer. Un- doubtedly Fisher played an important part in maintaining the general upper-class tone of the British Civil Service and in insisting on the backward looking economic orthodoxy which characterized the Treasury in particular and British policy in general. At the same time he was a convinced believer, in the 1930s, in a high-level of rearma- ment in the face of the German menace. Here he did not get his own way, and it is revealing of the relative strengths of a determined Con- servative Prime Minister and a top civil servant, that Neville Cham- berlain, in carrying through his appeasement policies, was able to operate through the slightly less eminent, but more congenial figure of Sir Horace Wilson, technically Chief Industrial Adviser to the government. Likewise the Permanent Under Secretary of the Foreign

Office, Sir Robert Vansittart, a strong anti-German, was virtually ignored by Chamberlain. These are policy differences within the upper class. The views of working-class Labour MPs, whatever they might be, were of relatively little importance. But Hugh Dalton, the upper-class Labour MP, was, as noted in Chapter 5, able to participate in private foreign policy discussions with Winston Churchill and other upper-class Conservative dissenters from Chamberlain's policies.

One important behind-the-scenes figure, with a finger in many pies, Thomas Jones, assistant secretary to the cabinet throughout the 1930s, provides a further example of how an apparent outsider, aided by a Celtic background, could, like Ramsay MacDonald, reach the centres of political power. Jones was born in an industrial village on the Welsh border, son of an employee in the company store of the Rhymney Iron Company. After attending local schools, he became a timekeeper with the Iron Company. But in an environment favourable both to learning and to non-conformist religion, young Jones, via being scripture gold-medallist and a noted lay-preacher, in 1890 entered the University College of Wales, Aberystwyth. In 1895 he moved on to the rather more prestigious Scottish University of Glasgow, where he graduated with first-class honours in economics. In 1909 he became Professor of Economics at Queen's University, Belfast. His upward movement within the Civil Service began when he joined the newly established National Health Insurance Commission for Wales, set up by Lloyd George's 1911 Act, as its First Secretary. Tom Jones had joined the Independent Labour Party in 1895, and though his later offices were incompatible with any political activity, he was certainly an important force behind the moderation and the collectivist social policies sometimes practised by the Baldwin and Chamberlain governments. In social behaviour, as his diary suggests, he adapted himself fully to the upper-class lifestyles of the time.[9]

Were British business leaders drawn from the same social class as political and administrative leaders? What power did they exercise compared with, say, political leaders? Is it a *class* which is exercising power, or just successful *individuals*? The pioneer study by Dr Charlotte Erickson of industrialists in the steel and hosiery industries, understandably enough, depends upon the Registrar General's classification: his social class I is not, of course, the upper class of popular usage. However, if we seek hard quantities, we have to take the figures the way they are served up. For the thirties, then, as Dr Erickson shows, over eighty per cent of business leaders in the steel industry had fathers in social class I: Dr Erickson brings us back on to more familiar ground when she tells us that: 'one of the most significant trends in the education of steel manufacturers has been an increase in gravitation to the particular schools which are today recognized as public schools.'[10] In the hosiery industry only forty-two per cent of business leaders had fathers in social class I. But on the national scale the heavily capitalized and concentrated steel industry was clearly a much more potent force than the less heavily capitalized hosiery industry with its multiplicity of small firms. J. M. Keynes argued at the time that British businessmen were too dependent on the fortunes made by their fathers and grand-fathers which had, of course, enabled them to develop the manners and lifestyle of the upper class.[11]

It is easy enough to demonstrate the power wielded by business leaders in the 1930s, and the close interrelationship between business and government; less easy to demonstrate that business leaders were born into the upper class rather than recruited into it. Those who were recruited from below almost invariably came from a small business or professional background within the middle class, very rarely indeed from the working class. The British Iron and Steel Federation, founded in 1934, worked very closely with the govern-ment in a programme of rationalization and reorganization which often resulted in increased unemployment in the older industrial areas, but also induced shifts of population to new areas. But the National Shipbuilders Security – a private company dominated by Sir James Lithgow, a number of shipbuilding firms, the iron and steel giant, Colvilles, and the Bankers' Industrial Development Cor-poration – acted unilaterally when it deliberately set out to buy up and close down shipyards, in so doing destroying the livelihood of most inhabitants of the Northumberland town of Jarrow. The director of the British Iron and Steel Federation was Sir William James Larke, son of a builder who, after a solidly middle-class education, trained as a professional engineer, and was helped into the important world in which business mixed with government by the First World War, during which he had a successful career in the Ministry of Munitions. His son became a general manager of the steel firm of Stewart and Lloyds. Most famous of the 'self-made' businessmen was the former bicycle mechanic, W. R. Morris, founder of the Morris Motor Company, who became Baron Nuffield in 1934 and Viscount Nuffield in 1938. Nuffield played no direct part in politics, but certainly his central role in the amalgama-tion and consolidation of an important sector of the British motor car industry involved the exercise of an enormous influence over the lives of many people. An earlier, largely self-made figure was William Lever, the first Lord Leverhulme, builder of the mighty Unilever combine. In the early twenties Leverhulme was unsuccessful in his attempt to bequeath the chairmanship of the company to his son. Instead Sir Francis D'arcy Cooper, impeccably educated scion of the family accountancy firm of Cooper Bros & Co., became chairman. Some mystery surrounds the origins of Arthur Balfour, first Baron Riverdale (1873–1957), chairman of the steel and engineering firm of Arthur Balfour and Company Limited, and frequent member of government committees and commissions. His birth was unregistered; he finished his education at the age of sixteen. In the same year that he became managing director of the Sheffield steel firm in whose office he had first been employed, he married the daughter of a partner in a local silver and electro-plating firm. His son succeeded to the title and as head of the business.

Middle-class, and indeed working-class *individuals*, rising in the world, could be extremely powerful. But what was the position of the middle class, as a *class*? In the depressed conditions of the 1930s the distinction between the upper-middle class and the lower-middle class was quite sharp. Those in lower-middle-class occupations – white-collar workers and primary schoolteachers, for example – had less job security than at probably any time since the middle of the nineteenth century. Those in upper-middle-class occupations would on the whole still continue to command good fees, and many, particularly doctors and solicitors, especially those who dealt with upper-class clients, were in a good position to cross the frontier into the upper class itself. The various professional organizations, whether established voluntarily or by statute, exercised control over standards and recruitment within the professions, and could operate a certain pressure-group influence on government and through sponsored members of parliament. But in the end, middle-class groups, whether upper- or lower-, had, essentially, influence rather than power. Most of the major decisions were taken by limited élites largely drawn from the upper class, whose decisions could indeed affect, if indirectly, the lives of middle-class people, though these in turn were much more effectively insulated from national political and economic decisions than were the working class.

The British working class was more highly unionized than that of either of the other two countries being studied. Free collective bargaining was by now widely accepted throughout most of British industry and in this way, through its organized representatives, the

British working class did have some little power in mitigating the full rigour of market forces and the self-interested demands of employers. The Labour Party was the official Opposition, though few influential Labour leaders came from anything like a typically working-class background. Official Labour representatives served on government commissions and committees, and one or two could now expect to receive knighthoods, a possible indicator of future individual movement towards the upper class, though no great help to the working class itself. The vicissitudes of unemployment policy in the thirties illustrate well how much, and how little power the working class possessed. The most hated facet of unemployment policy was the family means test, whereby all possible sources of family income were taken into account when assessing the amount of unemployment assistance. Working-class resentment was powerless in face of government determination to enforce the humiliating system, yet organized protests did secure some amendments in the new Unemployment Assistance Act of 1934, and, overall, unemployment insurance benefits ran at a consistently higher level than did health insurance benefits, over which there was little or no agitation. Organized working-class protest, then, could achieve something, probably uniquely when compared with similar efforts in France and the United States. But it must always be remembered that there was a great deal of upper-class and middle-class sympathy over the central social issue of unemployment.

POWER IN FRANCE

By comparison, France in the 1930s was characterized by an even tighter control of the positions of real power, particularly in finance and industry, by a distinctive upper class, though mediated by the strong influence over the National Assembly exercised by the provincial upper-middle class; in all areas the working class appears considerably weaker than its British counterpart. Thanks to the work of Professor Dogan, we have some useful statistical information on the social origins of French deputies and ministers (see table overleaf[12]).

The disproportionate strength of the upper class (nobility and high bourgeoisie together) is very apparent. However, the point is almost certainly overstated since a proportion of those classified by Dogan on occupation grounds as *high bourgeoisie* were probably perceived by themselves and French society as being middle-class rather than

| | SOCIAL ORIGIN OF DEPUTIES IN PERCENTAGES | | SOCIAL ORIGIN OF MINISTERS IN PERCENTAGES |
	1919	*1936*	*1899–1940*
Nobility	10	5	4
High Bourgeoisie	30	24	37
Middle Bourgeoisie	35	36	33
Small Bourgeoisie	15	20	17
Working Class	10	15	7
No information	—	—	2

upper-class. Other evidence, some of which is developed below, suggests the very tenacious hold of the provincial upper-middle class on ordinary parliamentary seats; though, of course, a parliamentary seat carried influence rather than power. The *small bourgeoisie* of Dogan's classification includes small tradesmen, artisans and peasants. The weak position of the working class is very clear. If we move from social origins (i.e. classification by parents' occupation or status) to men actually in working-class occupations, we find that even after the Popular Front victory of 1936 there were only 51 working men in the National Assembly, 8.5 per cent of the total: 37 of these were communists, out of a total Communist Party strength in the Assembly of 77; although the Socialists had a total of 145 deputies, only 12 of these were manual workers.[13]

Instead, now, of taking one entire cabinet as I did for Britain, I am going to attempt the same sort of biographical survey of all those Frenchmen who achieved the office of Prime Minister during the thirties; it was in the nature of French politics that almost all of those who from time to time surfaced as Prime Minister spent most of the rest of their time in some other major cabinet office.

Camille Chautemps came from an old established Savoy family. His uncle was a Senator, and his father both a former minister and vice-president of the Senate. He was educated at the lycée Charlemagne then at the lycée Marceau of Châtres, where his mother was a substantial property-owner.[14] His successor as Prime Minister, André Tardieu, was even more distinctively upper-class. As one of his biographers put it: 'spoiled child, privileged child, André Tardieu was the *gosse de riche* [rich kid] who went out to play in the Parc Monceau'[15] – the exquisite small park in one of the most exclusive parts of Paris, where even today governesses and nursemaids can be seen taking out the children of the very rich. After a brilliant academic career Tardieu went into the French Foreign Office but, with total aristocratic self-confidence, he shortly pulled out to become a journalist, writing in particular for the French establishment daily, *Le Temps*. In 1896 his father had published a copious volume tracing the family's history as leaders of Parisian society back to the seventeenth century; his mother was Charlotte d'Arpentigny de Malleville. Tardieu was followed by one of those occasional Prime Ministers whom nobody has heard of, the Alsatian, Théodore Steeg. He, in turn, was followed by the man everyone has heard of.

Pierre Laval, who was to become one of the most hated men of the Third Republic, is sometimes described as a peasant. In fact his parents owned a hotel, together with a café, a butcher's shop, a stable with five horses, and also ran the local coach service in the village of Chateldon in Puy-de-Dôme. Laval went to the local communal school, then took a job on his father's coach service; however his talents were such, as also the possibilities for mobility within the French system, that some local notables persuaded his father to send Pierre as an external pupil to the Lycée St Louis in Paris. Laval followed a somewhat restless career, moving to two other lycées, then to the lycée Ampère (where history was taught by Édouard Herriot, who became one of the leading statesmen of the 1920s) to study science. Laval then took a law degree at Dijon; he married the daughter of a deputy who was also granddaughter of the mayor of Chateldon. He joined the Bar, made a name for himself defending trade unionists, and, at the same time, a good deal of money playing the French stockmarket. In effect, through wealth and connections, he became, his biographer in the French parliamentary dictionary tells us, 'lord of the manor of Chateldon'; he also, a theme to look out for in French power politics, owned a newspaper. In 1914 he was elected deputy for the Seine. In origins, no doubt, Laval was not above the middle of the middle class; but he was certainly moving upwards.

With Édouard Herriot himself, we seem to go deeper into popular France. His grandfather had retired as a corporal and married a seamstress. His father served in the 1859 campaign in Italy and there conceived a great passion for the classics. His uncle was a priest. Herriot made his way up the élite educational system to the École Normale Superieure where he was top of his year at the age of twenty-two. He became established as a famous teacher at the lycée Ampère in Lyons, where he married one of his pupils, the daughter of a local upper-middle-class family. He became a municipal councillor and then was mayor of Lyons from 1905 till his death, with an interruption of only one month. Herriot can be placed firmly within the provincial middle class which numerically dominated French parliamentary politics. Joseph Paul-Boncour, however, was, quite definitely, from within the borders of the upper class. His father was doctor to Élie-Roger-Louis de Talleyrand-Périgord, Prince de Chalais, duc de Périgord, and belonged himself to a family of doctors, notaries and administrators. Paul-Boncour's mother belonged to a monarchist and Catholic Norman family which traced its lineage back to William the Conqueror – a boast as common among certain French aristocrats as it was among British ones.

With Édouard Daladier, we return again in that middle, or lower-middle-class milieu, where education and marriage produce upward mobility. Daladier's father was a baker and municipal councillor at Carpentras in Vaucluse. While the elder of the two sons went into the family business, Édouard showed great scholarly talent in winning bursaries for himself. After going to the lycée at Carpentras he went as an internal student to the lycée Ampère where he was taught by Herriot. From there the road led to the École Normale Supérieure; as a *professeur* Daladier was renowned at three different lycées in Nîmes, Grenoble and Marseilles. He founded two newspapers, became mayor of Carpentras, then married the daughter of a Paris doctor and was just about to start teaching in a Paris lycée when he was asked by the Radicals to stand for Avignon where he was elected in 1919.

Continuing to work our way through the rapid succession of French Prime Ministers of the 1930s, we come to Albert Sarraut. In Britain it was customary to speak of the 'press lords'; perhaps for France one should invent the term 'bourgeoisie of the press'. Sarraut, who became a deputy in 1902 at the age of thirty, and his brother Maurice (who became a senator in 1913) were closely associated with the most powerful political journal in the South West, the Radical *La Dépêche de Toulouse*. Sarraut's successor, Gaston Doumergue, came from an old established Calvinist family of wealthy peasant proprietors and wine growers in Gard. Doumergue went first to the communal school then at twelve he was sent as an internal student (always more expensive than being an external student) to the lycée at Nîmes. After he took his baccalauréat he studied law in Paris and was called to the Bar in Nîmes in 1885. If Doumergue's origins place him outside the national upper class (though his place in a *local* Protestant upper class, is significant) no such doubts attached to his successor Pierre-Etienne Flandin, whose family (formerly called Flandin des Aubues) rated three other entries in the French Biographical Dictionary, namely those of his father, grandfather and great uncle. His grandfather's grandfather had been a doctor; his father was first a deputy and then a senator. Pierre-Etienne Flandin studied at the lycée Carnot, took a diploma from the École des Sciences Politiques, a doctorate in law, and became an advocate at the Court of Appeal in Paris. For Flandin there need be no nonsense about serving as a municipal councillor or mayor: in May 1914 he was elected a deputy for Yonne, despite, or perhaps because of, the fact that he had just reached the legal age of twenty-five. Flandin was a trained pilot and served as such for the first year of the war before being allocated to political and staff duties. Fernand Bouisson is another of the lesser-knowns, perhaps in part because of his relatively undistinguished social origins. He was the son of the owner of a tannery in Provence. He had no higher education but became a director of the family business, and also a municipal councillor, and then mayor of his home town of Aubagne.

France's only socialist Prime Minister before the end of the Second World War was Léon Blum, head of the Popular Front government of 1936. Blum came from an Alsatian Jewish family which had established a prosperous book-selling business in Paris. Blum had a brilliant educational career and had already established himself as a writer and intellectual of distinction before the First World War. He also had a brilliant career in the law and served as a French government lawyer throughout the period of the First World War, coming directly into politics only at the end of the war. Blum, though his Jewishness was always a target for political opponents, is in many ways the prototype of the French meritocratic middle-class figure, presenting the manners and style of the intellectual aristocracy.

Let us persevere as far as the man who was called to the premiership after the outbreak of war, for his antecedents tell a fascinating story of nineteenth-century French social mobility. Paul Reynaud's was a long-established family of prosperous peasants in the French Alps. His grandfather was mayor of the village of St Paul and his grand uncle a doctor. His father went to college, but as an external pupil in order to save money. In 1857 at the age of seventeen he went to seek his fortune in Mexico and in fact returned eighteen years later a rich man, able to build himself a country mansion and take a flat in Paris. He now married the daughter of the most important man in the valley, a banker and mayor of Barcelonnette; this marriage Reynaud himself in his memoirs describes as 'a social promotion'.[16] While the father continued with his Mexican enterprises, the young Reynaud was brought up in Paris where he went to the same school as the Rothschilds. At his father's insistence he did two years at the École des Hautes Etudes Commerciales, then, as was fitting in this high bourgeois member of the upper class he turned to the law. As was also typical of certain members of his class, Reynaud travelled a great deal in England and was much given to dropping little hints about his familiarity with British ways.

Sixteen ministries in a decade (some of our potted biographees served as Prime Minister more than once): that was a symptom of the well-known weakness in the French political executive. The vacuum was filled by the French higher civil service, and, in some degree, by the interlocking group of financial magnates, the 'two-hundred-and-something families'. Where did the top civil servants come from? The high road ran through the private École Libre des Sciences Politiques, whose expensive fees confined entry to the very rich. Candidates from the 'Sciences Po.' dominated entry to the most prestigious and powerful Civil Service departments: the *Conseil d'État*, the *Quai d'Orsay* (Ministry of Foreign Affairs), the *Inspection des Finances*, and the *Cours des Comptes*. In the period 1901–35 113 out of 117 entrants into the Conseil d'État were from the 'Sciences Po.' which, in the same period, also provided 246 out of 280 entrants into the Foreign Ministry, 202 out of 211 entrants into the Inspection des Finances, and 82 out of 92 entrants into the Cours des Comptes.[17]

The most potent symbol of the power of the upper class was the control over the Bank of France exercised by the general assembly of the two hundred largest share-holders and by the fifteen Regents chosen by this assembly. A law of 24 July 1936, one of the main achievements, such as it was, of the Popular Front government, replaced the assembly of two hundred by an assembly of all share-holders and replaced the fifteen Regents by a council of twenty technical experts responsible to the government. The reality was that the Bank of France remained a private institution dominated by the major share-holders and still very much under the influence of the traditional families who had sat in 'the armchairs of the regents', the Vernes, the Mallets, the Rothschilds, the Wendels.[18] Private wealth dominated the vast nationalized enterprises, in part because of the weakness of political authority. Although the famous *Crapouillot* article on 'the Two-Hundred Families' went in for elegant rhetoric and a certain exaggeration, it was all in all a fine piece of investigative journalism, which built up a convincing biographical description of the families overlapping in their control of state enterprises, financial institutions, private industries and international corporations. Among the most influential names, apart from those already mentioned, were: de Neuflize, Tinardon, Duchemin, de Vogue, Mirabaud, Peugot, Hottinguer, Rothschild, Lebon, Dreux, Laurent, Cambon, Cordier, Benac, Schwob, d'Héricourt, de Tarde, Thion de la Chaume and Ville le Roux. Most representative of all, said *Crapouillot*, was the Belgian-originated, French-based and truly European family of Empain, subject, over forty years later, of a sensational kidnap case.[19]

Yet, a complex republican and democratic country such as France did set limits on the power of the upper class. The Popular Front government, certainly, faced the determined and, in the main, successfull resistance of representatives of this class. But it also faced the opposition, or, at best, neutrality, of large sections of the French population. Members of the upper class did a great deal to establish the Daladier government in power in the aftermath of the collapse of the Popular Front experiment, but were greatly aided by the very weaknesses of the experiment itself. The massive study by Jean-Noël Jeanneney (himself, it may be noted, the scion of an established upper-class family of public servants and academics) of *François de Wendel and the Republic: Money and Power 1914–1940* establishes clearly the extent of, and the limits on, the power of the French grand bourgeoisie. Undoubtedly de Wendel believed that 'what was good for the iron and steel industry, and particularly for his enterprises, was good for France.' In the 1920s he, more than anyone else, was the agent behind the political manoeuvres which, without benefit of a General Election, changed what had been elected as a leftish government (the *Cartel des Gauches*), into the rigidly right-wing government formed by Raymond Poincaré in 1926. But (at the risk of being repetitious) the Cartel had foundered in the first place for reasons deeply rooted in French society. Jeanneney's well-argued and convincing thesis is that de Wendel and his like were given the opportunity to exercise power by the post-war upsets to the stability of French society, the ignorance among politicians of contemporary economic problems, and the general weaknesses of the left. 1926, in any case, was an exceptional high-water mark, and, despite all the mythology of the Popular Front, such direct political influence was not again exercised in the 1930s. But certainly when it came to getting rid of a left-wing government, or the threat of the revival of one, de Wendel and his like added all the weight accruing from their wealth, ownership of newspapers, and tenure of positions of power.[20] Wendel's history, writes Jeanneney,

> sharply confirms the autonomy of the political sector from economic and financial forces and confirms the pointlessness of trying to explain the former entirely or even principally by the latter, and the falsity of giving too much importance to any one powerful magnate, or to the obscure and persistent designs of several dynasties, or of two hundred families: a useful slogan for some, and perhaps even a necessary one, *hic et nunc*, in the struggles for greater social justice, but quite unacceptable for the historian.[21]

The slogan of the 'two hundred families', then, and the notion of individual magnates exercising direct power is unacceptable. What clearly remains, however, is the reality of an upper-class 'reservoir' whose members exercised a grossly disproportionate power over French life.

POWER IN THE USA

In the United States, Professor G. William Domhoff has been the leading present-day proponent of the view that America, since at least the 1930s, has had a governing élite, either drawn from, or controlled by, the upper class which he takes as comprising just over one half of one per cent of the total population. At one point Domhoff suggests that parental class position is not important in determining whether a person is a genuine member of the American upper class or not; elsewhere, he takes the more reasonable line that the children of those who have moved rapidly upwards into governing circles may or may not become members of the upper class, depending 'on the stock accumulation of their fathers, the schools they attend, and the persons they marry.'[22] Discussion of power in American society is made difficult by the persistence of geographical sectionalism and the jealous protection of states' rights, by the uncoordinated growth of Federal agencies and commissions, and by the opportunities which a twentieth-century society, still practising much of the morality of the wild frontier, offered for gangsterism, bossism and union racketeering. However, if we concentrate on positions of nationwide power we can see that, as in Britain and France, a disproportionate number of upper-class figures, as well as substantial numbers of upper-middle-class ones appear in the seats of power; figures from the lower-middle and the working class are conspicuously absent, though it was possible for someone who had risen rapidly out of such a milieu into, say, a top business position to move quite smoothly over to a top political position. To get at the reality of national power we do best to look at the Presidency, presidential advisers, the more important cabinet officers, the major Federal agencies, and the main business leaders. While individual members of Congress could often wield more influence than was the case with their French or British counterparts, Congress, because of the pluralistic nature of American society and because it does not serve as a necessary base for cabinet office, can properly be left out of any brief study of the main distribution of power.

Roosevelt and his predecessor, Herbert Hoover, came from different sections of the upper class.[23] The distribution of power around President Roosevelt demonstrates, on the one side, the strength of the upper class, and, on the other, the strength of sectional interests cutting across class and the degree of mobility within the American system. Many of Roosevelt's closest advisers were Republicans: John G. Winant, one of the most important organizers of the social security programme, came from an aristocratic New York family, was educated at Princeton, and joined himself to an aristocratic Princeton family by marrying the daughter of Eleanor Roosevelt's father's law partner. Francis Biddle was another Republican grandee who joined the Roosevelt team. Among other close advisers were A. A. Berle, Jnr, a corporation lawyer featured in the pages of the New York *Social Register*; Raymond Morley, a criminologist and Professor of Public Law at Columbia; Gerard Swope, head of General Motors; but also Supreme Court Justice Louis Brandeis, a proper Bostonian by education and residence, yet a Jew by birth and faith, and Felix Frankfurter, Jewish immigrant at the age of twelve and Law Professor at Harvard by the age of thirty. Roosevelt's Secretary for the Interior was the Republican aristocrat we have already met, Harold D. Ickes. His first Secretary of the Treasury (later succeeded by Dean Acheson and then by Henry Morgenthau, Jnr, another member of the Jewish upper class and a neighbour of Roosevelt's) was William H. Woodin, a Republican magnate from the American Car and Foundry Motor Company, a director of eight other institutions including the Federal Reserve Bank of New York, and a listee in the *Social Register*. Secretary for Labor was that perfect Bostonian 'clubwoman', Frances Perkins. It might have been a reflection of the manner in which the Great Crash and economic depression had thrust domestic concerns in front of international ones, that the Secretary of State, Cordell Hull, was not a member of the upper class, as Hoover's choice, Henry L. Stimson, Wall Street lawyer, New York Social Register, Yale *and* Harvard, had been. Hull was, however, an important figure in Tennessee, a barrister, judge, congressman, and senator, and his appointment, above all, represented the need for any government to contain one or two influential Southerners. Joseph Kennedy, at the Federal Securities Commission, we have already encountered; the Business Advisory Council, which acted as the government's liaison with big business, was organized by one of the best known of hereditary aristocrats, Averill Harriman, who subsequently became a dominant force in Roosevelt's National Recovery Administration.

The involvement in high politics of certain important business leaders is easy to detect. What of the direct economic power of these business leaders? Are they all, in any case, upper-class? Two theories about American society are particularly relevant here. The first postulated that the 'managerial revolution' was removing power from the owners of capital, placing it instead in the hands of salaried managers. The second, more romantically, argued that the mobility inherent in American society enabled men of the humblest origins to rise quickly to positions of business leadership. The second theory was soundly trounced by the historian William Miller, writing in 1949: 'More likely,' he wrote, 'poor immigrant and poor farm boys who become business leaders have always been more conspicuous in American history books than in the American business élite.' Miller suggested that fifty per cent of business leaders came from the 'upper class', forty-five per cent from the 'middle class', and only five per cent from the 'lower class'.[24] The growth of salaried management is not to be controverted: but owners were often also top managers, and top managers were often also major share-holders. At the end of the thirties 'thirty-six per cent of the directors of the top industrials were also key officers in their respective companies'; the top officers and directors of each of the ninety-seven largest manufacturing corporations, at a conservative estimate, 'collectively owned an average of seven per cent of the *total* number of shares in their own company'.[25]

At the national level, then, there was a disproportionate share of power to be found concentrated in the hands of an upper class. At the same time, in contrast with Britain, and, in lesser degree, with France the highly developed institutions of local democracy in America entailed a great deal of real power in regard to matters of immediate concern to 'middle' Americans. Certain trade union leaders had already established positions of considerable power for themselves, though that certainly did not necessarily involve any considerable accretion of power to industrial workers as a whole, many of whom were even more powerless than their counterparts in France, and most of whom had not yet established the position occupied by British workers.

INCOME, WEALTH AND OCCUPATION

With regard to income, the situation in the three countries was slightly different. For manual workers *in employment* real wages were highest in America and lowest in France. Sharp distinctions between working-class incomes and middle-class incomes were clearest in Britain. True, workers in certain trades, such as printing, could earn as much as some white-collar workers at the bottom of the lower-middle class: but the crude reality can be seen in the difference between the average industrial *wage* in the thirties of just under £3 a week (about £150 a year) and the average annual *salary* of £350.[26] In France, differences between the petty bourgeoisie and the working class were often cultural rather than economic. In both France and America the big inequalities appear more clearly further up into the professional and business middle class. Since in all countries the upper class supported itself from investment income rather than from 'earned' income, it is not easy to present simple contrasts between its economic position and that of the middle class. What is true is that those professional jobs in the law, banking, medicine and government, which tended to go anyway to those with upper-class backgrounds, also yielded the sort of very high incomes which made possible the acquisition of substantial investments. France, with a much lower gross national income than the two Anglo-Saxon countries, had far fewer really rich people[27] than had Britain and America, which, naturally, had the most; there, in 1939, the top 1 per cent of all individuals owned 30.6 per cent of the wealth and the top 0.5 per cent owned 28 per cent of the wealth.

Such figures are familiar enough. Many books, and many tables, present the facts of income and wealth distribution. There would be little profit in quoting them extensively here: income statistics by themselves simply tell us that certain types of job are much better paid than others; wealth statistics alone simply tell us that wealth is divided in a grossly unequal way. Our question is whether or not social class is at the root of these inequalities. Taken in the context of everything that has been said so far, and remembering that there must always be an element of circularity in the relationship between class on the one side and income and wealth on the other (joining a higher income group *may* mean joining a higher class) the implication is that social class (as distinct, in particular, from natural talent) was indeed the most significant factor. This will emerge more clearly when we look at differences in lifestyles and material circumstances. To assist later study of the *changing* reality of class some simple points bear repetition now. The greatest inequalities at the top were to be found in the United States, but already there was an overall diffusion of relative affluence, so that the divide between middle class and working class was not so obvious as in Britain; on the other hand, at the very bottom of the social scale deprivation was very stark indeed. In France and in Britain, to be middle-class was usually to be comfortably off, save that among the French petty bourgeoisie many were no better off than the manual workers. To be upper-class, anywhere, was to have the wherewithal to indulge, at an early age, in the public service.

Central to class, and what class is thought to be, is occupation. Central to occupation are certain styles of life which become among the most important external indicators of the significance of class. There is no tautology here for in this book I shall be looking at working conditions over forty or fifty years: it is possible for jobs to move up or down the social scale; it is possible for conditions in a job once, say, firmly regarded as working-class, to move towards those formerly regarded as characteristic of a middle-class occupation. However, for the 1930s, a reading of the various surveys and accounts of working-class life does suggest a distinctive commonality of working-class experience in all three countries. Without taking a sentimental or an heroic view of working-class life, one can see at once that industrial work was usually long, physically taxing, carried out in unpleasant conditions, and often tedious.

THE GEOGRAPHY OF CLASS

Conditions of work join with level of income or wealth in helping to determine other obvious external evidences of the realities of class. It is possible, just about, to imagine a society in which everyone lived in the same kind of house, in which no locality was allowed to fall into decay, in which no deliberately shoddy, nor any ostentatiously exclusive, housing was ever built. In fact, as is well known, there are in Britain, France and America vast areas of housing where at a glance one could pin a class category on the occupants of the entire district. A distinctive feature of urban development has been the way in which different areas have emerged as the habitats of different social groups.

While other aspects of class might be ignored in the United States, the significance of the geography of class was well understood; an excellent contemporary source is the rigorous technical study published by the Federal Housing Administration in 1939 of *The Structure and Growth of Residential Neighborhoods in American Cities*. The report first of all discussed the inadequacies of the very simplistic concentric-circle theory of land-use, then fashionable among urban sociologists, which postulated that American cities had as their core a central business district, surrounded by a zone of working men's homes, surrounded by a residential zone, surrounded, finally, by the commuter zone. The report pointed out that since factories did not form a concentric circle around the central business district, thus neither did working men's homes encircle the central core of the city. The notion of the residential zone, it further pointed out, fell down in regard to both the Gold Coast of Chicago and Park Avenue in New York City 'where the socially élite pay the highest rents in the city for apartments located within a mile of the central business district.'[28] With regard to the so-called commuter zone, the report pointed out that 'some of these settlements are occupied by fine homes, but other towns may be middle class in character and others may consist of shacks', explicitly recognizing the existence of an upper class, a middle class and an under class. In every city there was bound to be at least one cluster of blocks in which the average rents paid were the highest in the city. From these high-rent poles, there was a gradation downwards on all sides, with successive rings of blocks of lower and lower average rent right down to the worst slums in the city. However, in some cities there was just one main high-rent area. In small cities or cities of slow growth this might be located near the centre of the city as in Charleston, South Carolina; Zanesville, Ohio; Santa Fé, New Mexico; and Portland, Maine. But in other cities the highest rent area was to be found on the periphery of one sector of the city, as in Wichita and Topeka, Kansas; Des Moines, Iowa; Washington DC; Atlanta, Georgia; Wilmington, Delaware; Greensboro, North Carolina; and Akron, Ohio. A substantial chapter of the report was, inevitably, almost exclusively concerned with problems of race and the manner in which the very worst housing tended to be the preserve of the blacks: however, the emphasis is on southern cities since as yet blacks were not very widely diffused among northern cities.

In my discussion of Hollywood images we encountered James Stewart in the character of a journalist from South Bend, together with Katherine Hepburn as the upper-class lady who thought that South Bend was a dance. The real South Bend, Indiana, together with the adjoining town of Mishawaha, was, for the bulk of its population, a town of automobile factories, machine shops, engineer-works, clothing and shoe factories, all of which gave employment to both men and women: seventy-one per cent of the male inhabi-tants surveyed in 1932 were factory workers, as were sixty-six per cent of the female inhabitants.[29] A survey of 1936 reveals the range of houses in this working-class industrial area, from those of an obviously 'lower-class' character to those occupied by families aspiring towards 'middle- class' status:

> The houses of the workers in one section of South Bend were frame cottages near the factories, making it possible for those employed to walk to and from their work. In the central part of the city the homes occupied by the workers were old residences that were deteriorating into tenements or rooming houses. The third area selected was one of small modern homes that the fami-lies had been interested in buying on the instalment plan. In Mishawaha, two-storey one-family homes were most common in the center of the city, while in most of the outlying districts smaller bungalows, surrounded by well-kept lawns and gardens, housed the workers interviewed.[30]

From Mishawaha let us jump to Paris: why not? Any tourist with half a nose in his guide book and half an eye for the urban environ-ment knows that the *arrondissements* and suburbs to the north east, east, and south east, had been solidly working-class since the be-ginning of the century. Try, for instance, a stroll along the rue Lénine in Ivry-sur-Seine. In the thirties the sixteenth- and seven-teenth-century palaces of Le Marais formed part of a particularly noisome working-class slum. Middle-class suburbs developed to the west, and it was in the thirties that the upper class began to move from St Germain-des-Prés to the sixteenth arrondissement, so con-venient for the Champs Elysées and the Parc Morceau (in the eighth arrondissement). Distinctive class areas can just as readily be mapped out for the smaller French towns as well.[31]

London's 'villages' are well known: those of the East End, other working-class areas south of the river – Lambeth, Brixton, Battersea, Wandsworth – giving way eventually to the new 'metro land' of the inter-war years, the neat estates of owner-occupied houses financed by low-interest mortgages and inhabited by the expanding lower-middle class; upper-class Mayfair and Kensington; middle-class Hampstead with upper-class pockets and working-class patches.[32] Throughout Britain, certain place-names automatically indicated definite class characteristics: Bognor Regis – retired upper-class; Birkenhead – disorganized working-class. Nowhere was this more true than in Scotland. The Gorbals in Glasgow immediately suggested the deprived lower-working class; Kelvinside meant the aspiring middle class, with phoney anglified accents. History had shaped the residential map of Edinburgh. Princes Street Gardens and the railway had become a social chasm between the Old Town, now left to the working class, and the elegant Georgian New Town. Nineteenth-century industrial developments had brought concentrations of working-class tenements in such districts as Gorgie and Easter Road. Morningside shared the odium of Kelvinside: 'sex', the local joke went, was what the people of Morningside put their coal in. Edinburgh was very much a town of lawyers, medical men, academics, civil servants, and agents and entrepreneurs of all descriptions: it was a middle-class town with a strong upper-class element, and with its solid stone-built houses, elegant tenements in the centre, detached two-storey houses further out, it looked the part. Britain stood out from the other two countries through the amount of public-authority housing already built in the 1930s. In most towns, and even in quite small villages, new frontiers of working class life were being established: new estates, often of well appointed houses, but houses which were nonetheless distinctively plainer than those in the private middle-class estates, were growing up, usually on the outskirts of towns and often very far from the normal urban amenities.

Ivry-sur-Seine, South Bend, Indiana, Gorgie: where has the argument taken us? Earlier, my case was that people in the thirties did indeed believe, with various particular reservations and qualifications, that class, in its different national manifestations, existed. At the beginning of this chapter I was endeavouring to demonstrate some of the concrete inequalities in the distribution of power and wealth associated with those very same classes of people's thoughts and imagery. Now I have been discussing the geography of class: patterns of housing development, together with the prevailing housing standards in any particular individual 'neighbourhood',

are about the best on-the-ground evidence we have of the actual
realities of class. (It is a matter of physical geography as well as
social geography: elegant houses were built along the sides of hills;
slums and shacks grew up in valleys, alongside railway lines; some
of the most miserable of America's 'lower class' were to be found in
the mountains of West Virginia, the dust bowls of Oklahoma, and
the swamps of Louisiana; in France and Britain the prevailing winds
are from the west – so lower-class districts tended to grow up to the
east of big cities, collecting all the soot and grime.)

LIFE CHANCES AND LIFESTYLES

Carr-Saunders and Caradog Jones, no longer denying that classes
existed, insisted that class distinctions were diminishing, that members of different classes were increasingly resembling each other. Undoubtedly many of the forces within what social historians now
usually agree to call 'modernization' were pushing towards a greater
standardization and homogeneity throughout societies: mass communications, mass production, high wages allied to high consumer
spending (principally in the USA) meant a greater sharing of similar
entertainments and a greater commonality in dress and appearance.
But these changes, vitally important, of course, in the evolution of
contemporary society, impinged only marginally on the basic
realities of class being discussed here, as would have been obvious to
Carr-Saunders and Caradog Jones had they followed George Orwell
to Wigan Pier or J. B. Priestley on his *English Journey*, or simply
looked around them, or even just absorbed the abundant newsreel
material on show in the cinemas (and available now as invaluable
primary source material on this very matter). Being less guilty about
class, the French, more secure in their ideas of a common citizenship
and of a hierarchy of talent sponsored by the state, and the Americans, still confident about the possibilities for the able and energetic
to get to the top, were less concerned to deny the realities of social
inequality.

Many of the most important of these, which can be grouped together as 'inequalities in life-chances', do not exactly correlate with
social classes as popularly conceived. Educational opportunity, or
lack of it, offers the closest correlation, inevitably, since educational
provision is one of the contexts in which class must be set, as well
as an indicator of the inequalities arising from class. It is in the
realm of education that the distinctiveness of the upper class in all

three countries stands out most strongly, as well as the relatively better opportunities of the American working class (as against the American 'lower class' and underclass) and the deprivation of the French 'popular classes' and working class, and the British working class.[33] In health, morbidity, adult mortality, infant mortality, nutrition and material conditions generally, the significant lines of distinction were, in Britain, between the working class on the one side, and the middle and upper classes on the other, and, in France, between the lesser peasantry, small independent proprietors and working class on one side, and the middle-middle class and above on the other.[34] There was then another more important divide between the upper-working class, and the unskilled and casual workers who were worst off of all. This was the kind of line which obtained in America, with the racial minorities being a substantial component of those on the wrong side of it. This less than clear-cut situation can perhaps be illuminated by introducing the carefully decanted phrase used much later by Richard Crossman: in his diaries Crossman spoke of himself as enjoying 'a facility of freedom and an amplitude of life' denied to most others.[35] This phrase, I believe, goes to the heart of the realities of class. In all three countries only the upper class enjoyed this 'amplitude of life' in the full sense intended by Crossman. But substantial sections of the various middle classes, and, in America, some of the best-off workers enjoyed something of it too. Freedom and amplitude became notably lacking as one moved down through the working class. 'As I say,' one former miner told Melvyn Bragg, 'it was rough. As far as meat was concerned, I know meat was cheap, but you just couldn't buy it. So therefore what we used to have, either dry bread and jam or butter and bread. If you got butter on your bread, you didn't get any jam. If you got jam on your bread, you didn't get any butter. If you fried, and very rare, a little bit of bacon or something, then when the fat was cold you put that on your bread.' Three different working-class interviewees told Melvyn Bragg the same story of how, by their own decision, they felt bound to miss out on educational opportunity. 'I had a feeling I might pass and I thought if I passed I know the scholarship's free but you got to have better clothes and there's a bit of uniform to buy and there's books and schoolbag and even though I knew me mother would somehow manage to get the money some way honestly as she always did I didn't feel like imposing on her anymore so I deliberately made some mistakes in my exams.'[36]

Some class differences may not necessarily involve inequalities, yet in one way or another it usually turns out that they do. High

culture is not necessarily 'better' than popular culture, and the enjoyment of much popular culture was anyway, in the thirties, shared
by the middle and working classes; where inequality enters is in the
diminished access to high culture as one moves down the social scale.
Accent, as a badge of class, is often thought to be a British phenomenon. Nothing could be further from the truth – even if it is difficult
to imagine the fuss over 'aitches' taking place in any other country.
The phenomenon, certainly, is confused in America by the great
range of sectional accents, so that, for example, a very rich southern
white could sound very like a very poor southern black. But without
any doubt at all there was a distinctive upper-class American accent,
or more accurately a very limited range of different accents running
from Boston through New York to Philadelphia. And there were
certain accents which, combined with poor grammatical construction, were distinctively lower class. Nor does it take great linguistic
skills to detect the variation in accents to be found in France. 'What
indicates that we are definitely among the people,' wrote Louise-
Marie Ferré,

> is above all language, often extremely gross, even among *com-
> mercants* of correct appearance whose style of life much more
> suggests the *petit bourgeoisie*. The use of the *patois* in certain
> provinces would also be a sign of class. Without doubt, the
> medium merchant, the medium industrialist, having reached the
> level of the *petit bourgeoisie* would also know the *patois*; they use
> it during their conversations with the servants and the peasants;
> they do not speak it amongst themselves.[37]

The last point is the significant one: use of the *patois*, variation in
accent and speech, was recognized as relating to social position
(again there is no exact correlation with class as popularly perceived,
but certainly a rough-and-ready correlation, since popular perceptions, also, fluctuated somewhat). An upper-class accent was the
sound of superiority, and was meant to be so. It could be mimicked,
but it was scarcely a cause for real hilarity. In Britain middle-class
business or professional people in the provinces might well speak
with a strong provincial accent, distinguished only from the working
classes around them, perhaps, by the 'educated' element contained
in it, and the correctness of the grammar; but very many British
middle-class families spoke with, or aspired towards a version of
the standard upper-class accent. If you could not always quite tell
what class a man belonged to by his accent, you could certainly tell
where his aspirations lay.

CLASS AND POLITICS

A person's command of power and authority, his income and wealth, his home, his lifestyle, his life chances, his education, his share in the amplitude of life, are all primary indicators of his social class; his politics are not. Much confusion has been spread by the determination to identify social classes rigidly with political ideologies: thus the upper class is declared conservative, the middle class liberal, and the working class socialist. Class *is* important in political behaviour, probably the most important single determinant of voting preferences in the 1930s, but it is not the same thing as political behaviour. As the forms of class differ in the three countries, so such correlations as there are vary. Historians of nineteenth-century Britain have poll books from which to make precise judgements about voting behaviour and class affiliation; the secret ballot has proved a bit of a nuisance for historians of a more recent period. Since opinion surveys began only at the end of the decade, and were then confined to America, most conclusions have to be based on political geography: how do predominantly working-class areas vote, how do farming areas vote, etc.?

The classic work of Georges Dupeux has thrown much light on the French scene.[38] Districts containing substantial owners of land tended, he noted, to vote to the right, though by no means completely so. Areas of peasant ownership, however, betrayed no consistent voting patterns. Of the areas of peasant proprietorship, those in Brittany and Normandy, in the West Pyrenees, and in the southern part of the Massif Centrale, were firmly wedded to the right; those in such western regions as the Landes, Charentes and the western borders of the Massif Centrale, together with La Beauce and Le Berry in the north, and part of the Alpine region to the south east, tended to vote Radical. In the interior of the Aquitaine basin, and, above all, on the northern slopes of the Massif Centrale the peasant proprietors actually tended towards the extreme left. As far as areas inhabited by the industrial working class were concerned, the north (i.e. Lille and its surroundings in particular) and the Paris region inclined to the extreme left; however the Champagne region tended to the Radicals; and workers in the eastern part of France had a clear preference for right-wing parties. Dupeux noted that areas consistently voting communist or socialist were certainly strongly working-class in composition; but that not all clearly working-class areas voted communist or socialist, this being especially true in eastern France. Summing up region by region, Dupeux pointed out that in the east of France both the working class and the peasant proprietors voted for the right, that on the northern slopes of the Massif Centrale both the peasants and the workers together tended towards left-wing candidates, and that on the shores of the Mediterranean peasant proprietors, industrial workers and agricultural workers tended to vote towards the left. Dupeux had noted, incidentally, that agricultural labourers did not vote consistently across the country. Dupeux's conclusion was that regional particularisms predominated over class as prime movers in political behaviour.

To illuminate this point further he reiterated that the three major right-wing blocks in the electoral map of 1936 were to be found in the west, a densely populated peasant region, the east, a densely populated, predominantly working-class area, and the south of the Massif Centrale, a lightly populated peasant area. This mapping was found to coincide exactly with another mapping indicating the areas of greatest religious vitality. Feeling that the clue must lie in historical tradition, Dupeux now compared the electoral map of 1936 with that of 13 May 1849. The two maps revealed the same patches of right-wing support along the Atlantic coastline and along that of the Channel, in Alsace and Lorraine, and in the southern part of the Massif Centrale. They also showed the same patches of left-wing support in a great semi-circular zone running from Lot-et-Garonne to Saone-et-Loire crossing the Dordogne, Haute-Vienne, la Corrèze, la Creuse, l'Allier, le Cher and la Nievre, and also the same patches of left-wing support in the south east and along the left bank of the Rhone. The only places where there were striking differences were the Paris region, the north region, and the Mediterranean coastline, which in 1849 did not show the strong left-wing support which was so apparent in the map of 1936. But these were the very areas affected by the great economic upheavals of the later nineteenth century. Thus Dupeux produced another map indicating which departments had a stable population (i.e. a high percentage of the inhabitants were born there) and those which did not. From this the conclusion was that right-wing voting tendencies coincided both with strong religious practice and with population stability. The left retained its own areas of stability, but gained the newly mobile areas, especially the Paris region, where class quite clearly was the most significant feature in voting patterns.

For America, we have the pioneer survey conducted by Paul Lazarsfeld and his helpers in Erie County, Ohio, in 1940.[39] Inevitably the interviewees were divided up by 'socio-economic status' not by anything as indefinite and vulgar as class. These status groups were A (three per cent of the sample), B (fourteen per cent), C+

(thirty-three per cent), C (thirty per cent), and D (twenty per cent). The report noted that there were twice as many Republicans on the A level as on the D level, and that with each step down the socio-economic scale, the proportion of Republicans decreased and the proportion of Democrats correspondingly increased. There is a muddled echo of France and old Europe in the conclusion that religion to some extent cut across this direct socio-economic correlation. Sixty per cent of Protestants and twenty-three per cent of Catholics had Republican voting intentions in May 1940 (the survey only measured intentions, or, more accurately, what people said were their intentions). This distinction seemed to depend more on history than on ethnicity, since German voters were split in almost exactly the same proportion between Protestants and Catholics. What did seem to be true was that 'out-group' elements (ethnic minorities) tended to look to the Democrats. Older Protestants tended to be more determined in their Republican allegiance as older Catholics appeared more determined in their allegiance to the Democrats. Another survey, conducted over a longer period of time, in New York City, also concluded that: 'social status, as described by income and religion, largely determines a person's vote and other aspects of his political behaviour. The voting trend in New York City over a long period appears to be a function of social status.'[40] Such surveys, however, don't really match up with the sketch of class, however fuzzy at the edges, that I have tried to draw. Taken with the general, though by no means exclusive, preference of trade unions for the Democratic party, they suggest a definite, but far from necessarily rigid, relationship between class and voting behaviour; as far as leadership was concerned, as we have noted, that could be just as likely to come from the upper class in the Democratic Party as in the Republican Party.

In the late nineteenth century, the working class in Britain had tended to vote Liberal, though in Lancashire, partly in hostile reaction to Irish immigration, it tended to vote Conservative, while in Scotland it was usually rather hostile to the Liberals. By the 1930s a fairly homogeneous picture had emerged of predominantly working-class areas tending to vote Labour:[41] the Conservative vote remained strong in Lancashire, whereas in Scotland the hostility to Liberalism had provided a fertile soil in which Labour support took root. Yet throughout the thirties, the Conservatives were the majority party in Great Britain; clearly a good third of the working-class vote was going to that party. Left-wing intellectuals tend to speak contemptuously of this as the 'deference' vote – in his last piece as editor of the *New Statesman*, Anthony Howard (in 1978) wrote furiously about the 'obedience-from-below attitude that still disfigures British life'.[42] Whether the working-class Conservative vote can properly be called deferential at all, let alone whether such 'deference' is disfiguring, is more of a moot point than is sometimes allowed. It could, rather, indicate a sense of occupying a secure position within a stable hierarchy. Not so much deference, more what Ernest Bevin called 'poverty of desire' characterized the British working class in the thirties.

Yet undoubtedly the most striking feature of the British political landscape was the very existence of the Labour Party, deeply rooted as it was in working-class political culture.[43] It is in Britain that the correlation between class and political behaviour (though not political ideology) is at its strongest: in Labour clubs throughout working-class areas the political and social attitudes voiced might often be centrist in domestic affairs and chauvinist in overseas affairs, while in middle-class areas young people of socialist sympathies might well join the local Conservative Club for the best tennis and most hopeful dances.

What of the larger dimensions of general history? What was the connection, if any, between the class relationships peculiar to each country and the particular developments and crises which took place in these countries? Did the existence of classes always and everywhere entail conflict? Was every major conflict, in fundamentals, a class conflict? Or could recognized class relationships be a force for stability and social cohesion? First of all major political decisions in both Britain and France were most often made by members of the two slightly different upper classes whose origins and opinions have been discussed. In France such decisions were made within the limits set by Republican traditions and the influence exercised throughout the country and in the National Assembly by the diverse middle class committed to notions both of popular government and of economic liberalism. In Britain such decisions were made within a tradition of public service, and broadly with the active support of much of the middle class and the tacit support of a substantial proportion of the working class. United in its acceptance of the fundamental conventions of British society and politics, the British upper class was not wholly united in its political affiliations: four of Labour's leading figures in the thirties were from this class, Clement Attlee, Hugh Dalton, 'the red squire' – Sir Stafford Cripps, and G. R. Strauss. In America the upper class was not quite so homogeneous or united, and did not have the same commanding position.

Roosevelt and some of his closest colleagues were upper-class; but more and more, especially after 1934 when business leaders organized the American Liberty League to fight the New Deal, he had to face virulent upper-class opposition, as well as other kinds of resistances which were as much of a sectional as of a class nature.

Many of the major domestic national crises of the period do contain within them strong elements of class antagonism or at least of class interest and class solidarity, as do most of the local incidents of virulent conflict. The minority Labour government collapsed in August 1931 because a substantial minority within the cabinet agreed with the General Council of the TUC that ten-per-cent cuts in unemployment benefits were unacceptable; the government, in that sense, foundered on working-class solidarity. The cuts, and the whole economic package which went with them, were not a deliberately designed expression of upper-class self-interest, but they did represent the prevailing orthodoxies and prejudices of that class. Throughout the thirties unemployment was the major domestic issue: in the struggles over the administration of unemployment benefits the solidarity and awareness of the British working class was not in doubt; yet the continuing scandal of mass unemployment brought no concerted working-class action against the government and its upper-class base.

The 'events' of February 1934 in France involved marches on the National Assembly by right-wing demonstrators, fifteen of whom were killed, a change in the complexion of the government from centre-left to centre-right, and, in protest, an impressive one-day general strike. Most French historians are now agreed that there was no deliberate attempt at a right-wing *coup-d'état*;[44] the change of government was enough. The General Strike was a fine demonstration of working-class awareness and solidarity, but it is hard to argue that it was something inherent in French class relationships (as distinct, say, from specific economic and social circumstances and longer-term political traditions) which safeguarded France, unlike Germany and Italy, from fascism. The Popular Front electoral victory in May 1936 can certainly be plausibly represented as indicating a determined effort on the part of working-class voters, along with many petty bourgeois ones, to see their wrongs righted. But it certainly cannot be represented as an overwhelming surge of working-class sentiment. As Georges Dupeux has shown, the victory was simply brought about by a series of shuffles to the left on the part of certain groups of voters: some former Radical supporters now voted Socialist; some former Socialist voters now voted Communist.[45] In overall popular votes, the Popular Front majority was a very narrow one. Thus the primary political fact remained the essential moderate conservatism of the bulk of the large French middle-class and peasant vote. A primary social fact revealed by the spontaneous sit-in strikes which followed the election victory was the class awareness, yet remarkable docility, of the workers. Towards the end of the decade, as we have seen, upper-class elements intervened actively, with much middle-class support, to ensure that there would be no revival of the Popular Front experiment.

Growing working-class consciousness was undoubtedly evident in the expansion, after the formation of the CIO between 1935 and 1937, of industrial unionism in the United States. Much of the turmoil in American society can legitimately be seen as part of an upper-class reaction against the new (and as it seemed) uncharacteristic attempt of American workers to adopt class solutions to their problems. But the New Deal policies themselves have to be seen as belonging to upper-class attempts to solve the problems of the whole society, meeting along the way the needs of business, and adapting to the prejudices of the middle class as well as those of the majority of the upper class, and in no way as responses to conscious working-class pressure on its own behalf.

Violent conflict took three rather different forms in the three countries. In France, there were several clashes between working-class *political* demonstrators (usually Communist-led) and police in each case leading to a number of deaths. In America there were extremely brutal confrontations between *strikers* and police or company representatives, with many deaths resulting; running all the time in the background was the continuous vicious oppression of blacks by whites of all classes. In Britain violence of a very much lesser character involving no loss of life centred on demonstrations by the unemployed. Britain, with the most clearly defined class structure and highest degree of class consciousness, yielded the least in the way of class-related violence.

THE SIGNIFICANCE OF CLASS

What then is the overall significance of class in the 1930s? Clearly, in all three countries your life chances were affected by the class into which you were born. There was greatest formal opportunity for mobility upwards in America and France, and most actual mobility in America; but there was also scope for it in Britain. In every case, a middle-class background made rising into the upper class a reasonable aspiration; in every case, though this was least true in the United States, a working-class background made such an aspiration highly unreasonable. Britain, with the most developed class structure, was the most stable and cohesive society. America, with the least developed class structure, also seemed unlikely to succumb to internal conflict, largely because the multiplicity of conflicting interest groups had not fully resolved themselves into classes, and because the working class was not in itself a threat to stability, nor did it provoke a strong right-wing counter-threat. France was the country most seriously affected by internal stresses. It was not that the stabilizing element of a large and variegated middle class allied with the peasantry had disappeared; rather that in difficult economic conditions this element proved unduly conservative. The working class was not strong enough to secure anything like the modest share in social advance and political processes won by the British working class. It demonstrated without hope, and succeeded only in arousing a spirit of reaction in the rest of society. The single most significant division in British society was that between the middle class and the working class, though when it came to a question of who ruled the country that between middle class and upper class was also important. The single most significant social division in the United States was not a class one at all, but that between white and non-white; the main class divisions were between upper class and middle class, and between the underclass and the rest of society. In France the major distinction was between the working class and the rest; yet even so the ordinary working man revealed indifference, rather than active hostility, towards his employer. Events within the separate countries, and comparisons across them, cannot be explained solely by reference to class, but they certainly cannot be fully understood without reference to class.

Notes

1. G. William Domhoff, *Who Rules America?* (1967); E. Digby Baltzell, *Philadelphia Gentlemen: the Making of a National Upper Class* (1958); Gabriel Kolko, *Wealth and Power in America* (1962); Pierre Birnbaum,

La classe dirigèante française (1978); J. Westergaard and Henrietta Resler, *Class in a Capitalist Society: a Study of Contemporary Britain* (1975).

2. David Dilkes in Lord Butler, ed., *The Conservatives* (1977), p. 273. Unless otherwise stated, biographical information is from the Twentieth Century volumes of the *Dictionary of National Biography* (1949–71).

3. Viscount Swinton, *I Remember* (1948), p. 14.

4. Imperial War Museum, London, Haslam Papers: W. H. Haslam to J. Winder, 19 January 1941.

5. Viscount Avon, *Another World, 1897–1917* (1976).

6. W. L. Guttsman, *The British Political Elite*, (1968). The quotation which follows is from p. 319, and the figures cited are from p. 105. See also T. J. H. Bishop and R. Wilkinson, *Winchester and the Public School Elite* (1967), p. 37.

7. *Report of the Royal Commission on The Civil Service* (1931), paras. 250–6.

8. R. K. Kelsall, *Higher Civil Servants in Britain* (1955), pp. 16ff. This paragraph draws heavily upon Professor Kelsall's standard work.

9. Thomas Jones, *Whitehall Diary*, 2 vols. (1968–9), edited by R. K. Middlemass.

10. Charlotte Erickson, *British Industrialists: Steel and Hosiery 1850–1950* (1959).

11. J. M. Keynes, 'The Position of the Lancashire Cotton Trade', the *Nation*, 13 November 1926.

12. M. Dogan, *L'Origine sociale du personnel parlementaire français* (1967).

13. Jean Charlot, 'Les Elites politiques en France de la IIIe à la Ve République', *Archives Européennes de Sociologie*, XIV, no. 1 (1973).

14. Unless otherwise indicated, biographical information is from Balteau, *Dictionnaire de biographie française*, and Jean Jolly, *Dictionnaire des parlementaires français* (1960).

15. Gabriel Puaux, in introduction to *André Tardieu* (1957), by Louis Aubert *et al.*

16. Paul Reynaud, *Mémoires* (1960), pp. 21–35. For Paul-Boncour, see Joseph Paul-Boncour, *Entre deux Guerres: souvenirs de la IIIe République*, vol 1 (1945).

17. Charlot, *op. cit.*

18. See Henri Dubief, *Le déclin de la IIIe République* (1976), p. 187.

19. *Crapouillot*, March 1936.

20. Jean-Noel Jeanneney, *Francois de Wendel en République: l'argent et le pouvoir 1914–1940* (1975), pp. 612–14.

21. *Ibid*, p. 626.

22. Domhoff, *op. cit.*, p. 9.

23. See Baltzell, *op. cit.*, p. 228. Biographical information is from *Who was Who in America*.

24. William Miller, 'American Historians and the Business Elite', *Journal of Economic History* (1949), pp. 184–208. Detailed figures can be

found in chapter 5 of Mabel Newcomer, *The Big Business Executive* (1955).
25. Kolko, *op. cit.*, pp. 60–1.
26. John Stevenson, *Social Conditions in Britain between the Wars* (1977), pp. 21–34.
27. G. Lecarpentier, 'Revenus et fortunes privés en France et en Grande-Bretagne', *Revue Politique et Parlementaire* (1937), pp. 73–81.
28. Federal Housing Administration, *The Structure and Growth of Residential Neighborhoods in American Cities* (1939), p. 23. For this paragraph, see also pp. 31–2, 34, 56, 75–6.
29. Department of Labor, Women's Bureau, *The Effects of Depression on Wage Earners Families* (1932).
30. Department of Labor, Women's Bureau, *A Second Survey of South Bend* (1936), p. 6.
31. See, e.g., Charles Bettelheim and Suzanne Frère, *Une Ville française moyenne: Auxerre en 1950* (1950), especially the map on page 183 showing well the 'geography of class'.
32. For 'Hampstead' see the brilliant short essay of that title by F. M. L. Thompson in M. A. Simpson and T. H. Lloyd, *Middle Class Housing in Britain* (1977), pp. 86–113. In general see Alan Jackson, *Semi-detached London: Surburban Development, Life and Transport 1900–39* (1973).
33. Alain Girard, *La Réussite sociale en France* (1961); Rayon Boudon, *L'Inégalité des chances* (1974); Kurt Mayer, 'Recent Changes in the Social Structure of the United States', *Transactions of the Third World Congress of Sociology*, vol. III (1956).
34. See R. M. Titmuss, *Birth, Poverty and Wealth* (1943).
35. R. H. S. Crossman, *The Diaries of a Cabinet Minister*, vol. II (1976), p. 190.
36. Melvyn Bragg, *Speak for England* (1976), pp. 125, 152.
37. Louise-Marie Ferré, *Les Classes sociales dans la France contemporaine* (1934), p. 202.
38. Georges Dupeux, *Le Front populaire et les elections de 1936* (1959), pp. 158–71, on which this, and the next paragraph is based.
39. P. F. Lazarsfeld, Bernard Berelson and Hazel Gaudet, *The People's Choice*, 2nd edition (1948), pp. 18–22.
40. Gerhart E. Saenger, 'Social Status and Political Behavior', *American Journal of Sociology* (1945), pp. 103ff.
41. See especially John Stevenson and Chris Cook, *The Slump* (1978), pp. 94–113.
42. *New Statesman*, 31 March 1978.
43. See Ben Pimlott, *Labour and the Left in the 1930s* (1976).
44. See Dubief, *op. cit.*, pp. 67–78, and the authorities cited there.
45. Dupeux, *op. cit.*, p. 107.

PART TWO

As it Became: from the Second World War to the Present

11

The Second World War and Class:
the Case of Britain

There have been many changes since the 1930s, though not all have been in the same direction. However, underlying them, in all three countries, have been those long-term economic and technological transformations – sometimes described as 'modernization', or as the movement towards 'post-industrial society' – involving the growth of multi-national conglomerates, an accelerated 'managerial revolution', the emergence of highly sophisticated technologies, particularly in communications and computerization, a decline in the size of the traditional heavy industrial base, and a continued diffusion of higher living standards and production of new consumer goods. To historians, as to other ordinary people, short-term discontinuities have significance as well as long-term trends; and this, and the next two chapters, examine the immediate effects of the war and its aftermath on class relationships. I then turn to that period of cultural dislocation, centred on the early 1960s, the period of 'cultural revolution'.

As noted in the Introduction, social scientists have offered two opposing interpretations of recent developments in class relationships. Marxists argue that classes are becoming more polarized between the bourgeoisie or ruling class on the one side, and the working class (including more and more of those elements formerly regarded as middle-class) on the other, with a consequent intensification of social conflict. At the other extreme, sociologists of the contemporary conservative school argue that classes have been disintegrating into a continuous gradation of status groups or strata, contributing on the whole to harmony within society. Neither theory really begins to cover the nature of changes in class and class structure in the three countries, nor even holds good for any one of our three societies. In reality, a growing sense of belonging to a particular class can often coincide with a wider trend favourable to the diminution of class distinctions. There have been many signs of class consolidation, if not exactly polarization, yet at the same time there has been greater social mobility and some evidence of a disintegration of classes.

213

Since the 1930s, class relationships in Britain and in France have in some respects become more like those in the United States, while in other aspects of class America has begun to resemble Britain and France. But in all three countries, many national peculiarities have been preserved, or even extended. First, to war!

It is some years since I first made the case that the effects on a society of a twentieth-century total war can best be expressed by looking in turn at four *dimensions* of war; nothing published since has made me change my mind.[1] The four dimensions are: *destruction/disruption*, including direct damage, dislocation and disruption of peace-time patterns of behaviour, but also, as some 'disaster' studies have suggested, involving a 'reconstructive' effect, a desire to rebuild better than before; the *test* dimension, which arises from the challenge war presents to society, imposing new stresses upon it, and inducing the collapse of some institutions and the transformation of others; *participation* in the national cause by hitherto underprivileged groups who thereby make social gains; and the *psychological* dimension – total war is a great emotional experience, and tends to reinforce 'in-group' feelings and, in general, to render change acceptable.

The three societies experienced the war and its aftermath in rather different ways, of course. America was not invaded and occupied, as was France, nor was it bombed as were parts of Britain. Nonetheless the consensus among American historians who have given thought to the subject is that expressed by William Miller in his standard short textbook: 'Wartime prosperity sparked a social revolution in the United States which continued with increasing momentum in the post-war years.'[2] At the same time America was profoundly affected by the Cold War, which, rather than fostering social change, engendered a strong re-emphasis on traditional American ideologies. In France the disruption and upheavals of war appear most obvious. The German invasion in May 1940 led rapidly to an armistice, the occupation of the north and west, and the setting up of the collaborationist Vichy regime in the south and east; in 1942 the Germans took over direct control of the whole of France; then from 1944 the Liberation regime was in power. Wartime austerity and privation continued in the post-war years, and American-style affluence did not reach France until the middle or late 1950s. Pressures for the maintenance of the values of the Third Republic proved stronger than seemed likely in 1944; at the same time economic and technological developments brought some fundamental changes including the very rapid diminution in France's rural population; by 1960 it accounted for about fourteen per cent of the total, as compared with almost a third in the 1930s. Britain, an embattled island for a crucial phase in the war, yet not occupied, and not subject to the terrible strains of collaboration and resistance, produced most comment from contemporaries on the war's effects on class. Much that was traditional also remained untouched. Austerity continued into the post-war years, and, as in France, significantly higher levels of consumer spending began to appear only in the later fifties.

Vivienne Hall was a middle-class spinster in her early thirties who lived with her mother in south west London, and worked as a shorthand-typist in the City of London. On the outbreak of war she volunteered to work with her local ARP Report Centre. She kept a diary of her war experiences, most of which her mother destroyed – a case here of the destruction dimension of maternal zeal, rather than that of war. Among the fragmentary remains are Miss Hall's thoughts on the second day of war, 4 September 1939: 'There is one thing, and one only, about this war – it is an instant and complete leveller of "classes".'[3]

Throughout the war, and after, there was much talk in this vein: of the war 'breaking down' the social structure, 'levelling' or 'mixing' social classes, and creating class unity. To talk of levelling or breaking down the class structure might be to imply that differences between classes, in power, wealth, life-styles, and so on, were so reduced as to lose almost all significance, so that everyone was left on the same social plane. More often what was probably meant (though wars do tend to provoke the exaggerations of genuine self-delusion as well as those of interested intent) was that significant reductions in class differences did indeed take place, but within a class structure which basically remained unchanged. Likewise with social mixing: this could imply that there was so much mobility, such a startling elevation of the material conditions of those lowest in the old hierarchy (the working class) and such an accretion of power to them, so many instances of miners hobnobbing with top civil servants, bank clerks issuing orders to barristers, and duchesses bunking down with dustmen, that the old class reference points had become meaningless. Or again mixing could simply mean that, within the recognizable continuance of the old structure, there was more mobility, and that, in greater numbers than ever before, members of different classes were associating with each other, 'mixing', indeed. Most of those who spoke of class unity were in fact recognizing the continued existence of classes: they did not usually mean that the nation was being united into one homogeneous class, but rather that the middle and upper classes were showing greater sympathy for, and understanding of the working class, and a greater willingness to support improvements in working-class conditions. In written and spoken comments about class in Britain during the war, there certainly was quite a strong emphasis on change; yet much of the imagery is remarkably unchanged. If we examine the realities – the objective indicators of inequality and class relationships – we find that there was a good deal of change, but that this came rather slowly and against strong resistance. The war was not over in one sudden flash; and certainly 4 September was somewhat early for a complete assessment of its social consequences.

A crucial reality of the war was the steadily increasing bargaining power of the working class (a facet of the *participation* dimension). The government deliberately sought to enlist its support and maintain its morale by using food subsidies to keep the cost of living under control; at the same time the high demand for labour in the war production industries pushed wages up. Average weekly earnings rose by eighty per cent from £2.13.3d in October 1938 to £4.16.1d in July 1945, when the cost of living had risen only by thirty-one per cent. The results of the major social policy programmes, developed towards the end of the war, again, in part, designed to enlist working-class support and to reward working-class participation in the war effort, could only be felt in the post-war years; but the deliberate policy of rationing, 'fair shares', and the raising of nutritional standards, did have immediate effects. No power on earth, however, could prevent poorer working-class mothers from pouring their free orange juice and other welfare foods down the drain, nor from adhering to their peculiarly British faith that if these had any value at all it must be for their laxative properties.[4] High levels of direct wartime taxation were in no way designed as a bulldozer of social differences, yet the reduction of the disposable income of many in the upper and middle classes meant that there was some compression of the economic distinctions between classes. Of even more immediate importance was the widespread austerity and shortage of consumer goods, though it has to be noted that the well-to-do still managed to eat rather well. Overall nutritional standards were levelled out at those of a prosperous artisan in the pre-war period, which meant a very definite levelling-up for much of the working class. As in the previous war, domestic servants left for higher wages and greater personal freedom in the war factories. Yet many upper-class families were able to keep up their establishments, so that where obvious class distinctions were being obliterated this was largely in the marcher lands between the middle class and the working class.

An important objective development of a slightly different sort, related to the *test* dimension of war, concerns the manner in which individuals, who in the pre-war years could only exceptionally have expected to be recruited into positions of power and influence, frequently attained such positions during the war. The real power behind the famous Beveridge report was the secretary to the Beveridge Committee, D. N. Chester, a wartime civil servant who had in the pre-war period made his way up part of the social ladder by becoming a lecturer in public administration at Manchester University. Under the test of war the class restrictions on recruitment to the higher civil service had to be much relaxed. Ernest Bevin had been an influential trade union leader in the pre-war years: suddenly in 1940, despite not having served the normal long apprenticeship in parliament, he was brought directly into the cabinet by Churchill. Labour, which had seemed like a permanent Opposition party in the 1930s, now had its representatives in the seats of power. J. B. Priestley, middle-class novelist of the thirties, became an influential broadcaster. Many of the government-supported films were made by film makers who had been part of an alternative culture in the thirties; many of them, though, were just as upper-class as the accepted media magnates of the thirties. Of the film director Penn Tennyson, grandson of the Victorian Poet Laureate, it was said that he had to do his 'huntin'' and 'fishin'' before he did his 'shootin''. The army provides the central and special case. Having 'a good war' was very important to individuals who, already making their way up in the thirties, would probably not in peacetime have got anywhere near the top: Edward Heath, whom we shall encounter again towards the end of this book, is a case in point. Here, however, we are talking of individuals, already relatively successful before the war, who found that the war helped their continued upward progress; we are not talking of changes in the relative positions of whole social classes, except to the extent that the successes of an Ernest Bevin and an Edward Heath made it a little easier for successors from similar social backgrounds.

In the period of the 'Invisible War' or 'Phoney War' up to the summer of 1940, and indeed during the 'blitz' (lasting till the summer of 1942) which followed, most of the traditional characteristics of British society were only too evident. In the private papers of the distinguished military historian Captain Liddell Hart, there are

many comments on the 'feudalism' which lay behind the recruitment
of officers to the original Home Guard. Certainly the evacuation of
mothers and children from potential danger areas was of profound
though confused, social significance. One businessman and former
naval commander, in a letter to an American associate in October
1939, shone a special upper-class light on it: 'The tremendous social
experiment of shifting the town population to the country has revealed, as far anyhow as the mothers and children are concerned,
that country people – living in many cases around the Manors as in
the old feudal days – are, though much poorer in worldly monetary
wealth, infinitely richer in standards of cleanliness, happiness, kindli-
ness, comfort and contentment than the townsfolk.' What, he asked,
'does America and its contempt of feudalism say to this?'[5]

However, Monica Cosens, a social worker who had been a muni-
tionette in the First World War, wrote of evacuation as a 'social
revolution'.[6] Her argument, which was to be repeated many times,
was that the revelation to middle-class families in the reception areas
of the appalling circumstances of children reared in the country's
slums would encourage class 'unity'. She was not utterly wrong. But
more often middle-class families were confirmed in their prejudices
about the dirty fecklessness of the working class. There was little
of the Christian spirit in a Christmas letter received by the wife of a
London barrister from an old school friend describing her experience
of evacuees sent from Liverpool to North Wales: 'It was terrible –
dirt and disease among the children and mothers. The wretched
local Red Cross had the job of "delousing". But most of them have
returned to Liverpool now, Anglesey was too dull with no pubs open
on Sunday. We do not want any more.' Earlier the barrister's wife
had herself recorded: 'After tea we watched numbers of strange
looking people with babies, children and odd parcels of clothes and
bedding struggling up West End Lane. They turned out to be East
Enders evacuated from bombed areas to empty houses all about
here.'[7]

It is in the second and real evacuation, when the bombs were
actually falling, that we begin to find hard evidence of the development of a genuine concern among middle-class families about the
appalling conditions which had bred the slum children billeted upon
them. However, it may be that too exclusive an attention has been
devoted to evacuation. Evacuation is best seen as a part, though an
important one, of a whole process in which middle-class and upper-
class people became involved in various kinds of social work and
social care for working-class families. The pre-eminent organization
in this respect was the Women's Voluntary Service. Organized by

Lady Reading, it was in many ways an extremely upper-class organization. We find one middle-class lady exulting that through her work with the WVS she was 'getting to know Wendover's "best" people. I help a Lady Something.'[8] On the other hand, in Coventry, one of the most blitzed areas, the WVS was run by a Labour Councillor, Mrs Pearl Hyde, the daughter of a publican.

As the Invisible War ended in the West, a new British government was formed under one of the most traditionally upper-class of all political leaders, Winston Churchill. But this government included representatives of the Labour Party. In his diary, Hugh Dalton explained how the Labour leader Clement Attlee made his selection of Labour members to be included in the government: 'A balance had to be maintained between bourgeois and working-class MPs.' He also reported that Churchill had told Harold Macmillan: 'My Government is the most broad-based that Britain has ever known. It extends from Lord Lloyd of Coleraine to Miss Ellen Wilkinson.'[9] As Ellen Wilkinson had been a shop workers' organizer it would appear that Churchill had no very clear idea about the social make-up of classes other than the one to which he and Lord Lloyd belonged.

Upper-class politicians and civil servants, so little faith did they have in the British working class, expected aerial bombardment to produce panic and a mass exodus. Undoubtedly the horrors of the blitz, the inadequacies of air raid precautions, and the bungling of the local authorities, did create dismay and resentment. Yet when in his chairman's address to the 1941 conference of the Transport and General Workers Union, Harry Edwards, a docker, expressed his conviction that this war was a 'People's War' he was echoing a sentiment which was remarkably widespread, as can be seen from the secret reports the government itself compiled on civilian attitudes, from letters sent abroad, which, naturally, passed through the hands of censorship, and from private letters and diaries. Henry Penny, a London bus driver who wrote up a diary on scraps of paper during the long nights in his air-raid shelter, noted in the early stages of the blitz: 'We are all in the "Front Line" and we realise it.'[10] Throughout, his diary is marked by a tone of reasoned self-confidence, of pride in himself and his fellow working men, and by an acceptance of the established order of society and Churchill's leadership. The notion of class unity, set within the reiteration of traditional class attitudes, comes through in the infinitely ambivalent diary of an upper-class lady living in London:

An aggressive Labour bus driver told me the East End people were saying their houses were destroyed, or allowed to be destroyed and no-one cared; but when the West End was touched the government started the barrage!

Bruton Street, Bond Street, Park Lane, all bombed yesterday; much damage to the two former, but people are carrying on as usual. Milkman delivers slowly, pushing his tricycle during raids; the paper comes and so on and so forth. Wonderful stoicism.

Three women, Legion officers killed in East End; Mrs. Knowle and the Misses Cooper; yesterday while running a mobile canteen. Several firemen too; and two were blown over a building on an escape ladder which was broken in half. One is just stunned to read of these happenings which often are beyond belief. Such heroism everywhere in all classes.

The Tube stations are filled with people packed together for the night. Wondered if I should join them, then concluded that even loneliness was best at *home*.[11]

The mix of real change from below engendered by the war, with attitudes and images at the top rooted in the past comes out clearly in the attempts of the Ministry of Labour to draft a memorandum on industrial morale in September 1942. The first draft was drawn up within the ministry and depended on reports sent in from all over the country by regional controllers, industrial relations officers, labour supply inspectors, employment exchange managers, welfare officers, and factory inspectors, all of whom were well qualified to present an authentic view of what was actually happening in the realm of industrial relations. Their draft provided a neat and deeply true encapsulation of how the participation dimension of war was modifying the class relationship between employers and workers: 'Many employers still cherish the right to discipline their workers and to manage labour in their own way and resent the alleged curtailment of managerial rights. Management are slow to realise that times are changing and that their relationship with their workpeople must change also.' Yet a small committee of senior civil servants insisted on redrafting the passage in a manner which brings out well the resistance to, and total unwillingness to accept, any change in relationships between employers and workers: 'Many employers still consider it important that they should have the right to discipline and manage their workers in their own way, and dislike curtailment of managerial rights.'[12]

The Beveridge Report, which was published in December 1942, though not overtly concerned with class, was in effect advocating the abolition of the official image of the working class. Social security provision (and also a National Health Service, mentioned in passing) should be 'universal', not simply confined to the statutory working class. The report also advocated the abolition of the distinctively working-class 'industrial insurance' – funeral policies touted round, often at exorbitant rates, by the private companies. The Prudential Assurance Company, however, remonstrated strongly that 'facilities for securing this benefit for the working classes are highly desirable and indeed a vital necessity.'[13] In the diary of Captain Crookshank, now Financial Secretary to the Treasury, there are no references at all to the Beveridge Report at the time of its publication in December 1942, and only three references to the House of Commons debate in February 1943 which was finally forced on a reluctant Churchill. They are for 16, 17 and 18 February, and read as follows: 'First of 3 days debate on Beveridge. John Anderson spoke well. Shakes had a goodbye cocktail party'; 'I went for a while to the House of Commons – Beveridge again'; 'Morrison wound up on Beveridge but Labour voted against us, 335–119 were the figures.'[14] Such was the laconic nonchalance of the upper class in the face of what has often been regarded as one of the greatest documents of social reform in twentieth-century history.

For a majority of younger men, the biggest upheaval of the war was service in the army. The army in many respects represented the ultimate parody of the hierarchic assumptions of the British class structure of the thirties. Since at the same time the propaganda idea was being steadily developed of this as a people's war on behalf of democracy, for many soldiers the contrast was all too sharp and engendered a powerful reaction against notions of hierarchy: a number of young officers of upper-class background were to form an important body of recruits into the Labour Party at the end of the war. For all that, the army did offer opportunities for education in political and social subjects which most men would not have received in peace time. Strongly against the wishes of both Churchill and the War Office, the Army Bureau of Current Affairs, thanks again largely to the influx of outsider figures of the thirties of which I have already spoken, became something of a centre for the propagation of democratic ideas. Whatever the exact train of causation there can be no doubt that sentiment among the rank-and-file in the army, who were after all simply civilians in uniform, was turning strongly towards the idea that Britain must be a more egalitarian society after the war. One Methodist minister reported of his encounters with the soldiers on leave: 'Most of them are thinking of a world where there will be better opportunities for everyone, and more economic security than there has been since the early ages of mankind.'[15]

Most of those who aspired to better opportunities or more economic security saw these as coming within a largely unchanged social
system. Within the trade union movement there was discussion of
the question of industrial democracy, particularly at the 1944 TUC
Conference, but there was very deep-rooted hostility to the idea that
workers should ever aspire towards being managers, save in the
nationalized industries. A true voice of the working class, respectful,
combative, resentful, can be heard in a sad letter to the Minister of
Transport concerning a mother's problems over visiting her
evacuated children:

Dear Sir,
I hope you will excuse me if I am intruding by writing to you as I
know you are a busy gentleman, but what I would like to know is
why parents and friends of evacuees in Wales can have cheap fares
to see their dear ones, yet there is no cheap fares for us to see our
dear ones evacuated to Somerset. It is 10/8 from Soton [*sic*] to
Hensbrady and Templecombe. We cannot afford it. We are
longing to see our child but cannot afford it. We have all her winter
clothes ready and if they run cheap trains would kill two birds
with one stone as the postal is dear, and if the fare was say a half-
penny a mile we could see the children as well as taking her warm
clothes. Not only that, she would love to see us as she is only seven
years old like hundreds of others get home-sick when they haven't
got anything to look forward to seeing them. We haven't got cars
to go and see them as the Directors of the Railways got. So they
want to bear in mind that our children are as valuable and dear
to us as any of the rich people's children. So I hope Sir this letter
won't be delayed or falling on deaf ears till the rough cold weather
sets in. Thanking you Sir to wake the railway officials up.
I am, Sir, faithfully. . . .[16]

As unchanging were the voices of the upper class. In the autumn,
winter and spring of 1940–41 Sir Stafford Cripps, who had been regarded as so far to the Left in the 1930s that he had been expelled
from the Labour Party, was marooned in cold and miserable isolation as Britain's Ambassador to Moscow. In his deepest agony he
did not turn to his Socialist cronies, but instead, as we saw, began a
fascinating personal correspondence with his Conservative contemporary and fellow barrister, Sir Walter Monckton, who was then
at the Ministry of Information. However, although the correspon-

dence is important evidence of the continued existence of a close-knit upper class, which transcended political frontiers, it is very important to note also that much of it was taken up with discussing the possibilities of, and indeed the necessity for, social change occasioned by the war. In a holograph letter of 25 September 1940, Cripps wrote from Moscow to 'My Dearest Walter' describing war as a 'pre-natal period'.[17] There is something of the old patronizing manner in his remark that: 'No-one can blame the ordinary man & woman with much too much to do at the moment and with no knowledge or opportunity of appreciating the needs of the future.' Cripps desired change, but he was not at all optimistic about it coming about in Britain:

What has temporarily brought Russia and Germany together is because historically they are both an attempt to get away from an effete civilisation which the countries we represent are trying desperately hard to cling to and to revivify. It is indeed a revolutionary war but we are on the side of the past – at the moment. We talk some of us about the old order changing but in our hearts we are clinging to it as the one solid thing we can visualise.

Cripps feared that an Allied victory would reinforce the old will against change thus making it 'more difficult to make any change without a revolution'. 'But why preach to the converted!', he concludes the letter, recognizing that his Conservative friend shared his own aspirations.

For his part, Sir Walter Monckton, in a self-typed letter from the Ministry of Information during an air-raid, commented rhetorically: 'doesn't it also mean showing now that we mean to get rid of the rotten parts of the established system. . . .' But apart from sharing sweeping political judgements with Sir Stafford, Sir Walter could also operate the establishment network to take care of his friends. On 10 August 1940, he wrote to R. A. Butler at the Foreign Office about Lady Cripps's forthcoming visit to Moscow:

I feel a little anxiety about Lady Cripps' journey to Moscow, particularly as I have in the last few days had a letter from Stafford begging me to take charge of her. I should not feel happy about it unless she were accompanied by some male companion throughout the journey. She, I know, would be content if Squadron Leader Norris who she and I both know were sent on this journey.

Then in a striking letter of 20 January 1941 he suggested that there was a good deal of upper-class, as well as popular support for the notion of Cripps as a successor to Churchill:

> The fact is that there is no satisfactory successor or alternative to Winston I am pretty clear now that Ernie Bevin will not fill the post. Anthony is too conventional a thinker to make a great leader, and one looks in vain among the rest for the right quality of mind and character . . . I have discussed you as a leader with the most diverse people, from Nancy Astor up and down. I find them all attracted by the possibility.

During 1943 and 1944, the government published white papers on *Social Insurance*, which followed Beveridge very closely; *Employment Policy*, which declared in favour of a high and stable level of employment; and *A National Health Service*, which announced the principle of free, comprehensive medical service. Yet, partly indeed because of opposition in high places to the expenditure and social reorganization implied in these proposals, the only major legislation actually carried through was in the realm of education, a topic, as it happened, central to questions of class. In theory, and to some degree in practice, the provision through this Act of 'Secondary Education for All' would eventually create greater social mobility. On the matter of the public schools, the Act was silent, though they had been much in the news throughout the war. A letter to *The Times* in January 1941 from Lt Col. R. C. Bingham appeared to put the cat among the pigeons:

> Never was the old school tie and the best that it stands for more justified than it is today. Our new armies are being officered by classes of society who are new to the job. The middle, lower-middle, and working classes are now receiving the King's commission. These classes, unlike the old aristocratic and feudal (almost) classes who led the old Army, had never had their people to consider. They have never had anyone to think of but themselves. This aspect of life is completely new to them, and they have very largely fallen down on it in their capacity as Army officers.

But the cat was blind and toothless, the pigeons plump and confident in their consciousness of the pecking order. Although Colonel Bingham was relieved of his commission, his view seems largely to have been shared throughout British society. Labour Party policy documents and Labour Party conferences almost totally ignored the question of what was to be done about the public schools. In the education debate at the 1944 conference C. E. M. Joad, the philosopher, pointed out the very large proportion of MPs drawn from public schools. Almost despairingly Harold Clay in his summing up for the National Executive retorted that 'it was the ordinary working-class voter, man and woman, who placed in the House of Commons the people who were there now.' A delegate from the National Union of Distributive and Allied Workers revealed one serious reason for Labour's lack of interest in the public schools: the basic working-class concern was with the abysmal nature of working-class education, not with intellectual theorizing about the inequities inherent in the highly remote public school system. One working-class Labour MP, together with a number of his colleagues, did conduct a personal investigation into five of the most famous public schools, Christ's Hospital, Eton, Harrow, Charterhouse, and Winchester. 'What did we find?' he asked:

> We found an utter absence of snobbery. After all, the average normal boy is the same all England over. Whether rich or poor, a young lad has to be made, under duress, to wash his neck as well as his face. . . .
> There was a fine simplicity of living. . . . Most of the boys made their own bed. . . . these public schools breed character. . . . in the mass these boys have independence and poise.[18]

The modest conclusion drawn from all this was that the door should be kept 'at least ajar for the boy who has passed the entrance examination to the local grammar school, whose parents are ready for their boy to go to a boarding school, and who is temperamentally suitable'. The Conservative Party had its own sub-committee on education; however the proposal to produce a report on the public schools was squashed by R. A. Butler, for whom the very idea of a public discussion of these bastions of privilege and tradition was an intolerable violation of good manners.

Nevertheless the report of the sub-committee provides a good summary of considered upper-class attitudes towards class at a time when the war had fostered much radical criticism of the old order. 'The slackening of moral fibre', said the report, 'is common to all classes, though it is the result of different causes and shows itself by different symptoms on different levels.' Looking for one class to blame, the report carefully avoided speaking of 'the upper class' or of 'the middle class', but instead singled out that useful collective entity 'the monied classes', with its overtones of the crass *nouveau riche*, or of the exceptional bounders among the established upper class (one recalls Sir Ian Fraser's contribution to the BBC's contortions on class mentioned in Chapter 9). Still, in roundly condemning these 'monied classes' the report implies that they do indeed make up an upper class which has duties of service and leadership: 'setting before themselves an ever higher standard of material comfort and enjoyment, they have weakened both their will and ability to serve the State and their powers of leadership.' All was not lost, however, for there have, said the report, been 'very many individual exceptions' – including, no doubt, the writers of the report.

But the example set has been general enough to infect the entire social body, whether with desire to emulate it or with envy or by making it hard for the better sort of citizens in all classes to retain faith in the virtue of a community which could still lose its sense of direction. At the other end of the social scale a wholly different reason, for which its victims cannot be blamed, has made it difficult for the instinct of social and national service to flourish. . . .

After this slightly muddled explanation of working-class readiness to exploit its favourable market situation by going on strike, and working-class willingness to assert its aspirations by supporting non-government candidates in wartime by-elections, the report continued with a traditional defence of the public schools, including a discrete new euphemism for the working-class aggressiveness which, towards the close of the war, began to look suspiciously like class consciousness: 'class discomfort'.

we think that much of the class discomfort, of which the nation has become so impatiently conscious, is due not to any dislike of educational privileges as such but to the belief that these privileges are too often given to the wrong people. . . . in our judgment, the special contribution made by public and preparatory schools to the end we are discussing (the education of talent and the development of leadership) is too valuable to be jeopardised; and that it would be jeopardised if they were to lose their independence and become a mere part of the State system. The aim should be on the contrary, to increase the value of their special contribution.[19]

It is not really surprising that the government committee which reported in 1942 on *The Public Schools and the General Educational System* (the Fleming Report) was not concerned at all with the possible abolition or absorption into the State system of the public schools, but simply with ways in which places in them could be made available to suitable children whose parents could not afford the high fees. In practice little was done even along these modest lines and the public schools remained as propagators of the upper-class ethos.

Many of the documentary films of the Second World War consciously presented the image of a progression towards greater democracy and 'class unity', though most of the feature films – for example, *In Which We Serve* (for the social backgrounds of naval officers and other ranks) or *Went the Day Well* (for the social hierarchy in an English village) – were more striking for their careful delineation of the traditional class structure. Something of a breakthrough, though rather an isolated one, came with John Baxter's film *The Shipbuilders* of 1943. It is instructive to compare this film with the 1935 novel of the same name by the Glasgow journalist George Blake, on which it is based. In its description of the relationship between the Clyde-side shipworker Danny Shields, and his boss Leslie Pagan, the novel is redolent of the older patronizing-deferential attitudes (the officer-batman relationship of the First World War was a recurrent stereotype in this type of presentation):

> A toff and a gentleman, thought Danny Shields as he walked eastward along the Dumbarton road that night of the Estramadura's launching; a toff and a gentleman.
> His admiration of Leslie Pagan was flawless. To this decent working man's sense of respect for a good and efficient master there was added his memory of courage in battle, or steadfastness and kindness in the long trial of trench and camp. He never ceased to praise in his private mind and in the presence of whomsoever cared to listen the uniqueness of the younger man he adored and trusted with a faith almost religious. A toff and a gentleman![20]

There is none of this in the film, which instead provides a convincing portrayal of the Glasgow working-class milieu, with Danny Shields emerging as a thoroughly rounded and independent-minded character.

In the BBC Written Archives for the early part of the war there is a file whose main title, 'Reconstruction-Political Talks', has the

illuminating explanatory parenthesis, 'Working Man'. The mix is
the familiar one: a new and positive desire to give working-class
aspirations a hearing, buried within the old patronizing manners
and sense of class distinctions. Detailed legislative proposals, a
producer explained, 'are better discussed by people with administrative experience and a knowledge wider than working-class people
can hope to have of the whole political and economic fabric'; but
'useful work' could be done 'in bringing to expression the background and vague aspirations of working class men and woman'.[21]
The director of the BBC in Scotland was rather less sentimental and
much more aware of the new readiness of workers to express their
grievances vociferously. He noted incisively that: 'the interests about
which workers in the industrial areas would want to talk are – the
war, home politics, industrial grievances, football, and the dogs. We
believe that the kind of things they would want to say about the first
three could not be broadcast.' In the event a series of somewhat
anodyne talks were broadcast. The old clashed obviously with the
new in a proposal in September 1942 for a programme on 'The
British Worker and his Wife During the War'. Ernest Bevin protested
at the cosy implications of the title and suggested 'Labour's War
Effort'; eventually the programme went on the air as *The Voice of
Labour*.[22] For a time in 1941 the news was read in the strong Yorkshire accent of Wilfred Pickles, the actor born in a 'soot-blackened
working-class house' in Halifax.[23] But this self-conscious experiment was short-lived. The muted controversy surrounding it showed
that class and accent were not the only areas of discrimination in
the BBC. Asked about the possibility of some Scottish programme
announcers (including two women) becoming newsreaders, a
spokesman, in the perfect syntax of icy upper-class dismissiveness,
commented: 'I hardly think we are considering women as newsreaders.'[24]

The longer-term implications of wartime developments will be
explored more fully in a later chapter. As far as the fundamental
inequalities of class are concerned it can be said that the position of
the upper class was not greatly altered by the war, though certainly
a door was opened to greater upward mobility, mainly from the
middle class. Much of the upper-class image of itself and of society
was unchanged, though the war did modify some upper-class political prejudices. The change is neatly capsulated in a letter from
Lord Arran to Leslie Scott discussing the Uthwatt Report on reform of land use: 'Personally I think that its principles are perfectly
fair although they hit my Essex property rather hard, but all of us

are beginning to realise that we live in a rapidly altering world and that we must accept it with a good grace.'[25] The 'people's war' spirit and the social welfare policies emanating from it were to prove valuable to many members of the middle class, particularly those in the lower half, but on the whole war-time developments put the middle class under pressure, so that some of the old easy assumptions of superiority were abandoned and a new perception emerged of the need for it to defend itself as a class. Mrs Diana Brinton-Lee, however, had concluded her diary of the years 1940–1 with a resounding assertion of upper-middle-class self-confidence: 'I believe the strength and civilisation of a nation is shown by the growth of its "middle classes", that is the number of people who are neither poor and oppressed or rich and idle.'[26]

For the working class, the relative changes were the greatest. I would say that the working class in 1945 assumed a position in British society analogous to that assumed by the middle class after the passing of the Great Reform Act of 1832. Just as the middle class then, having asserted its importance and the need to pay heed to its wishes, was thereafter prepared to go on being governed by aristocratic governments, so the working class, whose claims could henceforth never be ignored by governments, was on the whole content to leave both management and high politics to the classes which had monopolized them in pre-war years. Shortly before the General Election of 1945, Bevin, who understood the British working class better than any other front-rank politician, wrote to Attlee: 'We have faced many great problems together and have overcome them.' He then, referring directly to the war, added an aspiration which, on the whole, had come true: 'One thing it should have done is to remove the inferiority complex amongst our people.'[27]

Notes

1, Arthur Marwick, *Britain in the Century of Total War* (1968); *War and Social Change in the Twentieth Century* (1974). The approach has been fruitfully used in Neil A. Wynn, *The Afro-American and the Second World War* (1976).
2. William Miller, *A New History of the United States* (1958), 1970 edition, p. 351. See especially, Richard Polenberg, *War and Society: the United States 1941–1945* (1972).

230 *Class: Image and Reality*

3. Imperial War Museum [IWM], London, Vivienne Hall Diary.
4. For more detail on this and other points see my *The Home Front: the British and the Second World War* (1976).
5. IWM, Yates Correspondence, 6 October 1939.
6. Monica Cosens, *Evacuation: a Social Revolution* (1939).
7. IWM, Gwladys Cox Diary, 22 December, and 25 September 1939.
8. IWM, Herbert Strong Collection: Doris King to H. E. Strong, 15 August 1944.
9. British Library of Political and Economic Science [BLPES], Dalton Diaries, May 1940.
10. IWM, Henry A. Penny Diary, 12 September 1940.
11. IWM, Hilda Neal Diary, 18 September 1940.
12. Churchill College, Cambridge [CCC], Bevin Papers, BEVN 2/13.
13. BLPES, Beveridge Papers, VII, 36: 'Inter-Department Committee on Social Insurance and Allied Services: Memorandum submitted by the Prudential Assurance Company Limited'.
14. Bodleian Library [Bod. L], Oxford, Crookshank Diaries, MSS Eng Hist d. 360, vol. II, p. 188.
15. IWM, Reverend Mackay Papers: 'Archway Letter', 13 September 1940.
16. Public Record Office, HLG 900/59: copy of a letter to the Minister of Transport from a woman in Southampton, September 1940.
17. Bod. L, Monckton Papers, Dept. MT 4.
18. *The Times*, 8 July 1943.
19. Conservative Party Sub-Committee on Education, *Looking Ahead* (1944).
20. George Blake, *The Shipbuilders* (1935), p. 29.
21. BBC Written Archives: 'Reconstruction-Political ("Working Man") Talks', Acc. no. 1644.
22. *Ibid.*
23. Wilfred Pickles, *Between You and Me* (1949), p. 11.
24. *Manchester Guardian*, 2 February 1942.
25. Modern Records Centre, Warwick University, Lord Justice Scott Papers, MSS 119/3/P/AR: Arran to Scott, 29 December 1942.
26. IWM, Brinton-Lee Diary: 'Epilogue', May 1941.
27. CCC, Bevin Papers, BEVN 3/1: Bevin to Attlee, 31 May 1945.

12

The Second World War and Class
in France and the USA

At times the Second World War was a deeply frightening and very horrible experience for many British people. But the open discussion of matters related to class was not only possible but persistent. In France the story was altogether more grim. The German invasion led to an Armistice which came into effect on 25 June 1940. To begin with, a corner in the South-West remained as Unoccupied France. The French government established there at Vichy was responsible, in cooperation with the German forces occupying the remainder of France, for the administration of the entire country and for meeting the costs of the occupation. In November 1942 the Germans moved into the Unoccupied territory. From the end of 1940 a number of underground Resistance groups appeared. After the Allied invasion of France, Paris was liberated in August 1944, and the Occupation régime was replaced by the Liberation government. For most Frenchmen, for most of the war, the all-consuming task was that of keeping life going. The anonymous preface to the famous clandestine novel, *Le silence de la mer*, which appeared in February 1942, captures the essence:

> For three years France has lived under the mask of silence. Silence in the streets, silence in the home; silence because the German army parades at mid-day in the Champs Elysées, silence because an enemy officer is living in the next room, silence because the Gestapo has spies everywhere, silence because the child dare not say that he is hungry, because the execution of patriots every evening makes each new day another day of national mourning.[1]

Did the adversities of war bring 'unity' among classes (in the sense discussed in the previous chapter)? Or did the war make French society more thoroughly and bitterly divided than ever it had been in the 1930s? Dr Philip Williams, the British historian and political scientist, has sharply contrasted the First World War which 'had brought national unity' to France and this war, which 'had destroyed it'. But how about the war as 'a leveller of the social structure'? Dr Williams calls the Resistance 'a potentially revolutionary movement', and declares that the Liberation, 'was potentially a revolutionary change'.[2] However the American historian, Stanley Hoffmann, has argued that despite the apparent irreconcilability between Vichy and Liberation regimes, there was in practice an essential continuity in their policies which brought about important economic and social change in France. More than this: 'Common sufferings did a great deal to bridge over, if not to close, some of the fissures which the social fabric of France had suffered before the war.'[3]

The establishment of the authoritarian Vichy regime symbolized a defeat for the provincial upper-middle-class groups which had dominated Parliamentary politics if not executive decision-making. On the whole, Vichy rallied to it most of the upper class, as well as a wide cross-section of the nation. However, the Free French Movement, based on London, was itself led by an upper-class figure, Charles de Gaulle. Events inexorably pushed de Gaulle into the position of a social leveller: France, he declared in April 1942, 'has been betrayed by our ruling élites and privileged classes.'[4] In some respects the policies of the Vichy government were not antipathetic to the 'Popular Classes' (in the usage which excludes the organized working class). A major objective was to reverse the disastrous decline in the French birthrate, and a vigorous 'politics of the family' was promulgated. At the same time old-age pensions for retired workers were introduced. But Vichy policies, including the Labour Charter, were fundamentally antagonistic to the organized working-class movement, and to the hard core of French industrial workers. Businessmen seized the opportunity to take revenge for the Popular Front. The Liberation, therefore, necessarily involved a heavy blow to the upper class; yet the prestige of the political middle class was scarcely restored either. It seemed that only lower-middle-class groups and the working class could gain.

The Resistance began as a very tiny minority of all Frenchmen; it grew when the Germans took over the whole of France and as Nazi brutalities multiplied. Resistance appears more a personal phenomenon than a political one, but, in keeping with the intellectual and ideological context of French society, as much a political one as a class one. Dr H. R. Kedward, in his masterly *Resistance in Vichy France*, published eighteen 'profiles', abridged from interviews he conducted with former Resisters.[5] Of these eighteen, three were indisputably working-class: a railway-worker, a fitter and a metal-worker. Four fell into lower middle-class categories which in France *could* be closely associated with the working class: two teachers in local schools, both militant trade unionists; an engineer who, as a member of the Communist Party 'did not want to be caught in a factory between employers and workers' and so became self-employed; and a chemist who was also a member of the Communist Party: a fifth was a peasant, and, once again a member of the Communist Party. The curé who declared that he had 'always been known as a red priest' is difficult to place in the class structure, but the other nine were definitely middle-class, or, in two cases, upper-class: a university-educated engineer in a small factory, who was, however, a member of the CGT; a building engineer who was an active Christian Démocrat; an editorial secretary on a moderately right-wing newspaper; two rather different 'functionaries', one a minor civil servant, and socialist, the other a top local administrator with a doctorate in history from the Sorbonne, who as a Radical had opposed the Popular Front; another engineer who was also a municipal councillor; a young female student who was certainly at least upper-middle-class; and, at the top of the tree, a barrister who, as he said 'was of independent means and had plenty of money', and a landowner seized of the aristocratic particule. This last traced his family's domicile at Saint-Antoine-de-Breuilh back six hundred years: he declared himself 'a man of the Right, a man of order', who had opposed the Popular Front 'because it was revolutionary', and for whom the 'cardinal virtues' were *patrie* and *famille*.

Almost all of these people, so different socially and in political affiliation, showed themselves aware of the issues of class. The landowner noted of the Resistance: 'There were all types of people in the network by the end, though at the beginning it was the humble people who were most easily recruited. As Jaurès said, and Socialists do say something true occasionally, "The fatherland is the only wealth of the poor". No cottage door was ever closed to me in the Resistance.' The communist peasant declared that during the phoney war he 'saw the bourgeoisie use the pretext of the Nazi-Soviet pact to revenge themselves on the working class by turning the French people against the PCF [Communist Party].' The CGT engineer found that his position made him 'a mediator between the employers and the unions.' 'I never identified with the employers,' he continued, 'but because I was seen as a member of the ruling class my left-wing ideas were constantly under pressure.' The Resistance Group he organized consisted essentially of 'young workers'. He noted some signs of the Resistance as social leveller:

Within the Resistance, prejudices tended to disappear since people were united by something essential – the defence of liberty, justice, dignity, and the fatherland. For myself Resistance was the direct continuation of my pre-war ideas. I had always dreamed of revolution, the remaking of the economic and political structure, and the movement towards a peaceful world of people united in a common cause. Resistance was a sense of Utopia, and it is always necessary to envisage Utopia, even though serious-minded people at the time saw this Resistance as mad and ridiculous.

The Christian Democratic building engineer presented a class analysis of the two main attitudes to Collaboration or Resistance: 'The bourgeoisie did not like the idea of civil violence and preferred to keep the possibility of rebellious action at arm's length. The working class, on the other hand, were used to fighting for their rights and were more imbued with a revolutionary spirit.' The railway-worker 'had taken part in the strikes at Oullins in 1938 and had seen soldiers sent to occupy the factory, so I knew this was another action against the working class'. At this point he had joined the Communist Party. Both of the other working-class figures showed clear signs of both class awareness and class consciousness: the fitter was clearly proud of his status as a skilled worker. After stating that 'all sorts of people were involved' in the Resistance, the rightist newspaperman admitted that 'the active Resistance was mostly undertaken by ordinary people for whom Resistance was a movement of social progress'. According to the minor civil servant recruitment to the Resistance was 'mainly among workers and intellectuals'. While both the wealthy barrister and the self-employed engineer saw the Resistance as mainly recruiting among the workers, one of the teachers noted that two of the first Resisters in his area were a barrister and 'notable', and the son of a marquis. The other teacher, however, had a sharp explanation for the Fall of France: 'the ruling classes had betrayed the country'. In one or two of the 'profiles', notably those of the 'red priest' and the female student, the emphasis is exclusively ideological and, at times, personal, rather than related in any overt way to any clear perceptions of class and class structure.

The Resistance drew upon all social classes and many political persuasions. In itself it involved a 'mixing' of social classes. The weighting, however, was towards the working class, and towards the political left. Resistance publications put a great emphasis on the role and needs of the workers and much of the discussion of eventual victory took it for granted that victory would be accompanied by some kind of social revolution. In April 1942 Jean Moulin, parachuted into France to group together the various resistance organizations, set up a General Committee to draw up political and social policies for the Liberation. In a main report of 1943 the committee declared that 'the working masses expect from the Liberation the birth of a new world where everyone can develop to the full without constraint'. At the same time a Catholic Resistance journal could say: 'the working class is the most important. It has the right to speak and the right to responsibility.'[6] It fails to be noted, however, that much of this literature seems to be spoken *for* the working class, rather than *by* the working class. Furthermore, it covers quite a university of intellectual theorizing about the new world. For their part, trade union publications tended to play down notions of the class struggle and to stress class unity.[7]

The non-socialist Resistance group *Défense de France* published a revealing statement in March 1944:

The governing class has abdicated. The bourgeois class is shown to be incapable of directing by itself the destiny of the country. It senses obscurely the arrival of a new social structure and, while its best elements devote themselves already to trying to establish and to promote its main features, the rest weep for a dead past and whine uselessly over the uncertainties of the time.

The moment is propitious to ratify anew the social unity of the nation, destroyed by the birth of large-scale industry and by the accompanying birth of a capitalist bourgeoisie and of a proletariat of mechanical beings, whose work, cares, clothes and even the quarters to which they are relegated, separate them from the rest of the nation. The revolution must consist of re-integrating all classes of society into the nation, thus giving to the workers (*travailleurs*) the place which must be returned to them.[8]

Trade unions, the statement says, have improved the material conditions of the workers, but still there is a chasm between 'proletarians' and 'non-proletarians'. The very condition of being proletarian must be suppressed, and not through the windy delusions of the Pétain regime. There must be an end to the 'absolute dependence in regard to terms of employment, to the perpetually reborn fear of tomorrow, of the deprivation involved in an immense mechanistic organization in which the worker (*ouvrier*), an anonymous peone, is buffetted around at the whim of sovereign and mysterious forces'. Having long since achieved its political, administrative, and territorial unity, France is now, in the Resistance, 'forging its moral unity'.

Next it must establish its 'social unity'. To achieve this social unity, liberal capitalism would have to be abolished:

> It will be necessary to institute an economic structure in which all Frenchmen can participate both in prosperity and in common set-backs. It will be necessary to remake 1936, with different methods and a different spirit, suppressing not only the hostility of the Right towards the leaders of the popular masses, but also the efforts of the 'revolutionaries' to avoid real revolution, and the 'socialists' to save capitalism. It will be necessary to put the economy at the service of the nation. Then, having eliminated the material cause of the chasm between our children, France can hope to re-find her internal coherence and to march in harmony towards a better future.

The programme of the Lyons region of the *Mouvement de Libération Nationale* (into which *Défense de France* was merged) stressed the need for the whole war experience to yield benefits for the working class and for the peasants (*cultivateurs*). But it also stressed the need to look after the interests of artisans and small businessmen. *Organisation civil et militaire* (OCM) suggested that the companies of private capitalism might be replaced by 'groups of workers' brought together to carry out a common labour and using the help of capitalists; collective agreements would unite together the enterprises and the members of them.[9] Many Resistance organizations supported 'the politics of the family' very much along Vichy lines. OCM wanted a Ministry of Social Life to deal with abandoned mothers and children, and to rehabilitate criminals, prostitutes and beggars. The *Défense de France* statement declared solicitously, and apparently without intended *double-entendre*, that 'every man and every woman should be penetrated by the obligation to transmit life'. Calling for the equal distribution of the charges involved in bringing up children, it declared that 'an important part of the increase in salaries should be granted in the form of an increase in family allowances accompanied by marriage loans, tax relief, and a battle against abortion.'[10]

I have quoted these various policies in detail as a necessary background to an appreciation of the significance of the Programme of Action of the (united) National Resistance Council (15 March 1944), and of the summing up by Henri Michel, doyen of historians of the French Resistance, that 'in politics, economics, and in democracy, the members of the resistance were constructing a new

France.'[11] The 1944 programme[12] called for the institution of a 'true economic and social democracy', involving the removal from the direction of the economy of the 'great economic and financial feudalisms'. National production should be developed in accordance with a National Plan drawn up in consultation with representatives of all interests (including the workers). All sources of energy, all mineral wealth, the insurance companies and the big banks should be 'returned to the nation'. Workers in general should participate in the direction of the economy, and the direction and administration of individual enterprise should be open to workers 'possessing the necessary qualities'. The level of wages and pensions should be fixed so as to guarantee each worker (*travailleur*) and his family 'security, dignity, and the possibility of a full human life'. The independent trade union movement should be revived with a large say in the organization of economic and social life. There should be a complete social security plan, guaranteeing the means of existence to all citizens who, for whatever reason, could not secure these by their own labour, together with guaranteed security of employment. Agricultural workers should be granted the same rights as industrial workers. The final clause of the programme dealt with education and promised the opportunity for all French children to benefit from and to have 'access to the highest levels of education, whatever the income of their parents, so that the highest occupation may be truly accessible to all those who have the required abilities thus creating a true élite, not of birth, but of merit, constantly renewed by popular recruitment.'

Before attempting to assess what all this meant for the realities of class we must look at some of the main material developments of the time. Serious privation reigned throughout the war. According to the official index, prices rose by 185 per cent between 1938 and 1944, but the true rise was nearer to being six-fold, while salaries and wages had risen by only 63 per cent in 1944. The basic food ration never yielded more than 1200 calories a day, about half what is needed to maintain healthy active existence. Amid the disruptions of war, five main tendencies can be discerned. First, the tiny under-class of pre-war years was greatly swollen by people whose family lost its principal wage-earners, or who lost their means of livelihood, or in some way fell foul of the régime. Second, while middle-class incomes generally kept up fairly well with the cost of living, working-class incomes fell catastrophically behind; against that, thirdly, the *participation* effect did give the French workers some leverage – in the end the very survival of the German war effort depended upon some heed being paid to the claims of labour. Fourthly, many individuals, mainly from the middle classes, were able to exploit war conditions to amass considerable fortunes for themselves. Finally, the peasants on the whole did rather well out of the war. Here again we have a function of the *participation* dimension: the peasants could offer that vital commodity, food.[13]

Not only did material standards improve, but it appears that peasant lifestyles altered as well, drawing them eventually within the ambit of the contemporary urban-based class structure. Three surveys recording the views of village priests produced reports which are perhaps at once both unsurprising and exaggerated. Of the Normandy peasant it was said that 'the appetite for gain dominates everything and stifles the cries of conscience'; in the Loire-Inférieur the record was of 'a passion for work to earn yet more'; honesty in business, it was said, had lasted until the advent of the black market, but now the impression is that 'increasingly our people believe themselves to have been created and put in the world in order to make their fortunes.' The priests believed that the decline in business morality was accompanied by a similar decline in another kind of morality. 'The number of virgins', it was lamented, 'seemed to be very very small. It seems that in public opinion that counts for little. The young men speak with astonishment of any girl who refuses them.' Perhaps all sense of history had fled from the priests. Another reported:

> On Easter Sunday I had to baptise three children in the same family and of about the same age. Here is how their paternity was attributed: one by the father and the mother, another by the father and his step-daughter, that is to say the eldest daughter of his wife of whom he was the second husband. Then a third by one of his own daughters and a hired hand at the farm.

The surveys are quoted in Gérard Walter's authoritative *History of the French Peasants* in support of what is in general a convincing thesis about the effects of the war in improving, and in changing, the lifestyle of the peasant.[14]

Town-dwellers were infinitely worse off, as was shown by a social survey in April and May of 1944, which asked people what they felt to be their greatest deprivation. The survey divided the population into four classes, which, the peasants apart, coincide very well with the outlines of the five main tendencies described above. 'Class A' was defined as comprising rich people with their own mansion or luxury apartment, several servants and, in normal times, at least one car and a telephone. 'Class B' was 'bourgeois', involving ownership of a comfortable house or flat, with a maximum of one servant and one car and a telephone. 'Class C' included white-collar workers and industrial workers, having a small house or other cheap habitation, but no servant, no car, no telephone, and covered by social security. 'Class D' lived in obvious deprivation with very minimal resources. Topping the list of people's greatest deprivations was food: 70 per cent of class A, 82 per cent of class B, 85 per cent of class C, and 88 per cent of class D.[15] Here was a kind of social levelling, and as Jean Lhomme, the sociologist and public servant, commented in a pamphlet published in 1945, 'one would have greatly astonished a bourgeois if one had warned him that in 1944 or 1945 his lusts would be concentrated on butter or legs of mutton, and that his children would be going without shoes and slippers.' Professor Lhomme's summing up in 1945 is worth recording. Speaking of a trichotomous structure of 'proletariat', 'middle classes' and 'bourgeoisie', he argued that the proletariat were more removed than ever from all the other classes and that they were now animated by a particularly strong hostility against the bourgeoisie and also against the agricultural interest which they felt had looked after itself only too well during the war – class hatred among the proletariat, he argued, had not weakened though in recent years it had been veiled; the middle classes, he said, were becoming less homogeneous and in some ways closer to the working class with very strong hostility towards the bourgeoisie. With regard to the bourgeoisie, Lhomme's conclusion was that they were ready to be displaced, but that there was no class to displace them.[16]

The war affected certain forces cutting across class. The *psychological*, 'in-group', dimension created a certain rallying to Catholicism as the core of a French tradition menaced by Nazism; the participation of many committed Catholics in the Resistance brought the Church new credit and new strength. In the realm of party politics the most significant effect of the war was that it led for the first time in French history to the creation of a major Christian Democratic Party, the *Mouvement Republicain Populaire* (MRP), largely staffed by progressive Christians who had served in the Resistance and were committed to many of the ideals of the Liberation. The emergence of this party certainly confirmed the decline of the old upper-class élites, but it also provided a further source of political division within the working class, and offered a new vehicle for middle-class political aspirations. A major and convincing part of Professor Hoffmann's thesis is that the combined experience of Vichy and Liberation provided an impetus to the development of modern managed technocratic capitalism in France. Hoffmann lists four types of new organization set up under Vichy, and in effect continued by the Liberation: 'Organisation Committees' within the world of business itself, on which the post-war *Conseil National du Patronat Français* was modelled; the Vichy government's Peasant Corporation, which provided the structure for the Liberation's *Conféderation Générale Agricole* (established in reaction against the peasant corporation) and a leadership for the *Féderation Nationale des Syndicats d'Exploitants Agricoles* of post-war years; the workers' groups established within the Vichy Labour Charter, which continued to flourish in the post-war years; and finally the various professional organizations of lawyers, doctors and so on, which were also preserved and consolidated in the post-war period.[17] The process of professionalization and the rise of the technocrats had little influence on the position and status of the working class, but did involve a shifting of lines between the middle class and the old upper class.

Obviously the war was a difficult time for French film makers. Oddly, two of the most notable films were made by Jean Grémillion, who somehow missed success both before the war and after it. For my money, his *Lumière d'été* (1943) is one of the best evocations there is of the French class structure as it existed in the late thirties, and, in reinforced form, under the autocratic Vichy régime. There are three very distinctive class settings: an elegant middle-class country hotel, where we encounter a surgeon, a former principal ballet dancer, a dress designer, and a professional engineer; a construction site where a dam is being built, where, unusually, we see not just the engineer but a group of very carefully realized working-class figures actually at work; and an aristocratic mansion, home of M. Patrice, and scené of the greatest of all the fancy-dress balls so beloved of French film directors. Patrice is the corrupt and lascivious aristocrat, who finally meets his end at the hands of one of the workers on the dam site. *Le Ciel est à nous* (also 1943) is about two dedicated aviators, distinctly from the artisan, garage-owning class, with, noticeably, a richer class above them (especially at the aero-club). But in the end the message is a republican, democratic one of social harmony. Small-town life, a central feature of the real France, as well as of French films, is most bleakly represented in the poison-pen story, *Le Corbeau* (G-H. Clouzet, 1943).

In France there was no equivalent, at the end of the war, to

Labour's 1945 election victory in Britain. The French elections for a constituent assembly in October 1945 gave overwhelming support to the Communist Party, the MRP, and the Socialists, who got roughly 4 million votes, $4\frac{3}{4}$ million votes, and $4\frac{1}{2}$ million votes, respectively; the other $4\frac{1}{2}$ million votes or so were shared between the Radicals (a pathetic shadow of their former selves) and the various Conservatives. In the general election of 10 November 1946 the Communists won 183 seats, the MRP 166, the Socialists 103, the Conservatives 74, and the Radicals 70. There was a brief single-party Socialist government for a couple of months from 16 December under Léon Blum who, in contrast to the bitter hostility of the Popular Front days, was now treated by the newsreels with the respect due to a national hero.[18] But the likelihood of a powerful ministry governing in the interests of the working class quickly vanished as fissures opened up between Communists and non-Communists, and Catholics and non-Catholics. The working class, and its leaders, had definitely gained in prestige, a prestige symbolized in René Clement's film of wartime sabotage, *La Bataille du Rail*, in which the heroes are the engine-driver and the fireman who alone have the technical skill needed to carry out the sabotage operation correctly. The aborted reforms, and the frustrated emotions, of the Popular Front were now, as the main features of the Resistance Charter became law, institutionalized, so that the working class would never again occupy the outsider position of pre-war days. The upper class and the upper-middle class were dented, but with working-class politics stymied, the upper classes seized the opportunity to re-group, reinforced as they now were by the growing technocratic, managerial element. Certainly the war, as in Britain, and as, indeed, in America brought *individuals* from new social groups to the fore. When Georges Bidault, history teacher, became a member of the Liberation government, he was succeeded as head of the National Resistance Council by the trade unionist, Louis Saillaut.

In America, land of the gospel of social mobility, if not of its universal practice, a successful war offered glittering prizes of social promotion and, more than in the other two countries, raised a whole level of middle-class leadership to challenge the ascendancy of the old upper class: two significant examples were Dwight D. Eisenhower and Richard M. Nixon. Yet in some ways the Second World War (which showed its effects long before America's formal entry in December 1941) was almost as important for what it revealed about the fundamental nature of American society as for what it changed in American society. From the earliest days, America truly was the arsenal of democracy, which meant the rapid creation of new industrial complexes, major movements of population, and a sudden pullulation of war-boom communities. Such is the hustling, entrepreneurial spirit of American academia, that there was also something of a boom in the sociological study of war-boom communities, which in turn threw up some interesting evidence on class relationships in American society. Among the points which emerged most strongly were: the bitter hostility felt by long-time residents towards newcomers seeking war jobs; the appalling conditions in which many newcomers were housed; the deep resistance of local vested interests to attempts by the Federal government to regulate and ameliorate conditions; and the incredible – by European standards – social mix to be found among the war workers.

Most notorious, perhaps, of the war-boom communities – product of both the *disruption* and the *test* of war – was Willow Run, situated to the west of Detroit. Here the Ford company was requested by the government to establish what became the biggest bomber factory in the world, producing B24s. Altogether 250,000 people moved into (and, in some cases, out of again) what had been overwhelmingly a farming community; the factory itself employed 42,000. Whereas in Britain and France most of the great population movements of the time appear as responses to the impersonal forces of war, in America personal initiative, the entrepreneurial will to turn the opportunities of war to account, are very evident. According to the patient chroniclers of the Willow Run case-study in 'Industrialization and Cultural Inadequacy', the first newcomers had given up 'a good job or small business at home'. Subsequent arrivals ranged from 'lower-lower to upper-middle class status', and the last arrivals included hillbillies from Kentucky and Tennessee. The writers spoke also of 'Big People' and 'Little People', and explained: 'If we refer to the newcomers at Willow Run as "hillbillies", "bomber workers", "trailerites", it is not in disparagement but in order to speak the language of the area.'[19] The Ford company and local and state authorities strongly resisted government intervention in the realm of housing; instead, private enterprise provided shanty towns and trailer parks.

The American Army had its own ten-point scale for housing in this area, which is in itself an illuminating addition to the documentation on both images and geography of class. At the top of this scale 'movie magnates' and 'millionaires' had 'palatial mansions' with 'exquisite grounds' and 'private bath with each bedroom'; next, 'corporation owners' and 'very successful businessmen' had 'luxurious private homes or villas' with 'spacious gardens' and 'several bathrooms'; 'junior executives' had 'comfortable two-storey houses' with '3 or 4 bedrooms, small plot, lawn and flowers'; fourth came 'section heads of department stores, managers of A & P' and 'accountants' whose houses were 'not quite so roomy or comfortable' being 'single storey' with '1 or 2 bedrooms' and 'less privacy'; 'young bank clerks, junior insurance salesmen' and 'A & P butchers' had 'duplex dwellings' with '1 or 2 bedrooms, postage-stamp lawn' and 'practically no privacy'; 'small independent businessmen' and 'owners of corner grocery stores' lived in 'multiple units' with '2 or 3 bedrooms, private bath, common yard, laundry room, etc.'; for 'manual laborers' and 'fruit vendors' there were 'shacks, 2 rooms per family' with 'no bath or heat'; below them (eighth on the army scale) came 'employees of Lynndale hosiery mills and U.S. Smelter' in their 'frame houses built by companies for employees' with 'no improvements or maintenance'; ninth were 'unprivileged transients' in 'tumble-down shacks' or 'motor tourist courts' with 'common water pump' and 'Chic Sale toilets'; right at the bottom were those described as 'Poverty-stricken, only lowest type whose conditions haven't improved in recent years', living in 'chicken coops, old abandoned garages, lean-tos, etc.' The army image, it may be noted, is a middle-class one. There is no recognition of a comfortable working class; factory workers, indeed, come below 'manual laborers', and just above 'unprivileged transients'.[20] Most of the distinctions are within middle-class occupations, and there is a heavy emphasis on age as a factor in living standards.

However, to return to our immediate purpose: two further grades of 'housing', the Willow Run survey said, would need to be added to the army scale to describe some of the accommodation in use there, namely, grade eleven, 'shanties', and grade twelve, 'tents, open lean-tos'. Conditions were frequently sordid, with the dwellings and their surroundings swamped in mud and the inadequacies of primitive sanitation. Yet: 'Trailer occupants at Willow Run were all kinds of people from all over the United States. Middle-class professional and business people from Michigan and Minnesota parked cheek by jowl with rural hillbillies from Tennessee and urban foreign-born mechanics from Weehawken and St Louis. They came from everywhere, and they had all kinds of backgrounds: college degrees and middle-class comfort; fourth-grade semi-literacy and working-class insecurity.'[21] It is hard to conceive of such mixing in such conditions in either Britain or France.

The diary of a former teacher helps to throw some light on the matter. This lady had given up being a teacher in order to assist her husband in running his own business as a professional masseur in the family home, three miles from the nearest town. The young couple, who had one son, also marketed the produce from their five-acre farm and orchard. The summer months of 1942

> were short, happy ones. But towards the end of the summer it became apparent that gas rationing would be nation-wide. Our customers expressed the desire that we move our business into town in order that they might walk to get their treatment. We realised that we would need to do this in order to maintain a satisfactory business during the winter months. But my husband also realised that our business was a non-essential one and that sooner or later he should get into war work. There were no war industries in our home town, which meant seeking employment elsewhere.[22]

Which meant, in fact, joining the rush to Willow Run. There, class did count, of course, and he, after a course of training and study, became an Inspector; she herself was briefly a filing clerk, and then a teacher for the trailer-camp children. Living conditions, as described in the diary, were thoroughly squalid. It is impossible not to see something of the frontier spirit, the mobility as well as the acquisitiveness of American society, in the entry of middle-class citizens into an environment more readily associated with the lower segments of the working class and below. Our couple looked forward above all to being able to buy their farm back home and to add more land to it.

Whatever the apparent forced mixing of social classes among employees, relations between employers and employees remained as bleak as they had been in the thirties. Ford were particularly notorious for their management policies, and they did everything possible to resist unionization by the CIO. In one case, recorded in the diary, a junior personnel official was strongly reprimanded by his seniors for seeking to solve a minor but recurrent industrial problem through cooperation with the CIO. At the same time many of the incoming workers, particularly those with rural backgrounds, were very strongly resistant to union organization. Broadly, however, circumstances favoured growing unionization, and by April 1941 Ford were forced to accept the legitimate existence of unions.

Outside of Willow Run, social mixing in war-boom communities was more apparent than real. A survey of Seneca, Illinois, whose population rose from 1235 to 6600 because of the wartime plant for building Landing Ship Tanks, clearly revealed that newcomers of different social classes tended to associate with members of the same class in the native community rather than with other newcomers.[23] Persistence of traditional attitudes was very much the key discovery of Catherine Archibald, a young researcher who took a job in a wartime shipyard in Oakland, California.[24] Working-class Californians manifested a good deal of hostility towards incomers from the dustbowl, whom they described as 'Okies' and openly likened to the more disreputable characters portrayed in the film *The Grapes of Wrath*. The Okies for their part responded with a nice little ditty:

> The miners came in forty-nine,
> The whores in fifty-one;
> And when they bumped together
> They begot the native son.

In a chapter entitled 'Class Consciousness', Miss Archibald stressed that the shipyard workers accepted the existing social hierarchy. In a discussion concerning the distinctions between the quarters then being outfitted with chromium fixtures and luxurious bunks for the ship's officers, and the much more utilitarian quarters for the crew, she questioned whether the extent of these distinctions were necessary or desirable or just, but her doubts were not echoed. The general reaction, she reported, was neatly put in one worker's remark: 'Well, hell! It's a sweet setup if you happen to be Captain.' The use of first names was, she found, an 'ironclad' custom among the 'ordinary workers': whatever a shipyard worker's age or personality, 'he was John or Bill or Henry to his fellows and to all his supervisors'. It was only the foreman and those of higher rank who were invariably addressed by their last names, although if their work remained within the area of construction their names were seldom preceded by 'Mr'. But the men of the front office, 'who wore business suits and, carrying notebooks and briefcases, occasionally wandered through the yard, were always spoken of as "Mr" Jones or "Mr" Brown, and the worker who had occasion to talk with them did so with an air of servility and due respect which might extend to the removal of his hat.'

Behind their backs, the workers expressed much hostility towards management, and much anti-Semitism. But at most a worker would aspire to the position of foreman: 'Managerial positions were thought to be exclusively the gifts of pre-existent wealth and privilege.'

That no vision of an egalitarian society was abroad in the shipyard to challenge customary distinctions was clearly demonstrated to me in a discussion of the preamble of the Declaration of
Independence. 'We hold these truths to be self-evident,' I quoted
to a shipyard group, 'that all men are created equal,' and then I
asked what this fine phrase conveyed to them. 'Well,' remarked
one sharp-witted man, 'men may be created equal like the fellow
who wrote that Declaration said, but they sure as hell ain't born
that way, and so far as I can see, no bunch of fancy words is going
to change the world and make all poor men rich.' Unquestioning,
as if it were the immutable laws of the universe which he recited,
he proceeded to consider the various differences of power and
privilege which divided men: 'There are people, and you know it,'
he concluded, 'who wouldn't even let such bums as us come
through any door in their houses except the back one, and I guess
if we lived in the houses and they worked in the shipyards, we
would feel and do the very same.'

For all the shipyard worker's loudly asserted pride in his way of
life and the work he was doing, he was essentially not proud or
satisfied. Along with his acceptance of the hierarchical society as
natural, eternal, and inevitable, he also accepted its scale of values,
and felt in his heart that work with the hands and the useful toil
of the wage earner were less honorable and less pleasurable than
the dilettantism of leisured wealth. One shipyard worker expressed
what was no doubt a common view when he remarked, 'I never
really wanted to be a working man; I was just forced into it.'[25]

Here are important elements of American working-class self-
awareness: an acceptance of hierarchy, an acceptance of privilege,
and some sense of inferiority: still, in interpreting this document,
there is a careful balance to be established between the 'loudly
asserted pride in his way of life', and the author's subjective judgement that he was 'not proud or satisfied'. Probably there *was* pride,
but it was not in essence pride of class.

Nonetheless, changes were being wrought by the single most
significant fact about the war on the domestic scene: whereas capitalist America in depression had seemed to have no need of the ten
million workers thrown on the scrap heap, now the needs of war
required their full *participation* in industry as much as in the armed
forces. In 1941 American industry was booming as it had not boomed
since the 1920s: to take the characteristic indicator, a million more
cars were produced than in 1939. Now the majority of American

people were touched by affluence and endowed with bargaining power. For all workers, the average weekly wage went up between 1939 and 1945 from $23.86 to $44.39. Labour's consciousness of its new strength (and the employers' powerful resistance) was reflected in the industrial strife of 1941, which, with the exception of 1937, was the worst year for strikes since 1919. The advantage lay with the workers; and, of the major unions, the United Mineworkers, the Steelworkers Organizing Committee and the United Automobile Workers were all able to gain favourable terms. Furthermore, a particularly bitter strike throughout the autumn in the 'captive' coalmines of the Appalachians in effect destroyed Roosevelt's first attempt at controlling labour through the National Defense Mediation Board. While all these developments were taking place, the unions recruited a million-and-a-half new members. There was relative tranquility in 1942, followed by further outbreaks of industrial discontent in 1943. Against the President's veto, Congress forced through a swingeing piece of anti-labour legislation, the Smith-Connally Act of June 1943. The act laid down that before calling a strike union officials must obtain the support of the majority of their members and must observe a thirty-day cooling-off period. In the face of the realities of the industrial situation the act was of little consequence: strike ballots simply demonstrated the power and solidarity of the unions and in practice no rigorous attempt was made to enforce the Act.[26]

The growing power of the unions showed itself in the railroad strike of 1943 and in the coal strikes of the same year. Because it could not risk the disruption to the war effort involved in a stoppage of the railways, the government simply took them over for long enough to grant substantial wage rises. Brief strikes in the coal areas resulted also in the mines being placed under the authority of the Secretary of the Interior, Harold Ickes. Ickes neatly summed up the invincible bargaining position conferred by labour participation in time of war: 'There are not enough jails in the country to hold these men,' he told Roosevelt, 'and, if there were, I must point out that a jailed miner produces no more coal.'[27] Eventually, in November 1943, the miners gained practically all of their demands. The war, then, brought both the diffusion of prosperity and the development of union organization, suggesting an acceleration of the tendencies noticed at the end of the thirties towards the consolidation of working-class awareness, and even consciousness.

The language of class was still not nearly so widely used in America as it was in Britain, or, in a slightly different way, in France. The war stemmed the flood of complaining letters which provided such a marvellous source for class imagery in the thirties: the rather fewer letters to the Secretary of Labor, however, do show an increased use of the phrase 'working class'; the wish most often expressed by individuals was to have a union to represent them.[28] The close of the Second World War presented a unique moment in American working-class history. The unions had strength; they were also still, some of them, prepared to articulate their claims in European style. On the various labour disputes at the end of the war, particularly in the coal and railroad industries, and on President Truman's apparent softness towards the anti-union lobby, the National Union of Textile Workers resolved 'that President Truman be roundly denounced as a danger to the country as long as he insists on making slaves of the working people who built this country, in debasing the United States army by treating it as a concentration camp for the breakers of un-constitutional laws, and in destroying the labor movement in the country by reckless hysterical legislation', and that 'President Truman be condemned for his harsh and unjust attitude toward working people and their union in his refusal to place the responsi-bility for the strikes at the doorsteps of management where it belongs. . . .'[29]

In fact, all through the war, government policy was orientated towards giving recognition and status to the unions, and this was widely reflected in the way in which unions were now treated by the mass media. A 1940 *March of Time* item on 'Labor and Defense' presented images both of the workers' sense of class loyalty, and of the manner in which they, as a class, fitted harmoniously into the community as a whole: 'whatever its faults and virtues, Organised Labor has long since become one of the permanent and accepted institutions of American democracy.'[30] News items covering strikes referred favourably to such leaders as John L. Lewis and William Green, and stressed the importance of the government conciliation service.[31] It is in the media, too, that one finds the most insistent harping on the theme, quite central to issues of class, that this war was a war for democracy. In its most laboured form the theme came through in such government-supported documentaries as *War Comes to America* (1941); but Hollywood was only too happy to share fully in the wartime mood. In June and July 1942, NBC radio broadcast 'a series of six narrative letters', said to be 'based upon actual letters written to Hitler by representative Americans', entitled *Dear Adolf*. The third programme in the series presented James

Cagney, 'relating the views of an American working man, as he addresses a letter to Hitler.' The true addressees, of course, were the American radio audience: subtlety need not be wasted on them, any more than on Hitler:

> Dear Adolf. We are writing you a letter and it isn't in fancy words. It's written around the clock by the working stiffs of America – the guys with grease on their faces who know what work means. . . .
>
> Get it Adolf? That's us. More than twenty million workers, eleven million union members, all over the USA. Yes, I'm talking about unions. . . . over here, a union button's a union button. . . .
>
> We hear the divisive voices. We hear the voices of those who would set class against class, whites against Negroes, Christians against Jews. But we know they're playing Adolf's game – and we're onto them. We hear the voices of those – not many but a few – who would rather beat Labor than Hitler, rather muscle in on Labor than save the United States. . . .[32]

Entering the spirit of the war for democracy, Harvard University came up in 1942 with an offer of special scholarships for trade unionists. The executive of the United Auto-Workers had no illusions about the continuing relationship between Ivy League universities, mid-western universities and trade unions. 'Harvard University', it decided, 'was not quite the proper place to educate future labor leaders'; instead Wayne University (in Detroit) and the Michigan state university should be contacted to 'work out a plan which would give students advanced training in labor economics, history and such other subjects pertaining to labor and which would develop the high type of leadership for our organisation'.[33] The sentiments of democratic unity could be directed upwards as well as downwards. In November 1943, the CIO issued a *Political Primer for all Americans*, addressed 'to our friends outside the labor movement: teachers, ministers, editors, and members of civic groups and womens clubs'. Its message was that 'we must now make a concerted effort to protect the future of the common man'.[34]

On their side some clubwomen were showing distinct signs of insecurity. The board of the Association of Junior Leagues of America spent a good deal of time in 1943 discussing the concern of members over such matters as 'Misrepresentation of Junior League as a leisure class group'. The board itself noted more phlegmatically: 'The question of the stigma attached to League membership still comes up at times. Nothing can be done about it except to live it down.' Then the matter was mopped up magisterially by the new executive secretary, Mrs Winthrop Pennock: 'The Junior Leagues', she said, 'represent only a small proportion of the population so we have to emphasize community leadership as a major part of the program rather than just volunteer service.'[35]

In two important areas, already discussed in earlier chapters, the war did have a definite effect on the realities of class: domestic service and social welfare legislation. For domestic servants the war opened opportunities for higher paid work in conditions of greater personal freedom. In addition to their other worries, the Junior Leagues noted a loss of membership due, among other things, to the 'servant problem'.[36] The Women's Bureau files at the end of the war are choked with statements and clippings on the servant shortage (and there was a marvellous Laurel and Hardy film in which Stan and Ollie, rejected manservants in the thirties, are now lionized by desperate society ladies). The Buffalo *Courier-Express*, on 14 October 1945, declared that women workers, 'used to wartime liberty', were 'setting their own standards for household jobs' and spoke of Buffalo being in the 'throes of a domestic revolution'. Mrs Wayne Babcock, one of the founders of the Philadelphia Institute of Household Occupations, prophesized that there would never again be 'a servant class in America': 'Former maids will do almost anything before going back to housework.' Mrs Wayne Babcock perceived that not the war alone was responsible, but also the secular trend in America towards professionalization. 'Employers held too long to old-fashioned attitudes,' she said. 'For half a century they exploited the employee. Now the employee is exploiting the employer.' The Metropolitan Executive Director of the Philadelphia YWCA, Mrs Emily P. Yaple, pointed out that demand would decrease as well as supply. The war had also emancipated the servant-keeping classes: housewives had got used to doing without maids and many had enjoyed new-found freedoms and the opportunities offered by labour-saving equipment, frozen foods, and smaller, more efficient houses. The circle is joined up by an article on 'The Master Problem', by a 'Long Island Butler'. He has no objections to domestic service as a *career*, but recommends that servants *unionize*. During the war America had also taken a large stride towards the reality of the job-conscious, as distinct from the class-conscious, society.

One factor among many which had made domestic service unattractive was its exclusion from the original social security provisions. Under the *test* of war the gaps in the legislation of the 1930s were glaringly exposed. In the previous chapter I quoted *in extenso* a letter from a British working-class housewife to a political leader. Here now is a comparable one from an American housewife (from Buffalo) to Senator Robert Wagner. The problem is the lack of social security coverage offered by farm work; the standard of literacy is very low; but, such was the openness of American political democracy compared with British, the letter did produce a reaction.

Dear Sir,
   sence their is so mutch talk of men beeing Drafted from one job to an other wee are rather puseled on several questions, I mezan we mothers at the Mothers Club I'll take my own case as an example my Husband has worked 14 years on his job and as it is not Ascencel or at least so some say, you can see working these years he has payed a lot of money in this so caled socal security, now if he shood bee drafted to a farm this beeing the only other work he knows, he is now 55 years old by the time this war is over what will have happened to his securety writes, this question is bothering A lot of us Wommen who are reaching an age where he hafto look where we are at, if My Husband and the other Man his age are drafted to do Farm work will he still be aleagable for his Socal security Payments at 65 years?
   if you can put us strate on this wee will be very grateful to you,
                              Sincerely Yours

Senator Wagner passed the letter on to Wilbur T. Cohen, Technical Advisor to the Social Security Board. Replying to Wagner, Cohen wrote that he had had to translate the letter the first time he read it, had had to concentrate on understanding it during the second reading of it, was amused during the third reading, and in the fourth reading had realized that the letter really had an important point, leading him to believe that 'it may be vitally necessary to consider the extension of social legislation' to both agriculture and domestic service.[37] The disruptions of war affected those higher up the social scale as well: the government's attention was drawn to the possible plight of 'the man of 45 to 65, who has passed through the 1929 Depression and is faced with the possibility of absence from his profession and a return at some remote date at an age when it will be impossible to begin the practice of law or medicine again.'[38] Overall, the relevant files in the National Archives demonstrate that from the characteristic trend of the 1930s of employers trying to keep their employees out of social security, the swing during the war is to employees themselves striving hard to get themselves in. The war played a crucial part in the general move towards universal social security coverage which, at least in this one modest aspect, serves to hold Americans together in one kind of classless frame.

As in Britain and France, then, though in different degrees, the war both assisted the consolidation of classes and the disintegration of overt class distinctions. It also affected those facets of American life which tended anyway to cut across class. The war was a central phenomenon in bringing a new status and a new self-consciousness to the black American, and indeed helped to bring to birth the whole contemporary Civil Rights movement. A landmark in the shift of official opinion was the establishment by Truman of the Committee on Civil Rights. Yet the war also showed the enduring power of racial bigotry. There were riots in 1943 and again in 1946. When a Junior League magazine in August 1943 printed a black face in a group photograph there were violent repercussions. A Southern member told the board that 'Southerners felt that it was an attempt to propagandize and to put the negro on the same social level as the white.' Further discussion led to this resolution:

> Materials for the magazine which might have doubtful repercussions for any group of leagues either by creating difficult public relations for such a group or by causing tension between this group and the leagues in other sections of the country must be submitted to the president of the association for her consideration, and if she deems necessary, to the board. The board directs that this policy shall be applied only in cases where the editor and executive secretary feel that the material has definitely dangerous potentialities.[39]

And what more potentially dangerous topic than race?

The war, inevitably, increased still further the influence of one of America's most important pressure groups, the war veterans: in theory classless, in composition partially working-class, in practice usually strongly hostile to labour. In general the war did bring something of a rapprochement between labour and such organizations as the American Legion and the Veterans of Foreign Wars,[40] suggesting, if anything, a diminution in the significance of the politics of class. If the independent black Civil Rights movement itself gained an enormous boost, it might also contribute to a process whereby blacks could be incorporated within the existing white class structure. There was wishful thinking, but also truth, in the statement of the National Association for the Advancement of Colored People in February 1943: 'Every attack on labor is an attack on the Negro, for the Negro is largely a worker. . . . Organised labor is now our national ally. The CIO has proved that it stands for our people within the unions and outside the unions. . . . If labor loses a battle, the Negro loses also.'[41] But the complication was that just as the working class became stronger and more consolidated than it had ever been before, so also its high living standards, and its integration into bargaining procedures almost as characteristic of the pressure-group nature of American society as of relations between capital and labour, meant that there was also a blunting of any independent sense of working-class consciousness.

In popular mythology, and very much in reality too, British society, of the three studied in this book, shaped up best to the strains of war. Is class – to attempt now a final judgement on the *significance* of class in the war period – somehow the vital variable? Did British society 'pull through' (as the upper-class language of the time would have it) because of, or in spite of, her class system? The key to British morale and resilience, really, was civic loyalty. Class distinctions sometimes did come near to destroying that loyalty, but on the whole the structure was both subtle and flexible enough, and sufficiently widely accepted for class to be a useful framework within which national unity could develop. Sectionalism, racial and ethnic differences, and hostility to federal government were the main features affecting the efficiency of the American war effort, rather than the presence or absence of class distinction. In France, the surface, but very bitter, class conflicts of the late thirties undoubtedly flowed into the breaches driven into French society in 1939 and 1940 and thereafter: but the breaches themselves were created externally – by the Germans. Working-class solidarity was at the base of the Resistance, but its leaders came from all classes. Once again the particular nature of class in each of the three countries is an important factor in explaining their contrasting experiences in war, but it is not the only, nor in this case, the overriding one.

Notes

1. Vercors, *Le Silence de la mer* (1942), preface.
2. P. M. Williams, *Crisis and Compromise: Politics in the Fourth Republic* (1964), p. 18.
3. Stanley Hoffman, *France: Change and Tradition* (1963), pp. 34–5.
4. Henri Michel, *Les Courants de penseé de la résistance* (1962), p. 103.
5. H. R. Kedward, *Resistance in Vichy France* (1978), pp. 249–85.
6. Quoted in Henri Michel and Boris Mirkine-Guetzovitch, *Les Ideés politiques·et sociales de la résistance* (1954), pp. 159–61.
7. See, e.g., Kedward, *op. cit.*, pp. 106–7.
8. Michel and Mirkine-Guetzovitch, *op. cit.*, pp. 376–7.
9. Henri Michel, *Les Courants de penseé de la résistance* (1962), p. 400.
10. *Ibid*, pp. 405–6.
11. *Ibid*, p. 406.
12. Printed in Michel and Mirkine-Guetzovitch, *op. cit.*, pp. 215–18.
13. P. Arnoult and others, *La France sous l'occupation* (1959), pp. 65, 70 and 85.
14. Gérard Walter, *Histoire du paysan français* (1963), p. 461–3.
15. Jean Lhomme, *Classes sociales et transformations économiques* (1945), p. 21.
16. *Ibid*, pp. 23, 43.
17. Stanley Hoffman, 'The Effects of World War II on French Society and Politics', *French Historical Studies*, vol. II, no. 1 (spring 1961), pp. 28–63.
18. See Jean-Noel Jeanneney's excellent film, *Léon Blum ou la Républiqué* (1972).
19. Lowell J. Carr and James E. Sterner, *Willow Run: a study of Industrialization and Cultural Inadequacy* (1952), pp. xiii, 44.
20. The army's rating of housing is quoted in *ibid*, pp. 66–9.
21. *Ibid*, p. 89.
22. The diary is reproduced in *ibid*, pp. 95ff. The entry quoted here is for 2 November 1942.
23. Robert J. Havighurst and H. G. Morgan, *The Social History of a War-Boom Community* (1951), p. 15.
24. Catherine Archibald, *Wartime Shipyard: a Study in Social Disunity* (1947).
25. *Ibid*, pp. 170–1.
26. See Richard Polenberg, *War and Society: the United States, 1941–1945* (1972), esp. pp. 137–209.
27. Quoted by Polenberg, p. 164.
28. NA, RG 86, box 923.
29. Archives Division, the State Historical Society of Wisconsin, Madison, Textile Workers Organizing Committee Papers.
30. *March of Time*, vol. 7, no. 5 (1940).
31. See, for example, in NA Film Department, 200.143, 200.147, 200.149, 200 PN.40.100, 200 PN.41.4, 200 PN.41.54, 200 PN.41.61, 200 PN.41.63.

32. Tamiment Library, New York University Libraries, Max Zawitsky Collection.
33. Archives of Labor and Urban Affairs [ALUA], Wayne State University, Detroit, UAW: executive minutes, 7–9 June 1942.
34. Columbia University Library, New York, Frances Perkins Papers, box 72, CIO file.
35. Social Welfare History Archives [SWHA], University of Minnesota Libraries, Minneapolis, AJLA: Board of Directors files, January to September 1943.
36. *Ibid.*
37. NA, RG 47, box 239.
38. *Ibid.*
39. SWHA, AJLA board minutes, 20–4 September 1943.
40. See especially ALUA, UAW, box 23: United Auto-Workers Congress of Industrial Organizations, 'Veterans Conference', Washington, April 1944.
41. *NAACP Bulletin*, February 1943, quoted by James S. Olson, 'Organized Black Leadership and Industrial Unionism: the Racial Response, 1936–1945', *Labor History* (Summer, 1969), p. 486.

13

Image and Reality of Class
in Post-war Society

During the period studied in this chapter, which takes us well into the 1950s, the longer-term changes associated with the war shook themselves out. On the whole, America prospered; while austerity was a dominating characteristic in Britain until at least the early fifties, and France continued to suffer the greatest deprivations. Recovery from war was the major European preoccupation whereas the Cold War, with its perceived external and internal threat of communism, was the major American concern. The French continued to be the main originators of cross-cultural studies; and the French scene in this period is marked by an even greater insistence on the social and political (as distinct from the academic) importance of class, a stronger interest in the working class, and a hint that the old ruling bourgeoisie no longer carried its former weight. In America there was an elaboration of the view that class, if it existed at all, was a matter of subjective perception; and there was a move to reject class labels altogether, and to present America instead as a society characterized by a continuous gradation of status groups. Much of the sociological argument was over semantics and had the perfectly legitimate aims of securing the most precise use of such concepts as 'élites', 'strata', 'status' and 'socio-economic groups', of illuminating the different 'dimensions' of inequality, and of analysing the 'multiple hierarchies' that exist in complex contemporary society. Not our worry, if I can risk being tedious about that once more: whether or not ordinary Americans were speaking about 'classes' or, say, 'the working class', they were not speaking about stratification or multiple hierarchies, though they were, admittedly, beginning to talk about 'status' and 'status symbols'. In Britain, class began to be studied with a new professionalism, and some of the old shibboleths against discussing the nasty subject in good company (i.e. in learned books) was dispelled. There was a move away from surveys devoted solely to the working class and towards an interest in the so-called 'plight' of the middle class. In the wider sweep of European intellectual development there was a move towards producing overall theories which accepted the real existence of social classes while denying the Marxist conclusion that conflict must necessarily ensue.

FRENCH ACADEMIC IMAGES – INTERNAL AND EXTERNAL

One important personal example of the link (stressed by Hoffman) between the Vichy and Liberation régimes was Pierre Laroque, the very prototype of upper-class government man, who had been the brains behind the drafting of both Vichy social policies, and the new welfare-state legislation enacted at the end of the war. His *The Major Contemporary Social Problems* (1954–5) exemplifies French cross-cultural analysis at its best. Laroque recognized the emergence in modern society of multiple hierarchies – political, economic, administrative, spiritual and cultural – but argued that these could exist side-by-side with more traditional, historically determined, hierarchies. More than this, he maintained that contemporary societies still were made up of social classes, and defined them simply as 'relatively closed groups of unequal rank'.[1] Laroque's image of the French class structure is a familiar one: governing bourgeoisie; middle classes – made up of four main groupings, the artisans and small tradesmen, those elements of the liberal professions who are not definitely in the governing bourgeoisie, the technicians and managers of industry and commerce (but excluding the senior managers, who belong to the governing bourgeoisie), and the middle and lower civil servants; the rural classes; and the working class.

Laroque had the traditional anglophiliac image of Britain:

Great Britain brings us into the presence of an old country very attached to her traditions. The British social hierarchy is to a large extent one of the products of these traditions. It is an accepted hierarchy which is widely recognised and has never seriously been debated. The majority of the population even show a real attachment to this social hierarchy. As a result, there has never been deep class antagonism in Great Britain. This expresses itself in a whole collection of forms which are translated into the contemporary social structure of Great Britain and also, and perhaps more important, into the evolution of these social structures.

The tradition in Great Britain, he says, is to make a distinction between the middle class and, on the one side, aristocracy, and, on the other, the working class, and, furthermore, to break the middle class down into two elements: 'upper middle class' and 'lower middle class'. The upper middle class is equivalent to the French governing bourgeoisie, the lower middle class is 'the middle class properly so-called'. How is the upper middle class defined? By income, certainly, he says, also occupation, but still more by a collection of other elements gathered under a descriptive term which, he declares, is very difficult to translate into French: this term he gives as 'gentility' – a word which might have surprised British readers even in the early 1950s. However, if the label perhaps seems anachronistic, his description of its collection of elements is shrewd enough: 'a certain style of behaviour, a certain style of speech – accent plays an important part in determining whether one belongs to this social category – and also a certain type of education, equally certain distinctive leisure pursuits and membership of certain clubs.' He concludes that the dominating notion of this social category is that of being a 'gentleman'. The key institutions, he says, are the public schools, and Oxford and Cambridge. However this 'upper middle class' is not closed to recruits from below.

In 'the middle class properly so-called' or 'lower middle class', Laroque includes all who do not qualify for the label of 'gentility', as well as the 'artisans' and, since there is no separate rural class in Britain, the farmers. Although this class hasn't quite made it to gentility, 'the ideal of "gentility", the ideal of "gentleman"' is, according to Laroque, a potent aspiration for this social class. 'As soon as, in this case, a family has a sufficient income, the first thing it does is to send its children to a "public school", in order to let them benefit from a certain type of education which will give them access to the higher social category.' Then he moves on to the working class which, he says, covers nearly two-thirds of the population and is therefore 'a determining element' in British political life. The British working class is not homogeneous but it is very unified. The power exercised by British trade unions has been an essential element in the evolution of British social structures since trade union leaders have themselves been raised up into the traditional governing class. Laroque praises the social changes he detects in Britain, brought about not by guided policies aimed at the abolition of class distinctions, but simply through force of circumstances. Laroque gives his unstinted admiration to the 'upper class' for its flexibility, demonstrated by the appearance of trade unionists in the House of Lords, the provision of scholarships to the public schools, the 'democratization' of Oxford and Cambridge, and the rise of the provincial university. 'The fact that education is orientated towards the formation of the "gentleman", is favourable to upward social mobility' since it enabled individuals of diverse origin to be assimilated into the governing class. And while opportunities of getting to the top are increasing, so also the middle class and the working class are coming closer together. Thus, Laroque concludes, with all the enthusiasm and optimism of the early fifties, 'a progressive social revolution is being sketched out, peaceful and silent, which is apparent to those who after an interval of several months or several years return to England and take note of the profound transformation taking place there.'

Turning to the United States, Laroque says that country 'presents a social structure which is in large degree the exact opposite of the British social structure.' The three points to be stressed are, first, that America is a continent, yet, secondly, there is general equality of material conditions and lifestyles, and so, thirdly, a profound egalitarianism. Yet, paradoxically, there is well defined social stratification, determined by income, by occupation, and by family ties and lifestyle. America, he suggests, breaks down into 51 per cent working-class and 43 per cent middle-class; there is a small governing class, indistinguishable from the middle class. There are also hierarchies within the two major classes. Laroque touches on a theme, already mentioned, that a more 'European' class structure is beginning to form in the United States.

Laroque then returns to France for a development of his preliminary remarks. The working class he reckons at forty-to-fifty per cent of the population. It is not homogeneous: certain workers, such as those in the book trade or on the railways, enjoy specially high social prestige. But despite this heterogeneity, the working class is the most class-conscious of all classes in France. The middle classes represent a microcosm of the whole social structure of France. There are different prestige groups, with the self-employed carrying higher status than the salaried. The middle classes are essentially conservative, and 'have a more defined personality than in any other country'. The governing class, according to Laroque, embraces elements from the summits of different hierarchies – political, economic, administrative, spiritual and intellectual – as well as from families benefiting from traditional prestige. It is very heterogeneous, he maintains, and in contrast to Great Britain, the leaders of the various hierarchies do not necessarily come from the same social background: the governing class is therefore less sharply delimited than the other social classes and, in particular, there is a constant movement between this class and the middle classes. Despite this, Laroque concluded that there was less social mobility in France than in the United States or the United Kingdom: the material circumstances and the educational and cultural standards of the different classes were, he maintained, more sharply differentiated in France than in the other countries. Then, in a final brilliant phrase, he pointed to the French 'conjunction of a tacit recognition of the social hierarchies, and a refusal to admit to them openly'. This, he thought, was the key to the strong social antagonisms which might lead to another revolution in France.

While Laroque was completing his book, an interesting thesis on 'Social Classes in the United States' was being presented for a doctorate in law at the University of Paris.[2] Classes along traditional lines, with strong hints of the *ancien régime*, still existed in France, said Françoise Bouriez-Gregg, whereas:

> The criterion of class based on belonging to a particular family group does not have the same weighting in the United States as in Europe. The family cell in France, in particular, is much more stable. In spite of the great upheavals of the war and although a growing number of marriages across different classes have been observed in recent years a quite heavy ostracism still weighs upon these misalliances. Education of children is organised in this sense, impregnated as it still is with maxims, and with prejudices about the choice of school, of friends, and of career.[3]

Unlike France, said Mlle Bouriez-Gregg, America bore no trace of the ancient feudal 'estates'; instead, distinctions there were based on economic criteria. Thus for America Lloyd Warner's classification of 'upper-upper, lower-lower, etc.', fitted much better than the French classification which, in an interesting variation on Laroque, and something of a throwback to Louise-Marie Ferré's imagery of the thirties, she gives as 'aristocracy, grand, medium and small bourgeoisie, and people.' She then argues that the absence of such distinctive class labels as 'aristocracy', 'bourgeoisie', 'people' suggested a 'oneness in the notion of class', and that in America it was 'a case not of distinct categories, well defined and isolated from each other, but of the different steps within the heart of one single class.'[4] The image she sees of American society is a shining one when compared with her image of France:

> the French bourgeois and the American 'average man' have little

in common. The concept of the bourgeois is bolstered by that of property, but not necessarily by that of work. The opposite is the case for the ordinary American. The French bourgeois is thrifty, prudent, Sybaritic, sceptical and xenophobic. The average American is virtuous, dogmatic, religious, enterprising, comfortable and welcoming. One of these middle classes (the French) is defined by its place in the material order, the other (the American) by its place in the intellectual and cultural order.

It is difficult, in the American context, to speak of a proletariat:

America draws great pride from its middle class, the backbone of the nation, which reflects the truest image of it and which is quantitatively and qualitatively the most powerful force. America speaks with detachment of its aristocracy. It is with uneasiness and difficulty that Americans allude to the proletariat. The word itself is scarcely suitable. Even emptied of its ideological Marxist content, it implies a series of notions which only fit American society very imperfectly. In the first place, the proletariat by definition is that which has neither capital nor reserves, while in fact the United States is not so much a capitalist as an industrial country. The non-possession of capital does not place an individual on a lower scale, insofar as the word evokes a static condition without remedy which fits badly with the numerous opportunities and climate of social mobility of the country. Which is to come back to the point that the American proletariat would be morally responsible for its own condition, through laziness and bad intentions, or through being organically ill-adapted, infirm, stupid, or racially unassimilable (negro), or as yet unassimilated (immigrants of recent date).[5]

Upward mobility was 'rather difficult' in a 'relatively rigid society' like France. So was downward mobility: 'Even if mediocre, even if ruined, those belonging to the upper class remain in the upper class in their own eyes, in the eyes of their peers and in the eyes of the lower class.' The distance between the classes is great because the social system in France was founded not on economic, but on social and political considerations. In America, by contrast, while upward mobility is relatively easy, there is little to stop the mediocre, the lazy and incapable from sliding down the social scale. Extended family ties, which contribute so much to the underpinning of class in France, are weaker in America. Business recruitment in America was becoming more closed, and in areas of economic stagnation class lines were firming up; but against this there was constant flux in boom states such as Texas, the areas of industrial revolution in the south, and Alaska. But she firmly rejected the possibility of a convergence between American class structure and the European model on the grounds that the two dominant trends in America were a levelling of material and cultural standards, and the elaboration of distinct strata based on income.[6]

Bouriez-Gregg was endeavouring to interpret American society for the French academic community. At a Fabian Summer School held at Royaumont in August 1950, the French Socialist, Étienne Weill-Raynal, attempted to explain 'Social Classes and Political Parties in France' to British Socialists.[7] It appears, began Weill-Raynal with perspicacity, that our friends from other countries, and in particular our British friends, do not understand us very well. The essential fact to be grasped was that economic evolution in France had been relatively slow, so that all types of economic activity were still being practised with all types of social class still in existence. In 1946 the agricultural class was still thirty-two per cent of the active population compared with five per cent in Britain. Medium-sized industry, and the artisanry occupied a special position in France. Many artisans, such as the farriers and coopers, were still closely linked to country life. Large numbers of those working on the fringes of the new motor, electrical and radio-communications industries, as mechanics, or in accessory or repair shops or garages, had outlooks very different from factory workers, their sights being set on becoming independent proprietors. Whether or not Napoleon had ever been right in his comment on Britain, France was now 'the nation of shopkeepers'. There had been over a million retail shops in 1939; now there were nearly a million-and-a-half, with one shop-keeper (*commercant*) for every thirty inhabitants.

Even if the significance of the pure capitalists had declined, there had arisen a new generation of 'the economically strong' – those who drew their incomes from both management and shareholding. One other complication in French society was the existence of the socially important liberal professions, consisting in particular of lawyers and doctors. Although wage-earners made up more than half of the active population, they were very far from homogeneous: again, the railwaymen were singled out as having 'attitudes which verged on those of the minor functionaries in, say, the Post Office.' The smaller the enterprise the fewer the differences between the boss and the workers. Workers in small enterprises might often hope to acquire enough equipment to set up their own businesses. Still more people aspired towards setting up their own shop or similar commercial establishment, and there had been a proliferation of these since December 1945 when the old limitation on the number of *commercants* was abolished. Weill-Raynal's concluding points for his British listeners were that a multiplicity of social classes went with a multiplicity of political parties, but that it was impossible to make exact correlations between social class and political party. Certainly the majority of the big owners were conservative, and the largest number of Communists was to be found among the workers; but that was all that one could say. Out of every three workers one would vote Communist, one would vote Socialist, and one would vote for the MRP, 'for what separates them is not their social condition but their political or religious convictions.' Laroque, writing after the return of the Conservatives to power in 1951, was full of praise for the British system of, as he saw it, harmony and progressive change. Weill-Raynal, speaking when the post-war Labour government was still in office, expressed his admiration by quoting from a letter written by Léon Blum to Michael Foot describing the choice for Europe as being between Labour Britain and Soviet Russia, praised Britain for making great gains in justice, equality and liberty in advance of any revolutionary transformation of the system of private capitalism. These hymns of praise form a sharp contrast to the current dirges attributing British economic weaknesses to the rigidity of her class system.

Laroque referred to the refusal by official and political circles to admit the realities of class in France. Nonetheless, advances had been made since the thirties. A pamphlet produced by a militant section of the MRP, perceiving that 'bourgeois France', proud of the Revolution, had not wanted to recognize classes, declared that one of the great weaknesses of the parties of the Third Republic, outside of the extreme left, had been 'to have wished to ignore the problem of social classes', since this was a subject 'dominating contemporary political life'.[8] The classes described in the pamphlet were the working class, the middle classes, and the peasantry: there was no explicit reference to an upper class or 'governing bourgeoisie'. The main point that emerges from all these academic and polemical sources is of the continuing importance, and special character, of the French middle classes. These were as fully recognized by communist commentators[9] as by anyone else; and the classic study of *The French Worker* (1951),[10] by Michel Collinet, necessarily devoted a good deal of space to discussing the middle classes.

AMERICAN ACADEMIC IMAGES

One remarkable sign of the ideological climate among American academics in the Cold War era was the enthusiastic reception accorded to the republication in 1949 of Selig Perlman's *A Theory of the Labor Movement*,[11] the book which, in 1928, had suggested that the key to the American worker's harmonious integration into capitalist society lay in his 'job consciousness' (as opposed to 'class consciousness'). The same year saw the publication of the influential *The Psychology of Social Classes*,[12] in which Richard Centers argued, with all the force of the italics at his command, that social class is *'no more nor no less than what people collectively think it is.'* Now this, in part, coincides with the colloquial or popular approach favoured by me; but Centers made a sharp distinction between class, which was exclusively 'subjective', and the 'objective' hierarchy of social stratification: my own aspiration is to bring the two parts into a common focus. Of course sociological research in America proceeded under the impetus of its own internal logic and within cultural constraints which went far back into history. American sociologists continued to set the pace in the accumulation of detailed survey material on social stratification, almost all of it concerned purely with subjective perceptions since questions were not usually asked about property and power relationships. Some followed Centers in regarding the responses as being about 'social class'; many others said they were about 'prestige status', and used that concept to wish away any discussion of class. Numerous articles in American journals came up with this sort of conclusion: 'Data gathered in research on a southern New England mill town indicate that, while a prestige status system exists in that town, local residents do not perceive this system as a series of discrete social classes. They see it, instead, as a continuum.'[13] Others simply stepped to the side: 'no attempt is made to relate the concept of "prestige status" to other concepts in social stratification, such as those of social class.'[14] The famous Kinsey, in his own peculiar investigations, denied himself the use of class categories and thus twisted himself into delightful knots with such classic utterances as, 'lower level males, however, are likely to have a negative attitude toward petting and to demand sexual intercourse in preference to any other form of sexual release.'

One of the most balanced and perceptive contributions of the time was William Goldschmidt's article, 'Social Class in America: a critical review', published in 1950 in the *American Anthropologist*. Goldschmidt pungently pointed out the weakness of the small-town studies of the Lynds and of Warner and his fellows when they generalized from one local community to the nation as a whole: 'we know what short shrift Middlewestern upper-uppers would receive among the proper Bostonians.'

> The important fact is that the local community does not represent either a miniature or a cross-section of the nation; that is it contains no industrial leaders or international bankers, governors, presidents or bureau chiefs, nor any labor leaders or top church officials.

Goldschmidt also convincingly challenged the assumption of Warner and his associates (and implicit in many a Capra movie) 'that most of the people in the United States identified themselves with their community.' He had his own constructive view of the 'class system which appears to be emerging, though it is not yet clearly defined'. For my taste the attribution of a coherent ideology to each class is overstated, but Goldschmidt carries much conviction when he writes: 'This emerging pattern is toward four basic classes, each with its own basic cultural orientation, its own life ways, with differential degrees of power, and with sharply differentiated status':

> The smallest and most clearly established of these emerging social classes is an élite. It is characterized by the long-established possession of power and money, and by the adoption of an aristocratic orientation in its subculture stressing family background, leisure pursuits and the rejection of any employment. Its endeavors to draw itself completely apart are thwarted by the great technological growth of America and the consequent rise of great fortunes and fiscal power. Its powers are undermined by the democratic procedures in politics and the public protection of anti-élite interests, such as unions, in the economic sphere. This élite is not found in each or even most communities, and is but a small segment of the total social universe.
>
> The middle class, constituting about 40% of the population, if Centers is correct, is characterized by a set of values oriented toward the fiscal élite and by the acceptance of the thesis of absolute equality and its correlate, the individual's responsibility for his own status. Its values appear to be oriented about money but are not, for it is subordinated to the notion of the genteel occupation. . . . Members of this class act as the élite in the local community, but are not usually a part of the upper group. They

are rather a pseudo-élite, taking on its powers and social preroga-
tives within the narrower context of the local community.

The third class might be called a working or laboring class, or
perhaps a proletariat. It is a proletariat not merely because it is
made up of manual workers, but because it rejects, or tries to
reject, the middle-class ideal of economic advancement through
individual achievement, and accepts instead an identification with
labor and the ideal of collective action for social gains. . . .

The fourth sector is made up of laboring people who also accept
their laboring status, but who are reared in such a psychological
atmosphere of hopelessness that they do not expect to advance,
either individually or collectively, from a position of labor. . . .
They inhabit the slums, both in urban centers and the share-
cropper South. Their circumstances of life are always degrading,
and one might refer to them as being decultured. . . .

The lines of distinction between these classes are not sharply
drawn, and class orientation is not fully achieved. It is a tendency
rather than an accomplished system. An understanding of American society cannot be arrived at by asserting a fixity in class
orientation; rather the fluidity of class position and the force of
the cultural denial of class must always be kept in mind.[15]

But where on earth, one has to ask, are the blacks?

BRITISH ACADEMIC IMAGES

Carr-Saunders and Caradog Jones have been hunted through these
pages, stalwart representatives that they were of the changing
academic orthodoxy of their time. This is how it went in the 1950s:

Social class is a most elusive concept and one that has long interested sociologists, both as a subject in its own right and as a
method of classification to be used when investigating social conditions, behaviour, and attitudes. The difficulty of the concept lies,
not in deciding whether social classes have reality, in the sense that
social class attitudes have a share in everyday behaviour and
thought, but rather in defining appropriate class boundaries for
statistical purposes. Clearly there is no single measure of social
class. . . .[16]

The 1958 edition of the *Survey* then proceeds to a sophisticated study of social mobility which, thanks largely to the work of Professor D. V. Glass, was now also a flourishing area of scholarship in Britain: the publication in 1954 of the collection of essays on *Social Mobility in Britain*, under the editorship of Glass, was a landmark. The essay by C. A. Moser and J. R. Hall on 'Social Grading of Occupations'[17] lay at the core of an important trend of the time, the attempt to produce more precise classifications than those offered by the Registrar-General. Hall and Moser offered a seven-point scale running from 'Professional and High Administrative' to 'Unskilled Manual'. Since the early 1950s most British social investigators have used this scale or some variation of it. And this brings us back to the central problem posed by this book. Such scales are immensely valuable in establishing a reliable quantification of the realities of social inequality; but the scale itself in no way coincides with social classes as understood historically and colloquially. The same difficulty occurs with the scale developed in this period by market researchers, in which 'A's and 'B's (together covering all of the upper class and much of the middle class) are run together in one AB category; the 'C's (covering the rest of the middle class and the more prosperous working class) are split into C_1 and C_2; and the 'D's and 'E's (the unskilled and the poor) form one DE category. Here we touch on another fundamental phenomenon with which this book is concerned: the tendency of the upper class, apparent in much imagery and manifestly exercising real power, nonetheless to disappear from many taxonomies of the social structure.

The best commonsense taxonomy was presented by Anthony Crosland in *The Future of Socialism* (1956), in which he argued that 'the hierarchies of education, occupational prestige, and style of life' all showed pronounced and visible breaks in the classes, and that these breaks broadly coincided. They did so because they were causally related, with a segregated three-tier system of education (public schools, grammar schools, secondary modern schools) imposing a corresponding pattern on the other two criteria. Inheritance also contributed to this correspondence. Crosland admitted that ambivalent cases existed, but felt that the correlation was 'sufficiently close to impart a strong significance at least to the tripartite division of working, middle, and upper classes.'

People accept this division subjectively as a reality; it influences their behaviour towards other people, and their social judgements. And it is objectively real in the sense that it would emerge, without asking people for their subjective evaluations, from the external application of at least the three criteria mentioned above.

Crosland further thought that a more refined division of 'upper', 'upper middle', 'lower middle', 'upper working', and 'working' would also be real.[18] Crosland notwithstanding, there was still much resistance to the naked use of the phrase 'upper class'. Dudley Seers, in introducing his important study of *The Levelling of Incomes Since 1938* (1951), explained that he regarded the term 'middle class' as 'colloquially' including everyone not in the working class!

On the big questions of the role of class in social conflict and in social development there was little agreement among academic writers, and less among political writers. Whether they spoke of classes or of a continuum of status groups, Americans in the main, envisaged integration rather than conflict. There was some agreement among European observers that differences between the middle classes and the working class were diminishing: but this, said Michel Crozier, should be interpreted as part of a progression towards a society in which class distinctions would be less sharp, not as the beginnings of a polarization into two classes.[19] Perhaps the most important contribution of Marxist commentators was to resist any facile acceptance of the managerial revolution thesis, and insist on the continued existence of 'the economically strong' (if not exactly 'a ruling class') who combined management with ownership of shares.[20] A new twist was given to the debate by the German sociologist and politician, Ralf Dahrendorf, who accepted the Marxist proposition that conflict was endemic in society but saw this as involving 'quasi-groups' rather than traditional social classes.[21]

OFFICIAL IMAGES

We need not spend long on official images. Government classifications remained detached from popular concepts of class, though the 1951 British census did introduce an additional classification into fifteen socio-economic groups, echoing academic thinking on the subject. All three countries attempted to spread social security provision to the whole community rather than confine it to 'employees' or to the 'working class'.[22] The process went farthest in Britain where, indeed, the statutory working man was finally buried, with perhaps only a toe or two left sticking out. National Insurance and the National Health Service were available to the entire nation. Although for technical reasons the phrase 'for the working classes' could not be dropped from the 1946 Housing Act, Aneurin Bevan, the responsible minister, made it clear that he understood the working classes to include everyone who worked for a living (*travailleurs* as well as *ouvriers*, one might say). He also said that he wished to recreate the classless villages of the seventeenth and eighteenth centuries:[23] alas, his estimate of British social behaviour was even more inaccurate than his history. The 1949 Housing Act explicitly dropped the reference to 'the working classes'. The Blue Books and White Papers which poured forth from the presses of His Majesty's Stationery Office take on a complete change in tone from that of the thirties. In many, photographs and histograms proliferate; there is a clear intention to communicate with a wide audience. The Ministry of National Insurance emphasized its desire to be accessible to all: success came in the wet summer of 1948 when its offices were deluged by holiday-makers who 'apparently filled in their spare time during wet weather by seeking shelter and information at the same time.'[24]

In France, while social security provision was greatly extended, social security categories continued to come very near to replicating class lines. When the separate Social Security Code was established at the end of 1956 there remained a fundamental distinction between wage and salary earners on one side, and the self-employed (*non-salariés*) on the other. The latter comprised the artisans (as inscribed on the *Register of Trades*), those in industrial and commercial occupations (as enrolled in the *Register of Commerce*), those in agricultural occupations (as defined in article 1107 of the Rural Code), and the 'liberal professions', defined as follows: doctors, dentists, midwives, pharmaceutists, architects, chartered accountants, veterinary surgeons, solicitors, barristers, bailiffs, auctioneers, stockbrokers, trustees and official liquidators, lawyers at the *Tribunal de Commerce*, insurance brokers, registrars, legal valuers, agents, umpires at the *Tribunal de Commerce*, men of letters, artists, civil engineers, medical auxiliaries, insurance agents. Further separate provisions covered executives (*cadres*) and functionaries.[25]

As already noted, official attitudes to labour in America changed during the war period. In the post-war years organized labour was regarded as a sectional interest – rather than as representing a social class. The change of tone in official papers which I noted in Britain took its own special form in the USA. After the war the old *Annual Reports of the Secretary of Labor* have individual titles, each appealing to labour's status as a responsible element in the community:

To Promote the General Welfare (1949), *Strengthening the Economy* (1950), *Mobilizing Labor for Defense* (1951). In America, alone, official papers enter the realm of ideological combat. In 1956 the Department of Labor's *American Workers' Fact Book* was still fighting the Cold War:

> The American labor union movement has not embraced the ideology of class conflict advanced by some European unions. It hates communism. As a typically American institution, the labor movement of the United States believes in democratic government and a philosophy of gradualism. It sets its sights on things it has a practical chance of winning, but within the framework of American institutions. It supports our free-enterprise economic system, and seeks to strengthen and improve our economy, our democracy, and the welfare of workers. These goals labor unions attempt to achieve through both economic and political action.[26]

UNOFFICIAL IMAGES

Let us move on to popular and unofficial images: we are now in the era of reliable and broadly comparable social survey material. F. M. Martin's investigations, conducted in Greenwich and Hertford in September and October 1950, produced one unequivocal conclusion about British images of the class structure as a whole: 'The great majority of our subjects thought in terms of a three-class system, and most of them described these classes by the same set of names – upper, middle and working.'[27] Surveys conducted in France (by the Institut National d'Études Démographiques in 1950) and in the United States (presented by Richard Centers in *The Psychology of Social Classes*), and brought together in a pioneering American comparative study by Natalie Rogoff.[28] however, produced much less well-defined pictures, as the following table shows:

CLASS	PERCENTAGE OF RESPONDENTS	CLASS	PERCENTAGE OF RESPONDENTS
Bourgeois	7.9	Upper	5.4
Middle	22.5	Middle	45.2
Working	27.1	Working	10.6
Peasant	13.7	Farming	0.8
Poor	7.5	Lower	4.0
Other	2.3	Other	6.5
No Answer	19.0	No Answer	27.5

These figures tie in with much of the academic analysis given at the beginning of the chapter. The high proportion unable to answer, particularly in the United States, stands out – though the American response is definite enough to suggest that any wishing away of the existence of classes in America was wilful thinking. The recognition of the existence of a peasant class, and of quite a substantial working class in France, and the large proportion calling themselves middle-class in America, are all in keeping with other impressions that we have already formed.

A 'closed' survey, conducted under the auspices of UNESCO in Vienne-en-France in 1949–50, in which the interviewees were invited to assign themselves to one of three classifications, 'proletariat', 'middle-class' or 'bourgeoisie', produced the following results:[29]

	Men	Women
Proletariat	53%	45%
Middle Class	43%	50%
Bourgeoisie	4%	5%

A further breakdown by occupation revealed that this 'imposed' tripartite structure did not coincide well with the French self-image of their society. Twenty-four per cent of workers (*ouvriers*) did not declare themselves to be proletarians; many skilled workers put themselves in the middle class; two per cent declared themselves bourgeois: 'probably', explained one of the two sociologists who conducted the survey, 'they came from traditional bourgeois families.' Thirty-nine per cent of the small employers and white-collar workers did not put themselves in the middle class; many declared themselves to be proletarian. Seventy-nine per cent of top professional people refused to put themselves in the bourgeoisie; the great majority of them put themselves in the middle class; only the rich industrialists were prepared to call themselves bourgeois. Looking at things the other way round: about one-third of those who called themselves proletarians were not workers; about a quarter who called themselves middle class were workers, and fifteen per cent had been classified by the surveyors (perhaps incorrectly, they admitted) as being upper professionals; and among the self-styled bourgeoisie, only fifty-one per cent were in top jobs, the remainder being made up of workers, small employers and white-collar workers. To sum up, it appeared, rather as Weill-Raynal had said, that skilled workers had a strong tendency to detach themselves from the proletariat; at the same time white-collar workers, small employers and top managers had a tendency to under-estimate their social class; finally, there was much confusion over the term 'bourgeois' – professional people obviously preferred the simpler 'middle class'.

The more traditional source material suggests a remarkable continuity in many of the older attitudes about class. Among taxi-drivers the squabbles continued between the *artisans* and the *ouvriers*, and the constant appeal made by the former was to their rights as 'citizens'.[30] Within the 'nation of shopkeepers', and, still more within what one might call 'the community of hotel keepers' (320,000 hotel enterprises had half-a-million employees in 1951), the distinction remained formal between those who were *ouvriers* and those who were a cut above.[31] The older industrial working class maintained its awareness and cultural solidarity: a survey of miners' attitudes in the Centre-Midi spoke of 'the homogeneity and great cohesion of the milieu'. The same survey found that, in general, relations with the bosses and with the engineers and other professionals were good; only one miner in ten had difficulties with his chiefs. But the miners were prompt and self-confident in voicing their grievances. According to a phrase much used by the miners, it was not so much the bosses who ruled their lives, but the work itself: '*le travail commande*'.[32] The overlapping aristocratic and intellectual worlds continued. In several letters a crony of Gérard de Lacaze-Duthiers expressed his dismay at the upheavals of the war and the 'expropriations' which had followed: 'we must hope at all costs; for it is not the multitude who are the source of the great spiritual virtues but a certain number of the predestined'.[33] In 1953 there was a series of thirty radio broadcasts on *The Great Families of France*: these included Les Marquis de Chabannes, Les Princes Murat, and Les Ducs de Broglie – the current Duke, it was pointed out, had become a nuclear physicist. Also included was one working-class hero of the Resistance: 'M. Gaston Perrin is neither noble nor bourgeois. A worker, he belongs to a family of workers.'[34]

As American trade unions became integrated into American society, some of the pioneers lamented the days of struggle in the thirties. Henry Bridges, a leader of the great San Francisco strike of 1934, told a friend in 1950:

When we were all down at the heels and just starting to organize, I used to tear my guts out trying to tell them they were just as good as anyone else around here; that they could become respectable members of the community; that someday they'd be accepted.

They weren't afraid to fight for what they wanted then. Then they started to win better wages and conditions. They started to buy homes, and then property, apartment houses especially. I kept telling them they could be respectable. And now they've become too Goddamned respectable for me. Now they're starting to worry if I'm respectable enough for them![35]

The United Auto Workers' president in the North American Air-craft Corporation in California gave a nice account of how the new technological industries spread social ambiguity and hindered union recruiting:

You go into the plant, it is a dust-free plant, it is air-conditioned not because they want to be good to the workers but because the parts they work with and the machines they use just cannot be used under any other conditions. . . . They give these people or at least the people seem to think that they give them an awful lot of individual attention but they do not really care too much about this guy or gal but they are very particular to what happens or who touches this part they are building. But I am sure this is one of the reasons. They call them technicians and this gets into their minds that they are just a little better than a tool-maker or an assembler, the janitor or something of this sort and everyone else is barred from coming into their areas, they are a special breed, so to speak. I am positive this has an awful lot to do with the difficulty to organize. You talk to them. Again they will say, We are getting all of these things anyway. I am sure that they believe the company has just given it to the people. They are the age and type of people who know nothing about the struggle that was made by our union and other unions to get these benefits and make it possible for people to work under these conditions.[36]

Class ambiguity was compounded by the American tradition which gave white-collar workers a status much lower than their European counterparts. While on strike in August 1947, the National Federa-tion of Telephone Workers declared: 'Our twelve dollars a week wage demand is not excessive. At the present time the average wage rates of the telephone workers are the lowest paid of any worker even lower than that of school-teachers. . . .'[37]

In all this there is evidence of 'job consciousness' as well as of lack of class consciousness. The language of the unions echoes that of government: it is the language of a sectional interest; loyalty is to unionism itself rather than to a class; appeals are to social justice and human decency rather than to the rights of the working class. Making an emotional appeal for the creation of a national medical scheme, Walter Reuther reached for a standard American phrase to describe the plight of kinds 'born on the wrong side of the railroad tracks'.[38] This was a difficult period in American history. Union leaders, many of them professionally educated, were in fact becoming more and more detached from the manual workers. *Their* voice surfaces more clearly in a later period: we shall listen again then. The progress of the black Civil Rights movement also suffered a big hiccup in the late 1940s and early 1950s. At the same time the colossal war-time expansion of California and Texas had brought about a renewed influx of Mexican migrants to add another racial element to the composition of the under-class. In 1951 Mexican migrants were placed under the control of the Department of Labor, against the opposition of almost all the Californian farmers. The farmers regarded the migrants with the same pseudo-paternalistic contempt as had characterized Southern attitudes towards the blacks:

> Sometimes we wonder if the average migrant farm worker enjoys all the emotional slobbering that goes on over his busy body. Some of the migrant workers that we have met seemed, to us, the happiest people we have ever met. Life was one big camping trip and the family lived and worked together. We doubt if many of these people would be happy if you made them settle down to fixed responsibilities. It is nice to be able to run away from troubles, responsibilities and situations you don't like.[39]

Where class awareness, and even class consciousness, continued to be most obvious was, as our other sources would lead us to expect, in the unambiguously established business and professional middle class. In giving the Horace Mann lecture for 1960 on the 'Psychology of the Child in the Middle Class', Alison Davis was quite positive about the social hierarchy consisting of 'the upper class', 'the middle class' and 'the lower class'. Her paper was about the hardships of the middle-class child:

> Unlike individuals in the 'leisure class', or aristocracy, who inherit their positions of distinction in both the social and financial worlds, the middle-class individual usually has to achieve his position in the manufacturing or business world, and always must achieve it in the professional world. He must strive toward

the attainment of long-postponed goals, and compete effectively with others who are similarly striving.[40]

The witch-hunts of the fifties were aimed in many directions, but especially at the old-established upper class. Senator McCarthy himself insisted on writing into the Congressional Record this piece of class hatred:

> The reason why we find ourselves in a position of impotency . . . is the treacherous action of those who have been treated so well by this nation. It is not the less fortunate or members of minority groups who have been selling this nation out but rather those who have had all the benefits the wealthiest nation on earth has to offer – the finest homes, the finest college education, and the finest jobs in the government that we can give.

Dean Acheson, he called 'a pompous diplomat in striped pants, with a phoney British accent'.[41]

In Britain some of the attention previously lavished on studies of the working class switched to the middle class. In 1949 Mass Observation carried out two investigations into 'The London Middle Class Housewife and her Food Problems' and 'The London Middle Class Housewife and her Expenditure'. In the previous year the same organization had collected some fascinating interview material from its own national panel of observers. A woman civil servant aged fifty-six declared:

> I definitely think of myself as middle-class. It is difficult to say why. I had a typical middle-class education (small private school and secondary school). I have a middle-class job and I live in a middle class district. But none of these things would make me middle-class in themselves. If I had been clever enough to get a higher post or profession, or rebellious enough to choose a more attractive manual job, I should not thereby have changed my class. Nor should I change it by living in a different district. Besides, my education and job and residence (to a certain extent) were determined by the fact that my parents were middle-class so it is like the old riddle of the hen and the egg. Income has something to do with it but is not in itself a deciding factor nowadays as many working class people get higher pay than the lower middle-class, and many upper class 'new poor' get less.
>
> I suppose it is rather a question of being born into a family and

social group with particular customs, outlook and way of life – a group, that is (in my case), in which it is normal for the children to go to a secondary school, which usually chooses 'black-coat' or professional careers, but which cannot afford university education or the higher professions – which has a certain amount of leisure and culture and expects to have time for such things as books, music and social activities, but does not go in for extravagant entertainment, expensive dinners and hotels, and so on; which chooses theatres in the balcony or pit rather than the stalls or gallery – which lives, generally, in dining room or lounge rather than in the kitchen or in various rooms for different times of the day, which speaks and writes generally correct English, is, generally speaking, thrifty. And so on!

A housewife of the same age, after insisting that 'class distinctions are now so mixed up that nothing like firm classes exist', proceeded to explain why in her view she and her husband belonged 'to the Upper Middle Classes'. She listed the reasons as: 'Financial' – her husband earned a good income and they now lived on the interest from investments; 'Genealogical' – their fathers were respectively architect and headmaster; 'Occupation and Educational' – her husband was an MA of Cambridge and had been Director of Agricultural Research in the Sudan; 'Sartorial' – 'We know what is correct wear even though we may have to make do with our old clothes'; 'Cultural' – they enjoyed good music, books, plays, etc.; 'Conventional' – 'We eat in the dining room and use the conventional speech. We speak grammatical English in accepted pronunciation.'
Another wife declared herself to be 'lower middle class!'

Firstly because of my husband's position – production manager in an engineering firm, and secondly because our education is of a higher standard than most working-class people. This has produced a standard of tastes in music, art and literature different from those of working-class people. (There are exceptions of course.) Our speech is different than most working class people in this district, having particular dialect and a larger vocabulary. Our circle of friends is mainly of the same type of person as ourselves as with two or three exceptions they do not coincide with those of working class acquaintances. Do not think I am a snob. Can mix easily with working class people, and do so in church and Parents' Association activities. But as friends, I find them unsatisfying and in conversation limited in subject common to both.

A fourth housewife chose to describe herself simply as of 'professional' status because: 'I can hardly say "middle class" now, though I was brought up in it. Our threadbare conditions seem at variance with the comfortable plumpness one associates with the term "middle class".'[42]

Middle-class insecurity was counterpointed by a certain working-class complacency. Not that working-class anger had disappeared. In August 1947 the Labour MP Hartley Shawcross reported to the Prime Minister,

> the feeling that the burdens of the present situation are not being as equally shared as they might be, in that those with money are relatively unaffected by them. This obviously is to some extent inevitable, but there is very strong feeling about restaurant meals, about imports of the more expensive foods, e.g. pineapples, and about the curtailment of various mid-week sports which cater for the workers, without similar restrictions on the more fashionable entertainment, like Wimbledon and Goodwood . . .[43]

Perhaps one should not take too seriously the boast of Edgar E. Fryer (while noting the manner of its phrasing) to the Transport and General Workers Biennial Delegate Conference in 1949, of which he was chairman: 'Let there be no mistake about it, we have made substantial progress in working-class conditions during the lifetime of this Government.'[44] However the plumber interviewed by Elizabeth Bott in 1951 is well worth listening to:

> Before the war there was a little bit of slum clearance and other people saw it and realized what they might have and put on the pressure and got things started. Nowadays people have got the new flats and houses, but somehow we do not appreciate them. . . .
>
> People live more together now but they are miles apart. You do not get neighbours coming in so much for a ding-dong [sing-song]. Nowadays people tend to be frightened of their neighbours.

On change in the class system in general, he said that the old middle class, the boss class, had disappeared because:

> . . . there is now so much work to be done and so little unemployment so if the boss rattles at you or threatens you with the sack you can just up and leave. There is no poverty any more so that makes a lot of difference. The working people are better off and

the bosses have lost a lot of their grip. [The people he was talking about were the] ordinary factory boss and the building boss. The only bosses now are the snob class, the high-ups, senior civil servants, directors and such.[45]

For the upper-class self-image there are few better sources than the diary of Hugh Dalton, now, in the first years of the post-war Labour government, Chancellor of the Exchequer. In describing a visit to the Cambridge Union he shows all the boisterous élitism of an exuberant ex-public schoolboy and university oarsman back in familiar territory:

In high spirits . . . I went to Cambridge on 3.6.47 to speak at the Presidential Debate at the Union in opposition to a motion expressing no confidence in H.M.G. [His Majesty's Government]. There is supposed to be a Tory majority now, but I scored the first Labour victory of the term by 180 to 170 odd, which was very gratifying. Two points which I think turned votes were:

(i) my declaration that we were spending, and would continue to spend, substantial sums on the Universities, and

(ii) a new declaration of Government policy which I made on the Olympics. I said that I had been informed by the President of the C.U.B.C. [Cambridge University Boat Club] who had the good sense to belong to my old college, that in the Olympics the Boat crews would have to row in old British boats with old British oars against foreign crews in new British-built boats with new British-built oars. Thus, I said, we should meet the export drive coming back again along our rivers. This would, indeed, be most unfair discrimination – Imperial Preference in reverse etc. I was, however, very glad to inform them that that very day, before leaving London, I had been in touch with the Admiralty as well as with the Secretary of State for Air who was not only an old King's man and an old President of the Union, but also an old Olympic Captain, and I was able now to say that the Admiralty would give special consideration to providing, as a most exceptional case, suitable boats and oars for the British crews in the Olympics. 'After that declaration of Government policy' I cried 'I am confident that no rowing man will vote for this ridiculous resolution.[46]

Were there, though, signs of disintegration in upper-class morale in the fuss over 'U' and 'non-U' and 'the Establishment' of ten years later? It was in the September 1955 issue of *Encounter* that Nancy Mitford published her famous article on 'The English Aristocracy', in which she popularized Professor A. S. C. Ross's linguistic study of the distinctions between upper-class English usage (U) and non-upper-class usage (non-U). That issue – the English do love a lord after all – sold out, and the grateful proprietors of *Encounter* hastily prepared a special pamphlet containing the Mitford article, which, indeed, made some shrewd points. After referring to the 'basic aristocracy of about 950 peers', Nancy Mitford wrote: 'Most of the peers share the education, usage and point of view of a vast upper middle class, but the upper middle class does not, in its turn, merge imperceptibly into the middle class. There is a very definite border line, easily recognizable by hundreds of small but significant landmarks.' *Encounter* knew a good thing when they saw it, and in the November issue they had Professor Ross himself on, 'U and non-U: an Essay in Sociological Linguistics'. 'Today, in 1955,' he began, 'the English class-system is essentially tripartite – there exist an upper, a middle and a lower class.' No doubt it was non-U to say 'working class', though to say 'lower class' was scarcely true to real colloquial usage in the Britain of 1955. It was in the same period that the phrase 'The Establishment' as a pejorative term came into vogue. Henry Fairlie popularized it in the *Spectator* in 1955, and in 1959 Hugh Thomas published a motley collection of essays by different hands, entitled *The Establishment*. Most of those who used the phrase were themselves disaffected members of the upper class who used it as camouflage, to decry their more successful upper-class peers. Thomas's own contribution was a rich piece of upper-class twittery in which he divided society into Saxons, Normans, etc.

FILM IMAGES

That, perhaps, was a slight diversion towards the realm of the media. What of the film images of class in the post-war years? Hollywood produced a number of films with serious social and political themes, including *The Best Years of Our Lives* (returning servicemen), *Gentlemen's Agreement* (anti-semitism), *Pinky* (racism) and *Crossfire* (anti-semitism again). Only *Pinky*, where the conflicts were those of race in the rural South, set out to establish a detailed social milieu, and none dealt explicitly with working-class characters or working-class background, but all shed little assumptions about the nature of the American social structure. One of the main polarities in *The Best Years of Our Lives* is between a demobbed air-force captain and an infantry sergeant, respectively a 'soda jerk' and a banker in peacetime. In *Gentlemen's Agreement* Gregory Peck is a star journalist out to attack anti-semitism: his editor's niece refers to her own 'upper-class manner': and much of the action is among the exclusive Connecticut suburban set. In *Crossfire* the police captain (Robert Young) explains that 'this hating Jews business comes in lots of different sizes'. He gives three examples, which seem to suggest three different social categories: first, there's the 'you can't join our country club kind': second, there's the 'you can't live around here kind': and, third, uttered after a short pause, as if to herald the modulation to a lower class, there's the 'you can't work here kind'.

Many run-of-the-mill social comedies, such as Vincente Minelli's *Father of the Bride* (1950), presented the image of a contented middle-class apparently isolated from all other social classes. However Capra hounded some hoary class themes in *Here Comes the Groom* (1951). Bing Crosby is a Boston newspaperman who plays it cool towards his long-time girl friend, Emmie, daughter of a Boston-Irish fisherman, Captain Jones, a name which suggests ordinariness (i.e. middle classness) rather than Irishness (but then perhaps Capra confused Ireland with Wales). So Emmie, who works in an insurance office, gets engaged to her boss, Wilbur Stanley, scion of an old Boston family whose insurance company own 'about half the buildings in Boston'. Out come the old Capra headlines: 'Cinderella Jones', and 'Fisherman's daughter to marry $40,000,000'. The family view is that the 'Stanleys can't just get married like other people', but Emmie claims she is 'going to learn how to be a lady'. The Crosby character ('Pete') meantime works out a kind of reverse pygmalion (or 'my fair lady') deal with Wilbur's aristocratic cousin: he will teach her how to 'walk like a Jones' (in the hope that she can thus win back Wilbur). Eventually the wedding ceremony comes along, 'with a guest list like the *Blue Book* and *Who's Who* rolled into one': in the course of the traditional Hollywood marriage cliff-hanger, Wilbur drops out and pushes Pete into his place. So middle class sticks with middle class (one of Emmie's earlier insults to the man she now unprotestingly marries was, 'you used to be such a good reporter – now you sound like a journalist'); and the two aristocrats are free to marry each other.

A much more rounded social universe was presented in the James Dean Technicolor saga (directed by George Stevens from the novel by Edna Ferber) *Giant* (1956). John Benedict comes from Texas into a Maryland upper-class household – fine mansion, full-dress fox hunt, English style country-house breakfast – to buy a horse, and marries the daughter of the family, Lesley (played by Elizabeth Taylor). The social clash between Benedict, a powerful man in Texas, and Lesley and her traditional upper-class background is beautifully realized. James Dean plays a hanger-on and minor prospector in Texas: of Benedict he says, 'who gets so much land unless they took it off someone else?' When Elizabeth Taylor remarks, 'you're a working man,' Dean's reply is, 'that's something I'm going to fix'. Dean ('Jet' in the film) strikes oil, and a crude power-struggle begins between him and Benedict. At the same time the racial dimension is established as we see the Mexican-Indians treated as an outcast under class.

British films of the time covered a wider range than might be expected. *The Guinea Pig* (Boulting Brothers, 1948) was based on the West End comedy by Warren Chetham-Strode about a council schoolboy at a public school, and was popular enough for a 'book of the film' to be produced. The preface to this ran: 'Richard Atten-borough demonstrates once more his versatility and gives a con-vincing portrait of the working-class lad confronted with the manners and customs of the son of the rich. It takes time and mutual tolerance to reconcile the two vastly differing worlds, but young Jack Read does it triumphantly.'[47] Actually, Jack's father, played by Bernard Miles, is a tobacconist in Walthamstow in East London, and a former army sergeant. Broadly, though, the story is that, after initial rebellion, Jack is steadily socialized into upper-class attitudes. The key scene is between his traditionalist house-master and his father, when a definite rapport is established across the classes. The message is of social harmony and the value of public schools as trainers for leadership. Fine perception of class distinctions, within an overall frame of social harmony, is also the key-note of *His Excellency* (directed by Robert Hamer for Ealing Studios, 1951). An ex-docker (played by Eric Portman) is sent out to govern a colo-nial dependency where he comes into conflict with the Lieutenant Governor (played by Cecil Parker). It is the latter who finally admits to his Excellency the Governor, in a rather flabby phrase which sums up quite well the social ethos of post-war Britain, 'the answer lies somewhere between us'. In *The Chance of a Lifetime* (Bernard Miles, 1950), the workers take over the running of a factory, then find they are not competent to do so, and gladly hand over once more to their boss. *It Always Rains on Sunday* (Robert Hamer for Ealing, 1947) was a straightforward thriller about an escaped convict, but set within an authentic East End working-class setting: at one point the factory environment is clearly established by a notice in the background, 'machinists wanted', and there is, above all, a sense of a distinctive working-class culture. The better-known Ealing comedies tended to be set in a lower-middle-class milieu, with no very definite establishment of class culture or class relationships. However, in 1952, the government-supported experimental Group Three, under the supervision of John Grierson, produced the immaculate *The Brave Don't Cry*, based on the Knockshinnoch mining disaster. The reality of life in a working-class community is patiently established. The image is one of order and integration: at one point the local policeman is used to get a bookie for one of the miners trapped in the pit, and in the same scene the local doctor fits in harmoniously as a member of the community.

The Brave Don't Cry cries out to be contrasted with Louis Daquin's *Le Point du Jour* (*At Break of Day*, 1949), set in a very carefully realized mining community. But whereas the British film sees life, as it were, from the inside, Daquin, whose film contains much more polemical and intellectualizing content, felt bound to mediate his story through the person of a middle-class outsider, a young engineer from Paris. Daquin himself explained:

It was necessary to discover the mine in the company of someone who was himself discovering it. I had the choice between a young engineer or a young miner. I opted for the young engineer. Why? It was not simply an experience which I wished to describe; I wanted to go beyond that experience, to convince the spectator of the intolerable severity of the miner's work. Now the world of our audiences is made up of a vast heterogeneous mixture, but it is not the manual workers who are difficult, who have prejudices to overcome; above all they seek to understand things, to document them. At the other extreme, a bourgeois is, by his situation, by his occupations, by his style of life, completely alien to this world which is not his own. He is perhaps even hostile to it, and that was the case in the circumstances, a press campaign having, following the strikes of 1948, tried to prove that the miner was a 'privileged worker'. It was therefore through a bourgeois that I had to bring about the discovery of the mine to the audience, by a being having their reactions, their feelings, with whom they could identify with the minimum of difficulty. That is why, in the film, the mine is revealed through the mediation of a young engineer who comes out from Paris and who is acted by Jean Desailly.[48]

Two Jacques Becker films also repay study. *Antoine et Antoinette* (1947) is ostensibly about a working-class couple. He is in fact a skilled print worker in the book trade, while she is employed taking passport photos in a department store. They do not live in the south-eastern suburbs of Paris, but in the socially mixed area of La Fourche on the fringes of Montmartre. Such socio-economic conflict as is shown is between Antoine and the local grocer, who is said to be very rich, and between Antoinette and the store *directoire*, a stuffy middle-class type. Antoinette's closest friend sells tickets in the Metro. The other main family who come into the action – which concerns the loss and recovery of a winning lottery ticket – run the local café. Even the other lottery winner we meet belongs to this same social milieu: he is a butcher. The fundamental point of the film is that only by colossal luck, such as winning the lottery, can one escape from this milieu: there is no chance of upward mobility through the exercise of professional skill or personal talent. Here we have a basic contrast with *Édouard et Caroline*, in which class lines are quite clear. Édouard is a middle-class pianist, humiliated before Caroline's upper-class uncle, M. Beauchamp (he even has a camped-up aristocratic accent, and the contrast between his lavish establishment and their small flat is well made) and cousin. But a rich American recognizes his talent and so he hits the jackpot (and holds on to his wife).

REALITY OF CLASS

From the imagery of film, back to what I have termed the *realities* of class. Compared with the 1930s, there were, in all three countries in this period, changes in the type of recruit to positions of power, but within circumscribed limits. The Labour victory of 1945 meant the advent to political office of several men of working-class backgrounds. There were slight changes in the composition of the Conservative Party, dominant again after 1951: there were more small businessmen and fewer big businessmen, and more representatives of such new growth areas as investment trusts, insurance, property development, advertising and public relations, entertainment and communications. The shift in parliament was towards the middle class rather than the working class. The upper class still dominated many of the most important posts, nor did the character of recruitment to the higher levels of the civil service change markedly (of the successful candidates for open entry to the Administrative Class in 1949–52, seventy-four per cent came from Oxbridge).[49]

A survey of the social backgrounds of French ministers revealed that they came overwhelmingly from the upper class, with the old admixture of provincial middle-class parliamentarians; in the main they came from the same social background as other élite figures in French society. The effect of the Liberation and post-war reforms had been to carry even further the principle of careers open to talent: the '*Sciences Po.*' ceased to be an expensive and exclusive private institution and became part of the state system; recruitment nonetheless remained largely from the upper and upper-middle classes.[50]

In the United States the elevation to the Presidency of Harry S. Truman, the provincial mid-western figure who clearly lacked upper-class status, may have seemed a portent; but probably the significant fact is that Truman was never intended for the Presidency, he had simply been chosen as Roosevelt's Vice-Presidential running-mate. A more clear-cut setback for upper-class domination came when Eisenhower defeated Robert Taft for the Republican presidential candidature in 1952. The Taft family formed part of that American aristocracy which could move easily between local interests in Ohio, national business interests in New York and Boston, and political and judicial interests in Washington. Eisenhower, on the other hand, was 'the very embodiment of a middle class, middle income, middle-brow, wholly unanguished revolution which with the utmost of decorum had won a place of social and political dominance in this country after the end of the Second World War'.[51] The Eisenhower family had worked a three-acre plot in Abilene, Kansas, where the doctors, lawyers and businessmen lived on the north side of the railroad tracks while the Eisenhower family lived on the south side. Young Dwight Eisenhower did, however, attend school on the north side. Later he worked in a creamery to accumulate some capital, then, through making contact with his local Senator and performing capably in the entrance exam, he got himself into West Point.[52] Eisenhower's running mate, Richard Nixon, son of a store and garage owner, had, like Edward Heath in Britain, had a good war. Nor was his law degree from Duke University to be scoffed at. However, the solid bastion of the Eisenhower administration was the Secretary of State, John Foster Dulles, whose uncle and grandfather had both been Secretaries of State, and whose father was a Presbyterian minister in Watertown, New York. Both John Foster Dulles and his brother, Allen Dulles, had been pillars of one of the most influential Wall Street law firms. The new Secretary of State appointed his brother to be Head of the CIA. Meantime, by methods which we looked at in an earlier chapter, the Kennedy family had solidly established itself in the East Coast upper class. We shall join some of these colourful characters again in a later chapter.

Extensive nationalization in Britain and France did little to alter the distribution of economic power in those countries. The bosses of private enterprise simply became the bosses of state industry; the political and economic élites became, as had long been the case in France, still more closely intertwined. Though individual union leaders served on the boards of nationalized industries in Britain, the unions, in general, kept well clear of any involvement in the management of private industry.[53] There was a universal redistribution of income, largely due to the high levels of economic activity in all three countries: to that extent some of the material differences between classes were diminished.[54] Everywhere, organized labour had gained in strength, though in the American South, 'despite substantial gains during the war', it 'remained too weak to temper the rural orientation of most southern politics.'[55]

Earlier I cited at some length the global picture of the realities of American class structure offered by Goldschmidt, reviewing a wide range of survey material. I propose to conclude this chapter by pulling in material from two very important and detailed surveys conducted almost coterminously in France and Britain, the first carried out by Charles Bettelheim and Suzanne Frère in Auxerre between November 1947 and February 1950, the second conducted by Margaret Stacey in Banbury between 1948 and 1951 (though not published till 1960). The Auxerre survey brought out sharply the patterns of unity and of distinction between 'social categories'. Radio was a unifying factor, but theatre-going singled out the upper bourgeoisie; of the three cinemas, there was one which the bourgeoisie did not visit; there was an obvious distinction between the weekly public dances and the two or three annual 'society balls' which brought together 'the bourgeoisie and the personalities of Auxerre'. Housing was segregated socially, and the well-off had out-of-town summer residences. On one question to which I can promise no final answers, Bettelheim and Frère were certain: social differences were often more important for women than for men. Two final conclusions stand out: first, it was in *education* that social differences were absolutely fundamental; second, a person's 'social category' provided him with a more homogeneous entity to identify with, than did belonging to the town Auxerre (three-quarters of the population had not been born there anyway).[56]

In discussing 'Social Status and Social Class' in Banbury,[57] Margaret Stacey first referred to her own students' problems in talking about class: 'The reasons for this reticence are connected with the class system itself and with the changes which are taking place within it. There are certain social rules which say that the existence of status and class differences should be assumed but not spoken about.' She gave an example of this attitude from a Colonel's wife speaking to a new-comer to a village on whom she had called.

'I think you'll like the X's,' she said, 'and then there are the Y's and the Z's; otherwise I don't think there is anybody. But of course it's bad luck for you there are no children in the village.' (The new-comer had a young family.) Happily this startling picture of rural depopulation was contradicted by statistics which showed that the village had a population of about 500 with normal complement of children. Yet this woman, who referred to 98 per cent of her fellow villagers as 'nobody', as people you would not 'know', although in fact she knew a great many through the Women's Institute, saw no contradiction in saying: 'I shouldn't mind the socialists so much if they didn't bring class into everything.' Her real complaint was, of course, that the socialists, instead of taking class for granted, talk about class and, worse still, question it.

Professor Stacey found that 'it was impossible to ignore the existence of upper-class people'. Furthermore, 'in so far as this class sets the standards and the aspirations of traditional social class attitudes, if only indirectly below the level of its frontier with the middle class, it is important out of all proportion to its size'. At the same time, recent social changes meant that, while it was relatively easy to place 'traditionalists' within a clear-cut class structure, it was much less easy to do so for 'non-traditionalists', the products of an increasingly professional and technological society. Within 'the traditional class system' three classes could be identified, 'upper, middle, and working', though with ambiguous 'frontiers' between them. The single most important characteristic which divided the upper from the middle class was education: 'members of the traditional upper class in the Banbury district were all educated at one of the major public schools'. In contrast, a common educational background was 'by no means a characteristic of the Banbury middle class'.

Education, therefore, does not necessarily provide a distinction between the middle class and the working class, although it is true that the majority of the working class have received only an elementary education while a much higher proportion of the middle class received a secondary education. The single most important characteristic which divides the middle class from the working class is occupation. . . .

The working class itself was composed 'chiefly, but not exclusively, of manual workers'. The survey divided the working class (here is a theme I have touched on before) into three status groups: 'respectable', 'ordinary' and 'rough'. Other classes were also subdivided: for example, the upper class into 'county' and 'gentry', with a further 'upper frontier' group closely tied to it. The Banbury study concluded that the widest range of 'knowledge and social recognition' between status groups was 'two groups distant from your own (except, of course, in terms of business relationships, of master and man, or tradesman and customer, for example)'.

Thus members of the county do not 'know' anyone below some of the doctors (the 'upper frontier' ones), neither do the gentry, the gap made by the public school 'test' is too great; the upper frontier know members of the gentry and the middle class; the middle class range from upper frontier to lower frontier; the ordinary worker from respectable to rough, and so on. Beyond these ranges the gulf is so wide that informal contacts do not take place.

Notes

1. Pierre Laroque, *Les grands Problèmes sociaux contemporains* (1954–5), pp. 71–143, for this and the next few paragraphs.
2. Françoise Bouriez-Gregg, *Essai sur le problème des classes sociales aux États-Unis* (1954).
3. *Ibid*, p. 45.
4. *Ibid*, p. 96.
5. *Ibid*, pp. 103, 104.
6. *Ibid*, pp. 157, 192.
7. 'Les Classes sociales et les partis politiques en France', *La Revue Socialiste*, no. 42 (December 1950), pp. 545–61.

8. Centre de Documentation Internationale Contemporaine, Nanterre, MRP: Centre de Formation. des Militants, 'Les Classes sociales en France' (typescript, 1946).

9. See, e.g., Parti Communiste Français, *La Nation française et les classes sociales* (1955).

10. Michel Collinet, *L'Ouvrier français: essai sur la condition ouvrière 1900–1950* (1951).

11. See the excellent article by Andy Dawson, 'History and Ideology: Fifty Years of "Job Consciousness"', *Literature and History*, no. 8 (Autumn 1978).

12. Richard Centers, *The Psychology of Social Classes* (1949).

13. Gerhard Lenski, 'American Social Classes: Statistical Strata or Social Groups?' *American Journal of Sociology*, vol. 58 (1952), p. 139.

14. A. Reiss, 'Occupation and Social Status', *ibid*, vol. 61 (1955).

15. W. Goldschmidt, 'Social Class in America: a critical review', *American Anthropologist*, vol. 52 (1950), pp. 485–6, 494–5. Also particularly worth consulting is Kurt Mayer, 'Recent Changes in the Class Structure of the United States', *Transactions of the 3rd World Congress of Sociology* (1956).

16. A. M. Carr-Saunders and D. Caradog Jones, *A Survey of the Social Structure of England and Wales* (1958), p. 115.

17. C. A. Moser and J. R. Hall in D. V. Glass, ed., *Social Mobility in Britain* (1954), p. 31.

18. C. A. R. Crosland, *The Future of Socialism* (1956), pp. 178, 186.

19. Michel Crozier, 'Classes sans conscience ou préfiguration de la societé sans classes', *Archives Européennes de Sociologie*, I (1960), p. 247.

20. See Sam Aaronovitch, *The Ruling Class: a Study of British Finance Capital* (1961), especially pp. 7, 116–17.

21. Ralf Dahrendorf, *Class and Class Conflict in Industrial Society* (1957).

22. On this point with regard to France, see Collinet, *op. cit.*, p. 111.

23. *House of Commons Debates*, 17 October 1945.

24. *Report of the Ministry of National Insurance for the Period 17th November 1944 to 4th July 1949* (1950), p. 3.

25. Dalloz, *Précis de droit commercial* (1936).

26. US Department of Labor, *American Workers' Fact Book* (1956), p. 320.

27. F. M. Martin, 'Some Subjective Aspects of Social Stratification', in D. V. Glass, *op. cit.*, p. 58.

28. Natalie Rogoff, 'Social Stratification in France and in the United States', *American Journal of Sociology*, vol. 58 (1953), pp. 347–57; the tables are on p. 349.

29. N. Xydias, 'Classes sociales et conscience de classe à Vienne-en-France: aspects subjectifs et objectifs', *Transactions of Second World Congress of Sociology* (1953), pp. 246–51, on which the whole of this paragraph is based.

30. Centre d'Histoire du Syndicalisme, Paris, Archives Syndicat FO des Taxis, 37_2.

31. Marcel Gautier, *Métiers et main d'oeuvre dans l'industrie hôtelière* (1955); and Marcel Jeanne, *La Profession hôtelière* (1956).
32. Institut National d'Etudes Démographiques, *Les Attitudes des mineurs du Centre-Midi et l'évolution de l'emploi* (1957), p. 80.
33. Archives Nationales, Institut Français d'Histoire Sociale, archives Lacaze-Duthiers, envelope 9: Philéas Lebesque to Lacaze-Duthiers, 12 February 1946.
34. André Gillois, *Les grandes familles de France* (1953), p. 181.
35. Charles P. Larrow, *Biography of Harry Bridges* (1951), p. 87.
36. Archives of Labor and Urban Affairs [ALUA], Wayne State University, Detroit, Oral History by Jack R. Hurst.
37. ALUA, Merle E. Henrickson Collection, box 4.
38. Henry M. Christmas, ed., *Walter P. Reuther: Selected Papers* (1961), p. 42.
39. *California Farmer*, 13 January 1951.
40. Alison Davis, *Psychology of the Child in the Middle Class* (1960), pp. 4–5.
41. Richard Rovere, *Senator Joe McCarthy* (1960), p. 82; E. Digby Baltzell, *The Protestant Establishment*, pp. 284–5.
42. Mass Observation Archives, University of Sussex, file 3073.
43. University College, Oxford, Attlee Papers A, box 9: Hartley Shawcross to Clement Attlee, 1 August 1947.
44. Modern Records Centre, University of Warwick, Transport and General Workers archives 1/4/12.
45. Elizabeth Bott, *Samples from English Cultures* (1955), p. 184.
46. British Library of Political and Economic Science, Dalton Diaries, 35: entry for 24 May 1947 to 29 May 1947.
47. Arnold Meredith, *The Guinea Pig* (1948).
48. Louis Daquin, *Le Cinéma, notre métier* (1960), p. 158.
49. W. L. Guttsman, *The British Political Elite* (1968); R. K. Kelsall, *Higher Civil Servants in Britain* (1955); Kenneth Robinson, 'Selection and the Social Background of the Administrative Class', *Public Administration* (1955), p. 385.
50. Alain Girard, *La Réussite sociale en France* (1961); *Sondages, l'enseignement en France: (été 1950)*.
51. William S. White, *The Responsibles* (1972), p. 144.
52. Kevin McCann, *America's Man of Destiny* (1952), p. 37.
53. K. Coates and A. J. Topham, *Industrial Democracy in Great Britain* (1975).
54. See, e.g., Dudley Seers, *op. cit.*, and Guy Routh, *Occupation and Pay in Britain 1909–1960* (1965).
55. George B. Tindal, *The Emergence of the New South, 1913–1945* (1967), pp. 710–11.
56. Charles Bettelheim and Suzanne Frère, *Une Ville française moyenne: Auxerre en 1950* (1950), pp. 197, 183, 216, 217, 263.
57. Margaret Stacey, *Tradition and Change: a Study of Banbury* (1960), chapter 8.

14

The Cultural Revolution and
the New Historical Context

The changes effected by the war had scarcely worked themselves out when they were overtaken by another set of technological, economic, intellectual and political changes, often identified by such clichés as 'post-industrial society', 'affluence', 'permissiveness', 'end of ideology', 'liberation', 'black power', 'student power' and 'participation'. This 'cultural revolution', which came to full flood in the 1960s, though the tides were already rising in the late 1950s, involved: the diffusion of relative prosperity to sections of society which previously had never enjoyed more than the barest living standards; the wide availability of new technologies, particularly in communications and transport; and an attack, of unprecedented breadth and intensity, on established social controls, traditional hierarchies, and received assumptions. Economic change was least striking in the United States where high living standards had been developing continuously since the early years of the war; intellectual and cultural changes, on the other hand, were very much in evidence. In Britain, particularly, and to some extent in France, much of the attack was on the complacencies of the existing class structure; in America there was criticism of the complacent assumption that class distinctions did not exist. Thus, a result of the cultural revolution was to diminish the significance of class in the European countries, and to increase it in the United States.

The most important economic and occupational changes took place in France, where the proportion of the population employed in agriculture declined very rapidly, until it stood at eight per cent of the active population in 1970 – at last bringing France into line with the occupational structures of the other two countries. The proportion of industrial workers continued to increase until around 1970. The industrial base was already shrinking in both America and Britain, the main increases being recorded in the managerial and white-collar groups. In America the number of farmers fell by half since the war. The interpenetration between North and South continued, so that American society was becoming more homogeneous and less sectional, offering a *possible* basis for a more integrated nation-wide class structure akin to those of the compact European countries.

In the sphere of ethnicity, race and immigration, developments ran in different directions in the different countries, and even within the same countries. In America there was a significant merging of the white ethnic communities into the wider society, as evidenced by the number of foreign-language newspapers which faded away towards the end of the 1950s, or were transliterated into English-language newspapers.[1] An exchange of letters between the White House and a leader of the Boston Italian community, in which claims for special Italian representation in the Kennedy administration are lightly dismissed, already has an anachronistic air.[2] In a famous book, *Beyond the Melting Pot*, published in 1963, and in other publications, it was argued that the ethnics were now vigorously identifying themselves with 'middle America'. White ethnic sentiments were both obscured and intensified by the explosion of the Black Civil Rights movement after the relatively quiescent 1950s. From being aimed primarily at the abolition of formal discrimination in the South and the achievement of integration within white America, the movement developed into a concerted attack on all forms of discrimination, and began to turn away from white America. Formal equality was embodied in the two Civil Rights Acts of 1964 and 1965. Meantime the lineaments of a race problem were appearing both in France, where by the late 1960s there were over two million coloured immigrants, mainly from North Africa, and in Britain, where there were four million, from the West Indies, from Asian communities in East Africa, and from the Indian sub-continent itself. Britain's first major race-riots took place at Notting Hill, London, in 1959. White ethnic movements appeared in the European countries too: in France, outbreaks of peasant militancy dating back to the early 1950s began to focus into a positive Breton nationalism; in Britain, both Scottish and Welsh nationalism attained unprecedented levels of support.

It was part and parcel of this era of cultural change that when so many other assumptions were being challenged, so too were assumptions about class. By 1967 Ralf Dahrendorf, who earlier had argued that conflict was no longer generated by economic classes in the Marxist sense, but by a range of 'quasi-groups' competing for power, was now suggesting that group conflict had given way to individual competition: his 'theoretical concern' was with 'the fact that instead of taking part in a May Day parade, individuals change jobs, or buy a new house, or spend their holidays in Italy'.[3] There was much talk of 'the end of ideology',[4] though ideology, of course, is not the same animal as class. Still there were many other theories about the declining influence of class. In Britain some commentators spoke of an affluent 'new working class' which, through a process of *embourgeoisement*, was becoming middle-class in cultural and political behaviour. The *embourgeoisement* thesis was also publicized in France; but in both countries it was, in its more naive forms, subjected to convincing rebuttals, while Richard Hoggart had in 1957 published the highly influential insider's study of a separate British working-class culture, *The Uses of Literacy*.[5] A different 'new working class' was discovered by the French Marxist sociologist Serge Mallet. He used the term to embrace all the technical, white-coated, and minor managerial posts which had been proliferating up to the mid-1960s.[6] Members of the American New Left attempted to adopt this usage for their own country, where the industrial workers had shown no strongly politicized class consciousness. But the technicians and managers scarcely proved a better bet, and the term 'new working class' came to be applied more often to the truly under-privileged, casual workers, migrants, blacks, chicanos, and the deprived generally.[7]

But the major discovery of the period, hinted at by Glaiser and Moynihan in *Beyond the Melting Pot* in 1963, and dominating the media by 1969, was 'Middle America'. Glaiser and Moynihan envisaged a pluralistic, not a class society, and the notion of Middle America emerges as a description of a state of mind, or a political programme with components appealing to many different sections and groups, rather than as a social class: specifically, it opposed Civil Rights, the Peace Movement, the Student Movement, 'Welfare Intellectuals', and so on. Yet much of the discussion of this concept involved an enthusiastic, if confused, use of class labels. A volume of essays on Middle America, with the title *Overcoming Middle Class Rage*, had a foreword by Hubert Humphrey, the defeated Democratic presidential candidate in 1968, in which, having mentioned the prime attention hitherto given to 'our most disadvantaged groups – the very poor and the victims of racial discrimination', he stressed the problems of 'an even larger group of Americans – the near-poor, the lower middle-class, the "ethnics", the "blue-collar" worker'. The editor of the collection, Murray Friedman, contrived in one short paragraph of his own to run together 'working-class', 'ethnic', 'lower-middle-class', 'Middle Americans', and 'the common man':

> By the summer of 1969 and in subsequent months, the mass media began to focus on working-class and ethnic whites. The *New York Times* and *News Day* in Long Island carried feature-length articles on the personality, life-style, and economic plight of lower-middle-class Americans. *Time* featured 'The Middle Americans' on its front cover and analysed them in an essay on its inside pages. *Newsweek* developed A Special Report on the White Majority, 'The Troubled American', later expanded into a book. It quoted Eric Hoffer as warning, 'You'd better watch out – the common man is standing up'.[8]

However confused the usage, the unabashed resort to the language of class distinguishes American books, newspapers and television programmes in the late sixties from those of the previous decade.

In film, the most trumpeted intimation of innovation was the French 'New Wave', which is often reckoned to have begun with Claude Chabrol's *Le Beau Serge* (1958). It continued with such works as: *Les Quatre cents coups* (1959), *Tirez sur le pianiste* (1960) and *Jules et Jim* (1961), all directed by François Truffaut; *A Bout de soufflé* (1959), the Jean-Luc Godard film generally regarded as one of the key works in the movement, and *Hiroshima, mon armour* (Alain Resnais, 1959), which is similarly regarded. These film directors were all young, some of them were quite rich; they were making a conscious protest against the literary and literal characteristics of the post-war French cinema. Almost all the innovation was in style. They and their films appear to exist in a complete social vacuum. *Le Beau Serge* is a village melodrama and does point us, as do many of Chabrol's later films, to the centrality in the French social universe of integrated village, or small-town life. *Les Quatre cent coups*, the most traditional of these films, does, at the beginning, establish the Parisian petty bourgeois milieu in which no class relationships or antagonisms are apparent. As for the rest, and for the New Wave films of the sixties, science fiction, polemicist, or crassly commercial, one might as well search for clues to class attitudes in a string quartet. Of course, this is not in any slightest sense a criticism. These film-makers were, with absolute legitimacy, concerned with matters of style, and with the autonomy of film as a cultural artefact.[9] In the end we learn little about the Cultural Revolution in its relationship to class, but we learn a lot about the contrasting obsessions of the British and the French.

The noteworthy British films of the sixties were, in contrast, characterized by a patient, sympathetic recreation of the industrial working-class environment, and were often based on novels by working-class authors. (The more widely publicized movement of cultural innovation in Britain had, characteristically, been a literary and theatrical one: the so-called 'Angry Young Man', however, scarcely dealt with working-class environments, but rather with the frictions between lower-middle-class and upper-middle-class status; John Wain, one of the most distinguished of this group of writers, has recently recorded one of his own motives as outrage against the continuance into the fifties of all the old class shibboleths.[10]) However, if one had to select one film to represent the outbreak of 'cultural revolution' in Britain it would have to be *I'm All Right Jack* (Boulting Brothers, 1959). Films like *His Excellency* had carefully delineated all the nuances of class distinction, but had suggested that in the end classes would come together, making their own special contribution to the public welfare. *I'm All Right Jack* ruthlessly, rudely and hilariously painted a picture of a snobbish, arrogant and corrupt upper class, and a pig-headed, work-shy working class, perfectly secure in its own *mores* and *folkways*, with some rather unhappy middle-class elements in between: at bottom, the two major classes were, in fact, in cahoots to do the nation down.

I'm All Right Jack was a highly deliberate and historically sensitive social satire: there is a very self-conscious pre-credit sequence sketching the history of the decline of the old upper-class since 1945, when it had been rooted in the world of finance ('The City and Threadneedle Trust', 'Capital Gains Unlimited'), to the present, when its representatives are, somewhat shadily, involved in industry. Ian Carmichael plays Stanley, an earnest and gormless young man, who has been 'brought up a gentleman'. At his university appointments board he is told that what is required above all is 'an air of confidence'. We see the elegant, aristocratic household of Stanley's great-aunt (Margaret Rutherford), where the maid is addressed curtly as 'Spencer'. Stanley fails to get a string of 'suitable' appointments, and finally his uncle (Dennis Price), unknown to Stanley, fiddles him into a manual job in the factory that he owns. The great-aunt's comment is: 'I expect you just supervise, dear.' But Stanley goes to work with a fork-lift truck (the uncle, for nefarious reasons, to do with a shady arms deal with a shady Arab, intends that Stanley should create a strike). The atmosphere on the factory floor, the working-class accents and attitudes, are beautifully established, with only the necessary minimum of satirical exaggeration. Left-wing commentators at the time were outraged by the character of Kite (Peter Sellers), the communist shop steward. Kite has high intellectual aspirations: he speaks in a stilted, polysyllabic, and, in the end, ill-educated fashion; and that surely was the point – Kite with his immensely laudable aspirations has, in fact, been educationally stunted by the class society in which he grew up. Kite refers proudly to the week he spent at a summer school at Balliol (which he mispronounces beautifully – long 'a' instead of short). Balliol, one of the poshest, most academically demanding, and liberal in entry policy of the Oxford colleges, is an important symbol in the British class structure. In *His Excellency* the upper-class ladies who are so upset at the prospect of a docker as Governor-General remark on an upper-class socialist of their acquaintance: he 'came out of the right stable', he was at Balliol. A Labour leader of the sixties, George Brown, has referred in his autobiography to his days at Balliol.[11] Kite takes Stanley home to tea, and offers him lodgings. Compared with the austere working-class house of *It Always Rains on Sunday*, the Kite household betrays some signs of affluence. Stanley is a little taken aback by the tea, even more by the Australian Burgundy which is brought out in special celebration, and utterly appalled by Kite's verbosity. But he is captivated by Kite's daughter Cynthia (Liz Fraser), a spindle polisher: he takes the lodgings. The contrast between upper-class twit and working-class dumb blonde is cruelly done: 'are them your own teeth?', she asks: 'you keep them so nice and white'.

Personnel manager at the factory is Major Hitchcock, played by Terry-Thomas with that matchless plummy accent and manner which makes one suspect that the major either hasn't quite made it into the upper class or else has come down slightly in the world. In the best of many memorable lines, Hitchcock describes Kite, to whom in public he has to show the utmost matiness, as 'the sort of chap who sleeps in his vest'. Kite calls the inevitable strike. Stanley is sent back to work on his own by his great-aunt: 'unheard of that a gentleman should go on strike. Officers don't mutiny', she says. In the kind of scene beloved of British film makers, the mildly obsequious, but totally plain-speaking and self-assured Mrs Kite (Irene Handl) gets on famously with the condescending, but patently human, great aunt. Stanley breaks the picket lines (both police and pickets are shown as behaving in a most restrained 'British' way) and is sent to Coventry by Kite and his fellow workers. The shady deal planned by Stanley's uncle and the ghastly Mr de Vere Cox (Richard Attenborough), whose accent, at a moment of crisis, reveals his lower-class origins, progresses.

The film's climax comes in a television programme (sign of the times!) in which Stanley, the scales having dropped from his eyes, denounces both his uncle ('you're a bounder') and Kite. But virtue does not triumph. Bosses and workers are exonerated and continue in their dishonest, work-shy ways. Realistically, the film recognizes the barrier of class in not having Stanley marry Cynthia: he is bundled off to the terrors of a nudist camp.

The best of the 'working-class' films was *Saturday Night and Sunday Morning* (1960, directed by Karl Riesz from the novel by Alan Sillitoe who had himself been a worker in a Nottingham bicycle factory). The Raleigh bicycle factory at the beginning of the film is authentically presented; the scene then shifts to the working-class household where, after tea, Arthur Seaton (Albert Finney) selects his flash suit and goes out for an evening on the booze. One theme running through the film is the contrast between the older generation of the working class, beaten down into total acceptance of its lot, and the rebellious younger generation personified by Arthur Seaton. Yet, as with every sensitive film (or novel) about the working class, the point is that, despite youthful rebelliousness, being born into the working class is 'a life sentence', even if the sentence is served out in fine suits and at pubs and discos. Working-class boy meets working-class girl, Doreen (Shirley Anne Field). Doreen's aspiration in regard to their future house was not an empty one: 'I want a new one with a bathroom and everything.' The film presents (realistically, in the light of some of the evidence discussed in my next chapter) no sense of a class enemy, whether upper-class or middle-class: the enemy is organized society, with its tax demands, insurance contributions, and military service, and, as often as not, other stuffy members of the working class (Margaret Stacey's 'respectable' stratum, perhaps). The film portrays a complete industrial working-class environment from within, after a fashion which it is impossible to imagine in the French, or American, cinema of the time. Arthur Seaton settles for marriage to Doreen, the most beautiful girl around. In *Le Point du Jour* the rebellious miner was determined to get out of the pits and into middle-class life, even at the risk of losing his good-looking fiance. Somehow French intellectuals could never quite understand that a man might actually be proud of being working-class. Another significant contrast, this time entirely within the British context, can be made: while *The Guinea Pig* had been set in a public school, *The Loneliness of the Long Distance Runner* (Tony Richardson, 1962) was set in a borstal, and the working-class lad resolutely refused to accommodate himself to middle-class standards.

The age of cinema was giving way to the age of television: am I right to linger over film? Let me repeat: *any* film is part of the society which produced it, and must bear *traces* of some of the basic assumptions of that society. But a glance at British television of the time does yield a warning: every cultural medium has an internal logic of its own. While British films were reaching an unprecedented degree of sophistication in delineating some of the realities of contemporary society, television, still young and crude, blundered around perpetrating the worst banalities and clichés. Old television programmes are less accessible than old films, but fortunately there exists an excellent compilation programme made by Melvyn Bragg, Richard Hoggart and Tony Cash which brings out the total inability of the BBC at the time to create working-class characters who were not manifestly RADA actors speaking stock lines.[12] It was the rival commercial channel which made the great breakthrough towards the end of 1960 with the first edition of *Coronation Street*, whose characters had a completely real, independent, working-class existence. Actually the BBC written archives show that right back to the war the Corporation had been searching desperately for a means of putting authentic working-class life on the air. Radio's most successful soap opera was the very middle-class *Mrs Dale's Diary*. In the early fifties there was much talk inside the BBC of replacing it with a 'working-class *Mrs Dale's Diary*', but with that objective, not surprisingly, the project never materialized.[13]

Hollywood, meantime, was in the doldrums. A few worthy films were released, such as the Jack Lemmon/Lee Remick film about alcoholism, *Days of Wine and Roses* (1962), which presented the archetypal ethnic Middle American, in the person of Lee Remick's father, the Norwegian-American, Arneson, who runs his own nursery garden, and is totally contemptuous of Jack Lemmon's career in public relations. Style returned to Hollywood in 1967 with *The Graduate* (Mike Nichols) and *Bonnie and Clyde*. The former was set in the insulated middle-class world so common in American films; the latter (the action took place in the 1930s), together with such films as *Easy Rider* (Dennis Hopper, 1969), was set in classless environments of youth and anarchic violence.[14]

If films suffered a temporary eclipse in America, one special growth area was popular sociology. In 1959 Vance Packard published *The Status Seekers*, subtitled 'An Exploration of Class Behavior in America and the Hidden Barriers That Affect You, Your Community, Your Future'. Looking back to the thirties, Packard noted that 'a banker would never be mistaken for one of his clerks even at one hundred feet' (but note the white-collar imagery, nothing about miners, or construction workers). By the fifties, thought Packard, there was in America a mixing up of status and class, but yet a hardening into two distinct classes, which he somewhat elaborately defined as 'The Diploma Élite', and 'The Supporting Classes'. The Diploma Élite could be split into (I) 'The Real Upper Class', and (II) 'The Semi-Upper Class' (not the upper-middle class, since that would imply some sort of link with a middle class below, and Packard was insistent upon the sharp divide between his Diploma Élite and the rest). They, the Supporting Classes, divided into: (III) 'The Limited Success Class'; (IV) 'The Working Class (nearly forty-two per cent of the population by Packard's computation – a poke in the nose for the theorists of middle-class America); and (V) 'The Real Lower Class'. These were 'horizontal' divisions in American society; alongside them Packard placed the 'vertical dimension' of race. Apart from the stress on the working class, and on the racial dimension, Packard's book was notable for the comparisons he drew with Europe, which, contrary to the American dream, were to America's disadvantage. The American Real Lower Class, typically, lived in slums: 'slums', said Packard, 'are much less apparent in Europe's towns and cities'. Finally, Holland, England, Denmark 'have gone further than America in developing an open-class system, where the poor but talented young can rise on their merits. And they have done this while preserving some of the outer forms of class, such as titled families.'[15]

The French films of the New Wave say little about changing class relationships: perhaps there were none. Yet in 1977 President Giscard d'Estaing spoke of the 'hurricane' which had struck France in the previous twenty-five years. In France 'before the war, and even in the early fifties':

the gulf between social groups was immense, much wider than in comparable countries such as the United States and Germany. Now and again children from the State schools made their mark, but that did not conceal the compartmental nature of the society. The classes were sharply differentiated by standard of living, by food, dress and housing, even by thought and language. Pre-war films show clearly the contrast between the *grand bourgeois*, the *petit bourgeois*, the worker and the peasant. Everything conspired to separate the social classes, so that passing from one to another was a difficult feat, rarely achieved. . . .

In twenty-five years a sort of hurricane has struck this quiet world. A revolution more powerful than any political revolution has taken place at the heart of French society, affecting all its structures: family, school, university, church, moral standards. It has been caused by a combination of three factors: unprecedented economic growth, the massive spread of education, and the permanent irruption of the audio-visual media into everyone's life. . . .

Things change so quickly that words cannot keep pace. There are today half the number of peasants there were in 1950, but if we take the word peasants in the sense it had twenty-five years ago there are no peasants at all. The peasant has become a cultivator of land, a qualified factor in the economy. He has changed much as the wheat he grows has changed. . . .

. . . What is true of the agricultural worker, a symbol of stability, is true of every profession and every activity. Words have remained the same, but the country has not. It has changed more since 1950 than it changed in the eighty years before 1950.[16]

It may be, in the longer term, that the 'hurricane' was far more devastating in France than the coincident movements in the States. A new survey in 1977 of Muncie Indiana (*Middletown III*), led by Professor Theodore Caplow of the University of Virginia, was 'unable to find any trace of the disintegration of traditional social values described by observers who rely on their own intuitions'. Seventy-eight per cent of Muncie High School students found the United States 'unquestionably the best country in the world', and fifty per cent found the Bible 'a sufficient guide to all problems of modern life'. Forty-seven per cent (exactly the same figure as in the Lynds' original survey) thought it 'entirely the fault of a man himself if he does not succeed'. No doubt the very vastness of the country was serving to cushion the impact of cultural change. However, tradition and disintegration seem nicely blended in this sixteen-year-old's comment: 'Yeah, we smoke dope all over, in our cars, walking around before class, any time, but that doesn't mean we don't believe in God or that we'll let anybody put God down. That can get you in a fight.'[17]

THE NEW HISTORICAL CONTEXT

When I discussed the 'context' of class in the 1930s, I began with
physical geography. One would probably not expect that to change
much, yet what man can do and undo in the natural world is not to
be sniffed at. A wiser cultivation abolished the dust bowls whence
had come the itinerants and Okies. Clean air acts rendered the eastern
purlieus of the great European cities less insalubrious. Irrigation had
turned parts of California into playgrounds for the very rich. Geographical sectionalism still remained a factor of importance in considering the American class structure, though the development of
civilian jet transport, as well as that of the inter-state highways, had
brought the country much closer together The economic development of the South, particularly during the Second World War, and
the further migration at that time of Blacks from South to North
and West, brought some measure of homogeneity and inter-penetra-
tion as between North and South, though many of the traditional
differences remained. New waves of immigration had brought the
race problem to both Britain and France. Britain's non-European
population in the later 1970s amounted to four per cent of the total
population, that of France to seven per cent.

Most of the major points made in Chapter 2 about the different
historical legacies of the three countries remained true, despite the
war and the cultural upheavals I have just been discussing. All three
countries had been affected in greater or lesser degree by the enactment of social welfare legislation. In France and Britain deliberate
efforts had been made to deal with certain parts of the educational
system which seemed to distinguish them from the, in form, more
egalitarian American system. In America, legislation in this sphere
was directed towards redressing the more blatant racial, rather than
class inequalities. In the main, educational reform did create more
opportunities for upward social mobility. But, many authorities
now agree, the progressive modification of existing educational
systems cannot, of itself, remove deep-lying social inequalities.
Enhanced access to grammar school education, the British experience seemed to show, benefited most those already born in middle-
class homes, and only a small and exceptional number of those from
working-class homes. Under Labour governments and Labour local
authorities, therefore, the trend was towards the total replacement
of grammar schools by comprehensive schools. At the same time
an increasingly expensive private sector remained in existence. Thus
equalization of class opportunities in the middle and lower ranges

co-existed uneasily with a sharper polarization between the upper, and upwardly aspiring ranges, and the rest. In France, despite the development of the schools of a comprehensive type, the CEGs, for the first part of secondary education, the prestigious lycées remained, still taking the bulk of their intake from the better-off classes. In America, as before, it was the geography of class which set its brand upon national education. The disputed policy of bussing mainly black children from poor areas to schools in more prosperous areas was, at best, a palliative, and, at worst, a recipe for violent confrontation. The private schools continued to wax in fortune and prestige. Change was most marked at the top: the proliferation of bursaries, scholarships and more liberal entrance policies meant that the Ivy League and other high-prestige universities were now taking in students from a much broader range of social backgrounds – but only, perhaps, to socialize them into the upper-class ethos.[18]

When we turn to economic and industrial developments the most striking point overall is one already referred to (and stressed by Giscard d'Estaing who ought to know), the diminution in numerical significance of the 'peasant' class in France, though the agricultural sector still remained larger than in either Britain or the United States. In France the industrial working class had grown considerably since the 1930s, but by the later seventies was shrinking again, as was already the case in the other two countries as the industrial base shrank and the service trades grew. France, since the 1950s, had joined the world of large-scale national and international enterprises. Certainly the figures show a decline in the number of independent owners: the large industrialists, for example, formed 4.4 per cent of the active population in 1953, only 3.1 per cent in 1970. Undoubtedly the expansion in the numbers of managers and salaried executives in all three countries added further complexities to the middle and upper-middle ranges within society; many commentators continued to speak of the replacement of the entrepreneurial class by a managerial class, and the diffusion of economic power among a large number of shareholders. But any study of what has actually been taking place in France, Britain and the United States soon suggests that in fact there are a considerable number of people who combine an ostensible salaried position with a good deal of executive power, and in many cases considerable ownership of share capital. In some cases the former owners become salaried directors; in other cases successful directors acquire share capital. In France, nevertheless, between 1953 and 1970, the total number of salaried directors and top executives doubled.[19]

During the Second World War, and even more so, as far as France and Britain were concerned, in the later fifties, class relationships and class attitudes had been affected by rapidly rising living standards. In the seventies it seemed that the bubble had burst. The fall in industrial production, the ravages of inflation, and the cutbacks in living standards were greatest in Britain, but everywhere it was as if social structures and social conventions, having been heated to a point of flux in the sixties, were now subjected to a blast of icy water: would they settle in their new form, would they return to an older rigidity, would they crack? An elaborate metaphor is no substitute for analysis; the point is simply that in establishing the economic and technological context of class in the seventies, the facts of economic recession and high inflation must be included.

In trade-union history, recent developments were often no more than further twists on the historic past. The Communist-non-Communist split in France appeared stronger than ever towards the end of the seventies, the Catholic-non-Catholic one far from non-existent. In America the AFL and the CIO were united in one organization, but coloured rather by the collaborationist tone of the old AFL rather than the militant one of the early CIO. Though suffering with the shrinkage of the industrial base, the British trade union movement was still the most united and articulate in expressing a special working-class point of view, and in most respects seemed more powerful than ever in the late seventies. Although high living standards were widely diffused in America, it was still a country, as the West Virginia coal strike of 1977–8 revealed, of pockets of primitivism and ready resort to violence. In general, though, a high formal status had been established by American unions, in collective bargaining and on the shop floor, by the 1950s. It was in France that obvious contempt in manager-worker relations had been apparent before 1968, and were very much a factor in the events of that year. Since 1968, management-worker attitudes loosened considerably in France, though collective bargaining still did not establish itself as an inherent part of industrial relations. Too often wage negotiations were still conducted directly by the state. Thus working-class resentment could still show itself in the form of generalized protests against the state, rather than direct action against employers.

The war and post-war period had brought a real internationalization of social and economic ideologies. Whatever the disasters and heart-searchings of the seventies, a gospel of high mass consumption had certainly established itself in the European countries. In these countries, too, there had been shifts in the 'American' direction of giving some professional dignity to jobs formerly regarded as menial. There was no mass importation of such American euphemisms as 'redcap' for porter, but something of the shift can be seen, for example, in the virtual disappearance from English usage of the word 'charlady'. Most revealing of all, perhaps, of the international trend towards a 'one-dimensional' status social system was the appearance, particularly at airports, of the phrase VIP – not aristocrats, not upper-class personages, but simply 'very important persons'. Here we move into the realm of changes in vocabulary. Probably the most important change was the steady naturalization in the United States of a 'European' language of class.

Notes

1. The evidence can be studied in concentrated form in the Immigration History Research Center [IHRC], University of Minnesota Libraries, St Paul.
2. IHRC, Donnaruma Collection: Caesar L. Donnaruma to Lawrence F. O'Brien, Special Assistant to the President, 9 February 1961; O'Brien to Donnaruma, 16 February 1961.
3. Ralf Dahrendorf, *Conflict after Class* (1967), p. 20.
4. Daniel Bell, *The End of Ideology* (1960).
5. See, e.g., David Lockwood, 'The "New Working Class"' *Archives Européennes de Sociologie*, I (1960), pp. 248–59; and Jacques Delcourt et Gérard Lamarque, 'Un Faux dilemme: embourgeoisement ou prolétarisation de la classe ouvrière', *Etudies Sociales*, 52–3 (1963), p. 105. Richard Hoggart, *The Uses of Literacy* (1958).
6. Serge Mallet, *La Nouvelle classe ouvrière* (1965, 1969).
7. See, e.g., Arthur B. Shostack and William Gomberg, eds., *Blue-Collar World: Studies of the American Worker* (1964), and S. M. Miller and F. Riessman, *Social Class and Social Policy* (1968).
8. Murray Friedman, ed., *Overcoming Middle Class Rage* (1969), pp. 33–4.
9. For French films see Georges Sadoul, *Le Cinéma français 1890–1962* (1962), *Dictionnaire des films* (1965), and *Dictionnaire des cinéastes* (1965); and Roy Armes, *French Cinema since 1946* (2nd edition, 1970).
10. John Wain, introduction to new edition of *Hurry on Down* (1978), p. x.
11. George Brown, *In My Way* (1971), p. 29.

12. BBC TV: 'Mirror on Class', 29 May 1976.
13. BBC Written Archives, Caversham: Programmes: Industry. Acc. n. 32722.
14. For American films in the period see Robert Sklar, *Movie-Made America* (1975).
15. Vance Packard, *The Status Seekers* (1959), pp. 4, 10, 38.
16. V. Giscard d'Estaing, *Towards a New Democracy* (1977), pp. 19–20. I have not been able to obtain a copy of the French original.
17. *Middletown III*, previewed in *Time*, 16 October 1978, pp. 51–7.
18. In general, see Christopher Jencks, *Inequality* (1972).
19. Pierre Birnbaurn, *et al*, *La Classe dirigeante française* (1978); P. Sargent Florence, *Ownership, Control and Success of Large Companies* (1961).

15

Images of Class Today

In this chapter I look first at academic images, which, such has been the progress of sociological studies, are a little more international than they were in the 1930s. Then I take each country in turn, merging together official, unofficial and media images. Frankly, these images are shallower and cruder than I would have wished, because of my heavy dependence, in the contemporary period, on published sources; fortunately the deeper studies of earlier chapters help to project a little light and shade.

Two distinctive, and, in some senses, slightly contradictory trends are apparent in contemporary academic approaches to questions of class. On the one side there is at last a willingness in the Anglo-Saxon countries to accept whole-heartedly the continental tradition of a political sociology which envisages broad, nation-wide social classes; on the other, increasing stress is laid on the complexities of 'social stratification', so that, for example, just when many American sociologists were clasping the concept of class to their bosoms, some British ones were tush-tushing it away in puffs of mystification and jargon. There was still no end to the argument about what class actually meant: one man's 'class' remained another man's 'accorded status' and nothing to do with class at all; but, said the first man, class *is* accorded status and nothing but accorded status. Evidently class was not a simple subject: one could always try inventing a whole load of new labels, such as 'quasi-group', 'social level', 'buffer zone'[1] or 'unemployed slave labor classes'. Thus in contemporary complex, dynamic, loosely stratified society one might expect to estimate someone's social level by reference to his domicile in an unemployed-slave-labor-class housing estate, his failure to manage a decent buffer-zone accent, and his intention to sort out his blocked expectations through his quasi-group.

Happily, an American textbook tells us that 'there is good reason to believe that most Americans use and hear references to social class with some degree of understanding', though the author (Thomas E. Lasswell) was perhaps over-imaginative in his appraisal of American television when he continued that 'even the television "soap operas" entertain American housewives five days a week with the trials and tribulations of tormented characters in the throes of class maladjustment (Can the daughter of a poor-but-honest coal-miner rise to the glamor and security of High Society?).'[2] The second edition of *Beyond the Melting Pot*, published in 1970, contained a new introduction in which labels such as 'upper-middle class', 'middle class', 'lower-middle class', 'working class', as well as 'white collar' and 'blue collar', all noticeably lacking from the main 1963 text, were liberally bespattered.[3] As we have seen, such writers as Digby Baltzell and G. William Domhoff came out strongly in support of the view that America had a national upper class. Meantime a whole spate of books discussed the American working class. Herbert Gans wrote of 'the lower middle class and working class' as one category, and referred to 'the upper middle class' as another; but, he noted, 'class is a taboo subject, and the taboo is so pervasive, and so unconscious, that people rarely think in class terms'.[4] Harold L. Wilenski, in an essay on 'Class, Class consciousness, and American Workers', noted that social surveys 'indicate that most Americans think that classes exist, but there is little agreement about their nature and number, and there is great variation in how people of the same income and occupational level identify themselves'.[5] Lasswell, nearer this time to what was to become a well-worn mark, had concluded that 'Americans are uniform in their belief in the existence of social classes, but not uniform in their understanding of them.'[6] In an essay entitled 'How important is social class', in a collection on *The World of the Blue Collar Worker* edited by Irving Howe, Dennis H. Wrong took issue with Wilenski, arguing that 'he fails to distinguish between politically militant class consciousness in the Marxist sense and the more common emphasis in American sociology on class as the shaper of life styles and the source of a diffuse "consciousness of kind" that is hardly the same thing as Marxist class-consciousness.'[7] There was still mileage to be got out of the various types of 'new working class' discovered in the 1960s.

Whatever the messy details, the significant point is the wide use of European-style class labels which then passed from academic and polemical works into the newspapers and popular usage. Richard Sennett and Jonathan Cobb offered an interesting thesis on *The Hidden Injuries of Class* (1972): while British and French workers, they argued, took a pride in their class, the American workers, despite their relative affluence, suffered from hidden injuries: 'This fear of being summoned before some hidden bar of judgment and being found inadequate infects the lives of people who are coping perfectly well from day to day.'[8] In this respect, however, the blue-collar workers whom Sennett and Cobb interviewed sound just like all the other members of suffering humanity, aristocrats or middle-class professionals!

In one of the few British books to rival the breadth and sweep of French treatments of class, Anthony Giddens, in *The Class Structure of the Advanced Societies* (1973), argued that 'a three-fold class structure is generic to capitalist society', with the specific class systems of individual countries being determined by variations in economic and political development.[9] In France, Pierre Laroque brought out a fifth edition of his *Social Classes* in 1972. He still detected four in France: the rural class, the working class, the middle classes, which, compared with United States and United Kingdom, consisted relatively substantially of independent proprietors, and the ruling class.[10] However, Laroque had perhaps not sufficiently taken account of the drastic changes in the size and role of the former rural class. Daniel Bertaux, in the official journal *Economics and Statistics*, attempted to take account of this with a three-class structure: ruling classes, middle classes and, in a revival of an older phrase, popular classes. First he noted that the social structure defined by these categories has remained 'astonishingly stable from one generation to another: the respective proportions of 7 per cent, 30 per cent, and 63 per cent for the three categories are almost the same today as they were a generation ago.' However this superficial stability concealed very important structural changes. 'The popular classes defined as a combination of workers and peasants have passed from a peasant majority to a working class majority; the old middle classes, small merchants, artisans, have been replaced by new ones, lesser administrative executives, technicians, white collar workers.'[11]

If we look up the word 'class' in the *International* [i.e. American] *Encyclopedia of the Social Sciences* we are referred to 'Stratification, Social'. Here we have the matured wisdom of the senior generation of American sociologists, particularly Talcott Parsons and Seymour Martin Lipset, who in much of their writings had appeared as proponents of the idea that in America classes had disintegrated into a continuous gradation of strata or statuses. In a section written by Lipset himself, distinctions were made between: '(1) *objective* status, or aspects of stratification that structure environments differently enough to evoke differences in behaviour; (2) *accorded* status, or the prestige accorded to individuals and groups by others; (3) *subjective* status, or the personal sense of location within the social hierarchy felt by various individuals.' According to Lipset it is the second of these, 'accorded status', that sociologists are thinking of when they speak of 'social class'.[12] Gerhard Lenski no longer denied the existence of classes, but, in his comprehensive textbook on *Power and Privilege*, gave them a very wide meaning indeed. While the 'occupational class system is the chief determinant of power, privilege, and prestige', alongside it there exist an educational class system, racial, ethnic and religious class systems, a class system based on sex, and a class system based on age. Within the occupational class system, Lenski distinguishes ten classes: the entrepreneurial class (which he says has replaced the propertied class which belongs in a different system); the class of party functionaries; the managerial class; the military class; the professional class; the clerical class; the sales class; the working class; the farming class; and the unemployed slave labor classes.[13] Other recent American writers preferred to return to a European tradition in defining class as relating to inequality in regard to scarce resources; for them inequalities in regard to social evaluation such as respect and deference refer to status rather than class.[14] The point need not be taken further; if ordinary Americans are a little confused as to exactly what they mean by class, who can blame them.

In the post-war era one of the leading French social scientists on the international scene, Raymond Aron, had been denying all significance to social classes. Now he suggested that one might legitimately speak of 'class strata', and offered four separate criteria for distinguishing the class stratum:

(1) *The psychosocial cohesiveness of the stratum.* (How many workers live in the same way and have the same outlook toward society? How marked is this common feature?) (2) *Continuity from generation to generation.* (What is the degree of inequality at the start among children from different strata?) (3) *The individual awareness of belonging to a certain stratum and the value he attaches to this affiliation.* (For example, regarding his belonging to the working class as something higher than belonging to the French nation?) (4) *The self-awareness of the stratum in relation to other strata and a recognition of a common task.*[15]

The emphasis, here, is on political consciousness. Many American writers, as we saw earlier in the case of Goldschmidt, like to associate the notion of class with the notion of a shared social consciousness. Thus an older standard work by Joseph Kahl, cited approvingly by Lasswell, gave five classes, each with a specific characteristic: an upper class characterized by graceful living; an upper-middle class characterized by its orientation towards career; a lower-middle class devoted to respectability; a working class characterized by getting by, and a lower class characterized by apathy or hostility.[16] However, the most recent study, based on a detailed survey of 900 residents of Boston and Kansas City, conducted by Richard P. Coleman and Lee Rainwater in 1971-2, and published in 1978, offers, within 'three major classes' – Upper, Middle and Lower, a seven-fold structure which, in many respects, has a ring of colloquial authenticity to it. The classes from top to bottom are: 'the old rich of aristocratic family name'; 'the new rich, or success élite'; 'the college-educated professional and managerial class'; 'Middle Americans of comfortable living standard'; 'Middle Americans just getting along'; 'a lower class who are poor, but working'; and 'a non-working welfare class'. But, say Coleman and Rainwater, this structure forms an 'escalator' – a continuous series of gradations, encouraging mobility.[17]

We are getting back to national characteristics: French and American academics, in different ways, put a much heavier emphasis on ideology. In Britain, where the most sophisticated work along these lines divided working-class attitudes into 'traditional', 'deferential' and 'privatised' and the successful middle class into mobile 'spiralists' and stay-put 'burgesses',[18] occupation continued, pragmatically, to be taken as the main indicator of class. This often meant that Britain still continued to be presented as consisting solely of two classes: middle class and working class, with no upper class to be seen.[19] Anthony Giddens was one of the few non-Marxists to argue cogently against the thesis of the 'decomposition' of the upper class.[20] But the general thesis of the disintegration of classes had its most impressive empirical support from the second survey of Banbury conducted by Margaret Stacey and her (new) colleagues in 1966-8. Whereas the first survey in 1950 had validated the existence of the three traditional social classes, the new team found that 'there is no sense in which one can talk of a social class system or a stratification system in Banbury today.' Had Banbury changed that much, or just the sociologists? Banbury was, they agreed, 'composed of two or three social levels'![21]

OFFICIAL, POPULAR AND MEDIA IMAGES IN AMERICA

In the eyes of government and officials, America still had no classes, and the steady movement had been away from any suggestion that social security provision implied the existence of social classes. By now everyone, in any occupation, had a social security number, the doctors having, in 1965, been the last professional group to come in: the official image was of a vast classless majority being taxed in order to provide benefits for the tiny unfortunate 'low income group'. Thus an official study of *The Social and Economic Status of Negroes in the United States* (1970) remarked that 'about one-third of the black population and 10 per cent of the white population were in the low income group in 1970'. In the latest Bureau of Census, *Statistical Abstract of the United States*, the major division offered is 'by race': the percentage distribution by occupation is given in two columns, one headed 'white', the other 'black and other'. Here was official recognition of a major fact of contemporary American life. However, the two major occupational divisions are also of considerable interest: 'white-collar workers' and 'blue-collar workers'. The former include: professional, technical and kindred workers; managers and administrators; 'salesworkers'; and 'clerical workers'. Thus 'white collar' in American usage runs far further up the social scale than it does in British usage, which would centre on the last two of these categories. Blue-collar workers include craft and kindred workers, carpenters, construction craft workers, mechanics and repairers, metalcraft workers, and 'blue-collar supervisors'. There are three further smaller occupational divisions: 'operatives' who include drivers and labourers, 'service workers', and 'farmworkers'.[22] In 1973 the US Government Printing Office celebrated the twentieth anniversary of the Small Business Administration (a body, significantly, with no equivalent in Britain, though small enterprises in France had long had their special codes and help from the State) with a collection of essays written by academics, prefaced by a 'Message' from President Richard M. Nixon, *The Vital Majority: Small Business in the American Economy*. Academics could use language denied to bureaucrats, and one essay contrasted the 'middle class of successful business and professional men' with the 'wealthy aristocracy'.

In late 1978 a new edition of *The Amy Vanderbilt Complete Book of Etiquette*, revised and expanded by Letitia Baldridge, was published. Neither the book, nor the *Time* review of it, was directly aimed at questions of social class. The major source of difficulties over etiquette, indeed, were emancipated women: 'like dealing with blacks in the sixties', a sociologist had remarked, 'no one quite knows how to behave with women without giving offence'. Because it is not wittingly dealing with class, the *Time* article is good testimony on widely held assumptions about class. The 'dilemmas' over how to treat women 'extend from the most polished of society – where most hosts and hostesses have at last abandoned the practice of segregating the sexes after dinner (brandy and cigars for the boys, needlepoint chitchat for the girls) – to the working-class discos, where young women are cultivating a sexual aggressiveness that would have put Emily Post in an oxygen tent'. The adjective 'working-class' is noteworthy, though as we shall see 'blue-collar' had been used earlier in the same article: does 'blue-collar' perhaps have a too strongly occupational connotation to cover sexually aggressive young women? Earlier it had been admitted that,

> Americans do not always like to acknowledge class differences, even though one of the purposes of a more invidious etiquette for centuries has been precisely to establish one's own social superiority. I once said something about the lower class in the hearing of my mother, recalls Social Chronicler Stephen Birmingham. She slapped me and said, 'There are no classes in America!' Then she said, 'of course there are, but we *never* talk about it.'

A number of other miscellaneous points emerge: 'All kinds of elaborate dress rituals are still at work. In the great communal noise bath of a rock concert, males of any birth often take off their shirts. At baseball games, it is almost exclusively the blue-collar fans who remove their shirts and sunbathe in the bleachers; the Pierre Cardin numbers in the box seats are, if anything, unbuttoned only at the neck.' A quick change of gear: 'Children of the upper class generally seem to show less respect to their elders than the offspring of the upwardly mobile. The hulking, mouth-breathing surliness of adolescence knows no social distinction, of course. But the upper-class child, while able to engage easily in small talk that won't bore his elders, rarely says "Yes, sir" or "Yes, ma'am" when talking to his parents' friends. The custom still applies in those provinces of the middle-class where authoritarianism has not fallen into disrepute.' Finally, on the differences between true upper-class status and mere wealth: 'The upper class sees social pushiness as a trait of the new rich'; 'In Los Angeles, according to one observer, the basic rule is to defer to old money, and when that fails, defer to money.'[23]

The Coleman and Rainwater survey of Boston and Kansas City offered a variety of indications that Americans did indeed perceive class distinctions. A carpenter remarked that he wouldn't 'fit with doctors and lawyers or in a country club society. We have different interests and want to do different things'. Three rather obvious, though clearly deeply felt, utterances, were followed by quite a sophisticated analysis: 'of course, there's class. Look around you. A man driving a Cadillac feels he can thumb his nose at me because I'm driving an old VW'; 'You know there's class when you're in a department store and a well-dressed lady gets treated better'; 'most people look down on the poor like me because you have to live so shabby and can't help yourself'; *and* 'I would suppose social class means where you went to school and how far. Your intelligence. Where you live. The sort of house you live in. Your general background, as far as clubs you belong to, your friends. To some degree the type of profession you're in – in fact, definitely *that*. Where you send your children to school. The hobbies you have. Skiing, for example, is higher than snowbile. The clothes you wear . . . all of that. These are the externals. It can't be money, because nobody ever knows that about you for sure.'[24]

The American upper-class image of itself can, in a manner staggering to Europeans, be seen in the page upon page devoted to society gossip, above all in the *New York Times*. Here are to be found paragraph after paragraph on balls and dinner parties, and, above all, on forthcoming marriages. A bridegroom, we read, is a Phi Beta Kappa graduate of Harvard, and alumnus of the Harvard Law School, and his father is a partner in a Philadelphia law firm; a prospective bride 'was presented to Society at St Vincent's Debutante Ball in Rye in 1971'.[25] Alas, the violent disorder of American life, kidnap attempts for instance, could also bring the mighty under scrutiny. The Bronfman family, multi-million-dollar owners of the Seagram's whiskey business, were descended from a prosperous Jewish merchant from Bessarabia, who had settled in Canada at the end of the previous century. It was his son, Sam Bronfman, who built up the whiskey business in Canada in the 1920s so that when prohibition ended in the United States he had ready to hand a high quality product for thirsty America. More than this, it was declared by a major figure in the liquor industry in the Washington area, 'Mr. Sam . . . had an appreciation for the role of social class in American life. He liked to give his brands snob appeal. He personally designed the Seven Crown symbol – a crown on a velvet pillow – and encouraged advertisement for Seagram's VSO, a Canadian rye whiskey, which showed rich and glamorous people drinking it. Seagram's Chivers Regal Scotch, a luxury blend that trumpeted its high price, captured a large share of the market.'[26]

A further stage in the processes of assimilation and consolidation in the American upper class appeared to have taken place in the autumn of 1975 with the announcement that the various Social Registers from the different conurbations were to be amalgamated into one national *Social Register*. This in itself provided the occasion for a further round of society chat, so serious in its light-headedness:

San Francisco society showed rather little concern yesterday for the bold move disclosed in New York to consolidate all 12 handy local social registers into one absolutely unwieldy 'The' Social Register . . .

'As far as I am concerned,' Adelaide Kirkbride said 'I couldn't care less about New York and Chicago.' . . .

In Sausalito, Bill Turnbull – who gave a smashing cocktail party a few weeks ago for Diana Pryor (who had to duck out to have dinner with Jimmy Carter's advisers) – answered the telephone to say: 'I don't pay any attention to that little book at all.' 'Honestly,' said another socialite, 'what am I going to do with phone numbers for Buffalo?'[27]

The traces of an upper class are clear enough. After that the going gets more confused. In contemporary America the labels 'middle-class', 'upper-middle-class' and 'lower-middle-class' are often used in a quite British sort of way. But the 'middle-class', or, most certainly, the 'lower-middle-class' is still often conflated with the 'working-class'. 'White-collar', as already noted, often seems equivalent to the British 'middle-class'; on the whole the label 'middle-class' itself seems to be used when a sense of pride in class is being conveyed. After Mrs Sarah Moore had attempted the assassination of President Ford in San Francisco in September 1975, she reportedly described herself as an 'upper-middle-class suburban woman'.[28] The interloping female student in Alison Lurie's novel *The War between the Tates* is contemptuously described as 'lower-middle-class' by the wronged wife of the erring professor of political science.[29] In another, earlier study of Kansas City, Professor Coleman (in association with Bernice L. Neugarten) found that 'the status distinction most commonly used to divide the vast middle ranges of the status hierarchy was based upon occupation and can be called the *collar color line*', and the authors believed that this distinction was even truer for most of America than it was for Kansas City. In the words of one Kansas City woman, 'people who work in offices and wear white collars generally have more status than people who work in factories, work with their hands and are what you call blue-collar workers.'[30] But the authors felt that the demarcation was probably less important in Kansas City than in many other American cities. They found that many blue-collar families who were prosperous and maintained relatively high living standards were accepted as social equals by white-collar families. In his study of Levitt Town, Herbert J. Gans found a self-confident community which mixed blue-collar and white-collar occupations, and where the main fears had been of an influx of blacks; blacks of clear middle-class culture were just about acceptable, by contrast with manifest 'lower-class' blacks.[31] The sense of being in the middle, upper-middle-class on one side, poor on the other, is very apparent in the explanation a forty-year-old carpenter gave for his lack of interest in presidential elections. 'Are you kidding?' he asked in rhetorical demotic. 'Vote for what. You got to be an idiot to believe them political commercials. It's money that runs this country. Hell, even our welfare system is meant to give jobs to all them sociologists, social workers, bureaucrats, and political hacks. Welfare is a welfare system for the educated, upper middle class. That's what the liberal moaning for the poor is really about. It's for their own jobs. No politician is going to change that. Poverty is a going business. I just laugh at it and don't get involved.'[32]

A similar view was offered by a steelmetal worker, interviewed by a *New York Times* journalist: 'The Republicans are for the rich people. The Democrats are for the poor people. What we need is a happy medium.' More interesting, perhaps, was the gloss offered by the journalist: 'the steelmetal worker seemed to be saying that both parties are hostile to the interests of the middle class. Recent elections offered evidence that this view was widely held among middle-class voters and blue-collar workers who no longer seem inclined to call themselves working class.'[33] This apparent conflation of two differently labelled classes happens again and again. A plea for rehabilitation of a part of downtown Oakland declared that 'such a policy could foster the residence of stable working-class and middle-class families'.[34] However the *New York Times* had no equivocation in defining the district of Marquette Park in Chicago as 'an all-white, ethnic, working-class neighborhood'; the problem was that it was 'on the expanding edge of a poverty-stricken black community'. The wife of an electrician explained the attitudes of herself and her neighbours: 'it's not even integration they fear but their homes are all people have. This is not a community where people dabble in stocks and bonds. This is all they have, their only security'.[35]

Race: one just can't get away from it. And clearly it does not coincide with class lines. In some fascinating material collected among Detroit auto workers, John C. Leggatt found *both* racial antagonism *and* a sense of belonging to the working class, or to the poor. He asked black workers which people they felt were neglected by city officials. Among the responses he got were the following: 'poor people in general, but it's a little harder on Negroes than most'; 'Negroes don't get the breaks that they deserve'; 'Negroes, especially in the city services such as tree clipping, spraying, unpaved alleys, and things like that'; 'They try to keep us Negroes back far enough so that they will always have us working for them'; 'They spend millions of dollars on rockets, but there are people on welfare who can't put their kids through school – and don't get enough attention'; 'I realise that people have to help themselves, but look at the colored districts. Coloreds who earn the same as whites can't get properties in nice districts. The line is drawn so you can't get property'; 'the poorer class of people, the working class'; 'the working people aren't given an even break. The people, however, don't try to help themselves. They just don't care about helping themselves'; 'they don't pay attention to minority groups. They could improve welfare for poorer people.' The same question put to white workers produced these responses: 'lower-class folks like Italians, Polish, Negroes, and Southerners'; 'poor people'; 'In the poorer sections, playgrounds and things like that are run down, but not in the rich sections'; 'white working-class people don't get things as would Negroes. For example, the police are tougher on white working people who have dogs in the neighborhood'; 'they don't pay attention to the needs of workingmen. They want to keep him in the lowest place they can'; 'well, the ones with less, the poorer and older neighborhoods.'[36]

Without any doubt there is more pride in the dignity and significance of working-class occupations than we found among the Oakland shipyard workers in the Second World War. The interviews collected by Studs Terkel for his study of *Working* show how heavily the curse of work sits on everyone's shoulders. There is little or no overt sign of class feeling, though Terkel himself speaks of 'working class neighborhoods', 'a middle class suburb', and 'an upper middle class suburb on the outskirts of New York city' (inhabited by stockbrokers). But a strong voice, touching on many central issues, is heard from a labourer in a steel mill:

> Somebody has to do this work. If my kid ever goes to college, I just want him to have a little respect, to realise that his Dad is one of those somebodys. This is why even on – [muses] yeah I guess sure – on the black thing. . . [Sighs heavily]. I can't really hate the colored fella that's working with me all day. The black intellectual I got no respect for. The white intellectual I got no use for. I got no use for the black militant gonna scream three hundred years of slavery to me while I'm busting my ass. You know what I mean? [Laughs]. I have one answer for that guy: go see Rockefeller. See Harriman. Don't bother me. We're in the same cotton field. So just don't bug me. [Laughs].[37]

Compared with the 1930s, then, the language and labels of class are around in some profusion, though still often used inconsistently. The best defined images are of an 'upper class', or an 'upper middle class', or simply 'the rich', at the top, 'the poor' at the bottom – the word 'underclass' is now widely used in the journals and newspapers, but less so in popular speech – with 'the middle class' or 'the white-collar class' *and* 'the working class' or the 'blue collars' in the middle: though sometimes lumped together, there is enough evidence to suggest that when they really think about it, most Americans can see the difference. 'Lower class' is less used than in the thirties; when used it normally suggests the lower part of the industrial working class, together with agricultural workers and the various forms of transient labour, and excludes those workers sometimes seen as forming a part of middle America. Coleman and Rainwater's labels seem a little too elaborate. To accord with the vaguer language of everyday conversation, their first two classes (aristocratic 'old rich', and the 'success élite') could, I would suggest, be placed together in that upper class whose existence many Americans seem to sense, even if they never encounter members of it. 'College-educated professional and managerial class' does come close to the kind of labels people sometimes use; I would be inclined to regard this grouping as a kind of upper-middle class-fraction. 'Middle Americans of comfortable living standard' form the heart of the middle class. I would think that 'Middle Americans just getting along' and the 'lower class who are poor, but working', could without too much violence to colloquial actuality, be put together as forming the two slightly different elements in what is understood by the label 'working class'. The 'non-working welfare class', by whatever name, is certainly almost universally believed to exist. Race, sectionalism and job-consciousness all still run across the neat grain of British-style class categories. Job orientation seems to come through strongly in such a label as 'hard-hat', which has also assumed strong political overtones; yet, in the end, construction workers are surely quintessentially working-class.

The traditional ideologies endure. One worker, hit by the recession at the beginning of the 1970s, complained most about the repossession of his car: 'It's what burned me, the treatment, you know: I mean, I can get to work without the car, but nobody should get this kind of treatment in America.'[38] In the summer of 1977 the Georgia Republican Party, signalling that it was looking for recruits lower down the social scale, announced that it had plans to open its doors to the 'middle class'. To this a correspondent in the *Atlanta Constitution* offered what he called 'a friendly word of caution':

> Don't go too far in this ambitious plan before putting a lot of thought into it. It could lead to embarrassment and grief for the Party. Some of the 'lower class' will disguise themselves – even lie about their 'class' – and try to slip in if you crack the door too wide. And, as every sociologist knows, a member of the 'upper-lower class' and a member of the 'lower-middle class' are virtually undistinguishable, even when standing side by side in a GOP line-up. Believe me, some of these 'lower-class' devils will do anything to find out what goes on 'behind Closed Doors' . . . so be very careful in planning your selection process. . .
>
> It might appear presumptuous of me to give unasked-for advice to the GOP. But I feel that I can be reasonably objective in this 'class' matter, since I have never thought of myself as belonging to a 'class'. (My father used to urge me to be first class but never mentioned 'Upper', 'Middle' or 'Lower'.) I am a native-born American citizen and have always thought that fact eliminated any need to categorize myself as to 'class'.[39]

Professor Lasswell notwithstanding, American popular television is not notably preoccupied with problems of class distinctions, and daughters of coalminers are certainly not very prominent. Yet the little badges of class are there to be seen, usually in the context of some unscrupulous ex-blue-collar making his way to the top of society. Lomax, the self-made hotel magnate in *Washington Behind Closed Doors*, wants an ambassadorship, still a potent signal of upper-class status, for his wife. He at once reveals his lower-class origins: 'I don't owe nothing to nobody.' The Washington wheeler-dealers laugh at this solecism, which Lomax quickly converts to 'anybody'. In the Frank Sinatra film *Tony Rome* (to move briefly to the other medium), a similar figure (former bricklayer, now boss of a major construction company) says that he had had to buy 'class', in the shape of his aristocratic wife. The balance between upper-class status and the pull of wealth is well represented in the Elaine May film of 1971, *A New Leaf*: impoverished playboy Walter Matthau must find a rich wife for, as his English butler (played by George Rose) tells him, 'There is no such thing as genteel poverty here, sir.' At the same time, much was made of the manner in which, following the great success of the British soap opera about Edwardian class distinctions (hailed in America as educational television!) *Upstairs, Downstairs*, the attempt to produce an American version, *Beacon Hill* (named after the part of Boston in which proper Bostonians live) was a failure; the failure, no doubt due to other causes as well, was widely attributed to the unwillingness of the American public to view an open portrayal of class distinctions in American society, even American society of the 1920s. A further neat contrast can be made between American and British cops-and-robbers dramas. Kojak is the paradigm of the ethnic middle American: the Sweeney are aggressively working-class, exulting in the Cockney rhyming slang which provided the series with its title ('Sweeney Todd' equals 'Flying Squad').

American television offered a biting critique of the British class structure in the form of a programme prepared by the contemporary guru of market economics, Milton Friedman. The programme presented three very sharp class images: an upper class, indolent, uninterested in productive investment or serious work, seen in fancy togs, swigging champagne at the Henley regatta; a couldn't-care-less working class, straining to get out of the factory well before the end of the official working day, and ready to go on strike at the drop of a hat; then, squeezed in between, the hard-pressed middle class seen patiently waiting for their commuter trains. Apart from what the programme unwittingly reveals about a certain American assumption that America has no upper class and no working class (only, therefore, a relatively happy middle class), it added fuel, through the excerpts re-broadcast on British television, to a public discussion of class which was going on at that time (late 1976).

OFFICIAL, POPULAR AND MEDIA IMAGES IN BRITAIN

Class had long been a preoccupation of the British, though not thought a fit subject for public discussion. Now, when the statutory working class was dead, and when welfare policies were increasingly orientated towards the unfortunate, rather than towards the working class as such, there suddenly appeared, like a scarecrow leaping across the fields and into the kitchen garden, an official recognition of some of the realities of class. Throughout census reports had continued to make use of the (unsatisfactory) I–V classification; then the 1975 edition of the Central Office of Information publication, *Social Trends*, was devoted to *Social Class*. It was still a question of Classes I–V, as modified over the years (university teachers made it into Class I in 1961), but a profusion of tables made clear the continuing inequalities in life chances as between the working class (Classes III–V) and the middle class (Classes I–II), even if silence reigned over the tricky matter of the upper class. Some implied criticisms of the existing class structure were perceptible in the 1978 edition of *Britain: an Official Handbook*. While, in general, stressing the redistributive effects of taxation and welfare policies, the handbook did pick out the difference in the average weekly wage of the manual worker (£65.10) and the non-manual worker (£81.60), adding that: 'the normal working week in Britain is in the range of 39–40 hours for manual work, and 37–38 for non-manual work; a 5-day week is usually worked. Actual hours worked in manual occupations differ from these standard hours; in October 1976 they were 44 for men compared with 37.4 for women. Men and women in non-manual occupations generally work less overtime than manual workers.' Furthermore, 'non-manual workers generally have longer holidays than manual workers.'[40]

A Labour Party political broadcast on television at the end of 1976 was much discussed and abused for what was held to be its crude portrayal of a British upper class. There were letters and articles in many newspapers. Lynne Reid Banks summed up a view which was certainly widely expressed, if not necessarily widely held: 'Class is so deeply embedded in our national subconscious it is poisoning every aspect of our lives. Not just industrial relations and politics, but our choice of districts to live in, jobs, schools, friends – even which bar to drink in at our local. It's a kind of civil war we are perpetually fighting, wearing out our energy and emotions, wasting our time and money. It holds back progress, destroys prosperity, impedes social and working relations on every side.' A leftish Labour

MP welcomed the return to 'a fearless and radical examination and critique of class in Britain today'. The Labour Party, he said, did not seek to divide society, it was divided already. Nowhere was this more clear 'than in the factories where manual workers enter by one gate, eat in segregated canteens and work longer hours in worse conditions than their "betters".' Much the same point was made by a right-of-centre Labour MP, writing on 'Them and us: what we can do to heal our divided land': many managements, he noted, would not dream of sitting down to lunch with their shop stewards. The Conservative riposte was that 'some form of class structure is inevitable', but that Britain was a 'relatively open society' where class was not 'the major source of discontent'.[41] More recently, the right-wing Centre for Policy Studies published the pugnacious *Class on the Brain: the Cost of a British Obsession* by Professor Peter Bauer, whose thesis was that, if class-conscious and variegated, British society was also open and mobile; the easily detectable badges of class actually enhance mobility by providing incentives to hard work and enterprise.[42] The important point is that, whatever the political viewpoint, all of these statements do recognize the existence of classes. The last one is a defence, not a denial, of class distinctions.

What of the British people as a whole; how did they view their class structure? Kahan, Butler and Stokes in the middle sixties had insisted that 'the two-class formulation' – middle class and working class – had 'a profound hold on the perceptions of class found in British society'. Yet it is by no means clear that their own evidence supports this contention. When 'a random half-sample' was asked to volunteer what class they belonged to, twenty-nine per cent said 'middle class' and sixty-seven per cent said 'working class'. The remaining four per cent offered various categories, including 'one cheerful twenty-five-stone eccentric' who said he belonged to the 'sporting class'. But among these categories one per cent said 'upper class'.[43] This is dismissed as insignificant by Kahan, Butler and Stokes, which is rather cavalier, since the upper class only amounts to about one per cent of the population in any case. True enough, when it comes to voting preferences (which is what Kahan, Butler and Stokes were really on about) – the upper class isn't of much account; disposing of these votes may be a different matter. National Opinion Polls in 1972 gave ninety-five per cent of their respondents as identifying themselves with a social class, and ninety-one per cent as believing in the existence of different social classes.[44] Against this we have to put the testimony of those who conducted the second Banbury

study that when they attempted to 'tap the social images which Banbury people had in their minds, weak and confused conceptions of
social class emerged'.[45] Confusion of a sort not found in the starker
1930s must be allowed for, but we shall still be able to find some
pretty sharp class images.

Among those interviewed by Ronald Blythe in *Akenfield* was a
married lady who was a magistrate and chairman of the bench: 'I
suppose we would be called upper class – in fact, we could hardly
be called anything else.' On the social character of the bench she
remarked that 'we have always been upper class, which I think is a
bad mistake. We did have a working-class magistrate years ago and
he was always right.' Blythe also described a gardener who had
worked for Lord Covehithe: 'He is an easy loquacious man who
seems to be both ashamed of holding the key feudalistic ideas and
at the same time anxious to put in a good word for them. He uses
the word "calibre" as a euphemism for the word "class" – "people
of my calibre . . . people of their calibre".'[46] Simon Raven, the
novelist, offers lively, and suitably confusing images of the upper
class. Though his father was of independent means, and he was himself brought up in 'Surrey stockbrokers' country', educated at an
expensive prep school, at Charterhouse and at King's College, Cambridge, he denies being himself a member of the upper class, a term
which he uses rather as, in the previous decade, the term 'the establishment' had been used. His slightly hostile definition says something: the upper class 'control or consume the cream of the country's
resources, its cash, its offices, its perquisites, its youth – and only
have to open their mouths in a yawn to be assured of an attentive
and nation-wide hearing'. A piece of mock autobiography says more:

> On the one hand, being known to be no gentleman, I am not
> blamed by my acquaintance when I behave like a cad, maltreating
> a woman or failing to return a loan; it is what is expected of me,
> and is received with equanimity by all. On the other hand, since
> I am known to lack the steely self-sufficiency, the boundless ability
> to overlook the feelings or welfare of others, that is perhaps the
> purest characteristic of the upper class, no one is disposed to mock
> me for some pitiful display of bourgeois weakness, like apologiz-
> ing to the restauranteur if a member of my party has been sick on
> him. My upper-class acquaintance simply recognize my lack of
> assurance, and then deprecate but tolerate my condition.[47]

Raven's main point about the upper class is that people can get into it from different backgrounds and by different routes – in a later essay he defined these as 'birth or caste', 'wealth (acquired or inherited)'; and 'professional or personal merit'.[48] *My* main point is that there is still a recognizable upper class for them to get into. In giving one of its characteristics earlier, I borrowed a phrase from the diaries of the late R. H. S. Crossman. Here now is more of that entry, for 8 January 1967:

> Prescote is magnificent now the grey skies have blown off. I'm sitting here in comfort and am therefore bound to wonder whether that fierce old Tory, my brother Geoffrey, is reasonable when he says that I can't be a socialist and have a farm which makes good profits. I tell him the two are compatible provided that as a member of the government I'm ready to vote for a socialist policy to take those profits away and even, in the last resort, to confiscate the property. Nevertheless that isn't a complete answer. Having Prescote deeply affects my life. It's not merely that I'm more detached than my colleagues, able to judge things more dispassionately and to look forward to retirement, it's also more crudely that I'm comfortably off now and have no worries about money. I can eat, drink and buy what I like as well as adding 170 acres to Prescote Manor Farm. Anne and I have a facility of freedom and an amplitude of life here which cuts us off from the vast mass of people.[49]

Even the second Banbury study admitted to finding 'sets' of people who were very likely to refer to themselves as 'middle-class'.[50] Arguably, it is in the realm of middle-class perceptions that the biggest changes have taken place since the thirties. Without any doubt middle-class people then were very aware of being middle class; in the seventies *awareness* was moving towards *consciousness*. Yet, inevitably, it was not really as simple as that, above all because objectively there had been greater mobility than ever before out of the working class into the middle class. Colin Bell's study of middle-class families in Swansea (carried out in the sixties) contained two contrasting career autobiographies. A thirty-eight-year-old chemist remarked that there had been a time 'when I used to think that I was a cliché – the working-class boy who made good, a member of the new middle class, the meritocratic technocrat.' The 'whole question of identity' had been 'very difficult for me and my kind'. But this was no longer a problem 'because I now think I know where I am going.' If, he concluded, 'I can get another couple of notches up I will be able to send the boys to a boarding school. . . .' The family of the thirty-nine-year-old wholesaler, on the other hand, had 'always been comfortably off'. As he was the eldest, it had always been assumed that he, at least, 'would go into Dad's business'. Describing those now working for him in his warehouses, he remarked that 'about 22 men' were 'what you would call working-class'.[51]

The *Voices from the Middle Class* listened to by Jane Deverson and Katherine Lindsay in the early seventies belonged to the inhabitants of a newly built outer-London suburb ('Rivermead'), and a slightly grander Victorian inner-London suburb, 'Purlbridge', whose southern part contained large detached houses set in substantial gardens. Next to 'Rivermead' there stood a council estate and this certainly served to precipitate middle-class images of itself and of its working-class neighbours. Most usual were complaints about the vandalism and rowdiness of council-estate youngsters. But the council-estate had its uses. One woman felt that she owed her very presence in Rivermead to its existence, as it had reduced the price of the house to within her range. Another woman said how convenient it was to have the council-estate so near for a constant supply of cleaning ladies. 'We use them, and they use us, I suppose. They can come and clean our houses, but, quite frankly, if someone built a high wall down the middle and separated our estate and theirs, no one would mind. There is no real relationship between us.'[52] Purlbridge, too, was menaced with a council estate. A long-time resident, with some reluctance, said: 'We had to build our wall up at the back because you'd sit in the garden and be showered with stones, and you felt – it's the enemy over there!'

Nearly all middle-class self-images were expressed by means of contrast to an image of the working class. A public relations consultant, discussing his long hours in the office, remarked that if he was 'not prepared to put in the work' he might as well 'be a bus driver'. 'We struggle to buy our own homes and send our children to good schools, while the poorer people live in council estates and have everything done for them,' declared one Purlbridge couple. 'People don't get het up about whether my child or your child has a fair deal; after all, we're middle-class, we are paying for our mortgage and we're all right. But are we? I often think we are the most under-privileged section of society in many respects, and we won't make a fuss about it because of our middle-class pride; we just battle on for ourselves.' But the most violently class-conscious sentiments quoted by Deverson and Lindsay come from a lady from the substantial part of Purlbridge, who seems to me to be on the fringes of the upper class:

> I can't understand people who feel guilty about the working-classes. People will always be different, even if everyone has the same houses and the same money. We would always be richer in our minds than the working-classes, just by reading books. Labourers can earn a lot of money these days; God, they must have money, the prices they charge! But all they are concerned with is revenge, in the petty ways of their minds. Jealousy and bitching is their main occupation. Look, if everyone had the same amount of money, some people would manage their money better and then things would still be unequal. A person with a different background will live in a different way regardless of money.
>
> Anyway, the Capitalist system helps the poor. If the Stock Market is doing well and the country is richer, that helps the poor. The rich give jobs to the poor. There is always going to be envy, there's always going to be people who are better off than others. It annoys me when people vote Labour out of emotionalism. My best friend voted Labour once, just out of emotion, because she felt it was the right thing to do. Edgar said: 'Are you mad? They are going to nationalise everything and you'll lose all your shares!' She was horrified. 'Oh God, what have I done?' she said. She's mad, completely mad!

The second Banbury survey was unable to define any very distinct working-class images of self or of society. The famous Goldthorpe, Lockwood, Bechhofer and Platt survey of 'the affluent worker' in Luton, covering assembly line workers at Vauxhall Motors, machine operators and craftsmen servicing machines at the Skefko Ball Bearing Company, and process workers and craftsmen engaged on process maintenance at Laporte Chemicals, likewise, found the images of their respondents 'vague', 'confused' and diverse.[53] Some signs of the development of a more 'American' outlook among this particular group of workers is apparent in the fourteen per cent who claimed for themselves definite 'middle-class' status, and, even more so, in the eight per cent taking the view that they could be described equally well as 'working' or 'middle' class. According to the authors of the survey, 'affluent' workers tended to single out money as the most important determinant of class and (though the evidence in support of this is by no means clearly presented) to allocate themselves to a 'large central class' which was seen 'as being a mainly emergent one, resulting from the fusion of the more distinctive working and middle classes of an earlier period'. For all that, sixty-seven per cent of the sample apparently had no difficulty in allocating themselves to the 'working class' (or, in a few cases, apparently, to the 'lower class' – again there is an American ring, but again, also, the evidence is less clearly presented than one would wish).

If we now turn to a later survey of a more representative sample of factory workers, less affluent, but securely established in more traditional employment, we get some rather clearer images (the purpose of the survey was actually to contrast British and Swedish conceptions).[54] The first question asked was: 'Some people say that there are no longer social classes in this country. Others say that there are. What do you think?' Ninety-three per cent of the British workers thought classes *did* exist (ninety-seven per cent in Sweden, incidentally). Distinctive British perceptions emerged immediately in response to the follow-up question, 'why do you think this is the case?' Thirty-seven per cent of the British workers, certainly, opted for 'money, wealth and economic factors', but twenty-five per cent thought class 'an inevitable feature of life', making statements like 'you will always have leaders and followers', 'some people are bound to be better than others', and 'breeding makes social class inevitable'. Only 2.5 per cent singled out education (while over 20 per cent did so in the Swedish sample). Nearly 11 per cent opted for 'birth and family background' (under 2 per cent of the Swedes made this choice). Additionally, 12 per cent of the British sample were very conscious of notions of status and snobbery, making comments like 'there are those who think they are better than others', and 'some people will always look down their noses at you'. As to the most important determinant of class, 37.8 per cent of the British workers again singled out birth and family background (10.2 per cent of the Swedes), though 58 per cent picked 'money, wealth and economic factors' (68 per cent in the Swedish sample). Education was chosen by only 13.5 per cent of the British workers (38.1 per cent of the Swedish ones). Asked, 'Which are the major classes in this country today?' 74.8 per cent identified both the 'upper, top or higher classes' and the 'working class', and 75.6 per cent the 'middle class'; the only other main categories volunteered were 'the wealthy' (16 per cent) and the 'lower class' (17.7 per cent). Twenty-nine per cent had an overall image of a two-class society, 60 per cent of a three-class society; 11 per cent envisaged more than three classes. When asked to allocate themselves to one of the classes whose labels had emerged from the previous question, 69.8 per cent said 'working class', 19.3 per cent said 'middle class', 5 per cent said 'lower class', 3.4 per cent said 'the poor' and 1.7 per cent said 'average people'.

There is, then, some evidence of industrial workers in Britain beginning to use the term 'middle class' in one of the American senses of that term – the industrious middle, caught between rich and poor. But much more evidence, particularly from the 'affluent worker' study, shows how far away industrial workers still were from 'middle-class' job satisfactions, or from 'middle-class' aspirations after social mobility. The Luton workers stressed the unpleasantness of their work, giving the high pay as its only advantage (seventy per cent of white-collar workers, by contrast, did not mention pay, and two-fifths – the highest single group – gave the nature of their work as their greatest source of satisfaction). The Luton workers expressed no very strong feelings against separate canteens : 'I don't like the idea of the boss breathing down my neck at mealtimes,' said one; 'wouldn't want *them* listening in to my conversation,' said another. All three of the Luton firms encouraged promotions from the shop floor to supervisory, technical and managerial grades. 'Nevertheless,' recorded Goldthorpe, Lockwood, Bechhofer and Platt:

> it was clearly indicated by our interview findings that while the firms' promotion policies might be highly beneficial to certain individuals, they were of little effect in creating interest in advancement within the firm and in encouraging the mass of the labour force to think of themselves as one day likely to become something more than merely wage workers. We asked our respondents if they liked the idea of becoming a foreman (the first major step on the promotion ladder), whether they had ever thought about this seriously and, if so, whether they had taken any action to this end. The outcome was that only 20 per cent of the more skilled men and 15 per cent of the semi-skilled were both attracted to the idea of promotion and had given this serious consideration ; and that only 9 per cent of the former group and 8 per cent of the latter both wanted to become foremen and had actually done something about this, such as applying for promotion or attending a training course. In brief, for the large majority of men in our sample the possibility of promotion was of no real significance.[55]

All of these attitudes were echoed, and re-echoed by workers in the Ford motor plants: 'It's the most boring job in the world,' said one:

> It's the same thing over and over again. There's no change in it, it wears you out. It makes you awful tired. It slows your thinking right down. There's no need to think. It's just a formality. You just carry on. You just endure it for the money. That's what we're paid for – to endure the boredom of it.
>
> If I had a chance to move I'd leave right away. It's the conditions here. Ford class you more as machines than men. They're on top of you all the time. They expect you to work every minute of the day. The atmosphere you get in here is so completely false. Everyone is downcast and fed up. You can't even talk about football. You end up doing stupid things, childish things – playing tricks on each other.

'It's strange this place,' said another:

> It's got no really good points. It's just convenient. It's got no interest. You couldn't take the job home. There's nothing to take. You just forget it. I don't want promotion at all, I've not got that approach to the job. I'm like a lot of people here. They're all working here but they're just really hanging around, waiting for something to turn up. .... It's different for them in the office. They're *part* of Ford's. We're not, we're just working here, we're numbers.

Managerial and white-collar workers might be envied; foremen needn't be: 'The supervisors here are treated like dirt. The way they are shouted at in front of the men is terrible. The manager shouted at our foreman the other week: "You stupid fucking bastard you'll be sacked if you carry on like this." He said that in front of us. Their job isn't as secure as ours. All they get out of it is a white coat and you're married to the firm.'[56]

Besides the newer, and no doubt less homogeneous, working-class communities, there were still the older ones, such as the *Working-Class Community* (Huddersfield) studied by Brian Jackson and Denis Marsden in the sixties. Jackson laid stress on the continuing importance of the working-men's clubs, noting that there were very few businessmen or small tradesmen in the clubs and that these few preferred to keep a very low profile indeed. The view in Huddersfield was:

They've got their own clubs and political clubs. It's all working men here. Unlike even the pub, the club has the atmosphere of the working man's home: 'Ah never go into a pub at all now. Clubs are much more sociable like. Look at this. I couldn't rest my legs across a chair in t'pub. Here it is like being at home. As long as Ah don't put me feet on t'seat, I'm all right.'

There was a clear boundary to the community of mill workers; floor managers, clerical workers and minor officials were excluded. While they collected a general dislike and mistrust, there was, Denis Marsden found 'a grudging respect' for the mill owners. You could, said Jackson, 'trace a line through Huddersfield marking the point where the gap showed between middle-class and working-class life.'[57]
A series of interviews presented by Jeremy Seabrook indicated the disillusionment of older working-class activists over the break-up of many traditional working-class communities. They also brought forward a new voice and pointed to a new social divide:

Why do I fight for the National Front? Why, because I don't want parts of my country to become no-go areas, where I feel I can't walk without the risk of being knifed or mugged. I don't want to be with black people, I don't want a multi-racial country. Why should I? I've got nothing in common with them, they don't want to mix with me any more than I do with them. Why should I be forced to live with them? I want to be able to go into a pub, I want to be able to go to work without seeing a black face. The National Front is saying the sort of things I want to hear. I wouldn't be cruel. If I ran over a black in my car, I wouldn't just leave him lying in the road; I'd kick him into the gutter. I don't want them here. I want them to leave. I understand that this might be a bit disruptive. If the barricades do go up, it won't be middle class on one side and working class on the other; it'll be white on one side and black on the other, with just a few race traitors on their side. I want to be just with our own. I don't want to live in a system that falls over itself to favour blacks. If there's anything going in this country, I want it for myself. We've suffered enough in the past, and now it's our turn. We've had one flabby govern-ment after another saying, 'We've got to learn to live together.' Well, why? They don't have to live with them, killing goats, wailing at dusk and fasting and being a nuisance.[58]

The imagery of class in Britain in the 1970s is more varied and less clear-cut than it was in the 1930s. Carefully realized working-class settings had become quite commonplace on television and in films. Scenes of serious material deprivation were limited to programmes portraying earlier times. *When the Boat Comes In*, set in the Newcastle shipyards in the 1920s, also yielded up a nice piece of upperclass imagery: James Bolam plays the bright upwardly mobile former shipyard worker who is already paying court to the daughter of the local aristocrat – 'Daddy says our ancestors must have been a bit like you,' she tells him. In general what the media offered were total cultural enclaves, a working-class setting for one TV series, a middle-class one for another, with little sense of comparison or contrast, let alone conflict: class was now to be seen as very much a matter of culture, not of power or economics. After their great satire of the earlier period, *I'm All Right Jack*, the best Boulting Brothers film at the beginning of the seventies was *The Family Way*, the story of the stresses of an unconsummated marriage set entirely within a working-class environment – and with only the faintest hints of the 'life-sentence' being served by Arthur (Hywel Bennett), unable to realize his aspirations towards poetry and classical music. What often comes through most strongly (when comparisons are made with French and American productions) is the common *Britishness* of the middle and working class. Explicit class language is often used in a jokey, politically and socially neutral, fashion: Mr Dawson, a shop and restaurant owner, in *Coronation Street* (7 August 1978), says of two young carpenters who are working for him, 'Ah, the vulgarity of the working class.'

OFFICIAL, POPULAR AND MEDIA IMAGES IN FRANCE

Official France remains a country of codes and registers. While the *ouvriers* remain a juridically distinct entity, the great extensions of social security legislation have obliterated most of the overt class distinctions assumed in the somewhat fragmentary legislation of the thirties. The many labels – *artisans*, *industriels*, *professions libérales*, etc. – seeming to suggest a long and variegated middle class, still abound. The classification used by the National Institute of Statistics and Economic Studies is still not ordered in any class hierarchical sequence, but in grouping together owners, liberal professions, managers and civil servants, it comes close to recognizing an upper class. Officially the régime of Giscard d'Estaing projects a spirit of national unity and classlessness. Titles, save those of duke or prince, are no longer to be used. There is much talk of 'social partners', meaning government, employers, and unions. Yet opinion polls suggest a greater polarization into social classes: greater numbers of Frenchmen than ever before are willing to allocate themselves to 'the working class'. At the same time the events of 1968 boosted the notion of there being one 'popular class' of *travailleurs*, industrial, white-collar, and managerial workers (*ouvriers, employées, cadres*), who had a common cause against 'the tyranny of technocracy and bureaucracy', and a common 'encounter with the capitalist class'. 'You,' said a poster of 1968, 'are the class which is most deeply rooted in the nation.'[59] It remains true, then, that the language of class, when used in France, is influenced by historical, political and ideological associations; the same is not true of America or Britain.

The nobility, a phenomenon more agonized over in contemporary France than in Britain, is recognized to be more a matter of history than of politics or ideology. The distinguished French historian, Henri Lefebvre, in a preface to François de Negroni's *Noble France* (1974), an excellent guide to the contemporary upper-class self-image, described the book as 'an historical and philosophical analysis, a sociological study, and a polemical manifesto'. While the most recent *Dictionary of the French Nobility* lists only about 100,000 persons of aristocratic blood, from just over 4000 genuinely noble families, Francois de Negroni computed the nobility at 50,000 families, then added a further 400,000 individual members of high society (*mondains*) 'imperturbably practising the ancient and modern rites attached to their distinctive condition', and, as indeed it would seem, presenting the sort of upper-class image which has long existed in Britain, and which has become established in the United States. Negroni deliberately excluded the old country squireen, now more farmer than country gentleman, living a quiet rustic life which contrasted sharply with the ritual of high society. At the heart of this ritual was the summer migration to family domains in the provinces, and the re-grouping in the autumn in particular sections of Paris, or, less characteristically, in some of the main provincial towns: 'it is, of course, in Paris that the world of high society is centralized and has its bureaucratic apparatus'; it is to Paris that the young provincial debutantes are sent to be launched into the world. Aristocratic families tend to be large, and, by virtue of an 'old taboo', births take place in high-class nursing homes well away from the ancestral domain. Births are announced in the *Carnet Mondain* or *Le Figaro*, and at the end of the year in the *Bottin Mondain*, together with the father's titles and decorations and the 'divers properties, yachts or race horses' which he may possess. In a very French and formalistic sort of way, the birth and betrothal announcements in *Figaro* serve a function similar to that of the society gossip columns in the *New York Times*. Of twenty-three birth announcements, one cold day in December 1977, two were, respectively, to a princess and to a countess, eight to families boasting of at least one *particule*, and one to a general's wife. Of eight engagements announced in the same issue, one involved the daughter of a count and a countess on one side, and the son of a viscount and viscountess on the other, another involved the daughter of a baron, and another two involved at least one family with the *particule*. Of the seven marriage announcements, three involved families with claims to nobility.[60]

From his first steps, the 'noble' child will learn the life of the group. Accompanied by his nurse, he, along with the children of his parents' friends, will play in certain public parks, the Ranelagh, the Parc Monceau, the Tuileries, or the Pré-Catelan. On Sundays he'll meet the same children coming out of such churches as Saint-Honoré-d'Eyleau, Notre-Dame-de-Grace-de-Passy, Saint Philippe-du-Roule, and Saint Pierre-du-Gross-Caillou. At the Madeleine, the *mal* de Passy, or the Avenue Victor-Hugo, says Negroni, 'he will meet them again, like him following their mother in the weekly round of the high-society Parisian shops.' In the summer the child will take part in great family gatherings at the paternal or maternal chateau, and meet members of the international aristocracy. He grows up in a world of servants, but spends part of his time during the holidays with farmers' children in order to imbibe the 'popular virtues'. He will go to an exclusive school: Saint-Louis-de-Gonzague, Gerson, Les Roches, or Sainte-Marie. There will be a strong emphasis on intellectual and cultural activities, but also on such 'aristocratic' sports as tennis, horse-riding, fencing, and sailing. Around the age of fifteen the adolescent is enrolled in a special sort of club or fraternity (*Rallye*) responsible for looking after his 'final apprenticeship to high society life.' At seventeen there are formal dances lasting from five to nine in the evening. At eighteen the hours move to six until midnight; despite strict controls, says Negroni, there is a considerable black market in tickets for these dances, centred on the Café du Trocadéro. At nineteen comes the ball, held either at some place such as the Crillon or the Ritz, or at the country chateau. At the same time serious studies proceed:

At *l'école du Louvre*, at the Catho, or at the School of Art and Archaeology, the feminine intellectual élite convincingly bring to perfection their training as future society women, the others making up for their lack of scholarly success by brief and episodic careers as nurses or *cheftaines*. At *Saint-Cyr*, *Polytéchnique*, *Sciences Po* or the ENA, the more brilliant males perpetuate the university and professional monopolies traditionally exercized by aristocratic students; but at the *École des cadres* or at the *École supérieure des arts modernes*, the less brilliant elements without difficulty find plenty of old companions of like tastes with whom to share their modest lot.

In full adulthood, the man will serve in the diplomatic corps, in the more prestigious civil service departments, on the boards of major industries, or as municipal councillors, and, especially, as mayors. They will join the *Jockey Club*, the *Tir aux Pigeons*, the *Nouveau Cercle*. Like American 'clubwomen', the members of top families will tend to dabble in good works.

So much for the upper class. A study of the press, and of the activities of such organizations as the General Confederation of Small and Medium Enterprises (PME) and the Association of Iniatory and Responsible groups (GIR), suggests a high level of middle-class *consciousness* in contemporary France. *Figaro* spoke of PME as being the interpreter for '150,000 industrialists, 800,000 artisans, and 2,000,000 shop-keepers, who, with the 250,000 Frenchmen practising in the liberal professions, make up a large part of the "*silent, but active, majority*", the determinant element in the social and economic fabric of the country.'[61] Private voices, in contrast, suggest a recognition of how the higher sections of the middle class, at least, stand apart from the majority of society. A top manager, thirty-seven years old, head of a division containing sixty people, including four executives, felt the strain of work, but recognized that he had 'a good job'. There were problems over

> the employees who are sometimes congenial, but with whom our status as executives does not permit us to sympathise, for society lives in such a way, imposes such a form of relationships, that such sympathies can only be 'platonic'; and then besides, they themselves, 'the employees' (I too am an 'employee', but no one says so, above all I am a director), the employees, then, don't wish it. To them we are part of a monster called MANAGEMENT, for we are the ones who say: 'You must work longer, harder, more quickly, no, you do not deserve a rise. No, we do not have enough money to share out. We can't give it to you.'

What has my work brought me? Money. I make a good living. Much better than my father. That allows me comfort, holidays, my house which we bought last year and which is certainly not yet fully paid up.

But also a certain sense of personal success. I feel, because I have 'succeeded' quite well and because I am 'recognized' by others, more confidence in myself than fifteen or twenty years ago, when I was at school (not very bright) and a student (mediocre).

What has my work taken from me?

Time, which today seems to me the one luxury of life. Time to live in tranquility. My true life rhythm is that of a peasant, yet I live like a Parisian who races along the corridors of the metro.

A young schoolteacher in this same survey, conducted in November and December 1976 by the French Institute of Public Opinion on behalf of *Télérama*,[62] found that he could never switch off from work, while some aspects, such as marking essays, bored him: 'But I am clear that I am one of the privileged: my economic power, though modest, is superior to that of most Frenchmen. My free time allows me to participate in many activities. My job, concerned with human relationships, suits my out-going personality.'

Broken down by family head, the survey was described as comprising 84 farmers, 191 top executives, members of the liberal professions, teachers and artists, 209 supervisory staff, 343 workers, and 236 not in employment. Here is a fifty-year-old electrician from La Varenne: 'I get up at 5.55. It takes me an hour to get to the factory at Vitry. A works bus picks me up 500 metres from here and brings me back at 5.30 p.m. At the factory, we never talk about personal matters. Conversation centres on football, cards and telly.... Those who are interested in politics keep to themselves and form a ghetto. It's exhausting.' Replying to a question about how work *ought* to be organized in the factory, he continued:

First of all, it is scandalous to ask men to produce something without them knowing what purpose it serves. Workers should have the economic situation explained to them; then, workers' councils, made up of delegates, should decide the level and quality of production. That would end the power of the technocrats and put the whole hierarchy in question. But it is difficult to talk about this with your mates; most of the time they say: 'There you are, you're on your hobby-horse again, but the road is barred up there.'

Class: Image and Reality

Clearly this was an exceptionally politically conscious worker, but
in any case no British or American worker would have used any
such word as *prolo* ('prole' in British usage being purely and simply
a term of abuse and contempt), as he did in dealing with a question
about the possibility of escaping from the working-class condition:

> The son of the *prolo*, in the majority of cases, turns towards a
> technical career. By making many sacrifices he might become a
> professional engineer. But since he has nothing at all to lean on,
> he feels bound to conform to the utmost. This explains why the
> engineer of proletarian origins is before anything else a social
> copper. Only the engineer of bourgeois origins can allow himself
> to be a liberal. In any case, in industry, there is no true point of
> contact for individuals from different classes.

Finally, an elderly lady who worked as a night concièrge in a grand
hotel in Nice:

> My work, or my presence, extends from eight at night to eight in
> the morning; one week I have one day off, the next week, two. I
> said 'presence' because we do not pretend to be working continu-
> ally throughout the twelve hours. There are certain hours, known
> as 'equivalents' in the hotel trade, when we are permitted to rest
> while being on the spot and at the mercy of anything that happens.
> Now, in a big hotel there is always a continual coming-and-going,
> which makes resting difficult. But there are certain advantages:
> one can read, write and get to know foreign languages better, an
> essential condition in the hotel business.
> Despite all that, I like my work because it is lively and it permits
> me to rub shoulders with all sorts of people, from the well-off
> class and from different nationalities, as well as personalities from
> the world of politics and art and literature.

This sixty-one-year old woman, with her alternating sixty-hour and
seventy-two hour week, was, like the electrician's fellow workers,
devoid of class consciousness. And this remained very much in tune
with the findings Alain Touraine's classic study of *Working-Class
Consciousness*, published in the previous decade. Building workers,
Touraine found, 'reveal a type of consciousness strongly orientated
towards their job experience. They regard themselves as producers
more than as wage-earners; they are more sensitive to the labour
market than to the power of the boss.' Mining was the only sector

in which a majority found working conditions unsatisfactory. Miners did express their work situation in terms of classes more frequently than other workers, but, Touraine continued, it would be more true to say that they were orientated towards the practical improvement of conditions than to class consciousness.[63] The doctrinaire conception of class consciousness should, concluded Touraine, be replaced by an 'historical' and sociological conception, by which, it would seem, he meant very much what I mean when I speak of 'class awareness'.

Two French films of the 1970s address themselves explicitly to some of these issues. Godard's *All goes Well* (*Tout va Bien*, 1972), like *I'm All Right Jack*, opens with an historical sequence that makes jokey use of the various political, social and quasi-juridical labels that we have encountered so often in the course of this book: we meet the *ouvrier*, the *paysan*, the *bourgeois* (*petit et grand*) and, finally, *un bourgeois qui bourgeois*. Marin Karnutz's *Blow for Blow* (*Coup pour Coup*) was a non-commercial, explicitly political film, yet it shares with *Tout va Bien* (and here there is a link right back to *Le Point du Jour*) the device of filtering events through the eyes of middle-class intellectuals (and their television programmes). The strikers in both films appear more like media constructs than like real working people. At the same time, the strong element of ritualization is very relevant to the reality of French society, where, typically, strikes are brief, often confined to one locality, and trapped out with much of the ritual of ideological conflict. Neither *Tout va Bien* nor *Coup pour Coup* gives any broad sense of working-class solidarity. The *women* strikers in the provincial textile factory of *Coup pour Coup* (feminism is probably the single strongest political colouring in this film) say that they are sick of unions. Godard could hardly have stressed further the indignity of labour than he does by setting his strike in a sausage factory: the workers scarcely do more than join with the sausages in providing a background for the personal and ideological posturing and writhing of the two intellectuals (Jane Fonda and Yves Montand). André Tchechiné's *Souvenirs of France* (*Souvenirs d'en France*) is an ambitious panorama of French industrial life in a small town, from pre-war barbarity, through German occupation to contemporary affluence. Nowadays, we learn, small employers and their workers are facing together a hostile world.

Souvenirs d'en France certainly shows a two-class society, but with distinctions between employers and workers softening over time. Most contemporary French films do not present any overt industrial environment. In Bertrand Tavernier's *The Watch-Maker of St Martin* (*L'Horloger de St Martin*, based on a Simenon novel) the murder of a factory cop by a factory girl and her boyfriend, a student at a technical college, takes place, as it were, off-stage. The film is set in the milieu of a petty-bourgeois, *artisan*, inner-city quarter of Lyons: the relationship explored is that between the student's father, the eponymous watch-maker, and the police detective on the case, a hard-working lower-middle class figure, who savours his wine like a *gourmet*, but whose son will also go into the police. No social doubt is expressed over the watchmaker's son's liaison with a factory girl. We are in the world of republican citizens, menaced by rapacious lawyers and uncomprehending justice crushing those who 'talk back', the world of '*les classes populaires*'. Many French films are set in a comfortable upper-middle-class milieu, often isolated from any real sense of a surrounding class structure, and Claude Chabrol has said publicly[64] that his love of blood is rivalled by his desire to put '*the bourgeois*' in an embarrassing situation. However the butcher and other characters in *Le Boucher*, belong to the small-town artisan class, rather than the comfortable bourgeoisie. Seen through the imagery of French films, France today is a country where class distinctions are not strongly marked, where the most important people are intellectuals or artisans, and where the workers perform ritual functions in the background. A manifestly upper-class family, with the son deliberately sent to a local, low-class school, does intrude upon Bertrand Blier's delicious *Preparez vos Mouchoirs* (1977), but the main trio, schoolteacher, schoolteacher's wife and the friend (who has a faint air of manual work about him) are studiously classless.

French television need not detain us for more than a moment. Although it imports fewer programmes than any European Broadcasting system, French TV also presents very few programmes related to contemporary society, preferring instead the safety of costume dramas. A Canadian observer, Denise Bombardier, shrewdly contrasted the liveliness of everyday conversation in France with the pomposity and stiffness of French television, where every spokesman must have some sort of a title – a facet, she thought, of the growing *hierarchization* of French society.[65] And this leads me to final reflection on the imagery current in the three countries. *Hierarchization* and use of functional titles ('M. le President', 'Mr President', 'M. le Secrétaire-générale', 'Congressman'), as well as such 'honours' as the *Légion d'honneur*, need not represent an elaboration of class distinction, but class does tend to be bolstered by sycophancy and worship of rank, and weakened by casual disrespect. Only in Britain do newspaper headlines refer to leading politicians as 'Jim' or 'Maggie'.

Notes

1. 'Buffer zone' is the invention of Frank Parkin in *Class Inequality and Political Order* (1971), p. 56. The other labels reappear in my text.
2. Thomas E. Lasswell, *Class and Stratum: an Introduction to Concepts and Research* (1967), p. 3.
3. Daniel Moynihan and John Milton Glaiser, *Beyond the Melting Pot* (second edition, 1970).
4. Herbert Gans, *The Levittowners: Ways of Life and Politics in a New Suburban Community* (1967), p. 179.
5. Harold L. Wilenski, in William Haber, ed., *Labor in a Changing America* (1966), pp. 12–28.
6. Lasswell, *op. cit.*, p. 16.
7. Dennis H. Wrong, 'How Important is Social Class?', in Irving Howe, ed., *The World of the Blue-Collar Worker* (1972), pp. 297–309.
8. Richard Sennett and Jonathan Cobb, *The Hidden Injuries of Class* (1972).
9. Anthony Giddens, *The Class Structure of Advanced Societies* (1973).
10. Pierre Laroque, *Les Classes sociales* (1972).
11. Daniel Bertaux, 'L'Héridité sociale – France', *Economie et statistique*, (February 1970).
12. *International Encyclopaedia of the Social Sciences*, p. 310.
13. Gerhard Lenski, *Power and Privilege* (1966), pp. 351–86.
14. See Edward O. Laumann and Richard Centers, 'Subjective Social Distance, Occupational Stratification, and Forms of Status and Class Consciousness: a Cross-Cultural Replication and Extension', *American Journal of Sociology*, vol. 81, no. 6 (1976), pp. 1304–38.
15. Raymond Aron, *Progress and Disillusion: the Dialectics of Modern Society* (1968), 1972 edition, pp. 35ff.
16. Joseph A. Kahl, *Social Class in America* (1957), pp. 184–220. See Lasswell, *op. cit.*, p. 229.
17. Richard P. Coleman and Lee Rainwater, *Social Standing in America: New Dimensions of Class* (1978), pp. 26, 119.
18. David Lockwood, 'Sources of Variation in Working-Class Images of Society', *Sociological Review*, vol. 14 (1966), pp. 249–67. W. Watson, 'Social Mobility and Social Class in Industrial Communities', in M. Gluckman and E. Devons, eds., *Closed Systems and Open Minds* (1964).

19. See Michael Kahan, David Butler and Donald Stokes, 'On the analytical division of social class', *British Journal of Sociology*, vol. XVII, no. 2 (June 1966).

20. Anthony Giddens, 'Elites in the British Class Structure', in Peter Stanworth and A. Giddens, eds., *Elites and Power in British Society* (1974).

21. Margaret Stacey, Eric Batstone, Colin Bell and Anne Murcott, *Power, Persistence and Change: a Second Study of Banbury* (1975), pp. 131, 135.

22. US Bureau of the Census, *Statistical Abstract of the US* (1977), p. 407.

23. *Time*, 27 November 1978, pp. 50–2.

24. Coleman and Rainwater, *op. cit.*, pp. 80–3.

25. *New York Times*, 5 August 1977, etc., etc.

26. *Washington Post*, 14 August 1975.

27. *San Francisco Chronicle*, 1 November 1976.

28. *Chicago Tribune*, 25 September 1975.

29. Alison Lurie, *The War between the Tates* (1974).

30. Richard P. Coleman and Bernice L. Neugarten, *Social Status in the City* (1971), p. 18.

31. Gans, *op. cit.*, pp. 373–8.

32. *Chicago Tribune*, 4 November 1976.

33. *New York Times*, 2 December 1976.

34. *San Francisco Chronicle*, 28 October 1976.

35. *New York Times*, 7 August 1977.

36. John C. Leggatt, *Class, Race and Labor: Working Class Consciousness in Detroit* (1968).

37. Studs Terkel, *Working* (1974), pp. 19, 205, 280.

38. Quoted in Sennett and Cobb, *op. cit.*, p. 32.

39. *Atlanta Constitution*, 26 August 1977.

40. *Britain: an Official Handbook* (1978), p. 318.

41. *The Times*, 3, 9, 15 December 1976, 9 May 1977.

42. Peter Bauer, *Class on the Brain: the Cost of a British Obsession* (1978).

43. Kahan, Butler and Stokes, *op. cit.*

44. Cited in Ivan Reid, *Social Class Differences in Britain* (1977), p. 24.

45. Stacey, Batstone, Bell and Murcott, *op. cit.*, p. 121.

46. Ronald Blythe, *Akenfield*, pp. 101–8.

47. Simon Raven, *The English Gentleman* (1964), p. 10.

48. Simon Raven, 'Class and the Novel', in Richard Mabey, ed., *Class* (1968).

49. R. H. S. Crossman, *The Diaries of a Cabinet Minister*, vol. 2 (1976), p. 190.

50. Stacey, *et al.*, *op. cit.*, pp. 117–18.

51. Colin Bell, *Middle Class Families* (1968), pp. 28–32.

52. Jane Deverson and Katherine Lindsay, *Voices from the Middle Class* (1975), p. 18. Other quotations are drawn from pages 38, 70 and 191–2.

53. J. Goldthorpe, D. Lockwood, J. Bechhofer and J. Platt, *The Affluent*

Worker, vol. 3 (1969), p. 146. The rest of this paragraph is drawn from pp. 140–56.

54. Richard Scase, 'English and Swedish Concepts of Class', in F. Parkin, ed., *The Social Analysis of Class Structure* (1974), pp. 149–77.
55. Goldthorpe, *et al.*, *op. cit.*, pp. 70–3.
56. Huw Beynon, *Working for Ford* (1973), pp. 118, 121, 125.
57. Brian Jackson and Denis Marsden, *Working-Class Community* (1968), chapters 4, 5 and 10.
58. Jeremy Seabrook, *What Went Wrong?* (1978), p. 93.
59. Archives Nationales, Institut Francais d'Historie Sociale, Mai 1968 (14 AS 238).
60. *Figaro*, 10 December 1977. Otherwise this section is drawn from Francois de Negroni, *La France noble* (1974), pp. 17–33.
61. *Figaro*, 2 December 1975.
62. Published as, Janick Arbois and Joshka Schidlow, *La Vraie vie des français* (1978). My quotations are from pages 169, 172, 150 and 166.
63. Alain Touraine, *La Conscience ouvriére* (1966), pp. 60–8, 116–19.
64. On the BBC Television programme, *Monitor*, 12 December 1978.
65. Denise Bombardier, *La Voix de France: les français et leur télévision vus par un observateur étranger* (1975), pp. 73, 253.

Inequality, Distinctions and the Significance of Class

The inequalities of income that exist between different occupations can be measured. So also, in broad outline, can the major inequalities in the distribution of wealth and power (the actual execution of power is almost impossible to quantify though many attempts to do so have been made[1]). Inequalities of educational opportunity as related to occupational background can also be shown quantitatively, as can degrees of mobility between broad occupational categories, particularly between manual and non-manual occupations. Surveys can show the hierarchy of prestige in which different occupations are held. (The results, though, are often intriguing rather than useful. A *Nouvel Observateur* survey in September 1973 found that the French public put the great financial official, the Trésorier-Payeur Générale, at the top, and the unskilled labourer at the bottom, while the Parisian lawyer, the university professor and the strip-tease artiste were all placed on the same level, sixth from the top.[2]) The various inequalities appear to be related to each other, and to the distinctions which people do make in everyday life, and which they usually describe as 'class distinctions'.

INCOME AND WEALTH

It is not easy to make exact comparisons of income distribution in the three countries and thereby determine which country has greatest, or least inequality. Two generalizations can be made however: there has been a considerable levelling up of incomes since the 1930s, together with *some* levelling down, most obvious in Britain and least obvious in the United States; secondly, apart from a few sharp changes, the broad outlines of the inequality of distribution of income are not wildly different from those of the 1930s. The American government is the most open of the three in publishing comparative income statistics, indicating again an official pride in the generally high level of all incomes, the very high incomes attainable at the top, and the mobility suggested by the continuous range of gradations in income levels. The comparable statistical abstracts for Britain and France are much more coy; but it emerges that discontinuities between income levels are sharper in France and Britain than in America: in particular, while in America 'white-collar' incomes are one-quarter higher than 'blue-collar' incomes, they are one-third higher in Britain, and as much as fifty per cent higher in France. The *Statistical Abstract of the United States 1977* offers these examples of 'median annual earnings of workers': 'farm laborers', $6114; 'blue-collar workers', $12,469; 'white-collar workers', $15,852; 'salaried managers', $17,537; 'self-employed physicians and dentists', $37,117.[3] Crude figures derived from the French National Institute of Economics and Statistics offer the following contrasts: 'managerial staff', 7466 francs per month; 'medium salary staff', 3693 francs per month; 'office workers', 2153 francs per month; 'foremen' 3035 francs per month; 'workers', 1780 francs per month; 'service personnel', 1588 francs per month.[4]

For Britain, the measure of income inequality is reflected in the official handbook, *Britain 1978*. Average weekly earnings of full-time male adult manual workers in April 1976 were £65.10, that is an annual income of £3385. The corresponding figure for non-manual workers was £81.60, that is £4243 per annum. 'Most of the senior posts in business, the professions and the Civil Service', the handbook says, 'command salaries in the range £8000 to £15,000 a year gross before tax.' It then lists jobs commanding £15,000 to £30,000: 'cabinet ministers, top-ranking judicial appointments, the highest positions in government departments and the largest municipal authorities, editors of daily newspapers, some persons outstanding in their professions and in the higher managerial posts in industry, commerce, and banking.' Chairmen of major companies 'exceptionally' receive more than £50,000 a year gross 'though highly successful people (such as star entertainers) often receive more through fees or fixed contracts.'[5]

It seems likely that positive redistribution of wealth has gone further in Britain than in the other two countries, though there are plenty of commentators from the left to point out that even so it has scarcely gone very far, whereas commentators from the right would point approvingly to the much greater opportunities of accumulating wealth in the United States. The British Central Office of Information confessed that there was very little knowledge about long-term trends in the distribution of wealth, but found that 'such estimates as there are show a substantial fall in the share owned by the richest people in the community. In 1974 about twenty-five per cent of personal wealth was owned by the top one per cent of the adult population, and over seventy-eight per cent by the top twenty per cent. The value of state pension rights has a marked effect on these figures; in particular the share of the top one per cent falls by over forty per cent while the share of the bottom eighty per cent of the adult population is nearly doubled. The proportion of personal wealth held in the form of physical assets rose from less than a third in 1960 to almost sixty per cent in 1974, reflecting especially the increasing importance of dwellings. There has been a marked decline in the relative importance of company securities in the composition of personal wealth.'[6] What really stands out is that wealth is still very unequally shared. With regard to the United States, two recent authorities, J. D. Smith and S. D. Franklin, concluded that although 'wealth in the United States has become less concentrated in the last half century ... the diminution has not been great.'[7] The same conclusions hold true for France.[8]

POWER

In the world of politics, too, the biggest changes have taken place in Britain, where perhaps there was most room for change. The successive premierships of Wilson, Heath, Callaghan and Thatcher have been described as representing 'the rise of the meritocracy'. Wilson, Heath, and Thatcher were all educated at Oxford, while Callaghan was the first Prime Minister since Ramsay MacDonald to have been neither to Oxbridge nor to a public school.

In comparing the Labour cabinet of 1977 with that of 1964, Timothy May made a broad distinction between working-class members and middle-class members, then divided the latter into two sub-groups: 'The "patricians" (those from established middle-class backgrounds who were educated at expensive and prestigious public schools and Oxford University) and the "meritocrats" (those from more marginal middle-class backgrounds who attended state secondary schools and in some, but not all, cases went to a university).'[9] I'd be inclined to label his first sub-group 'upper-class', and to remark that his second sub-group contained both those from established middle-class backgrounds who managed to move upwards by making use of Oxford University and those from more marginal backgrounds. Whatever labels one uses, Dr May's findings definitely indicate the growing influence of the solid middle class at the expense of those above them, and the declining influence of the best public schools; but they also stress the continuing influence of the old methods of socialization into the upper class, particularly Oxford University. Traditional upper-class figures ('patricians') formed more than a third of the cabinet of 1964. Of the 1977 cabinet a quarter had been educated at public schools and Oxford (or in one case, Cambridge). Only Anthony Wedgwood Benn had been at one of the Clarendon schools – which had produced six cabinet members in 1964. Fred Mulley was the paradigm of mobility by merit, being the son of a labourer who had won his way to a minor public school on a scholarship. May detected thirteen meritocrats in the 1977 cabinet, as against eight in the 1964 one. But the majority of them had in fact been to Oxford, which still provided one-third of the 1977 cabinet. May, however, stressed the fact that eight Ministers had graduated from universities other than Oxford; whereas only two had done so in 1964. He concluded that 'the movement towards a middle class cabinet is undeniable', and continued 'the stratum of the middle class predominant in the contemporary Labour cabinet is much more typical of the British middle class than was the case ten years ago.' Many of the middle class, of course, still do not go to university at all. Revising the conclusion to meet with the class categories which have emerged in this book so far, I would say that the old upper-class dominance was certainly being reduced (though even in a Labour government, very far from being eradicated), and that the members of the professional middle class (which had always been reasonably well educated), together with members of the lower middle class and the working class, who had taken advantage of new educational opportunities, were beginning to improve their position.

Movement, then; but still quite a weight of old tradition. The points can be interestingly illustrated by looking at the career of Edward Heath, which also illuminates a number of themes which have arisen in the course of this book. Although he was born within a few miles of the Kent coalfield, there was nothing of the solid industrial working class in Edward Heath's background. His great-grandfather had been a merchant seaman, his paternal grandfather first ran a small dairy business which failed, and then became a porter at Broadstairs Station on the Southern Railway. His son, Will, Heath's father, became a carpenter. His maternal grandmother was the wife of an illiterate farm worker. On leaving school at fourteen, her very good-looking daughter had gone into domestic service with a middle-class family from Hampstead who spent their summers in Broadstairs. Her mother was proud of this position with its opportunity for learning middle-class ways but she was not at all pleased with her daughter's association with Will Heath. Firmly stressing one of the most important elements in female social mobility, she lamented that 'with her looks she could do a lot better.'[10]

The First World War, that great engine of social mobility, provided Will Heath, with the opportunity to take a job building air frames at the Vickers aircraft factory in Crayford in North Kent. After the war, he was employed at a good wage by a local builder, while at home his wife worked hard to introduce the middle-class standards she had learned in service. Around 1930 Will Heath took over a small firm which became 'W. G. Heath, Builder and Decorator' and the family, as Andrew Roth puts it, 'crossed the line' between the skilled working class and the lower middle class.

At the age of ten Heath won a scholarship to a grammar school in Ramsgate, which not only set high academic standards but imitated the forms of the public schools. He failed his Open Scholarship to Balliol but his parents, assisted by a loan, were prepared to fund him; then, after a year, he won the Balliol Organ Scholarship. Heath was well on the way; and the Second World War, in which he ended up a Lieutenant Colonel in the prestigious Honourable Artillery Company, consolidated his position. He entered the House of Commons in 1950; 'that intake in the Commons was exceptional in the large proportion of its new Tory entrants who were ex-officers – and who were professionally competent and had made their way without benefit of family wealth and connections'.

Significantly, however, Heath remarked that 'for the new member who has been a member of the Oxford or Cambridge Union, coming to those benches is like coming home'. And Heath quickly showed a knack for associating with the traditional upper-class members of the Conservative Party, though curiously, particularly for a man of his musical talents, he never managed to get the accent right. David Wood of *The Times* noted perceptively that for all his image of 'Wilsonian classlessness', Heath was well in with the Tory 'magic circle', and that 'his is the kind of classnessness that takes on the protective colouring of the company he keeps. . .'[11] Heath became the first-ever elected leader of the Conservative Party in 1965; he was Conservative Prime Minister from 1970 to 1974, in which time he brought into his cabinet four figures who had clearly not been born into the Conservative upper class: Anthony Barber, Geoffrey Rippon, Peter Walker and Margaret Thatcher. It was the lower-middle-class, though Oxford educated, Margaret Thatcher who successfully challenged Heath's leadership of the party, thus jumping ahead of the upper-class traditionalist, William Whitelaw. However, apart from having a wealthy second-generation businessman as a husband (a nice contemporary twist to the question of social mobility through matrimony), Mrs Thatcher showed great readiness to merge into the Tory upper class, from which she chose many key cabinet ministers. Similar developments were detectable in the rise of Eisenhower and Nixon in the 1950s. Nixon's defeat by John F. Kennedy in the 1960 presidential election was an extremely narrow one, and one which Nixon himself attributed to all the forces of the establishment being arrayed against him, the lower-class outsider. Kennedy's assassination left the way open for a man who was certainly not of the national upper class, and who had not been intended for presidential office. Lyndon Johnson's mother had had money, education, position and respect, being the daughter of a lawyer, educator and Baptist lay preacher, who had been a member of the Texas legislature and Texas secretary of state; she herself attended Baylor University. Here we perhaps have an example of initial female mobility downwards, resulting in eventual upward mobility for the family. Lyndon Johnson's father was a small-time farmer and trader in real estate and cattle, who also became a member of the Texas state legislature. The wide educational opportunities of the United States (compared with France and Britain), and also the early professionalization of American life, are apparent in Johnson's career. He went to San Marcos College in south west Texas and was a teacher for fifteen months; but then he went straight into professional politics, becoming secretary to a Congressman.[12] Some forty or fifty years before, an outsider figure in British politics like Ramsay Macdonald had had to do something similar, but in general the routes to high politics in France and Britain were rather different from those in the USA: the upper-class Conservative in both countries, after the correct education, entered parliament young and did other jobs as well; others served apprenticeships in journalism (particularly in France), in local government, or (particularly in Britain) in trade unionism.

The traumas of the sixties threw the East Coast Establishment into disarray. Johnson's sweeping victory against Goldwater in 1964 was followed by the Democratic collapse in 1968 against Richard Nixon who, if he had not meantime exactly acquired class, had certainly acquired considerable wealth (partly through work in a powerful law firm, partly through influential associates) and the sort of contacts which can be developed in the interstices of a pluralistic society in which the ethics of the frontier had never disappeared, and in which there were strong resentments against the liberal Establishment.

From the first, brief, perfectly struck, and highly evocative, sentence of his *Memoirs*, 'I was born in a house my father built', Richard Nixon portrays himself as one of the 'little people' rising up to fight against the might of the East Coast Establishment. Any dirty tricks he used, he argues, were no worse than those long used by his opponents.[13] Whatever the rights and wrongs of that, the disgrace and collapse of the Nixon presidency did not clear the way for the reassertion of upper-class control of the next Democratic presidential nomination. Jimmy Carter's accent and manners were certainly mocked by those who saw themselves as guardians of an older political tradition. Being, obviously, cast in strictly American terms, Carter's attacks were on Washington bureaucracy, rather than on an upper class as such. Yet the Kennedy family retain their charisma.

The first chapter of Xavier de la Fournière's *Giscard d'Estaing and Us* is entitled 'Le "Kennedy Gaulois" '[14]; the 'us' of the title emerges as a close-knit, upper-class group, enjoying something of the lifestyle described by de Negroni. That the 'd'Estaing' was added to the family name only in the 1920s reinforces the sense of conscious upper classness (though, *officially*, Giscard is opposed to the badges of class). Giscard had a brilliant career at the École Polytechnique and the École Nationale d'Administration before becoming an inspector of finances, then at the age of twenty-nine he became a deputy for the ancestral territory in the Auvergne. The build-up of the President's own political grouping in parliament, the UDF, however, indicated rather the growing influence of the middle-class specialist politician. A survey of the period up to 1967 had concluded that French ministers 'are a cross-section of the upper bourgeoisie rather than of the population as a whole.'[15] With regard to French members of parliament the most recent study has concluded that 'among those sitting today in the National Assembly, the proportion belonging to the directing categories (*catégories dirigeantes*) has been growing.'[16]

In the three countries which we are studying, there was in the 1930s, a distinct hegemony exercised over political power by a recognizable upper class, though least obviously so in the United States because of the variousness of the country and the variety of competing pressures being exercised on the centres of power. By the 1970s this hegemony had considerably weakened, mainly in the sense that positions of power were now more open to able members of the middle class or lower middle class and, in lesser degree, members of the working class who were moving up into the middle class (the 'meritocrats' and 'professionals' or 'specialists'). In Great Britain, there had come about, in addition, a special sense in which the working class could now also exercise power. The leaders of organized labour in the United States, that is to say the leaders of the AFL-CIO, could exercise power within the accepted context of American political campaigning by offering or withholding support from one candidate or another. But the leaders of British organized labour, that is to say the officials of the TUC, were in the 1970s exercising a certain amount of direct power in the establishment of the main lines of government economic policy. The paradox of the British situation is that while on the one hand the working class, through its formal representatives, has, and is seen to have, formal power, these representatives are also clearly seen to be acting as a pressure group for the special interests of the working class; union representations in the United States are merged into the general political pattern, whereas in Britain they emphasize the unchanging distinctiveness of the working class.

The continuing development of large-scale industrial organization has provided at least as much opportunity for the concentration of power as it has for its diffusion. An upper class with disproportionate economic power has not lost its place to a revolution of managers; but its powers are constrained by the growth of other countervailing forces in modern society. The question really is not whether finance-capital controls society, but whether persons of a certain social background tend, disproportionately to their numbers, to gain positions in the higher realms of the world of finance capital. Such evidence as there is suggests that in the seventies they still do, even if their power to make decisions affecting other members of society may be constrained by broad government strategies, and by the fact that many local decisions affecting people most nearly are indeed made by the duly constituted local authorities. Pierre Birnbaum concluded from his careful and detailed study of French owners and managers that

> the ruling categories of the dominant class in France truly constitute a ruling class. Recruiting themselves from the same social milieu in the heart of the same social class, the French ruling class appears as a definite social group, closed in on itself: practically no one from lower social classes can penetrate this group. The sons, as a result, possess the same characteristics as their fathers: all they do, in some cases, is move into different sectors, or different jobs.[17]

Earlier, Peter M. Blau, in his presidential address to the American Sociological Society, had noted that 'while inequality in education has declined in the United States, and inequality in income has at least not increased, the concentration of resources and powers in giant organizations and their top executives has grown.'[18]

EDUCATION AND LIFESTYLES

The overwhelming weight of informed opinion now maintains that whatever the value of the educational changes in recent years it is far from easy to eliminate the influence of social background upon educational opportunity. Despite moves towards comprehensive styles of education, French education, though more encouraging than ever to the bright poor child, still retains much of its traditional stratification. The move to comprehensives in Britain has in some ways simply replicated the American situation where schools, theoretically equal in status, are of much higher quality in some districts than in others. In all three countries private education remains, and in Britain is a growth area as former high quality grammar schools disappear into what are thought to be lower quality comprehensives.

The geography of class has remained remarkably unaltered since the 1930s. No traveller going north out of Detroit can fail to observe the social frontier as he passes suddenly from the mean working-class houses to the lavish splendours of upper-middle-class, and then upper-class, Grosse Pointe. William Kornblum has recently published a carefully delineated study of the steel mill community of south Chicago, which 'similar to steel-towns throughout the United States' is 'predominantly working-class'. South Chicago is not a homogeneous community, but only by stretching words could even the most prosperous part be described as anything other than working-class.

> Some neighborhoods are separated by mile-wide no-man's-lands of scrap yards, slag-dumping areas, and the giant glowing mills themselves. Crowded at the entrances to the mills along the Calumet River, the neighborhoods are often hidden under clouds of sulfurous red smoke and dust. Here and there in the open industrial expanses there are clusters of taverns, inviting refuges against the bitter cold of winter and the humid heat of Chicago summers ... in the old tenement neighborhoods of the area,

where Mexican, black, and European newcomers now raise their families, money is tight and life for large families is hard. Life is easier in the newer South Chicago bungalow neighborhoods, but here also the well-paid rollers, railroad engineers, foremen, and other skilled workers seek every available opportunity for extra money to keep up payments on the mortgage, the central air-conditioning, the furniture, and the new car. Established families in the area can point to one or more of their members who have made it out of the steel industry and now own small businesses or hold jobs 'with the city'. But for every adult who succeeds in earning a living outside the mills there are many more inside the plants who dream of making a 'killing at the track' and place their bets faithfully with bookmakers in the mills or at their local taverns.[19]

In all three countries much of the public-authority housing of the post-war years and of the sixties fast turned into slums. In Britain, Aneurin Bevan's dream of classless village communities had long been replaced by a nightmare of high-rise, low-cost housing. Of the 'deck' housing at Hulme in Manchester, it was said that, with lots of doors open, you could easily walk into the wrong house. One slight modification of the old geographical contours was that decaying areas, and the worst of the modern developments, tended more and more to be occupied by the under class of racial minorities, the unfortunate and 'problem families'. Kornblum noted the regular night working, and the long hours of overtime which were needed if the skilled worker was to keep up his Middle American standards. Gold-thorpe and his associates made exactly the same point in regard to the Luton factory workers: to earn their 'middle-class' incomes they had, as it were, to do peculiarly working-class work, often at night, and almost always for hours that were a quarter as long again as those of white-collar workers.[20] The way in which the upper class continues, also, to separate itself off was well encapsulated in Colin Bell's study of middle-class families in Swansea: Swansea, he said, 'may appear in the first chapters of the autobiographies of the famous', but, 'it rarely appears in the last.'[21]

THE SIGNIFICANCE OF CLASS

There are various ways of explaining the broad bands of inequality, the differences in opportunity, lifestyles, material standards, and working and home conditions which exist in each of the three countries. A different group of explanations could be advanced for each type of inequality. But if one single, convincing explanation is required then class, in the colloquial and historical sense of this book, fits the bill. To have been born into the upper class is to be automatically a member of that reservoir from which membership of the various élites is drawn. To have been born into the middle class means that special talent, energy and dedication will be needed to enter these élites, but encouragement and opportunity will be there; arrival will, however, probably come a little later. But the middle class does offer ready access to many of the posts in social welfare, planning, and petty bureaucracy, which carry some influence in contemporary society. (The French prefects are overwhelmingly drawn from this class.) As between upper and middle class there is no detectable difference in standards of health and mortality and so on, though to be upper-class is to have that 'amplitude of life' generally denied to members of the middle class. To be born into the working class, though no longer without many compensations, is to suffer from a distinct disadvantage when it comes to questions of power, influence, wealth and earning opportunities. Standards of living are still highest in the American working class, and, in contrast with the 1930s, it could no longer be said that there is either poverty or serious deprivation among the working classes of any of the countries under review. Poverty and serious deprivation is now less a class matter; it is more related to other forms of inequality and discrimination and to personal misfortune.

Apart from class, in the comprehensive and colloquial sense in which I am using the term, inequalities arise from age, sex and race. It is not possible to compare these directly with class as sources of inequality (one can only compare like with like), but one can make a number of points. First of all, sex and race are now regarded as very major issues in discussions of equality and so in that sense have obscured, and perhaps even diminished, the importance of class in this respect. But, secondly, questions of sex and race inequality often turn out to be tied in with class. The articulate middle-class feminist would seem to have advantages over the reticent factory cleaner; the black doctor or lecturer similar advantages over the black railway porter. It is, however, true that the aged, women and members of racial minorities are most likely to slip into the realm of poverty and serious deprivation: the deserted wife with children to bring up, the old couple without adequate pension rights, the unemployed black.

I want to turn again to the question of the significance of class in political behaviour and in major political, economic and social issues. The trend everywhere in voting behaviour is of a slight weakening, but no really sharp disruption, of traditional class allegiances. In Britain it is not just a case of the working class being less consistently and solidly Labour, but of the middle class showing greater volatility and less utter devotion to the Conservatives. The middle class, of course, is expanding, the working class contracting. Middleclass voters of working-class origin tend to take their Labour voting preferences with them, though one of them admitted that while he still voted Labour, he had ceased to worry if the Conservatives won.[22] Britain had two General Elections in 1974. The study by Butler and Kavanagh of the October election indicated that Labour obtained forty-nine per cent of the skilled working-class vote, compared with twenty-six per cent for the Conservatives, and forty-seven per cent in the February election; and Labour got fifty-seven per cent of the unskilled vote (fifty-five per cent in February), compared with twenty-two per cent for the Conservatives. But the 'coloured' vote had now emerged as the single category most favourable to Labour, who took seventy-two per cent, seventeen per cent going to the Conservatives.[23] The 1979 election brought out regional as well as class differences: manual workers in the north and in Scotland were still voting solidly Labour, but the more prosperous workers of the Midlands and south were apparently joining with the middle class in voting Conservative.

In the United States, greater consistency in voting behaviour is shown in congressional elections than in presidential elections. In his presidential election victory, Carter received very strong support from those firmly in the working class and below, but many of those on the upper fringes, leaning into middle America, voted for Ford out of fear of Washington welfarism, whilst sticking to class lines in the congressional elections by voting Democrat. In France the growth of the working class and of working-class self-awareness proved not to be sufficient to disrupt traditional sectionalism. The elections of 1978 were a triumph for the government coalition of parties, and particularly Giscard d'Estaing's part of it, 'the majority' as the French right-wing papers like to say. The working class had no unified political movement of its own, and the squabbles between communists and socialists proved fatal. Rock solid working-class communist seats remained rock solid; but when it came to the second round of voting it was clear that many working-class voters preferred to move right rather than vote for a communist candidate. Thus, in America and France, too, voting can be correlated with class, but, because of the existence of other cross fissures, not as consistently as in Britain.

What part has class played in the major conflicts and confrontations of recent years? The French 'events' of 1968 began with a student strike in November 1967 at Nanterre, one of the most insalubrious of the newer waste-land campuses of the University of Paris (stark housing-estate architecture, industrial smells permanently in the air), and, after other student demonstrations, was followed by the General Strike called by the trade unions for 13 May, and then by a second phase of militant trade union action. At the time, Marxist commentators saw these events as marking the beginning of a new phase of class conflict in which 'the new working class' of technicians, scientists, teachers, communicators, students and white-collar workers would unite with the industrial workers. However the most authoritative contemporary study, by Alain Touraine, minimized the role of the industrial workers, while stressing that of the professional workers in revolt against technocracy and bureaucracy.[24] In the upshot the 'events' passed off with remarkably little change in the political structure – the 'majority' rallying to de Gaulle at the polls; some modifications were made in the more authoritarian and bureaucratic features of French industry and higher education. A survey conducted shortly before the May events, and directed towards establishing the extent to which the French felt 'alienated', or 'powerless' in face of the economic and political organization of their society, offers a few clues. The replies showed

> an unusual degree of cross-class similarity in the level of alienation (powerlessness) in France. To be explicit, where 76 per cent of the manual workers say that there is 'not much they can do', 78 per cent of the white collar workers agree; and even among the better educated 64 per cent of both groups agree. Where 60 per cent of the better-educated manual workers say there's no use seeking redress from public officials, 52 per cent of the white collar workers hold the same opinion. Where 62 per cent of the manual workers say they have little hope of protecting their own interests against pressure groups, 60 per cent of white collar workers agree.[25]

Further clues are to be found in the collection of fly-sheets and other documents relating to 1968 in the French Social History Institute of the National Archives. Students appeal to the industrial workers:

> Your struggle is our struggle. We occupy the universities, you occupy the factories. We and you, are we fighting for the same

thing? Ten per cent of the workers' children get into higher education. Are we fighting to increase this figure, to make universities
more democratic? That would be an advance, but it's not the most
important issue. These workers' children become students just
like the others. That the son of a worker should become a director,
that is not our programme. We wish to abolish the distinction
between all those who work and workers who become directors.

However, a poster addressed to managerial and white-collar, as well
as industrial workers, inciting them against 'the tyranny of technocracy and bureaucracy' speaks contemptuously of those in 'the
golden overalls, children of the bourgeoisie' who join in 'mob rule'
with those in 'black overalls'.[26]

The events of 1968, then, were brought about by a coming together
of elements drawn from the working class, the middle class, the
upper class, and from some of the children of the upper class, in
protest against the stifling, authoritarian nature of the Gaullist
régime. That particular class mixture was very potent, but only for a
brief period. The deeper cultural differences between working class
and middle class soon reasserted themselves, as did the traditional
weight of the artisans, the farmers and the small businessmen: the
protestors soon went their divided ways and the classes separated
out into their historical patterns. In the end, as so often in France,
the confrontations were between ideologies, rather than between
classes. The vital ingredient was the sense of frustration across most
of French society; the vital context was that provided by the nature
of class in French society. Class was not an inevitable force for conflict and violence; but the particular shape of class relationships both
created the crisis, and set the final limits on it.

Further light on the significance of class is shed by the affair of the
provincial watch factory of Lip. This affair had its origins in 1967
when the Swiss multinational Ebauchés took over, and rumbled on
through the seventies. The Lip factory presented the very paradigm
of Serge Mallet's 'new working class', employing as it did, in 1973,
23 engineers and managerial workers, 167 white-collar workers,
technicians and foremen, and only 81 *ouvriers*. The occupation of
their own factory by the Lip employees was attended by the usual
verbal battle: officially the CGT recognized 'a major struggle' in
which the Lip workers were fighting in the interests of the nation,
yet at the same time both the CGT and the French Communist Party
were attacked for their passive 'bourgeois and revisionist' roles in
the struggle. At a more mundane level it was clear that the Lip

employees were widely regarded as privileged 'white-coated' workers: 'At Lip it's better than the army: there's a corporal for every two privates.'[27] The salient feature would appear to be the separateness of the white-collar middle class, rather than its unity with the industrial working class.

Rioting in America in the sixties and into the seventies had its origins in race, the revolt of youth against authority, and in protests against the Vietnam war. Opinion surveys on the whole validate the conventional stereotype of the 'hard hat' American working class as hostile to the claims of both blacks and students[28] and, therefore, as a force for stability, or, occasionally, confrontation with black protest movements. At the same time there is evidence of the integration of 'respectable' blacks into both middle-class and working-class communities.[29] The further development of an integrated class structure has, on the whole, save for occasional episodes of violent confrontation, tended towards the social harmony which observers had predicted in the 1930s, but with one awesome side-effect, the aggravated embitterment of those stranded in the black under class. As Charles Silbermann summed up in his *Criminal Violence, Criminal Justice*: 'Today the mythic has become real; cheap handguns and narcotics have become the outlets for aggression. Ironically, desegregation is partly responsible. Middle-class blacks, once a restraining force in the ghetto, have moved out and left behind lower-class enclaves.'[30] Here, then, we are speaking neither of race, nor of class, as a prime motor in violence, but of a particular combination of developments in class and race relations. In pluralistic American society, naked class war on a universal scale seems unlikely: but that long-lasting local engagements of high intensity are still very possible was shown by the great coal strike of 1977–8.

For industrial action on a more national scale, we have to turn again to Britain. Here the everyday cold war of the work-place several times in the seventies erupted into large-scale strikes. In 1973–4 the Conservative Government of Edward Heath found itself in hopeless confrontation with the miners; in January 1979 there were more workers out on strike than at any time since the General Strike of 1926. But there *was* no General Strike (as, for single days at a time, there was in France). No more than before was the British working class committed to the theory of class conflict; but, for practical economic gains, it was, occupational group by occupational group, prepared to demonstrate both its strength and its sense of apartness from employers, government and middle-class society generally.

Throughout the twentieth century many of the major movements of disaffection in the United States were not directly related to class. By the sixties and seventies, with the advent of Breton, Scottish and Welsh nationalism as major forces, the same could be said of France and Britain. However, class cannot be totally left out of account: many of the leaders of the various nationalist movements were drawn from the same professional and white-collar groups whose frustration with technocracy, bureaucracy and centralization has been noted elsewhere.

What of the specially vexed question of the relative economic performances of the three countries? No doubt as to the objective facts that industrial productivity per head of the population has always remained highest in the United States, whereas in Britain it has fallen considerably behind that of France. It has become a commonplace to attribute Britain's poor economic record to its being a 'class-ridden' society.[31] The epithet is an ambiguous one. France and America, this book has argued, are both class societies. In France the social gulf between management and workers is often at least as great as in Britain; there is more formality and more stress on the dignity of titles and status. There is less educational mobility than in Britain (fewer working-class children at university, for example). Formality, to the extent of pomposity, is also a feature of American society. Yet it is true that the forms of class are, historically, more deeply entrenched in British society: they were not seriously challenged in the forties, when they might have been, and they were only slightly modified in the sixties. In the end, formality and authority in both America and France are related to function: a boss behaves like a boss because he is a boss. In Britain a boss behaves as he does because he belongs to, or has been socialized into, a particular social background. In all the recent British industrial confrontations, the accents stick out: when an employer's representative opens his mouth he immediately associates himself, not so much with employers as such, but with the upper class; if he happens to have a working-class, or regional middle-class accent, we register that immediately. The pride, traditions and class awareness of the British worker have, over a period extending back into the nineteenth century, brought him to a position where he wages a constant, but usually very mild, cold war against his employers on the factory floor itself. He expresses little ideological hostility to the employer, and no desire to expropriate him. Feeling no sense of inferiority, his instinct is to stick among his own kind. He feels little involvement in the success of the enterprise in which he works. The French worker is either much more ideologically committed than his British counterpart, or, committed solely to his family and private interests, he goes in for the occasional ritual protest, typically the one-day strike, but otherwise co-operates efficiently with his employer, either because the day of revolution has not yet come, or because he sees it as in his own private interest to do so. The difference here is not between class and absence of class, but between the different ways in which the historical conditioning of the two classes has taken place. In Britain, the persistence of upper-class power, and the advent of organized working-class power, mean that there is a constant refrain of hostility towards the middle-class small businessman, who in America, and France, is praised and protected by special legislation.

The differences in social habits and culture are greatest in Britain. Most Frenchmen find it important to eat reasonably decent food, almost invariably accompanied by wine. The British working man eats one kind of rubbish; many middle-class workers eat a similar, more expensively presented, form of rubbish; the upper class does retain some claim to good taste. Most Americans eat much the same sorts of rubbish. In France, and, in large degree in America, high social status has tended to go with a really good, and in many ways eminently practical, education; this has not been the case in Britain. Managers in Britain are often distinguished most by their clothes, accents and manners; since these are their main qualifications, they go out of their way to stress them. French managers, though often more dictatorial and status conscious than their British counterparts, are better educated and better at doing what they are there to do. That is true, too, of American managers.

Class is a product of history. The particular nature of class relationships in Britain in the 1940s was probably to her advantage; in the 1970s they were much to her disadvantage. But other factors come in, only indirectly related to the different class structures of the three countries. French governments, however lacking in humanity they often seem, have simply been better at planning the French economy and directing it positively towards higher productivity than have British. Size and natural wealth have contributed much to America's overall economic success. At the same time a ruthlessly led labour movement has tended to join in the American ethos of expansionism rather than stand on pride in itself and its older traditions as the British labour movement has tended to do. The quirks and trimmings of class are a British preoccupation, and, in the upper reaches, playing the right part has too often been more important than getting things done. The upper class continued to hold too much political power for too long in Britain because there was no effective challenge to it; in America there are always challenges coming from all directions, and the fight to the top is a long and demanding one; in France a marked absence of the democracy, which, in different ways, is apparent in America and Britain, has at least left the higher civil servants to get on with it, and they, at least, are men who have got there by merit as well as by birth.

Notes

1. For the 'issue' method, as well as the 'reputational' and 'possessional' or 'sociology of leadership' methods, see Christopher J. Hewitt, 'Elites and the Distribution of Power in British Society', in P. Stanworth and A. Giddens, eds., *Elites and Power in British Society* (1974), chapter 3.
2. *Nouvel Observateur*, September 1973.
3. *Statistical Abstract of the United States 1977*, p. 411.
4. Marc Dandelot and François Froment-Meurice, *France* (1975), p. 22.
5. *Britain 1978: an Official Handbook*, pp. 317–18.
6. *Ibid*, p. 315.
7. J. D. Smith and S. D. Franklin, 'The Concentration of Personal Wealth, 1922–1969', *American Economic Review, Papers and Proceedings*, vol 64 (1974).
8. See Jane Marceau, *Class and Status in France: Economic Change and Social Immobility 1945–1975* (1977), pp. 39–43.
9. Timothy May, 'A Government of Meritocrats', *New Society*. 12 May 1977. See also R. W. Johnson, 'The British Political Elite, 1955–1972', *Archives Européenes de Sociologie*, XIV (1973), pp. 35–77; and Colin Mellors, *The British M.P.* (1978).
10. Andrew Roth, *Heath and the Heathmen* (1972), pp. 18–19. This section, and all its direct quotations, are drawn from Roth's excellent book.
11. David Wood, *The Times*, 29 July 1965, quoted by Roth, *op. cit.*, pp. xii–xiii.
12. Doris Kearns, *Lyndon Johnson and the American Dream* (1976).
13. *The Memoirs of Richard Nixon* (1978).
14. Xavier de la Fournière, *Giscard d'Estaing et nous* (1977).
15. Edward G. Lewis, 'Social Backgrounds of French Ministers, 1944–1967'. *The Western Political Quarterly*, vol. 23 (1970), pp. 564–78. See

also Jean Charlot, 'Les Elites politiques en France de la IIIe à la Ve République', *Archives Europeénnes de Sociologie*, XIV (1973).

16. R. Cayrol, J.-C. Parodi and C. Ysmal, *Le Deputé français* (1973), p. 43.

17. Pierre Birnbaum, C. Barucq, M. Bellaiche and A. Marié, *La Classe dirigeante française* (1978), p. 187.

18. Peter M. Blau, 'Parameters of Social Structure', *American Sociological Review*, vol. 39 (1974), pp. 615–35.

19. William Kornblum, *Blue Collar Community* (1974), pp. 18–19.

20. Goldthorpe, Lockwood, Bechhofer and Platt, *The Affluent Worker* (1969), p. 58.

21. Colin Bell, *Middle Class Families* (1968), p. 10.

22. Quoted in J. Deverson and K. Lindsay, *Voices from the Middle Class*, p. 56.

23. D. Butler and J. Kavanagh, *The British General Election of October 1974* (1975), p. 278.

24. Alain Touraine, *Le Mouvement de mai* (1968), p. 25.

25. Melvin Seeman, 'The Signals of '68: Alienation in Pre-Crisis France', *American Sociological Review*, vol. 37 (1972), p. 399.

26. Archives Nationales, Institut Français d'Histoire Sociale [IFHS], brochures et tracts de Mai 1968 (14 AS 238).

27. IFHS, dossier sur l'affaire Lip. See *Le Monde*, 15 September 1973.

28. E. Edward Ransford, 'Blue Collar Anger: Reactions to Student and Black Protest', *American Sociological Review*, vol. 37 (1972), pp. 333–46.

29. William A. Muraskin, *Middle-class Blacks in a White Society* (1975); Charles E. Hurst, 'Race, Class and Consciousness', *American Sociological Review*, vol. 37 (1972), pp. 658–70; Studs Terkel, *Working* (1974), pp. 177–8.

30. Charles Silbermann, *Criminal Violence, Criminal Justice* (1978), p. 180.

31. The case is most powerfully made in the Hudson Institute, Europe, *Britain in 1980: The Hudson Report* (1974).

CONCLUSION

17

Convergence and 'National Character'

It is as if the Christmas jigsaw had got drenched in the Christmas Veuve du Vernay. The cardboard has softened, the paper is torn, the pieces have swelled and buckled. The series of pictures that I have assembled in this book do not fit at every point; set out together, they lack tidiness. That, I believe, is in the nature of the subject, class. Of course, if you have a simple conceptual model of class, or if you argue that, since the bits do not all fit together, therefore class does not exist at all, both approaches make for a kind of clarity. My approach has not been anti-Marxist, nor has it been anti-sociological: it has simply been atheoretical. Much of my source material, I admit, has refused to be smoothed into the shape of any acceptable generalization and has perhaps stood for nothing more than the intractability of the subject.

That being so, I should now, perhaps, endeavour to set out the main points of my own discourse. Class, I have argued, has its origins in the Industrial Revolution and in the industrialization process which, at varying speeds, took place in the three countries during the nineteenth and twentieth centuries. Industrial societies were, and are, grossly unequal in the distribution of power, wealth, income and life chances, and contain marked distinctions in behaviour and lifestyles. In trying to describe these inequalities and distinctions, which they clearly perceive all around them, most people resort to the language of class. The different images of class held by different individuals and different groups roughly coincide with the broad bands of inequality and distinction which can be objectively established. In discussing inequality I have presented nothing that is new: the novelty, such as it is, lies in the attempt to accumulate composite images of class for each of the three countries at different points in time, and to relate these images to the objective realities of inequality.

Thus I have entered into the game of saying how many, and what, classes each country has. In the Introduction, I joked about sociologists saying 'status' or 'stratum', when ordinary people would say 'class'. Yet, if such a degree of precision is being sought that invented labels have to be used, then perhaps it *is* better to speak of 'status' or 'stratum'. If we wish to speak of classes, then better that these classes should have a touch of vagueness about them, and should be classes which people themselves recognize. Thus, when Professor Coleman divides American society into seven classes with such titles as 'the college-educated professional and managerial class', 'Middle Americans of comfortable living standard', and 'Middle Americans just getting along', I have some doubts, though I recognize that these 'levels' coincide with observable distinctions within American society, and also reflect the slight American reluctance to make whole-hearted use of the more obvious British labels such as 'middle class' and 'working class'. My argument is that Americans do use the language of class often enough to make it worthwhile trying to keep within the limits of that usage. My doubts about one of the best pieces of recent British work are slightly different. Margaret Stacey and her colleagues came out against attempting to divide present-day Banbury into social classes, though they concluded that it could be seen to be composed of two or three 'social levels'. What then becomes of all the discussion which certainly took place over the role of class in Britain's industrial problems? The answer is that Margaret Stacey and her colleagues were addressing themselves to one very specific question, rather than to a general one: to be fair, what they said was that Banbury had no *neat* social class system (my italics). My argument is that class is certainly not neat, but that it is general; that if your approach to class rules out any reference to the big debates about the role of class in current events, then that approach misses much that is significant in the study of class.

However, I have to admit that my own attempt to establish composite images of class has not been totally successful, particularly with regard to 'the upper class' in all three countries, and 'the working class' in the United States. It is a basic theme of this book that there has indeed been, and still is, an upper class in each of the three countries, a 'reservoir of persons economically free and accustomed to responsibility from an early age', and one of my aims has been to show how it is that the upper class, though real, tends so easily to disappear from people's perceptions, particularly the perceptions of census-takers, pollsters and consumer researchers. I stress the importance of the language that people use, but have to admit that in this realm the language used is far from consistent. Most used in France is some phrase involving the word *bourgeoisie*, most often *grande bourgeoisie* or *bourgeoisie dirigeante*. More recently, it is true, the phrase *la classe dirigeante* has come into greater use. There is still talk, as we have seen, of the aristocracy or the nobility. But, even if referred to by different phrases, or by a grouping together of several phrases, there has been, I would argue, throughout the period studied, a very strong image of the existence of a coherent upper class. In Britain, confusion arises from the way in which the phrase 'middle class' is used as a sort of polite anglicization of the unacceptable 'bourgeoisie'. Behind the confusion, there is also a certain amount of muddled history, a belief that somewhere in the nineteenth century the 'middle classes rose to power'. Thus, 'middle class' or 'upper middle class' are often to be found in British usage to connote a powerful class which is, however, thought to be distinct from the true upper class, or aristocracy. Still, as I have shown, there are plenty of examples of the simple phrase 'the upper class' also being used; and the overwhelming imagery, I would suggest, is of a single upper class embracing successful elements from finance, industry, government and the professions, but containing within it the remnants of the older aristocracy. The phrase 'aristocracy' is in much wider usage in the United States than might be expected; 'the upper class', too, is often spoken of, but the problem here is that frequently what is meant is a purely local upper class, which certainly would not rate as such on any realistic national scale. For all that, I believe that the evidence that there is a pretty clear image in the United States of a coherent national upper class is persuasive.

There can be no doubt that the phrase 'the working class', though it is to be found in the documents of the 1930s, and still more in those of today, is much less generally used in the United States than in either France or Britain. On the one hand, the facts are that the borders between working class and middle class in the United States are fuzzier than elsewhere; on the other hand, the individual's perception of himself sometimes differs from the perceptions other members of society have of him. Broadly, in this book, a person is working-class, if he is perceived as such by other members of society, *and* if his condition matches the main objective realities of the working class condition as presented in this book. By that token, there is indeed an American working class.

However, my fundamental thesis is that the exact forms of class, which differ quite significantly from country to country, are determined by the historical evolution of the particular country. It is when we look at the different images in the different countries, set within the different historical contexts of the different countries, and then at the different realities in regard to inequality, that we begin to see more clearly the manner in which image and reality can be joined together. It is a concomitant thesis that under the pressure of economic and technological developments and of the great political and social upheavals of war and peace, class has changed between the 1930s and the present. Two competing hypotheses have been considered: that classes have steadily become more consolidated and polarized; and that classes have been disintegrating into a continuous range of statuses. Since levels of industrial development were still very low in many of the areas studied in the 1930s, there was, in fact, plenty of scope for classes to continue to take shape and become more consolidated in the more recent period. At the same time, mobility between classes has increased, and the cruder distinctions between classes have been modified; in that sense, there has, at the same time, been a disintegration of classes. My policy, though, is to try to avoid generalizations which at once embrace all three countries: the two generalizations which I have deliberately stressed by featuring them in the title of this chapter, are both, I fear, of dubious lineage. Nonetheless, simplistic though it undoubtedly sounds, I would stand by the case that in regard to class structure and attitudes towards class, America today has become much more like the European countries than she was in the 1930s: the upper class, though also weakened in many ways, has become more of a national institution; the working class has certainly developed greater coherence than ever it had in the 1930s. Race is no longer the absolutely inescapable brand of inferiority that it once was. France and Britain, on the other hand, have both become more mobile, more affluent societies; they now are troubled by problems of race and ethnicity. In all three countries attention is more and more focused on the needs of, and the problems created by, those forming the 'under class', though again I must admit that the imagery for this category is weak and fragmented.

For all that there has been convergence, the distinctive national shaping of class structure and class attitudes remains strongly in evidence. It is many years now since any historian dared use the phrase 'national character' for any descriptive, let alone explanatory, purpose. I have deliberately put it in headlines, for I believe that where this book has failed to shed light on class, it has at least shed a little on the differences between the three societies studied.

But were there really only three societies? Have I not, for example, been generalizing from English experience, when, so it is often said, class is altogether a different matter in Scotland? I can only say that

I do not believe this to be so; indeed, the sort of class differences I have been discussing are made all the sharper in Scotland by virtue of the fact that the upper class there tends to be anglified, and therefore even more sharply cut off from the rest of society. I speak as a Scotsman born and bred. And that, of course, brings me right back round to that excellent document which popped through my letterbox just as this investigation was beginning, and, was quoted in the opening paragraph of this book. That document spoke volumes about its own writer's preoccupation with class; it also, alas, suggested an insensitivity to the true nuances of accent, or, more probably, a readiness to overvalue an assumed proletarian appearance at the expense of a considered appraisal of accent. My accent is, actually, that of middle-class Edinburgh (though, as is the case with other Scottish accents, and with the various accents of provincial England, there is indeed little, if any, difference between middle-class and upper working-class pronunciation).

This book, like a bedsitter doubling as an amateur bordello, is littered with evidence. Some I have scarcely tried to interpret, some I have probably misunderstood. My *attitudes* are more relevant than my *accent* (though obviously they are related to each other). My maternal grandfather was a civil servant; my paternal grandfather was a minister and missionary in the Church of Scotland who dissipated the family fortune in trying to establish himself as a London literary figure. Although my mother had a degree in medicine and was a pioneer of birth control in Scotland, and my father was a pioneer of adult education and a noted Scottish economic historian, I was brought up in one of those housing estates technically intended for the 'working classes'. I was educated at a (working-class) village school (Edinburgh is a city of villages), and at a direct grant (shopkeepers') day school (founded in the seventeenth century, and given to producing Scottish rugby fullbacks – but, even now, *I* play *football*, every Sunday, in the Milton Keynes fifth division), at Edinburgh University, and at Balliol. That brief autobiographical diversion was by way of recognizing that in endeavouring, pragmatically and atheoretically, to interpret a vast mass of documentary evidence, one cannot entirely escape from one's background or upbringing. But the main message of this book is that in studying class, as with any other phenomena related to human societies, one cannot escape from history.

APPENDIX

Gainful Workers in the United States
Classified into Social-Economic Groups,
by Sex and Occupation: 1930

GROUP AND OCCUPATION	MALE	FEMALE
All gainful workers	38,077,804	10,752,116
1. *Professional persons*	1,497,934	1,447,863
Actors and showmen	54,511	20,785
Architects	21,621	379
Artists, sculptors, and teachers of art	35,621	21,644
Authors, editors, and reporters	46,922	17,371
Chemists, assayers, and metallurgists	45,163	1,905
Clergymen	145,572	3,276
College presidents and professors	41,774	20,131
Dentists	69,768	1,287
Designers, draftsmen and inventors	93,518	9,212
Lawyers, judges, and justices	157,220	3,385
Musicians and teachers of music	85,517	79,611
Osteopaths	4,554	1,563
Photographers	31,163	8,366
Physicians and surgeons	146,978	6,825
Teachers	202,337	860,278
Technical engineers	226,136	113
Trained nurses	5,452	288,737
Veterinary surgeons	11,852	11
Other professional pursuits	43,847	70,546
Chiropractors	9,203	2,713
Healers (not elsewhere classified)	7,866	9,774

Religious workers	11,339	19,951
Proprietors, managers, and officials	9,159,896	505,644
2a Farmers (owners and tenants)	5,749,367	262,645
2b Wholesale and retail dealers	1,675,193	111,854
Retail dealers	1,593,366	110,166
Wholesale dealers, importers, and exporters	81,837	1,688
2c Other proprietors, managers, and officials	1,735,336	131,145
Foresters, forest rangers and timber cruisers	8,042	15
Owners and managers of log and timber camps	6,889	10
Operators, managers, and officials—extraction of minerals	30,755	141
Builders and building contractors	167,310	202
Manufacturers	202,190	5,711
Managers and officials—manufacturing	302,334	10,422
Captains, masters, mates, and pilots	24,482	3
Garage owners, managers, and officials	69,543	422
Owners and managers—truck, transfer, and cab companies	40,508	576
Conductors—steam railroad	73,332	—
Officials and superintendents—steam and street railroads	37,963	26
Postmasters	20,818	13,603
Proprietors, managers, and officials*—transportation	34,987	3,003

*Not otherwise specified.

GROUP AND OCCUPATION	MALE	FEMALE
Bankers, brokers, and money lenders	212,312	9,192
Managers and officials—insurance companies	27,556	1,752
Proprietors, managers, and officials*—trade	42,201	3,104
Managers and officials—real-estate companies	5,124	479
Undertakers	32,192	1,940
Officials and inspectors—city and county	69,431	8,064
Officials and inspectors—State and United States	49,881	1,819
Billiard room, dance hall, etc., keepers	28,819	310
Directors, managers, and officials—motion-picture production	1,888	35
Keepers of charitable and penal institutions	9,408	5,552
Keepers of pleasure resorts, race tracks, etc	9,741	977
Radio announcers, directors, managers, etc	1,639	160
Theatrical owners, managers, and officials	18,691	1,032
Owners and proprietors—cleaning, dyeing, and pressing shops	15,207	1,068
Managers and officials—cleaning, dyeing, and pressing shops	4,615	1,226
Hotel keepers and managers	39,538	17,310
Laundry owners, managers, and officials	22,482	2,003
Restaurant, cafe, and lunchroom keepers	125,398	40,006
3. *Clerks and kindred workers*	4,877,235	3,072,220
Inspectors, scalers, and surveyors—log and timber camps	2,183	1
Baggagemen and freight agents—railroad	16,361	16

*Not otherwise specified.

Ticket and station agents—railroad	25,370	1,790
Agents—express companies	4,102	74
Express messengers and railway mail clerks	25,600	8
Mail carriers	120,204	1,129
Radio operators	4,909	46
Telegraph messengers	15,997	179
Telegraph operators	51,699	16,122
Telephone operators	13,625	235,259
Advertising agents	43,364	5,656
Clerks in stores	238,844	163,147
Commercial travelers	219,790	3,942
Decorators, drapers, and window dressers	13,911	6,238
Inspectors, gaugers, and samples—trade	10,923	5,820
Insurance agents	243,974	12,953
Newsboys	38,576	417
Real estate agents	203,119	31,308
Salesmen and saleswomen	1,508,283	560,720
Abstracters, notaries, and justices of peace	9,848	1,908
Architects', designers', and draftsmen's apprentices	2,436	220
Apprentices to other professional persons	3,861	74
Officials of lodges, societies, etc.	11,513	3,002
Technicians and laboratory assistants	8,288	7,700
Dentists' assistants and attendants	770	12,945
Librarians' assistants and attendants	502	1,363
Physicians' and surgeons attendants	689	13,353
Agents, collectors, and credit men	182,630	13,477
Bookkeepers, cashiers, and accountants	447,937	482,711
Clerks (except clerks in stores)	1,290,447	706,553

Appendix

GROUP AND OCCUPATION	MALE	FEMALE
Messenger, errand, and office boys and girls	81,430	8,949
Stenographers and typists	36,050	775,140
4. *Skilled workers and foremen*	6,201,542	81,145
Farm managers and foremen	66,259	963
Foremen—log and timber camps	3,910	—
Foremen, overseers, and inspectors—extraction of minerals	34,274	12
Blacksmiths, forgemen, and hammermen	147,460	9
Boilermakers	49,923	—
Brick and stone masons and tile layers	170,896	7
Cabinetmakers	57,890	7
Carpenters	929,376	50
Compositors, linotypes, and typesetters	173,363	10,269
Coopers	11,347	—
Electricians	280,279	38
Electrotypers, stereotypers, and lithographers	16,448	244
Engineers (stationary), cranemen, hoistmen, etc.	316,942	22
Engravers	18,747	690
Foremen and overseers—manufacturing	310,037	28,467
Puddlers	1,597	—
Glass blowers	3,209	59
Jewelers, watchmakers, goldsmiths, and silversmiths	37,408	1,254
Loom fixers	19,180	35
Machinists, millwrights, and toolmakers	761,075	20

Mechanics*	638,190	63
Millers (grain, flour, feed, etc.)	15,906	40
Molders, founders, and casters (metal)	105,139	19
Painters, glaziers, and varnishers (building)	429,982	123
Paper hangers	26,872	1,456
Pattern and model makers	29,711	39
Piano and organ tuners	6,799	24
Plasterers and cement finishers	85,477	3
Plumbers and gas and steam fitters	237,813	1
Pressmen and plate printers (printing)	31,215	—
Rollers and roll hands (metal)	30,705	—
Roofers and slaters	23,636	—
Sawyers	35,984	80
Shoemakers and cobblers (not in factory)	76,127	261
Skilled occupations (not elsewhere classified)	12,227	31
Stonecutters	22,887	1
Structural iron workers (building)	28,966	—
Tailors and tailoresses	147,476	21,807
Tinsmiths and coppersmiths	83,421	6
Upholsterers	49,097	2,355
Bus conductors	1,002	—
Conductors—street railroad	35,680	17
Foremen and overseers—steam and street railroads	79,682	55
Locomotive engineers	101,201	—
Locomotive firemen	67,006	—
Aviators	6,031	66
Foremen and overseers*—transportation	52,061	74
Inspectors—transportation	50,965	1,155

*Not otherwise specified.

GROUP AND OCCUPATION	MALE	FEMALE
Floorwalkers, foremen, and overseers—trade	33,368	4,795
Firemen—fire department	73,008	—
Marshals, sheriffs, detectives, etc.	39,247	2,576
Policemen	130,838	849
Foremen and overseers—cleaning, dyeing, and pressing shops	470	349
Foremen and overseers—laundries	3,583	2,754
5. *Semiskilled workers*	5,448,158	3,529,414
5a Semiskilled workers in manufacturing	2,881,022	1,676,971
Apprentices to building and hand trades	40,105	28
Apprentices (except to building and hand trades)—manufacturing	33,450	3,869
Bakers	131,884	8,916
Dressmakers and seamstresses (not in factory)	452	157,928
Dyers	17,425	294
Filers, grinders, buffers, and polishers (metal)	76,264	2,336
Milliners and millinery dealers	4,846	40,102
Oilers of machinery	31,169	41
Enamelers, lacquerers, and japanners	4,622	1,136
Painters, glaziers, and varnishers (factory)	89,546	3,522
Operatives*—manufacturing	2,451,259	1,458,799

*Not otherwise specified.

	2,567,136	852,443
5b Other semiskilled workers		
Boatmen, canal men, and lock keepers	5,603	40
Sailors and deck hands	64,692	8
Chauffeurs and truck and tractor drivers	970,916	1,502
Boiler washers and engine hostlers	18,300	—
Brakemen—steam railroad	88,197	—
Motormen—steam and street railroads	60,718	5
Switchmen, flagmen, and yardmen—steam and street railroads	102,484	289
Telegraph and telephone linemen	71,624	1
Apprentices—transportation	6,097	54
Other occupations—transportation	83,794	1,923
Apprentices—wholesale and retail trade	2,337	107
Deliverymen—bakeries and stores	159,328	116
Other pursuits in trade	96,069	29,106
Guards, watchmen, and doorkeepers	147,115	1,000
Soldiers, sailors, and marines	132,830	—
Other public service pursuits	40,369	1,268
Other occupations—semiprofessional pursuits	8,765	1,756
Attendants—pool rooms, bowling alleys, golf clubs, etc.	16,047	121
Helpers—motion-picture production	1,234	979
Theater ushers	9,308	3,153
Other attendants and helpers—professional service	28,890	21,480
Barbers, hairdressers, and manicurists	261,096	113,194
Boarding and lodginghouse keepers	17,093	127,278
Other operatives—cleaning, dyeing, and pressing shops	42,313	18,321
Housekeepers and stewards	20,383	236,363
Deliverymen—laundries	20,558	15

GROUP AND OCCUPATION	MALE	FEMALE
Other operatives—laundries	45,087	149,414
Midwives and nurses (not trained)	13,867	143,142
Other pursuits—domestic and personal service	32,022	1,808
Unskilled workers	10,893,039	3,115,830
6a Farm laborers	3,746,433	646,331
6b Factory and building construction laborers	3,248,622	125,321
Firemen (except locomotive and fire department)	127,293	1
Furnace men, smelter men, and pourers	18,627	—
Heaters (metal)	14,941	1
Laborers*—manufacturing	3,087,701	125,519
6c Other laborers	2,871,744	31,321
Fishermen and oystermen	73,071	200
Teamsters and haulers—log and timber camps	9,242	1
Other lumbermen, raftsmen, and woodchoppers	146,803	93
Coal mine operatives	621,545	116
Other operatives in extraction of minerals	296,990	490
Longshoremen and stevedores	73,944	10
Draymen, teamsters, and carriage drivers	111,178	45
Garage laborers	66,536	157
Hostlers and stable hands	6,654	—
Laborers—truck, transfer, and cab companies	40,920	50

Laborers—road and street	300,980	47
Laborers, including construction laborers—steam and street railroads	459,090	3,384
Laborers*—transportation	50,998	65
Laborers in coal and lumber yards, warehouses, etc.	113,027	642
Laborers, porters, and helpers in stores	199,296	9,392
Laborers—public service	155,903	1,107
Laborers—professional service	23,762	1,621
Laborers—recreation and amusement	29,458	435
Stage hands and circus helpers	4,099	175
Laborers—cleaning, dyeing, and pressing shops	3,910	639
Laborers—domestic and personal service	67,337	4,350
Laborers—laundries	11,001	8,292
6d Servant classes	1,026,240	2,312,657
Bootblacks	18,747	37
Charwomen and cleaners	20,943	40,989
Elevator tenders	55,255	12,359
Janitors and sextons	273,805	35,830
Launderers and laundresses (not in laundry)	4,565	356,468
Porters (except in stores)	127,436	52
Servants	364,174	1,634,959
Waiters	161,315	231,973

*Not otherwise specified.

BIBLIOGRAPHY

A PRIMARY SOURCES

I *Archives*

(a) Britain

Bodleian Library, Oxford [Bod. L]
    Crookshank Diaries
    Monckton Papers
BBC Written Archives, Caversham [BBC A]
British Library of Political and Economic Science, London [BLPES]
    Beveridge Papers
    Dalton Diaries
    Fisk Papers
    Lansbury Papers
    Laski-Hubsch Correspondence
Churchill College, Cambridge
    A. V. Alexander Papers
    Attlee Papers
    Bevin Papers [BEVN]
    Page Croft Papers
    P. J. Grigg Papers
    Maxwell Fyffe Papers
    Margesson Papers [MRGN]
    Sir Archibald Sinclair Papers
    Weir Papers
    Willink Papers

Imperial War Museum, London [IWM]
    Hilda Neal Papers
    Herbert Strong Collection
    Reverend Mackay Papers
    Vivienne Hall Diary
    T. H. M. McHutchison Diary
    E. L. Evans Papers
    Yates Correspondence
    H. A. Penny Diary
    Brinton-Lee Diary, 1940–1
    Haslam Papers
    Gwladys Cox Diary

Labour Party Archives, Transport House, London
Liddell Hart Archives, King's College London (formerly at Medmenham, Bucks)
Mass Observation Archives, University of Sussex
Modern Records Centre, Warwick University [MRC]
    ASST/ASTMS (MSS 79)
    NUBE (MSS 56)
    Typographical Association (MSS 39)
    NGA (MSS 28)
    Lord Justice Scott Papers (MSS 119)
    Transport and General Workers (MSS 126)
National Library of Scotland, Edinburgh
    Scottish Secretariat Papers
Public Record Office, London
    CAB 66–68
    ED 12, 63, 66, 69, 102, 107, 110
    HLG 27, 30, 31, 36, 37, 41, 101
    LAB 8, 10, 11, 18, 19, 23
    MAF 59, 67
    MH 52, 55, 61, 62
    POWER 1
University College, Oxford
    Attlee Papers
University of Edinburgh Library [EUL]
    C. M. Grieve Papers
    A. Berriedale Keith Collection

(b) USA

Atlanta University Library [AUL]
    Association of Southern Women for the Prevention of Lynching Collection [ASWPL]
    McDuffie Collection
    Neighborhood Union Collection
    Columbia University Library, New York [CUL]
    Frances Perkins Papers
    Robert W. Woodruff Library, Emory University, Atlanta [RWWL]
    Mildred Seydell Collection
    Immigration History Research Center, University of Minnesota Libraries, St Paul [IHRC]
    St Paul [IHRC]
    Capraro Collection
    Crivello Collection
    Cupelli Collection
    Donnaruma Collection
    National Archives, Washington DC [NA]
    Social Security Administration Records (RG 47)
    President's Organization for Unemployment Records (RG 73)

Women's Bureau Records (RG 86)
Department of Labor Records (RG 174)
Bureau of Employment Security Records (RG 183)
War Manpower Commission Records (RG 211)
Department of Health, Education and Welfare Records (RG 235)
Archives of Labor and Urban Affairs, Wayne State University, Detroit [ALUA]
      George Addes Collection
      Airline Pilots Association Records
      American Federation of Teachers Records [AFT]
      American Newspaper Guild Records
      Agricultural Workers Organising Committee Records
      Auto Workers' Organizing Committee Papers [AWOC]
      United Auto Workers Papers
      CIO: Secretary Papers
      Treasurer's Office Collection
      Merle E. Henrickson Collection
      United Packinghouse Workers Archives
      United Community Services of Detroit
      Oral History Collections:
         Norman Bully
         Charles Conway
         James Couser
         Daniel Gallagher
         Nat Ganley
         Catherine Gelles
         Jack Hurst
         John McDaniel
         Stanley Nowak
         Joseph Pagano
         Sam Sage
Social Welfare History Archives, University of Minnesota Libraries, Minneapolis [SWHA]
      Association of Junior Leagues of America Papers [AJLA]
      Family Service of St Paul: Correspondence with
      Unemployed Men
      National Federation of Settlements Papers
Tamiment Library, New York University Libraries
    Max Zawitsky (Collection 6)
    Rose Schneiderman (Collection 18)
    Mark Starr (Collection 19)
    John Lyons (Collection 25)
Archives Division, the State Historical Society of Wisconsin, Madison [SHSW]
      American Federation of Hosiery Workers Papers
      American Federation of Labor Papers
      NBC Archives
      Textile Workers Organizing Committee Papers

(c) France

Archives Nationales: Institut Francais d'Histoire Sociale, Paris [IFHS]
    CFDT-PTT (Don Daniel Dubois) (14 AS 245)
    Dommanget (14 AS 258 and 261)
    Garmy (14 AS 304)
    Instituteurs (procès verbaux du Conseil Féderal de la Fédération)
        (14 AS 207)
    Lacaze-Duthiers (14 AS 212²)
    Dossier sur l'affaire Lip (14 AS 317)
    Mai 1968 (brochures et tracts) (14 AS 238 and 250)
    Pericat (14 AS 205)
    Renault regie (tracts 1962–5) (14 AS 238)
    Rougeron (14 AS 229)
    Vassart (14 AS 206)
Centre d'Histoire du Syndicalisme, Paris
    Fonds Delery
    Archives Compère-Morel
    Archives Salembier
    Fonds Lefranc
    Archives Syndicat FO des Taxis

II *Official Printed Sources*

(Parliamentary and Congressional records and statutes have been con-
sulted, as necessary, on an *ad hoc* basis. Listed here, chronologically,
country by country, are the more valuable individual items.)

(a) Britain

Ministry of Reconstruction, *Housing in England and Wales: Memorandum
    by the Advisory Housing Panel on the Emergency Problem*, Cmd 9087
    (1918)
Registrar-General, *Decennial Supplement, Part IIA: the Five 'Social
    Classes'* (1931)
Report of the Royal Commission on the Civil Service, Cmd (1931)
Department of Health for Scotland: Consultative Council on Local Health
    Administration and General Health Questions, *Report of the Con-
    sultative Council in regard to the steps necessary to secure that State-
    aided houses will in future be let only to persons of the working classes*
    (1932)
Ministry of Labour, *Report of the Unemployment Insurance Statutory
    Committee on Remuneration Limit for Insurance of Non-manual
    Workers* (1936)
Board of Trade, *Report by the Council for Art and Industry: the Working
    Class Home: its Furnishing and Equipment* (1937)

Report of Committee on Holidays with Pay, Cmd 5724 (1937–8)

Commissioners for the Special Areas (England and Wales), *Report of the Committee of Enquiry into Land Settlement* (1939)

Wartime Social Survey, Food Supplement: *An Enquiry for the Ministry of Food* (April 1944)

Report on Post-war Organisation of Domestic Employment, Cmd 6650 (1945)

National Income and Expenditure of the United Kingdom 1938–46, Cmd 7099 (1947)

The Social Survey, *The British Household* (April 1947)

Board of Trade, *Distribution and Exhibition of Cinematograph Films*, Cmd 7837 (1949)

Report of the Ministry of National Insurance for the period 17th November 1944 to 4th July 1949 (1950)

Central Statistical Office, *Social Trends*, no. 6 (1975)

Annual Abstract of Statistics 1977 (1978)

Britain 1978: an Official Handbook (1978)

(b) USA

Department of Labor, Women's Bureau, *The Effects of Depression on Wage Earners' Families* (1932)

USA Bureau of the Census, *A Social-Economic Grouping of the Gainful Worker of the United States* (1933)

Social Security Board, *Social Security Bulletin* (1935–50)

Department of Labor, Women's Bureau, *A Second Survey of South Bend* (1936)

Federal Housing Administration, *Third Annual Report* (1936)

USA Bureau of the Census, 'A Social-Economic Grouping of Gainful Workers in Cities of 500,000 or more: 1930', typescript (1938)

Federal Housing Administration, *The Structure and Growth of Residential Neighborhoods in American Cities* (1939)

Social Security Board, *Employment and Wages of Covered Workers in State Unemployment Compensation Systems 1939* (1942)

US Social Security Administration, *Handbook on Federal Old-age and Survivor's Insurance* (1947)

US Department of Labor, *'To Promote the General Welfare': 37th Annual Report of the Secretary of Labor 1949* (1950)

US Department of Labor, *The American Workers' Fact Book* (1956)

Louis Winnick, *American Housing and its Use: the demand for shelter space* (1957)

US Bureau of the Census, *Social and Economic Characteristics of the Population in Metropolitan and Nonmetropolitan Areas: 1970 and 1960* (1971)

Deane Carson, ed., *The Vital Majority: Small Business in the American Economy* (1973)

US Bureau of the Census, *Statistical Abstract of the United States* (1977)

(c) France

Statistique Générale de la France, *Recensement des Industries et Professions: Nomenclature des Industries et Professions* (April 1934)
Annuaire Statistique de la France 1933 (1934)
Institut Nationale de la Statistique et des Etudes Economiques, 'Nomenclature 1896 à 1936', in *Resultats statistiques du recensement générale, 1946*, vol. III (1952)
Marcel Bresard (de l'Institut National d'études demographiques), *La Mobilité sociale en France* (1952)
Institut National de la statistique et des études economiques: Code des catégories socio-professionnelles, 3rd edition (1954)
Annuaire Statistique de la France 1951 (1952)
Annuaire Statistique de la France 1977 (1978)

III *Guides, Codes, Dictionaries, Legal Text Books etc.*

Christian Chavanon, *Les Fonctionnaires et la function publique* (1950–1)
Dictionary of National Biography (1949–71)
Dictionnaire de biographie francaise (1933–75)
Dalloz, *Précis de droit civil*, 6th edition (1939)
Dalloz, *Précis de droit commerciale*, 6th edition (1936)
Dalloz, *Précis de legislation industrielle*, 4th edition (1936)
Encyclopedia of the Social Sciences (1933 and 1968)
Jacques Etienne and Jean Beylac, *Manual-Guide pratique de l'artisan* (1941)
Marcel Gautier, *Métiers et main-d'oeuvre, dans l'industrie hotelière* (1955)
Denis Gifford, *British Film Catalogue, 1897–1970* (1973)
H. A. Hill, *The Complete Law of Housing* (1938)
Marcel Jeanne, *La Profession hotelière* (1956)
W. Ivor Jennings, *The Law of Housing* (1936)
Jean Jolly, *Dictionnaire des parlementaires francais* (1960–)
Paul Pic, *Traité élementaire de législation industrielle: les lois ouvrières* (1937)
Georges Ripert, *La Régime démocratique et le droit civil moderne* (1936)
A. Rouast and P. Durand, *Précis de législation industrielle* (1934)
Georges Sadoul, *Dictionnaire des cinéastes* (1965)
Georges Sadoul, *Dictionnaire des films* (1965)
Jean Saratier, *La Profession libérale: étude juridique et pratique* (1947)
Who Was Who (1941–72)
Who Was Who in America (1943–76)

IV *Newspapers etc.*

Newspapers were not studied at all systematically, save at certain points of crisis, e.g. the French 'events' of February 1934, and for the very recent period. I have drawn heavily on the collections of clippings to be found in many of the archives, e.g. the Liddell Hart Archives, the Women's Bureau Records in Washington, the Dossier on the Lip Affair in Paris.

As well as daily and weekly newspapers, and such political and union journals as *American Federationist, Onlooker* and *Railway Review*, serials which proved particularly useful were: *Crapouillot, Nouvel Observateur, L'Express, Life, Fortune, Time, Picture Post* and *Encounter*.

V *Works containing Survey Material, Oral testimony, Interviews etc.*

Janick Arbois and Joshka Schidlow, *La vraie vie des français* (1978)
Katherine Archibald, *Wartime Shipyard: a Study in Social Disunity* (1947)
E. Wight Bakke, *Insurance or Dole?* (1935)
E. Wight Bakke, *Citizens Without Work* (1940)
E. Wight Bakke, *The Unemployed Worker* (1940)
H. L. Beales and R. S. Lambert, eds., *Memoirs of the Unemployed* (1934)
Bennett M. Berger, *Working-Class Suburb* (1960)
L. Bernot and R. Blancard, *Nouville, un village français* (1953)
Charles Bettelheim and Suzanne Frère, *Une ville française moyenne: Auxerre en 1950* (1950)
Huw Beynon, *Working for Ford* (1973)
Ronald Blythe, *Akenfield: Portrait of an English Village* (1969)
Melvyn Bragg, *Speak for England* (1976)
Harvey Cantril, 'Identification with Social and Economic Class', *Journal of Abnormal and Social Psychology*, vol. 38 (1943)
Lowell J. Carr and James E. Sterner, *Willow Run: a Study of Industrialisation and Cultural Inadequacy* (1952)
P. Clement and N. Xydias, *Vienne-sur-le-Rhone* (1955)
Richard P. Coleman and Bernice L. Neugarten, *Social Status in the City* (1971)
A. Davis, B. B. Gardner and M. R. Gardner, *Deep South* (1941)
Jane Deverson and Katharine Lindsay, *Voices from the Middle Class* (1975)
J. Dollard, *Class and Caste in a Southern Town* (1937)
Les Évenements survenus en France de 1933 à 1945: témoignages et documents recueillis par la commission d'enquête parlementaire, 9 vols. (1947–54)
The Gallup Poll 1935–1971, 3 vols. (1976)
Herbert J. Gans, *The Urban Villagers: Group and Class in the Life of Italian Americans* (1962)
Herbert J. Gans, *The Levittowners: Ways of Life and Politics in a New Suburban Community* (1967)
Geoffrey Gorer, *Exploring English Character* (1955)
Roy Greenslade, *Goodbye to the Working Class* (1976)
Robert J. Havighurst and H. G. Morgan, *The Social History of a War-boom Community* (1951)
Institut français d'opinion publique, *Sondages* (1938–75)
Institut français d'opinion publique, *Bulletins d'Informations* (1945)

Institut National d'études demographiques, *Les Attitudes des mineurs du Centre-Midi a l'evolution de l'emploi* (1957)

Brian Jackson and Dennis Marsden, *Working Class Community* (1968)

Brian Jackson and Dennis Marsden, *Education and the Working Class* (1962)

M. Kahan, D. Butler and D. Stokes, 'On the Analytical Division of Social Class', *British Journal of Sociology*, vol. (1966)

Josephine Klein, *Samples from English Cultures* (1955)

William Kornblum, *Blue Collar Community* (1974)

J. C. Legget, *Class, Race and Labor: Working Class Consciousness in Detroit* (1968)

David Lockwood, 'Sources of Variation in Working-Class Images of Society', *Sociological Review*, vol. 14 (1966)

Edith E. Lowry, Velma Shotwell and Helen White, *Tales of Americans on Trek* (1940)

Helen and Robert Lynd, *Middletown* (1928), and *Middletown in Transition* (1937)

Jerome G. Manis and Bernard N. Meltzer, 'Attitudes of Textile Workers to Class Structure', *American Journal of Sociology*, vol. 60 (1954)

F. M. Martin, 'Some Subjective Aspects of Social Stratification', in D. V. Glass, ed., *Social Mobility in Britain* (1954)

H. F. Moorhouse, 'Attitudes to Class and Class Relationships in Britain', *Sociology* (1976)

J. M. and R. E. Pahl, *Managers and their Wives* (1972)

Richard Scase, 'English and Swedish Conceptions of Class', in F. Parkin, ed., *The Social Analysis of Class Structure* (1974)

Jeremy Seabrook, *What Went Wrong?* (1978)

Nancy Seifer, *Nobody Speaks for Me!: Self-portraits of American Working-class Women* (1976)

H. Llewellyn Smith, ed., *New Survey of London Life and Labour*, 9 vols. (1930–5)

Margaret Stacey, *et al.*, *Tradition and Change: a Study of Banbury* (1960), and *Power, Persistence and Change: a Second Study of Banbury* (1975)

Studs Terkel, *Working* (1974)

Alain Touraine, *La Conscience ouvrière* (1966)

Unemployment Committee of the National Federation of Settlements, *Case Studies of the Unemployed* (1931)

Arthur J. Vidick and Joseph Bensman, *Small Town in Mass Society: Class, Power and Religion in a Rural Community* (1958)

W. Lloyd Warner and Paul S. Lunt, *The Social Life of a Modern Community* (1941)

W. Lloyd Warner and Paul S. Lunt, *The Status System of a Modern Community* (1942)

W. Lloyd Warner, *Democracy in Jonesville* (1949)

Simone Weil, *La Condition ouvrière* (1951)

James West, *Plainsville, U.S.A.* (1945)

Peter Wilmott and Michael Young, *Family and Class in a London Suburb* (1960)
N. Xydias, 'Classes sociales et conscience de classe à Vienne-en-France: aspects subjectifs et objectifs', *Transactions of Second World Congress of Sociology* (1953).

VI *Published Letters, Diaries, Autobiographies and Reminiscences (Select List)*

Dean Acheson, *Morning and Noon* (1965)
Julian Amery, *Approach March: a Venture in Autobiography* (1973)
Vincent Auriol, *Hier demain* (1945)
Vincent Auriol, *Journal du Septennat*, 5 vols. (1970)
Viscount Avon, *Another World* (1975)
Leon Blum, *L'Oeuvre de Leon Blum*, vol. IV pts. 1 and 2 (1964–65)
Robert Brasillach, *Notre Avant Guerre* (1941)
D. G. Bridson, *Prosper and Ariel* (1971)
Duc de Brissac, *En d'autres temps: 1900–1939* (1972)
George Brown, *In My Way* (1971)
Lord Butler, *The Art of the Possible* (1971)
Sir Henry Channon, *Chips: the Diaries of Sir Henry Channon*, ed. Robert Rhodes James (1956)
Henry M. Christman, ed., *Walter P. Reuther: Selected Papers* (1961)
Walter Citrine, *Men and Work: an Autobiography* (1964)
Walter Citrine, *Two Careers* (1967)
B. L. Coombes, *Miners Day* (1945)
A. Duff Cooper, *Old Men Forget* (1953)
Frank L. Crawford, *Memoir of Henry Augustus Shute of the Class of 1879, Harvard College* (1943)
R. H. S. Crossman, *The Diaries of a Cabinet Minister*, 3 vols. (1975–8)
Louis Daquin, *Le Cinéma, notre métier* (1960)
J. C. C. Davidson, *Memoirs of a Conservative: J. C. C. Davidson's Memoirs and Papers 1910–37*, ed. Robert Rhodes-James (1969)
Peter Donnelly, ed., *Mrs Milburn's Diaries* (1979)
Xavier de la Fournière, *Giscard d'Estaing et Nous* (1977)
P. J. Grigg, *Prejudice and Promise* (1948)
Ronald Hayman, ed., *My Cambridge* (1977)
Harold L. Ickes, *The Secret Diary of Harold L. Ickes*, 3 vols. (1955)
Lord Kilbracken, *Living like a Lord* (1955)
Cecil King, *With Malice toward None: a War Diary* (1970)
Cecil King, *The Cecil King Diaries 1965–1970* and *1970–1974* (1972, 1975)
Thomas Jones, *Whitehall Diary*, ed. Keith Middlemass (1969)
Jennie Lee, *Tomorrow is a New Day* (1939)
Jennie Lee, *This Great Journey* (1963)
Harold Macmillan, *Winds of Change, 1914–1939* (1966)
Harold Macmillan, *The Blast of War, 1939–1945* (1967)

Harold Macmillan, *Tides of Fortune 1945–1955* (1969)
Harold Macmillan, *Riding the Storm 1956–1959* (1971)
Harold Macmillan, *Pointing the Way 1959–1961* (1972)
Harold Macmillan, *At the End of the Day 1961–1963* (1973)
Cléo de Mérode, *Le Ballet de ma vie* (1955)
Jessica Mitford, *Hons and Rebels* (1960)
J. T. Murphy, *New Horizons* (1941)
Georges Navel, *Travaux* (1945)
Richard M. Nixon, *The Memoirs of Richard Nixon* (1978)
Joseph Paul-Boncour, *Entre deux guerres: souvenirs de la IIIe république* (1945)
Goronwy Rees, *Chapter of Accidents* (1975)
Jean Renoir, *My Life and My Films* (1973)
Paul Reynaud, *Mémoires* (1960)
Lord Robens, *Ten Year Stint* (1971)
Robert Roberts, *The Classic Slum* (1971)
Eleanor Roosevelt, *The Autobiography of Eleanor Roosevelt* (1962)
The Roosevelt Letters, edited by Elliott Roosevelt (3 vols, 1949–52)
Denis de Rougemont, *Journal d'un intellectuel en chômage* (1937)
George Tomlinson, *Coal-Miner* (1937)
Viscount Swinton, *I Remember* (1948)
Ann Thwaite, ed., *My Cambridge* (1977)
John Wain, 'Introduction' to new edition of *Hurry on Down* (1978)
Marcia Williams, *Inside Number 10* (1972)
Edwin E. Witte, *The Development of the Social Security Act* (1962)

VII *Academic and Polemical Works, Published Records of Parties and Unions etc. and other contemporary printed material (including fiction)*

(Pamphlets and tracts not available in the major copyright libraries were studied at the Centre de Documentation Internationale Contemporaine at the University of Paris, Nanterre, at the Fondation Nationale des Sciences Politiques, Paris, and at the Conservative Research Department, London.)

Sam Aaronovitch, *The Ruling Class: a Study of British Finance Capital* (1961)
Alain, *Les Eléments d'une doctrine radicale* (1926)
American Federation of Labor, *Report of Proceedings of Annual Convention* (1939–42)
Stanley Aronowitz, *False Promises: the Shaping of American Working Class Consciousness* (1973)
Association d'Entraide de la Noblesse Francaise, *Recueil des personnes ayant fait leur preuves devant les assemblées générales 1932–1949* (1950)

Peter Bauer, *Class on the Brain: the Cost of a British Obsession* (1978)

Daniel Bell, *The End of Ideology* (1960)

Alfred M. Bingham, *Insurgent America: Revolt of the Middle Classes* (1935)

George Blake, *The Shipbuilders* (1935)

Gordon F. Bloom and Herbert R. Northrup, *Economics of Labor Relations* (1954)

Francoise Bouriez-Gregg, *Essai sur le problème des classes sociales aux Etats-Unis* (1954)

A. L. Bowley, *Wages and Income in the United Kingdom since 1860* (1937)

A. L. Bowley and J. Stamp, *The National Income 1924* (1927)

Marcel Bresard, *La Mobilité sociale en France* (1954)

British Medical Association, 'Hospital Policy' (June 1939)

Richard Buckle, *U and Non-U Revisited* (1978)

Martin Bulmer, ed., *Working-class Images of Society* (1975)

A. M. Carr-Saunders and D. Caradog Jones, *A Survey of the Social Structure of England and Wales* (1927, 1937, 1957)

A. M. Carr-Saunders and P. A. Wilson, *The Professions* (1937)

Richard Centers, *The Psychology of Social Classes* (1949)

CGT, *Le Plan de la CGT* (1936)

Henri Clerc, *Pour Sauver les classes moyennes* (1939)

Robert Coles, *The Middle Americans: Proud and Uncertain* (1971)

Michel Collinet, *L'Ouvrier français: essai sur la condition ouvrière 1900–1950* (1951)

Congress of Industrial Organizations, *Congress Reports* (1939–42)

Conservative Party Sub-Committee on Education, *Looking Ahead* (1944)

A. Duff Cooper, *Why Workers Should be Tories* (1926)

Jilly Cooper, *Class: A view from Middle England* (1979)

Lewis Corey, *The Crisis of the Middle Class* (1935)

Monica Cosens, *Evacuation: a Social Revolution* (1939)

Oliver C. Cox, *Caste, Class and Race* (1941)

C. A. R. Crosland, *The Future of Socialism* (1956)

Ralf Dahrendorf, *Class and Class Conflict in an Industrial Society* (1959)

Ralf Dahrendorf, *Conflict after Class* (1967)

Alison Davis, *Psychology of the Child in the Middle Class* (1960)

Michel Débré, *L'Artisanat: classe sociale* (1934)

Jacques Delcourt and Gerard Lamarque, 'Un faux Dilemme: embourgeoisement ou prolétarisation de la classe ouvrière', *Etudes Sociales* (1963)

Jacques Dubois, *Les Cadres, nouveau tiers état* (1971)

Alba M. Edwards, 'A Social-Economic Grouping of Gainful Workers', *Journal of the American Statistical Association* (1933)

Louise-Marie Ferré, *Les Classes sociales dans la France contemporaine* (1934)

Donald Fraser, 'Newsreel: Reality or Entertainment?', *Sight and Sound* (Autumn 1933)

Murray Friedman, ed., *Overcoming Middle Class Rage* (1969)

René Garmy, *Pourquoi j'ai été exclu du Parti Communiste* (n.d.)

Alan Gartner, Colin Greer and Frank Riessman, *The New Assault on Equality: I.Q. and Social Stratification* (1974)

André Gillois, *Les Grandes familles de France* (1953)

V. Giscard d'Estaing, *Towards a New Democracy* (1977)

Nathan Glazer and Daniel Moynihan, *Beyond the Melting Pot* (1964 and 1970)

Edmond Goblot, *La Barrière et le niveau* (1925)

Maurice Halbwachs, *Les Classes sociales* (1937 and 1942)

G. W. Hartmann and T. Newcombe, eds., *Industrial Conflict* (1939)

J. R. Hicks, *The Social Framework* (1942)

Richard Hoggart, *The Uses of Literacy* (1957)

Arthur N. Holcombe, *The Middle Classes in American Politics* (1940)

Hudson Institute Europe, *The United Kingdom in 1980: The Hudson Report* (1974)

H. D. Hughes, *Towards a Classless Society* (1947)

Patrick Hutber, *The Decline and Fall of the Middle Class and How It Can Fight Back* (1977)

Inventaires III: Classes Moyennes (1939)

Alfred Winslow Jones, *Life, Liberty and Property* (1941)

Léon Jouhaux, *La CGT* (1937)

Suzanne L. Keller, *Beyond the Ruling Class: Strategic Elites in Modern Society* (1963)

Joseph P. Kennedy, *I'm for Roosevelt* (1936)

J. M. Keynes, 'The Position of the Lancashire Cotton Trade', *Nation* (13 November 1926)

Labour Party, *Reports of Annual Conferences* (1931–78)

Gérard de Lacaze-Duthiers, *Manuels et intellectuels* (1932)

Pierre Laroque, *Les Classes sociales* (1959 and 1972)

Pierre Laroque, *Les grands Problèmes sociaux contemporains* (1954–55)

Marghanita Laski, *Tory Heaven or Thunder on the Right* (1948)

G. Lecarpentier, 'Revenus et fortunes privés en France et en Grande-Bretagne', *Revue Politique et Parlementaire* (October 1937)

Gerhard Lenski, 'American Social Classes: Statistical Strata or Social Groups?', *American Journal of Sociology*, vol. 58 (1952)

R. Lewis and A. Maude, *The English Middle Classes* (1949)

Jean Lhomme, *Le Problème des classes* (1938)

Jean Lhomme, *Classes sociales et transformations économiques* (1945)

David Lockwood, *The Black-coated Worker* (1958)

David Lockwood, 'The "New Working Class"', *Archives Européennes de Sociologie*, vol. I (1960)

Alison Lurie, *The War between the Tates* (1974)

Richard Mabey, ed., *Class* (1967)

Serge Mallet, *La Nouvelle classe ouvrière* (1963)

Herbert Marcuse, *One-dimensional Man: Studies in the Ideology of Advanced Industrial Society* (1964)

André Maurois, *Histoire d'Angleterre* (1938)

André Maurois, *Histoire des États Unis* (1943)

S. M. Miller and F. Reissman, *Social Class and Social Policy* (1968)

C. Wright Mills, *White Collar: the American Middle Classes* (1951)

Jougla de Morenas, *Noblesse 38* (1938)

MRP, Centre de formation des militants, *Les Classes sociales en France* (1946)

Gunnar Myrdal, *An American Dilemma* (1944)

Gunnar Myrdal, *Beyond the Welfare State* (1960)

Francois de Negroni, *La France noble* (1974)

Theo Nichols and Huw.Benyon, *Living with Capitalism: Class Relations and the Modern Factory* (1977)

Vivian Ogilvie, *The English Public School* (1957)

George Orwell, *The Road to Wigan Pier* (1937)

Vance Packard, *The Status Seekers* (1959)

Franklin C. Palm, *The Middle Classes Then and Now* (1936)

Frank Parkin, *Class Inequality and Political Order* (1972)

Parti Communiste français, *La Nation française et les classes sociales* (1955)

Parti Communiste français, *L'Economie et les classes sociales en France* (1945)

Parti Socialiste français, *Congrès Nationals* (1936–8)

T. H. Pear, *English Social Differences* (1955)

Selig Perelman, *A Theory of the Labor Movement* (1928)

Francois Perroux, *Le Problème des classes* (1943)

Henri Prouteau, *Les Occupations d'usine en Italie et en France* (1938)

Simon Raven, *The English Gentleman* (1964)

A. Reiss, 'Occupation and Social Status', *American Journal of Sociology*, vol. 61 (1955)

Dudley Seers, *The Levelling of Incomes since 1938* (1951)

Semaines Sociales de France, XXXI, *Bordeaux, 1939, Le Problème des classes dans la communauté sociale et dans l'ordre humain* (1942)

Richard Sennett and Jonathan Cobb, *The Hidden Injuries of Class* (1972)

Arthur B. Shostack and W. Gomberg, eds., *Blue-collar World: Studies of the American Worker* (1964)

Francois Simiand, *Cours d'économie politique* (1929)

Louis Stark, *Labor and the New Deal* (1936)

Douglas Sutherland, *The English Gentleman* (1978)

R. H. Tawney, *Equality* (1931)

Tchao Tchung-han, *Etude sur la définition et la situation juridique du fonctionnaire dans le droit administratif français* (1942)

R. M. Titmuss, *Birth, Poverty and Wealth* (1943)

Alain Touraine, *La Société postindustrielle* (1969)

Alain Touraine, *Le Mouvement de mai* (1968)

Vercors, *Le Silence de la mer* (1942)

W. Watson, 'Social Mobility and Social Class in Industrial Communities', in M. Gluckman and E. Devons, eds., *Closed Systems and Open Minds* (1964)

Étienne Weill-Raynal, 'Les Classes sociales et les parties politiques en France', *La Revue socialiste*, no. 42 (December 1950)

Rupert Wilkinson, *The Prefects: British Leadership and the Public School Tradition* (1964)

Raymond Williams, *Culture and Society* (1958)

Edith Elmar Wood and Elizabeth Ogg, *The Homes the Public Builds* (1940)

Workers' Bookshop Ltd, *The Banned Broadcast of William Ferrie* (1934)

M. Wurmser, 'Le Milieu administratif en France et à l'étranger', in *Institut technique des administrations publiques* (no 69, 1951)

VIII *Select Filmography*

(Films were viewed at the National Film Archive, London, the Imperial War Museum, London, the Library of Congress, Washington, the State Historical Society of Wisconsin, Madison, the Pacific Film Archive, Berkeley, California, the Museum of Modern Art, New York, and privately in Paris by courtesy of Marc Ferro and Pierre Gauge, and in Paris and London by courtesy of the BBC.)

(a) Britain

Hindle Wakes (Victor Saville, 1931)
Black Diamonds (Charles Hanmer, 1931)
Letting in the Sunshine (Lupino Lane, 1933)
The Lucky Number (Anthony Asquith, 1933)
The Last Journey (Bernard Vorhaus, 1935)
No Limit (Monty Banks, 1935)
Broken Blossoms (Hans Brahm, 1936)
The Show Goes On (Basil Dean, 1937)
Spring Handicap (Herbert Brenan, 1937)
A Yank at Oxford (Jack Conway, 1938)
They Drive at Night (Arthur Wood, 1938)
The Stars Look Down (Carol Reed, 1939)
Shipyard Sally (Monty Banks, 1939)
The Proud Valley (Penn Tennyson, 1940)
Love on the Dole (John Baxter, 1941)
This England (David MacDonald, 1941)
Cottage to Let (Anthony Asquith, 1941)
Hard Steel (Norman Walker, 1941)
In Which We Serve (Noel Coward, 1942)
Let the People Sing (John Baxter, 1942)
San Demetrio London (Charles Frend, 1942)
Went the Day Well? (Peter Cavalcanti, 1942)
Millions Like Us (Launder and Gilliatt, 1943)
The Shipbuilders (John Baxter, 1943)

Waterloo Road (Sidney Gilliatt, 1945)
Fame is the Spur (Roy Boulting, 1947)
It Always Rains on Sunday (Robert Hamer, 1947)
Easy Money (Bernard Knowles, 1948)
The Guinea Pig (Boulting Brothers, 1948)
Here Come the Huggetts (Ken Annakin, 1948)
Flood Tide (Frederick Wilson, 1949)
Passport to Pimlico (Henry Cornelius, 1949)
The Cure for Love (Robert Donat, 1950)
The Blue Lamp (Basil Dearden, 1950)
Chance of a Lifetime (Bernard Miles, 1950)
The Man in the White Suit (Alexander MacKendrick, 1951)
Mr Denning Drives North (Anthony Kimmins, 1951)
His Excellency (Robert Hamer, 1952)
The Brave Don't Cry (Philip Leacock, 1952)
Street Corner (Muriel Box, 1953)
I'm All Right Jack (Boulting Brothers, 1959)
Room at the Top (Jack Clayton, 1959)
Saturday Night and Sunday Morning (Karl Riesz, 1960)
The Loneliness of the Long-distance Runner (Tony Richardson, 1962)
A Kind of Loving (John Schlesinger, 1962)
Nothing But the Best (Clive Donner, 1966)
The Family Way (Boulting Brothers, 1970)

(b) USA

Platinum Blonde (Frank Capra, 1931)
American Madness (Frank Capra, 1932)
I am a Fugitive from a Chain Gang (Mervyn le Roy, 1932)
Faithless (Harry Beaumont, 1932)
Heroes For Sale (William Wellman, 1933)
Black Fury (Michael Curtiz, 1934)
Broadway Bill (Frank Capra, 1934)
Mr Deeds Goes to Town (Frank Capra, 1936)
Black Legion (Archie Mayo, 1936)
You Can't Take It With You (Frank Capra, 1938)
Holiday (George Cukor, 1938)
Mr Smith goes to Washington (Frank Capra, 1939)
Philadelphia Story (George Cukor, 1940)
Grapes of Wrath (John Ford, 1940)
Sullivan's Travels (Preston Sturgess, 1941)
The Lady Eve (Preston Sturgess, 1941)
Now Voyager (Irving Rapper, 1942)
Mildred Pierce (Michael Curtiz, 1945)
The Best Years of Our Lives (William Wyler, 1946)
Crossfire (Edward Dmytrgk, 1947)
Gentlemen's Agreement (Elia Kazan, 1948)

Pinky (Elia Kazan, 1949)
Father of the Bride (Vincente Minelli, 1950)
Here Comes the Groom (Frank Capra, 1951)
Giant (George Stevens, 1956)
Days of Wine and Roses (Blake Edwards, 1962)
The Graduate (Mike Nichols, 1967)
A New Leaf (Elaine May, 1972)
Rocky (John Arildsen, 1976)
A Wedding (Robert Altman, 1978)
The Deer Hunter (Michael Cimino, 1978)
Blue Collar (Paul Schrader, 1978)

(c) France

Marius (Marcel Pagnol/Alexander Korda, 1931)
A Nous la Liberté (René Clair, 1931)
Fanny (Marcel Pagnol/Marc Allégret, 1932)
Joffroi (Marcel Pagnol, 1933)
L'Atalante (Jean Vigo, 1934)
Angèle (Marcel Pagnol, 1934)
Le Crime de Monsieur Lange (Jean Renoir, 1935)
César (Marcel Pagnol, 1936)
Les Bas Fonds (Jean Renoir, 1936)
Quai des Brumes (Marcel Carné, 1938)
La Femme du Boulanger (Marcel Pagnol, 1938)
La Bête Humaine (Jean Renoir, 1938)
Hotel du Nord (Marcel Carné, 1938)
La Règle du Jeu (Jean Renoir, 1939)
Le Jour se lève (Marcel Carné, 1939)
Lumière d'Été (Jean Gremillion, 1943)
Le Ciel est à Nous (Jean Gremillion, 1943)
Le Corbeau (G.-H. Clouzet, 1943)
La Bataille du Rail (René Clément, 1946)
Antoine et Antoinette (Jacques Becker, 1948)
Le Point du Jour (Louis Daquin, 1948)
Nous Sommes Tous des Assassins (André Cayatte, 1952)
Edouard et Caroline (Jacques Becker, 1952)
Les Amants (Louis Malle, 1958)
Le Beau Serge (Claude Chabrol, 1958)
A Bout de Souffle (Jean-Luc Godard, 1958)
Les Quatre Cent Coups (François Truffaut, 1959)
La Vérité (G.-H. Clouzot, 1960)
Le Bonheur (Agnes Varda, 1966)
La Femme Infidèle (Claude Chabrol, 1969)
Le Boucher (Claude Chabrol, 1970)
Le Souffle au Coeur (Louis Malle, 1971)
Coup pour Coup (Marin Karmitz, 1971)

Tout va Bien (Jean-Luc Godard, 1972)
Scènes d'en France (André Tchechiné, 1974)
L'Horloger de St Paul (Bertrand Tavernier, 1975)
Préparez Vos Mouchoirs (Bertrand Blier, 1977)

B SELECT LIST OF SECONDARY SOURCES

(The literature is far too extensive to itemize here; works containing useful bibliographies are asterisked.)

Paul Addison, *The Road to 1945* (1976)
John Ardagh, *The New France* (1970)
Roy Armes, *French Cinema since 1946* (2nd edition, 1970)
P. Arnoult *et al.*, *La France sous l'occupation* (1959)
Raymond Aron, *Progress and Disillusion: the Dialectic of Modern Society* (1968)
Raymond Aron, 'Social Structure and the Ruling Class', *British Journal of Sociology*, vol. 1 (1950)
Raymond Aron, *Main Currents in Sociological Thought*, 2 vols. (1968)
A. B. Atkinson, *The Economics of Inequality* (1975)
Louis Aubert *et al.*, *André Tardieu* (1957)
Jerold S. Auerbach, 'Southern Tenant Farmers: Socialist Critics of the New Deal', *Labor History*, vol. 7 (1966)
Philip Bagwell, *The Railwaymen* (1963)
E. Digby Baltzell, *Philadelphia Gentlemen: the Making of a National Upper Class* (1958)
E. Digby Baltzell, *The Protestant Establishment* (1964)
Charles Barr, *Ealing Studios* (1977)
Jean Baumier, *Les grandes Affaires français: des 200 familles aux 200 managers* (1967)
Colin Bell, *Middle-class Families* (1968)
R. Bendix and S. M. Lipset, eds., *Class, Status and Power* (2nd edition, 1966)
*Leslie Benson, *Proletarians and Parties: Five Essays on Social Class* (1978)
S. Berger, *Peasants against Politics* (1972)
Andrew Bergman, *We're in the Money: Depression America in the Movies* (1972)
Daniel Bertaux, 'L'Heredité sociale en France', *Economie et Statistique* (February, 1970)
Stephen Birmingham, *The Right People: a portrait of the American Social Establishment* (1966)
Stephen Birmingham, *Certain People: America's Black Elite* (1977)
Pierre Birnbaum *et al.*, *La Classe dirigeante française* (1978)
T. J. H. Bishop and R. Wilkinson, *Winchester and the Public School Elite* (1967)

Fay M. Blake, *The Strike in the American Novel* (1972)

Nelson M. Blake, *Novelist's America: Fiction as History, 1910–1940* (1969)

Peter M. Blau, 'Parameters of Social Structure', *American Sociological Review*, vol. 39 (1974)

J. Blondel, *Contemporary France: Politics, Society and Institutions* (1974)

Denise Bombardier, *La Voix de France: les français et leur télévision vus par un observateur étranger* (1975)

Elizabeth Bott, *Family and Social Network* (1957)

T. B. Bottomore, *Classes in Modern Society* (1966)

T. B. Bottomore, 'La Mobilité sociale dans la haute administration française', *Cahiers Internationales de Sociologié*, vol. 13 (1952)

F. Bouriez-Gregg, *Les Classes sociales aux États Unis*, 2 vols. (1954)

Richard Bourne, 'The Snakes and Ladders of the British Class System', *New Society* (8 February 1979).

M. Bouvier-Ajam and G. Mury, *Les Classes sociales en France*, 2 vols. (1963)

T. Brennan, 'The Working Class in the British Social Structure', *Transactions of the 3rd World Congress of Sociology* (1956)

Asa Briggs, 'The Language of Class in the Early Nineteenth Century', in Asa Briggs and John Saville, eds., *Essays in Labour History* (1960)

Asa Briggs, *History of Broadcasting in Great Britain*, 4 vols. (1968–79)

Charles William Brooks, 'Jean Renoir's *The Rules of the Game*', *French Historical Studies*, vol. VII (1972)

Nathaniel Burt, *The Perennial Philadelphians* (1963)

Nathaniel Burt, *First Families: the Making of the American Aristocracy* (1970)

Lord Butler, ed., *The Conservatives* (1977)

David Butler and J. Kavanagh, *The British General Election of October 1974* (1975)

Cahiers de la Fondation Nationale des Sciences Politiques, *Leon Blum: Chef de gouvernement* (1967)

Angus Calder, *The People's War* (1970)

David Caute, *Communism and the French Intellectuals* (1964)

R. Cayrol, J.-C. Parodi and C. Ysmal, *Le Député français* (1973)

J. Charlot, 'Les Élites politiques en France de la IIIᵉ à la Vᵉ république', *Archives Européennes de sociologie*, vol. XIV (1973)

M. Chavardes, *Un Ministre educateur: Jean Zay* (1960)

P. Chevallier, *L'Enseignement français de la revolution à nos jours*, 2 vols (1968)

Ely Chinoy, *Automobile Workers and the American Dream* (1968)

P.-H. Chombart de Lauvre, *La Vie quotidienne des familles ouvrières* (1956)

Allan Churchill, *The Upper Crust* (1970)

Peter Clarke, 'Electoral Sociology of Modern Britain', *History*, vol. 57 (1972)

Richard P. Coleman and Lee Rainwater, *Social Standing in America: New Dimensions of Class* (1978)

Michel Collinet, *L'Ouvrier français* (1951)

P. Collison and J. N. Mogey, 'Residence and Social Class in Oxford', *American Journal of Sociology*, vol. 64 (1959)

Colin Crouch, *Class Conflict and the Industrial Relations Crisis* (1977)

Colin Crouch and Alessandro Pizzorno, eds., *The Resurgence of Class Conflict in Western Europe since 1968* (1978)

M. Crozier, *The World of the Office Worker* (1971)

*Howard H. Davis, *Beyond Class Images* (1979)

Andy Dawson, 'History and Ideology: Fifty Years of "Job Consciousness" ', *Literature and History*, no. 8 (1978)

John P. Diggins, *The American Left in the Twentieth Century* (1973)

M. Dogan, *L'Origine sociale de personnel parlementaire français* (1965)

G. William Domhoff, *Who Rules America?* (1967)

G. William Domhoff, *The Higher Circles: The Governing Class in America* (1970)

*Henri Dubief, *Le Déclin de la III*ᵉ *république* (1976)

Georges Dupeux, *Le Front populaire et les élections de 1936* (1959)

Raymond Durgnat, *The Mirror for England: British Movies from Austerity to Affluence* (1970)

*Maurice Duverger, *Parties politiques et classes sociales en France* (1955)

Glen H. Elder Jr, 'Appearance and Education in Marriage Mobility', *American Sociological Review*, vol. 34 (1969)

John Ellis, 'Made in Ealing', *Screen*, vol. 16 (1975)

Charlotte Erickson, *British Industrialists: Steel and Hosiery 1850–1950* (1959)

P. Sargent Florence, *Ownership, Control and Success of Large Companies* (1961)

J. E. Floud, A. H. Halsey and F. M. Martin, *Social Class and Educational Opportunity* (1957)

Tom Forester, *The Labour Party and the Working Class* (1976)

Edward F. Frazier, *Black Bourgeoisie* (1957)

Lawrence M. Friedman, *Government and Slum Housing* (1968)

Jonathan Gathorne-Hardy, *The Rise and Fall of the British Nanny* (1972)

Jonathan Gathorne-Hardy, *The Public School Phenomenon* (1977)

Anthony Giddens, *The Class Structure of the Advanced Societies* (1973)

Anthony Giddens, 'Elites in the British Class Structure', in P. Stanworth and A. Giddens, eds., *Elites and Power in British Society* (1974)

Eli Ginzberg, *The Middle-class Negro in the White Man's World* (1967)

Alain Girard, *Le Réussite sociale en France* (1961)

R. Girod, *Mobilité sociale* (1971)

D. V. Glass, ed., *Social Mobility in Britain* (1954)

Norval D. Glenn, Adreain A. Ross and Judy Corder Tully, 'Patterns of Intergenerational Mobility through Marriage', *American Sociological Review*, vol. 39 (1974)

W. Goldschmidt, 'Social Class in America: a critical review', *American Anthropologist*, vol. 52 (1950)

J. H. Goldthorpe, D. Lockwood, F. Bechhofer and J. Platt, *The Affluent Worker*, 3 vols (1968–9)

J. H. Goldthorpe, *Social Mobility and Class Structure in Modern Britain* (1980)

Milton M. Gordon, *Social Class in American Sociology* (1958)

Martin Green, *Children of the Sun* (1977)

Pierre Guiral and Emile Témine, *La Societe française, 1914–1970, à travers la littérature* (1972)

W. L. Gutsman, *The British Political Élite* (1968)

William Haber, ed., *Labor in a Changing America* (1966)

A. H. Halsey, *Change in British Society* (1978)

A. H. Halsey, ed., *Trends in British Society since 1900* (1972)

A. H. Halsey, *Origins and Destinations* (1980)

Richard Hamilton, *Affluence and the French Worker in the Fourth Republic* (1967)

Richard Hamilton, *Class and Politics in the United States* (1972)

Molly Haskell, *From Reverence to Rape: the Treatment of Women in the Movies* (1974)

Henri Hatzfeld, *Du Paupérisme à la securité sociale, 1850–1940* (1971)

Godfrey Hodgson, *In Our Time: America from World War II to Nixon* (1976)

Stanley Hoffman, *France: Change and Tradition* (1963)

Stanley Hoffman, 'The Effects of World War II on French Society and Politics', *French Historical Studies*, vol. II (1961)

John D. Hogan and Francis A. J. Ianni, *American Social Legislation* (1956)

Serge Honoré, *Adaptation scolaire et classes sociales* (1968)

Irving Howe, ed., *The World of the Blue-collar Worker* (1972)

*Charles E. Hurst, 'Race, Class and Consciousness', *American Sociological Review*, vol. 37 (1972)

H. Montgomery Hyde, *Baldwin* (1973)

John N. Ingham, *The Iron Barons: a Social Analysis of the American Urban Elite* (1978)

Alan Jackson, *Semi-Detached London: Suburban Development, Life and Transport, 1900–1939* (1973)

Brian Jackson and Denis Marsden, *Education and the Working Class* (1966)

Brian Jackson, *Working-class Community*

Jean-Noel Jeanneney, *Francois de Wendel en république: l'argent et le pouvoir 1914–1940* (1975)

Christopher Jencks, *Inequality* (1972)

R. W. Johnson, 'The British Political Elite, 1955–1972', *Archives Européennes de Sociologie*, vol. XIV (1973)

Z. A. Jordan, ed., *Karl Marx: Economy, Class and Social Revolution* (1971)

Joseph A. Kahl, *Social Class in America* (1957)

Michael B. Katz, *Class, Bureaucracy and Schools: the Illusion of Educational Change in America* (1971) . .

Doris Kearns, *Lyndon Johnson and the American Dream* (1976)

H. R. Kedward, *Resistance in Vichy France* (1978)

R. K. Kelsall, *Higher Civil Servants in Britain* (1955)

Gabriel Kolko, *Wealth and Power in America* (1962)

Gabriel Kolko, *Main Currents in American History* (1976)

Laurence Lafore, *Philadelphia: the Unexpected City* (1966)

P.-O. Lapie, *Herriot* (1967)

Charles P. Larrowe, *Life of Harry Bridges* (1955)

Thomas E. Lasswell, *Class and Stratum: an Introduction to Concepts and Research* (1967)

P. F. Lazarsfeld, Bernard Berelson and Hazel Gaudet, *The People's Choice* (1944)

Georges Lefranc, *Histoire du front populaire* (1965)

Georges Lefranc, *Le Mouvement syndicale sous la troisième republique* (1967)

*Gerhard Lenski, *Power and Privilege: a Theory of Social Stratification* (1966)

Olgierd Lewandowski, 'Differenciation et mécanismes d'intégration de la classe dirigeante: l'image sociale de l'élite d'apres le *Who's Who in France*', *Economie et Statistique* (1970)

Edward G. Lewis, 'Social Backgrounds of French Ministers, 1944–67', *Western Political Quarterly*, vol. 23 (1970)

R. Lewis and R. Stewart, *The Boss: the Life and Times of the British Business Manager* (1958)

H. F. Lydall and D. G. Tipping, 'The Distribution of Personal Wealth in Britain', *Bulletin of Oxford University Institute of Statistics*, vol. 33 (1965)

Kevin McCann, *America's Man of Destiny* (1952)

Robert Mackenzie and J. Silver, *Angels in Marble* (1968)

Ross McKibbin, 'Working-Class Gambling in Britain 1880–1939), *Past and Present*, no. 76 (1977)

A. Allan MacLaren, *Social Class in Scotland: Past and Present* (1976)

*Jane Marceau, *Class and Status in France: Change and Social Immobility 1945–1975* (1977)

T. H. Marshall, *Citizenship and Social Class* (1950)

Arthur Marwick, *The Home Front: the British and the Second World War* (1976)

Arthur Marwick, *War and Social Change in the Twentieth Century* (1974)

Timothy May, 'A Government of Meritocrats', *New Society* (12 May 1977)

Kurt Mayer, 'Recent Changes in the Class Structure of the United States', *Transactions of the 3rd World Congress of Sociology* (1956)

A. Allan MacLaren, *Social Class in Scotland: Past and Present* (1976)

Colin Mellors, *The British M.P.* (1978)

Henri Mendras, *Sociologie de la campagne française* (1965)

Henri Michel, *Les Courants de pensée de la résistance* (1962)

Henri Michel and Boris Mirkine-Guetzovitch, *Les Ideés politiques et sociales de la résistance* (1954)

William Miller, 'American Historians and the Business Elite', *Journal of Economic History*, vol. 9 (1949)

R. N. Morris and J. Mogey, *The Sociology of Housing* (1965)

Leonard Mosley, *Dulles: a Biography of Eleanor, Allen and John Foster Dulles and their Family Network* (1977)

Roland Mousnier, 'Le Concept de classe sociale et l'histoire', *Histoire Sociale*, vol. 3 (1960)

William A. Muraskin, *Middle-class Blacks in a White Society* (1975)

Howard Newby, *The Deferential Worker* (1977)

Howard Newby, Colin Bell, David Rose and Peter Saunders, *Property, Paternalism and Power: Class and Control in Rural England* (1978)

Mabel Newcomer, *The Big Business Executive* (1955)

Eric Nordlinger, *The Working-class Tories* (1967)

John E. O'Connor and Martin A. Jackson, eds., *American History/ American Film: Interpreting the Hollywood Image* (1979)

S. Ossowski, *Class Structure in the Social Consciousness* (1963)

Charles H. Page, *Class and American Sociology: from Ward to Ross* (1940)

Frank Parkin, ed., *The Social Analysis of Class Structure* (1974)

M. Parodi, *L'Economic et la société française de 1945 à 1970* (1972)

Talcott Parsons, 'Social Classes and Class Conflict in the Light of recent Sociological Theory', *Essays in Sociological Theory* (revised edition, 1964)

Marguerite Perrot, *Le Mode de vie des familles bourgeoises 1873–1953* (1961)

Ben Pimlott, *Labour and the Left in the 1930s* (1976)

Richard Polenberg, *War and Society: the United States 1941–1945* (1972)

J.-C. Poulain, *L'Église et la classe ouvrière* (1960)

René Prédal, *La Société française (1914–1945) à travers le Cinéma* (1972)

H. Edward Ransford, 'Blue Collar Anger: Reactions to Student and Black Protest', *American Sociological Review*, vol. 37 (June 1972)

Alfred B. Rawlins Jr, 'Franklin Roosevelt's Introduction to Labor', *Labor History*, vol. 3 (1962)

John Raynor, *The Middle Class* (1969)

Ivan Reid, *Social Class Differences in Britain* (1977)

T. Rémond and J. Bourdin, eds., *La France et les français en 1938–1939* (1978)

John Rex, 'Capitalism, Elites and the Ruling Class', in P. Stanworth and A. Giddens, eds., *Elites and Power in British Society* (1974)

John Rex, *Approaches to Sociology* (1974)

F. Ridley and J. Blondel, *Public Administration in France* (1964)

Kenneth Robinson, 'Selection and the Social Background of the Administrative Class', *Public Administration* (Winter, 1955)

Natalie Rogoff, 'Social Stratification in France and in the United States', *American Journal of Sociology*, vol. 58 (1953)

Andrew Roth, *Heath and the Heathmen* (1972)

Guy Routh, *Occupation and Pay in Britain, 1906–1960* (1965)

Richard Rovere, *Senator Joe McCarthy* (1960)

J. A. Roy, *Histoire du Jockey Club de Paris* (1958)

W. D. Rubinstein, 'Wealth, Elites, and the Class Structure of Modern Britain', *Past and Present*, no. 76 (1977)

W. G. Runciman, *Social Science and Political Theory* (1960)

Georges Sadoul, *Le Cinéma français 1890–1962* (1962)

Gerhart E. Saenger, 'Social Status and Political Behavior', *American Journal of Sociology*, vol. 51 (1945)

Anthony Sampson, *Anatomy of Britain Today* (1965)

A. Sauvy, *Histoire economique de la France entre les deux guerres* (1965–67)

Charles I. Schottland, *Social Security Programs in the United States* (2nd edition, 1970)

Melvin Seeman, 'The Signals of '68: Alienation in Pre-Crisis France', *American Sociological Review*, vol. 37 (June 1972)

André Siegfried, ed., *Aspects de la société française* (1954)

Charles Silberman, *Criminal Violence, Criminal Justice* (1978)

M. A. Simpson and T. H. Lloyd, eds., *Middle-class Housing in Britain* (1977)

Robert Sklar, *Movie-Made America* (1975)

J. D. Smith and S. D. Franklin, 'The Concentration of Personal Wealth, 1922–1969', *American Economic Review, Papers and Proceedings*, vol. 64 (1974)

Pierre Sorlin, *La Societé française 1914–1968* (1971)

Philip Stanworth and A. Giddens, eds., *Elites and Power in British Society* (1974)

John Stevenson and Chris Cook, *The Slump: Society and Politics in the 1930s* (1978)

John Stevenson, *Social Conditions in Britain between the Wars* (1977)

William Stott, *Documentary Expression and Thirties America* (1973)

Elizabeth Strebel, 'French Social Cinema and the Popular Front', *Journal of Contemporary History*, vol. 12 (1977)

Ezra N. Suleiman, *Elites in French Society* (1978)

A. J. P. Taylor, *Beaverbrook* (1972)

*A. J. P. Taylor, *English History, 1914–1945* (1965)

Stephan Thernstrom, *The Other Bostonians* (1973)

Hugh Thomas, *John Strachey* (1973)

George B. Tindal, *The Emergence of the New South 1913–1945* (1967)

Richard Titmuss, *Income Distribution and Social Change* (1962)

J. Urry and J. Wakeford, eds., *Power in British Society* (1973)

Bernard Waites, 'The Language and Imagery of "Class" in Early Twentieth-Century England (c. 1900–1925)', *Literature and History*, no. 4 (1976)

G. Walter, *La Vie à Paris sous l'occupation* (1960)

G. Walter, *Histoire du paysan français* (1964)

W. Lloyd Warner and James Ableggan, *Big Business Leaders in America* (1963)

W. Lloyd Warner, *Social Class in America: the Evaluation of Status* (1960)

Donald Watt, *Personalities and Policies* (1965)

Dorothy Wedderburn, ed., *Poverty, Inequality and Class Structure* (1974)

Aubrey Weinberg and Frank Lyons, 'Class Theory and Practice', *British Journal of Sociology*, vol. 23 (1972)

John Westergaard and Henrietta Resler, *Class in a Capitalist Society: a Study of Contemporary Britain* (1975)

*John Westergaard, Anne Weyman and Paul Wiles, *Modern British Society: A Bibliography* (1974)

R. J. Whalen, *The Founding Father: the Story of Joseph P. Kennedy* (1965)

Dann F. White and Timothy J. Crimmins, 'Urban Structure, Atlanta', *Journal of Urban History* (February 1976)

William S. White, *The Responsibles* (1972)

Alfred Willener, *Images de la societé et classes sociales* (1957)

Philip M. Williams, *Crisis and Compromise: Politics in the Fourth Republic* (1964)

Louis Winnick, *American Housing and its Use: the Demand for Shelter Space* (1957)

Michael Wood, *America in the Movies* (1975)

Maurice Zeitlin, eds., *American Society, Inc.* (1970)

Maurice Zeitlin, 'Corporate Ownership and Control: the large Corporation and the Capitalist Class', *American Journal of Sociology*, vol. 79 (1974)

Theodore Zeldin, *France 1848–1945*, vol. 2 (1977)

R. Zick, 'Do American Women Marry Up?' *American Sociological Review*, vol. 33 (1968)

Fernand Zweig, *The Worker in an Affluent Society* (1961)

INDEX

Aaronovitch, S. 288n
accent, incidence of 200, 258, 355
Acheson, Dean 99–101, 126n, 191, 275
Action socialiste chez les ruraux, L' (Peters) 141n
Addison, Paul 12, 23n
Affluent Worker, The (Goldthorpe *et al*) 338–9n, 358n
Afro-American . . ., The (Wynn) 229n
Alain – *see* Charpentier
Allégret, Marc 167
All goes Well 335
Altmeyer, A. J. 75, 109
America – *see* United States
American Anthropologist 264, 288n
American Federationist 43n
American Journal of Sociology 209n, 288n, 337n
American Madness 148
American Revolution 16, 17
American Sociological Review 23n, 358n
American Workers' Fact Book 288n
American Man of Destiny (McCann) 289n
Amulree, Lord 70
Amy Vanderbilt . . . Etiquette (Baldridge) 310
Anderson, John 221
André Tardieu (Lowry *et al*) 208n
Angèle 167
Antoine et Antoinette 283
Arbois, Janick 339n
Archibald, Catherine 245, 254n
Archives Européennes . . . 208n, 303n, 357n, 358n
aristocracy/nobility 15, 30, 47, 98, 137, 361
Armes, Roy 303n
Arnoult, P. 254n
Aron, Raymond 49, 57n, 308, 337n
Art of the Possible, The (Butler) 97n

Aspects de la société française (Siegfried *et al*) 142n
Attlee, Clement 204, 219, 229, 230n
Auerbach, J. S. 43n
Austin, Sir Herbert 160

Babcock, Mrs Wayne 250
Bakke, E. Wight 52, 53, 57n, 110–112, 127n
Baldridge, Letitia 310
Baldwin (Hyde) 97n
Baldwin, Stanley 39, 92, 99, 173
Ballet de ma vie, Le (Mérode) 42n
Balteau, 208n
Baltzell, E. Digby 23n, 98, 99, 126n, 207n, 208n, 306
Banks, Lynne Reid 319
Banned Broadcast of W. Ferrie 171n
Barber, Anthony 344
Barucq, C. 358n
Barrie, Philip 145
Barrière et le niveau, La (Goblot) 141n
Bataille du Rail, La 241
Batstone, Eric 338n
Bauer, Professor Peter 320, 338n
Baumier, Jean 141n
Baxter, John 170, 227
Beales, H. L. 80, 83, 84, 87, 96n, 97n
Beaumont, Harry 147
Beau Serge, Le 293
Bechhofer, J. 324, 326, 338n, 339n, 358n
Becker, Jacques 283
Bell, Colin 322, 338n, 349, 358n
Bell, Daniel 303n
Bellaiche, M. 357n
Bendix, R. 23n
Benn, Anthony Wedgwood 343
Benson, Leslie 23n
Berelson, Bernard 206
Bergman, Andrew 150–1, 156n
Berle, A. A., Jnr 191
Bertaux, Daniel 307, 337n

Best Years of Our Lives 279–80
Bettelheim, Charles 209n, 285, 289n
Between You and Me (Pickles) 230n
Bevan, Aneurin 269, 349
Beveridge, Sir William 68, 89, 97n
Bevin, Ernest 70, 217, 228, 229, 230n
Beyl, Jean 77n
Beynon, Huw 339n
Beyond the Melting Pot 291, 292, 306
Bidault, Georges 241
Biddle, Francis 191
Big Business Executive, The (New-comer) 209n
Bingham, A. M. 52, 57n
Bingley, Lord 176
Biography of Harry Bridges (Lar-row) 289n
Birnbaum, Pierre 207n, 304n, 347, 358n
Birth, Poverty and Wealth (Titmuss) 209n
Bishop, T. J. H. 208n
Black Fury 150–1, 155
Black Legion 152, 155
Blake, F. M. 156n
Blake, George 230n
Blau, Peter M. 348, 358n
Blow for Blow 335
Blue Collar Community (Kornblum) 358n
Blue Collar World . . . (Shostack & Gomberg) 303n
Blum, Léon 40, 168. 187, 241
Bombardier, Denise 339n
Bond, B. 23n
Bonnie and Clyde 297
Boothby, Robert 93, 97n
Bott, Elizabeth 289n
Boucher, Le 336
Bourdin, J. 141n, 142n
bourgeoisie – see also under France – 13, 15–16, 52
Bouriez-Gregg, Françoise 260–2, 287n
Bout de Soufflé, A 293
Bowden, R. D. 98
Bowley, A. L. 54, 58n

Boyd-Orr, John 176
Bragg, Melvyn 86, 97n, 199, 209n, 297
Brandeis, Justice Louis 191
Brasillach, Robert 141n
Brave Don't Cry, The 282
Bridges, Henry 272–3
Bridson, D. G. 171n
Briggs, Asa 16, 23n, 171n
Brighouse, Harold 169
Brinton-Lee, Diana 95, 96, 97n, 229, 230n
Britain, agricultural workers in 33; audience research 164–5; aristo-cracy in 30, 95, 137, 178, 257, 279; BBC and class 80, 157–66, 171n, 226, 227–8, 230n; Beveridge Report 217, 220–1; Board of Trade 71, 77n, 176; British Medi-cal Association 89–90, 97n; Cen-tral Office of Information 319, 341; class, and films 162–4, 169–70, 198, 217, 227, 294–5; class, and power in 173–83, 215, 283, 342–5, 356–7; class, and war 213–30, 253; class im-ages in 54–5, 79–97, 157–70, 220, 228, 275–9, 283, 285–6, 318–29; class structure in 62f, 157–70, 206–7, 257–8, 270, 318–29; Con-servative Party 39, 85, 91, 93–4, 173, 203–4, 225, 283, 344–5, 351, 354; council houses 65–7, 197, 323; education in 32, 64, 71, 136, 199, 221, 224–7, 258, 267, 285, 286–7, 300–1; Education, Board of 71, 158, 177; Fleming Report 227; General Strike 84, 174; Great Reform Act 1832 229; Health, Ministry of 67, 70, 177; holidays with pay 70; House of Lords 258; housing 64–7, 70, 196–7, 209n; Housing Acts 64, 65, 269; immigrants in 291, 328, 351; income levels 340–2; indus-trial relations in 36, 38, 220; infant mortality in 62, 199; Lab-our, Ministry of 68, 77n, 220; Labour Party (Socialist) 39, 71, 84, 85, 173, 178, 180, 183, 203–4, 205, 219, 221, 222, 224–5, 278,

283, 300, 319–20, 343, 351; language of class in 55, 279; legislation in 63–5, 67–9, 71, 88, 180, 183, 224, 300; Liberal Party 87, 173, 203; means tests in 84, 183; medical care 69, 89–90, 224; 'meritocracy' 342–3; middle classes in 55, 67, 85–90, 156, 165–6, 176, 178, 181, 182, 197, 199, 204, 209n, 229, 257–8, 275–7, 279, 322, 342–3, 351, 361; national census in 62–3, 268; National Front 328; National Government 173, 175; National Health Service 221, 224, 269; National Insurance 67, 69, 183, 224, 268; National Insurance, Ministry of 269; parliaments, class character of 12, 173–8, 219, 342–5; pensions 69, 342; politics and class 91, 92, 94–5, 162, 173–8, 201, 203–5, 283, 342–5, 347, 351; provident associations 89; public schools in 225–7, 258, 267, 342–3; slum clearance 65–6, 277; social security in 68–70, 205, 220–1; television 297, 329; Trade Union Acts in 88; Trade Union Congress 71, 87, 205, 222, 347; trade unions in 33, 37, 55, 71, 81, 83, 85, 87, 88, 160, 182, 258, 302; universities and class 258–9, 278, 283, 295, 342–3; upper classes 55, 56, 90–6, 136, 157–9, 162, 166, 170, 173–81, 183, 197, 204, 219, 222, 225–6, 228, 295, 342–3, 356; Uthwatt Report 228; working classes in 55, 56, 63f, 70–1, 79–85, 86, 92, 160–4, 166, 169–70, 175, 178, 182–3, 197, 199, 203–5, 216–19, 222, 226, 228, 258, 287, 294–7, 324–5, 355–6; workmen's compensation 64, 67
Britain – an Official Handbook 319, 338n, 341, 357n
Britain in 1980 (Hudson Report) 358n
Britain in . . . Total War (Marwick) 229n
British Film Catalogue, The (Gifford) 171n
British General Election (Butler & Kavanagh) 358n
British Industrialists (Erickson) 208n
British Iron and Steel Federation 181
British Journal of Sociology 338n
British M.P., The (Mellors) 357n
British Political Elite, The (Guttsman) 208n, 289n
Broadway Bill 147–8
Brockway, Fenner 101
Broken Blossoms 169
Brooks, Charles William 168, 171n
Brown, George 303n
Brown, Ernest 177
Bruhat, Jean 142n
Bryant, Arthur 85, 91, 97n
Buchanan, J. P. 75
Burdon, Albert 169
'burgesses' 309
Butler, David 320, 338n, 351, 358n
Butler, Lord 92, 97n, 223, 225

California Farmer 289n
Callaghan, James 342
capitalism 34, 37–8, 138, 236, 240, 307, 324
capitalists 13, 45, 48, 52, 53, 89, 235, 324
Capra, Frank 143–4, 147, 148, 150, 280
Carné, Marcel 167
Carr, Lowell J. 254n
Carr-Saunders, A. M. 54, 57n, 88, 97n, 157, 198, 266, 288n
Carter, Pres. Jimmy 117, 346, 351
Case Studies of the Unemployed . . . 57n
Cash, Tony 297
Centers, Richard 264, 270, 288n, 337n
Cayrol, R. 358n
César 167
Chabrol, Claude 293
Chamberlain, Neville 94, 99, 173–4, 179
Chance of a Lifetime, The 281
Change in British Society (Halsey) 23n
Chapter of Accidents (Rees) 97n

Charlot, Jean 208n, 358n
Charpentier, Emile (Alain) 134, 141n
Chautemps, Claude 184
Chetham-Strode, Warren 281
Children of the Sun (Green) 97n
Christmas, H. M. 289n
Churchill, Sir Winston 180, 217, 221, 224
Ciel est à nous, Le 240
Cinéma français, Le (Sadoul) 303n
Citizens Without Work (Bakke) 52, 57n, 127n
civil servants 31, 74, 102, 136, 219, 234, 257, 357
civil service, and class 178–9, 188, 204; incomes in 341
Clarke, P. 18, 23n
Class (Mabey ed.) 338n
Class and Class Conflict (Dahrendorf) 288n
class, and beauty 95; and culture 143f, 193, 200, 290–304, 356; and demography 28; and films 22, 143–55, 166–71, 196, 198, 217, 248, 279–83, 292–9, 318, 335–6; and history 17, 21, 22, 27–43, 143, 204–5, 300–3, 356–7, 361, 363; and Hollywood image 143–56, 196, 279–80, 297–8, 318; and housing (*see also* under countries) 194–5; and income 54–5, 64, 66, 67, 68, 72, 89, 110–22, 162, 193–4, 237–8, 247, 258, 324, 333, 340–58; and lifestyles 67, 70–1, 74, 194, 196, 198–9, 213, 218, 238, 242–3, 245–6, 259, 267, 275–7, 298–9, 302, 348–9, 356; and moral standards 225–6, 238; and politics 91–2, 94–5, 99–103, 162, 173–8, 184–90, 201–4, 219, 239, 241, 256, 263, 283–4, 343–8, 350–1; and religion 203; and social context 17, 19, 48, 50, 82–3, 165, 167–9, 194, 202, 245, 275–6, 286, 302; and status 16, 18, 50, 59–60, 67, 69, 84, 115, 167, 203, 213, 240, 264–5, 305, 307–9, 314, 360
Class and Status in France (Marceau) 357n

Class and Stratum . . . (Lasswell) 337n
class, and the Second World War 214–55
class, changing realities of 194, 213f, 250, 259, 277, 286, 305–39, 362; definitions of 14, 16, 18–19, 45, 59, 61, 63–9, 73–4, 76, 85–7, 159, 165–6, 172, 258, 305; determinants of 324–6; evidential material 18, 21, 22, 44f, 172, 194, 198, 363; existence of 12, 14, 17, 21, 49, 54, 79, 91, 113, 157, 172, 195, 215, 271, 306, 325; geography of 27, 194–8, 201–2, 242, 348; images of (*see also* under countries) 13, 14, 21–2, 34, 44–171, 172, 256–87, 268–89, 305–39, 359; importance of 12, 21, 206–7; inequalities of 12–13, 14, 16, 18–19, 82–3, 193–4, 197–200, 216, 228, 246, 298, 300, 308, 312, 340–58, 359; mobility of 151, 213, 215, 241, 244, 260, 261, 267, 300, 309, 320, 340–1, 343–4, 345, 346–7, 362; realities of 172–209, 216, 217, 237, 256–87, 263, 283–7, 305–39; significance of 352–8.
Class Conflict . . . (Crouch) 23n
class consciousness/awareness 19, 29, 50, 53, 79–80, 83, 84, 90–1, 110, 112, 130, 132, 140, 150–2, 205–6, 233, 245–6, 250, 253, 259, 274, 322, 332, 351, 355; distinctions of 11, 12, 18, 27, 51–2, 55, 59f, 68–9, 70, 82–3, 86–7, 91, 94, 96, 112–14, 143–56, 159, 165, 167, 168, 179, 182, 193–4, 198–9, 206–7, 240, 243, 245–6, 261, 269, 272, 274, 287, 310–12, 320, 340, 342, 353, 359; distinctions, diminution of 213, 215, 217, 252, 259, 268, 362
Class in a Capitalist Society (Westergaard & Resler) 208n
Class Inequality . . . (Parkin) 337n
Class on the Brain . . . (Bauer) 320, 338n
Class, Race and Labor (Leggatt) 338n

class relationships 204–5, 213–20, 222–3, 242, 246, 281, 287, 294, 302, 328, 352, 356; solidarity 85, 245, 248, 253
Class, Status and Power (Bendix & Lipset, eds) 23n
Class Structure . . . (Ossowski) 23n
Class Structure of the Advanced Societies, The (Giddens) 23n, 307, 337n
class struggle 53, 83, 105, 111, 116, 138, 204, 213, 253, 330, 351–4
Classe dirigeante . . . La (Birnbaum) 208n, 304n
classes, disintegration of 309, 362; division of 267–8, 314; polarization of 19, 140, 213, 268, 280, 301, 330, 362
Classes sociales, Les (Halbwachs) 141n
Classes sociales . . . (Lhomme) 254n
class unity 215, 218, 219–20, 231–2, 233–4, 235–6, 249, 272, 285, 308, 327–8, 355
Clay, Harold 225
Clement, René 241
Clerc, H. 49, 57n
clergy 52, 108
Clouzet, G.-H. 240
Coal-Miner (Tomlinson) 85, 91–2, 96n, 97n
Coates, K. 289n
Cobb, Jonathan 306–7, 337n, 338n
Cohen, Wilbur T. 251
Coleman, Professor R. P. 309, 312, 313, 316, 337n, 338n, 360
collective bargaining 36, 52, 88, 247, 302
Collinet, Michel 263, 288n
Collins, Sir Godfrey 176
Complete Law of Housing (Hill) 77n
Conflict after Class (Dahrendorf) 303n
Conservatives, The (Lord Butler, ed.) 208n
Cook, Christopher 209n
Corbeau, Le 240
Corey, L. 52, 57n
Coronation Street 297
Cosens, Monica 218, 230n
cost of living 216

Courants de pensée, Les (Michel) 254n
Cour d'économie politique (Simiand) 57n
Crapouillot 134–5, 136, 141n, 188–9, 208n
Criminal Violence (Silbermann) 354, 358n
Crimmins, T. J. 127n
Cripps, Sir Stafford 93–4, 97n, 204, 222–4
Crisis and Compromise (Williams) 254n
Crisis of the Middle Class, The (Corey) 52, 57n
Cronin, A. J. 170
Crookshank, Capt. H. 93, 97n, 221
Crosland, Anthony 267, 288n
Cross Fire 279–80
Crossman, Richard H. S. 199, 209n, 322, 338n
Crouch, Colin 23n
Crozier, Michel 268, 288n
Cukor, George 145
'cultural revolution' 21, 213, 290–304
Culture and Society (Williams) 23n
Cunliffe-Lister, Sir Philip 175–6
Curtiz, Michael 150

Dahrendorf, Ralf 268, 288n, 291, 303n
Daladier, Édouard 134, 186, 189
Dalloz 76n, 77n, 288n
Dalton, Hugh 93, 97n, 180, 204, 219, 278
Dandelot, Marc 357n
Daquin, Louis 282, 289n
Davis, Alison 51, 57n, 274, 289n
Dawson, Andy 288
Days of Wine and Roses 297
Déclin de la République, Le (Dubief) 208n
Deep South (Davis *et al*) 51, 57n
Delcourt, Jacques 303n
Deputé français, Le (Cayrol *et al*) 358n
Desailly, Jean 282
Development of the Social Security Act . . . (Witte) 77n, 126n
Deverson, Jane 323, 338n, 358n

Diaries of a Cabinet Minister (Crossman) 199, 209n, 322, 338n
Dictionary of National Biography 174, 175, 179, 208n
Dictionary of the French Nobility 330
Dictionnaire de biographie française 208n
Dictionnaire des parlementaires français (Jolly) 208n
Dilkes, David 208n
doctors 108, 182, 193, 262, 269
Dogan, Professor M. 183, 208n
Dornhoff, Professor W. 98, 126n, 190, 207n, 208n, 306
Doumergue, Gaston 186
Dubief, Henri 208n, 209n
Duff Cooper, A. 91, 96, 97n
Dulles, Allen 284
Dulles, John Foster 284
Du paupérisme à la sécurité sociale (Hatzfeld) 77n
Dupeux, Georges 201–2, 205, 209n
Durand, Paul 76n
Durkheim 44

Easy Rider 297
Economics and Statistics 307, 337n
Eden, Anthony (Lord Avon) 177, 208n
Édouard et Caroline 283
Education and class 31–2, 64, 71, 198–9, 285, 286–7, 300–1, 308, 348–9
Edwards, A. M. 61, 62, 77n
Eells, K. 23n
Effects of Depression, The (Dept of Labor) 209n
Eisenhower, Dwight D. 241, 284, 345
Elder, G. H., Jnr 23n
Eléments d'une doctrine radicale, Les (Charpentier) 141n
Élites and Power (Stanworth & Giddens, eds) 338n, 357n
Elliott, Walter 176–7
Encounter 279
End of Ideology, The (Bell) 303n
English Gentleman, The (Raven) 338n
English Journey (Priestley) 198

En habillant l'époque (Poiret) 141n
Entre deux guerres (Paul-Boncour) 208n
Equality (Tawney) 54, 57n
Erickson, Dr Charlotte 180–1, 208n
Essays in Labour History (Briggs & Saville, eds) 23n
Essai sur les problemes des classes sociales . . . (Bouriez-Gregg) 287n
Essays in Sociological Theory (Parsons) 23n
Estaing, Pres. Giscard d' 12, 298, 301, 304n, 329, 351
Etienne, Jacques 77n
evacuation 218–19
Evacuation . . . (Cosens) 230n
Eyres-Monsell, Sir B. 176

Faithless 147
Fanny 167
Fascisme et les paysans, Le (Archives Nationales) 141n
Father of the Bride 280
Femme du boulanger, La 167
Ferber, Edna 280
Ferré, Louise-Marie 46, 47, 48, 50, 55, 57n, 200, 209n, 260
Ferrie, William 160
Field, Shirley Anne 296
Figaro 11, 330–1, 332, 339n
First World War 55, 64, 67, 179, 187, 231–2, 344
Fisher, H. A. L. 158
Fisher, Sir Warren 179
Fisk, Charles 84
Fiske, Bess 96n
Flandin, Pierre-Etienne 186–7
Florence, P. Sargent 304n
Ford II, Henry 99
Ford, John 153
Fortune 105–7
Founding Father, The (Whalen) 126n
Fournière, Xavier de la 346, 357n
France, agricultural class 262, 269, 290, 301; anticlericalism in 28, 41; birthrate 232; bourgeoise class 42, 45–7, 49, 59, 128, 132–4, 137, 140, 183–4, 234–5, 257, 260–1, 271, 282, 285, 298–9,

360–1; Christian Democratic Party 239; class, and films 166–9, 240, 241, 293, 335–6; class, and power 183–90, 301; class, and war 231–41, 253; class images in 44–9, 72, 74, 128, 130–2, 136, 139, 140, 270–2, 360; class structure (*see also* bourgeoise) 59–60, 128–44, 166–9, 236, 238, 240, 257, 270–1, 307; *commerçants* 129, 131, 262–3; Communist Party 128, 184, 201, 233, 241, 263, 351; *Confédération française de professions* 128–9, 133, 141n, 142n; *Défense de France* 235–6; education in 31–2, 299, 300–1, 348; family, and class 260; Fascism in 132, 205; German occupation 231–4, 237–8, 253; housing 196, 285, 298, 352; immigrants in 28, 291; income levels 340–2; industrialization 33, 36, 140, 290, 302; *intellectuels* 128, 129, 137–9; language of class in 45–9; legislation in 46, 60, 72–6, 232, 300, 329; middle classes 12, 46, 48–9, 131–2, 183, 186, 187, 196, 206–7, 241, 257, 259, 263, 271, 284, 332; national census 59–60; National Resistance Council 236–7, 241; 'New Wave' films 293, 298; nobility in 137, 140, 330–2, 361; opinion polls in 129, 330; *ouvriers* 42, 45, 59, 128, 138, 139–41, 167, 235, 271–2, 329–30; patois, use of 200; peasant class in 45, 46, 47, 48, 49, 59, 129–32, 141, 201–2, 236, 238, 271, 299, 301; pensions 232; politics, and class 184–90, 201–2, 205, 241, 256, 257, 284, 346, 351–3; Popular Front 36, 39–40, 131, 136, 139, 184, 187, 188–9, 205–6, 241; proletariat in 48, 49, 132, 138, 139, 235, 271, 334; Radical Party 30, 134, 186, 201, 205, 241; religious groups in 28, 202; Resistance, and class 232–7, 241; Socialist Party 130, 184, 187, 205, 241, 263; social security in 46, 72, 269; strikes in 36, 352; trade unions in 33, 131, 235, 352; *travailleurs* 42, 48, 74, 128, 134, 235, 237, 330; upper class 30, 134–6, 183–4, 186, 188–9, 196, 204, 206, 232, 241, 284, 286, 330–2, 361; Vichy, and class 232, 240–1; war deprivation in 237–9; working class (*see also ouvriers*) 11, 33, 42, 45, 48, 72, 131, 132, 139–40, 141, 184, 196, 201–2, 205, 207, 234, 240, 259, 301

France (Dandelot & Froment-Meurice) 357n
France, Change and Tradition (Hoffmann) 254n
France et les Français (Remond & Bourdin, eds) 141n
France noble (de Negroni) 339n
François de Wendel . . . (Jeanneney) 189, 190, 208n
France sous l'occupation (Arnoult et al) 254n
Frankfurter, Felix 191
Franklin, S. D. 342, 357n
Fraser, D. 43n
Fraser, Sir Ian 158–9, 171n, 226
French Cinema since 1946 (Armes) 303n
French Historical Studies, Vol VII (Brooks) 171n: Vol II (Hoffmann) 254n
French Revolution 16, 17, 45, 131
French Society 1914–1945 (Prédal) 168, 171n
French Worker, The (Collinet) 263
Frère, Suzanne 20, 285, 289n
Friedman, L. M. 78n
Friedman, Milton 318
Friedman, Murray 292, 303n
Froment-Meurice, F. 357n
From Max Weber . . . (Gerth & Wright Mills) 23n
Front Populaire . . . (Nixon) 209n
Future of Socialism, The (Crosland) 267, 288n

Gallagher, Dan 43n
Gans, Herbert J. 306, 314, 337n
Gardner, B. B. 51, 57n
Gardner, M. R. 51, 57n

Garmy, René 141n
Gaudet, Hazel 209n
Gaulle, Charles de 232, 352, 353
Gautier, Marcel 289n
Gentlemen's Agreement 279–80
George, Lloyd 180
Gerth, H. H. 23n
Giant 280–1
Giddens, Anthony 17, 23n, 307, 309, 337n, 338n, 357n
Gifford, Denis 171n
Gillois, André 289n
Giono, Jean 167
Girard, Alain 209n, 289n
Giscard d'Estaing . . . (Fournière) 346, 357n
Glaiser, John Milton 292, 337n
Glass, Professor D. V. 267, 288n
Glenn, N. D. 23n
Goblot, Edmond 133–4, 141n
Goldschmidt, William 264–5, 285, 288n, 308
Goldthorpe, J. 324, 326, 338n, 339n, 349, 358n
Goldwater 345
Gomberg, William 303n
Governance of Medieval England (Richardson & Sayles) 23n
Government and Slum Housing (Friedman) 78n
Graduate, The 297
Grandes affaires françaises, Les 141n
Grandes familles, Les (Gillois) 289n
Grapes of Wrath, The 153
Green, M. 93, 97n
Green, W. 31, 248
Greenwood, A. 64
Grieg, Robert 154
Grémillion, Jean 166, 240
Grierson, John 282
Grigg, P. J. 97n
Guinea Pig, The 281, 289n, 296–7
Guttsman, W. L. 178, 208n, 289n

Haber, William 337n
Halbwachs, M. 47, 48, 49, 57n, 128, 141n
Halifax, Viscount 175, 176
Hall, Helen 52, 57n
Hall, J. R. 267, 288n

Halsey, A. H. 23n
Hamer, Robert 281
Harriman, Averill 192
Harrisson, Tom 165
Hatzfeld, Henri 77n
Havighurst, R. J. 126n, 254n
Heath, Edward 217, 342, 343, 354
Heath, William 343–4
Heath and the Heathmen (Roth) 357n
Here Comes the Groom 280
Heroes for sale 150
Herriot, Édouard 185–6
Hewitt, Christopher 357n
Hicks, G. 70
Hicks, J. R. 54–5, 58n
Hidden Injuries of Class (Sennett & Cobb) 306, 337n
hierarchies, multiple 256–7, 267; prestige 340
Higher Circles, The (Domhoff) 126n
Higher Civil Servants . . . (Kelsall) 208n
Hill, H. A. 77n
Hills, Judge 176
Hindle Wakes 169–70
Hiroshima, mon amour 293
His Excellency 281, 294–5
Histoire du front populaire (Lefranc) 142n
Histoire du paysan français (Walter) 238, 254n
History 23n
History of Broadcasting, The (Briggs) 171n
Hitler, Adolf 248–9
Hoare, Sir Samuel 175
Hobson, J. A. 39
Hoffmann, Professor Stanley 232, 239–40, 254n, 257
Hogan, J. D. 77n
Hoggart, Richard 292, 297, 303n
Holcombe, A. N. 53, 57n
Holiday 145
Homes the Public Builds (Wood & Ogg) 103–4, 126n
Hoover, Pres. Herbert 34, 72, 191
Hopper, Denis 297
Hotel du Nord 167
Howard, Michael 12, 23n

Howe, Irving 306, 337n
Hull, Cordell 192
Humphrey, Hubert 292
Hunt, W. C. 61
Hurry on Down (Wain) 303n
Hurst, Charles 358n
Hyde, H. Montgomery 91, 96, 97n

I am a Fugitive . . . 152
Ianni, F. A. J. 77n
Ickes, Harold L. 101, 126n, 191, 247
Idées politiques . . . (Michel & Mirkine-Guetzovitch) 254n
ideology, economic etc 37, 39–40, 41, 44, 302, 309, 317, 355–6
Illustrated 162
I'm All Right, Jack 294, 335
I'm for Roosevelt (Kennedy) 102, 126n
Industrial Democracy in GB (Coates & Topham) 289n
industrialization 16–17, 27, 33, 140, 242–3, 347, 359
industrial relations 32, 36, 37, 38, 116–17, 272, 326–7; violence in 35, 36–7, 116, 151
Industrial Revolution 16, 17, 79, 359
Inequality (Jencks) 304n
inflation, incidence of 302
In my Way (Brown) 303n
Insurgent America (Bingham) 52, 57n
Inventaires III . . . (Halbwachs) 58n
In Which We Serve 227
I Remember (Swinton) 208n
Isaacs, George 165
It Always Rains on Sunday 281–2, 295–6

Jackson, Alan 209n
Jackson, Brian 327–8, 339n
Jeanne, Marcel 289n
Jeanneney, Jean-Noël 189–90, 208n, 254n
Jencks, Christopher 304n
Jennings, W. Ivor 77n
Joad, C. E. M. 225
job consciousness 111–12, 250, 264, 273, 317

Joffroi 167
John Strachey (Thomas) 97n
Johnson, Lyndon 345
Johnson, R. W. 357n
Jolly, Jean 208n
Jones, B. Caradog 54, 57n, 157, 198, 266
Jones, Thomas 180, 208n, 288n
Jordan, Z. A. 23n
Journal of Economic History 208n
Journal of an Unemployed Intellectual (de Rougemont) 137, 142n
Journal of Urban History 127n
Jour, se lève, Le 167

Kahan, Michael 320, 338n
Kahl, Joseph 309, 337n
Karl Marx: . . . (Z. A. Jordan, ed.) 23n
Kavanagh, J. 351, 358n
Kearns, Doris 357n
Kedward, Dr H. R. 232, 254n
Keith, A. Barriedale 97n
Kilsall, R. K. 208n
Kennedy, John F. 345
Kennedy, Joseph 101–2, 126n, 192
Keynes, J. M. 39, 181, 208n
Kolko, Gabriel 207n, 209n
Korda, Alexander 167
Kornblum, William 348–9, 358n
Ku Klux Klan 152

Labor in a Changing America (Haber, ed.) 337n
Labour and the Left . . . (Pimlott) 209n
Labor and the New Deal (Public Affairs Cttee) 57n
Labor History 43n, 126n, 254n
Lacase-Duthiers, Gérard de 137–9, 142n, 272, 289n
Lady Eve, The 146
Lamarque, Gérard 303n
Lambert, R. S. 80, 83, 84, 87, 96n, 97n
Lansbury, George 84, 96n
Laroque, Pierre 257, 258–60, 263, 287n, 307, 337n
Larrow, Charles P. 289n
Lasswell, Thomas E. 306, 309, 317, 337n
Laumann, Edward O. 337n

Laval, Pierre 185
Law of Housing (Jennings) 77n
lawyers 108, 182, 193, 262, 269
Lazarsfeld, Paul 202, 209n
Lecarpentier, G. 58n, 209n
Lefebvre, Henri 330
Lefranc, Georges 142n
Leggatt, John C. 315, 338n
Lenski, Gerhard 228n, 308n, 337n
Léon Blum . . . (Prost) 142n
Léon Blum ou la République 254n
Levelling of Incomes, The (Crozier) 268
Leverhulme, Lord 182
Levittowners, The (Gans) 337n
Lewis, Edward G. 357n
Lewis, J. L. 31, 248
Lhomme, Jean 47, 57n, 58n, 140, 142n, 239, 254n
Liberal Yellow Book 87
Liddle Hart, Capt. 217–18
Life and Labour (Smith, ed.) 54
Lindsay, Katherine 323, 338n, 358n
Lipset, S. M. 23n, 307–8
Listener, The 80, 171n
Literature and History 288n
Lithgow, Sir James 181
Littlewood, Joan 163
Lloyd, T. H. 209n
Lockwood, D. 303n, 324, 326, 337n, 338n, 339n, 358n
Londonderry, Lord 94, 97n, 173
Loneliness of the Long Distance Runner 297
Lothian, Lord 101
Love on the Dole 170
Lowry, Edith E. 127n
Lumière d'été 240
Lunt, P. S. 57n
Lurie, Alison 338n
Lynd, H. and R. 44, 50, 57n, 265
Lyndon Johnson (Kearns) 357n
Lyons, J. 127n

Mabey, Richard 338n
McCann, Kevin 289n
McCarthy, Senator 275
McCrea, Joel 154
MacDonald, Malcolm 175
MacDonald, Ramsay 39, 173, 342
Maconachie, Sir Richard 159, 171n

Macmillan, Harold 219
Major Contemporary Social Problems (Laroque) 257
Mallet, Serge 292, 303n, 353
Manchester Guardian 230n
Manual-guide de l'artisan (Etienne & Beyl) 77n
Manuels et intellectuels (Lacaze-Duthiers) 142n
Marceau, Jane 357n
Mar esson, apt. 94, 97n
Marié, A. 357n
Marius 167
Marsden, Denis 327–8, 339n
Marshall, Professor T. H. 166
Martin, F. M. 270, 288n
Marwick, Professor Arthur 229n
Marx, Karl 18, 23n, 41, 44
Marxism 14, 15, 19, 36, 41, 47, 54, 62, 125, 128, 150, 152, 160, 213, 268, 352
Mavor, Ronald 176
Maxton, James 176
May, Timothy 342, 357n
Mayer, Kurt 209n, 288n
Meeker, M. 23n
Melchett, Lord 101
Mellors, Colin 357n
Memoirs (Nixon) 346, 357n
Memoirs of the Unemployed (Beales & Lambert) 96n, 97n
merchants 31, 48, 132
Meredith, Arnold 289n
Mérode, Cléo de 30, 42n
Métiers et main d'oeuvre (Gautier) 289n
Michel, Henri 236, 254n
Middle Class, The (Raynor) 15, 23n
Middle-Class Blacks . . . (Muraskin) 358n
Middle Class Families (Bell) 338n, 358n
Middle-Class Housing . . . (Simpson & Lloyd) 209
middle classes (*see also* under countries) 13, 16, 33, 76, 199, 346
Middle Classes, The (Bingham) 57n
Middletown . . . (H. & R. Lynd) 50, 57n, 299, 304n
Middletown in Transition . . . (H. & R. Lynd) 50, 57n

Miller, William 192, 208n, 214, 229n
Mills, C. Wright 23n
Minelli, Vincente 280
miners 34–5, 80–1, 85, 92, 150–1, 152, 247, 272, 335, 354
Mirepoix, M. le duc de Lévis 137, 142n
Mirkine-Guetzovitch, Boris 254n
Mitford, Nancy 279
Monckton, Sir Walter 94, 97n, 222–4
Monde, Le 358n
Morenas, Jougla de 137, 142n
Morgan, H. G. 126n, 254n
Morgenthau, Henry, Jnr 191
Morley, Professor Raymond 191
Morning and Noon (Acheson) 126n
Morrison, Herbert 221
Moser, C. A. 267, 288n
Mouvement de Mai, Le (Touraine) 358n
Movie-Made America (Sklar) 304n
Moyne, Lord 176
Moynihan, D. 292, 337n
Mr Deeds goes to Town 148
Mrs Dale's Diary 297
Mr Smith goes to Washington 149
Mulley, Fred 343
Muraskin, William A. 358n
Murcott, Anne 338n
Murphy, J. T. 97n

Nathan, Major H. L. 87, 97n
Nation, The 208n
National Income 1924, The (Bowley & Stamp) 58n
national insurance 64, 67–9
nationalism 291, 355
Nation française, La 288n
Navel, Georges 28, 42n
Negroni, François de 330–1, 339n
Neugarten, Bernice 313, 338n
Newcomer, Mabel 209n
New Deal 34, 38, 51, 52, 117, 122
New History of the United States, A (Miller) 229n
New Horizons (Murphy) 97n
New Society 357n
New Statesman 204, 209n

New Survey of London Life and Labour (Smith) 58n
New York Times 11, 293, 312, 314, 338n
Nichols, Mike 297
Nixon, Pres. Richard M. 241, 284, 310, 345–6, 357n
Nobility, The (Morenas) 137, 142n
Noble France (Negroni) 330
Notre Avant Guerre (Brasillach) 141n
Nouvelle classe ouvrière, La (Mallet) 303n
Nuffield, Lord 181

occupation, and class 13, 14, 41, 44, 59, 61, 63, 87–8, 104, 194, 267, 271, 287, 308, 309, 310
Occupation and Pay . . . (Seers & Routh) 289n
Occupations d'usine, Les (Prouteau) 142n
Ogg, Elizabeth 126n
Old Men Forget (Duff Cooper) 91, 97n
Origine sociale du personnel, L' (Dogan) 208n
Ormsby-Gore, W. 177
Orwell, George 198
Ossowski, S. 18, 23n
Ouvrier français . . . L' 288n
Overcoming Middle Class Rage (Friedman, ed.) 292, 303n
Ownership . . . (Florence) 304n

Packard, Vance 297–8, 304n
Pagnol, Marcel 166–7
Parkin, Frank 337n, 339n
Parodi, J.-C. 358n
Parsons, Talcott 18, 23n, 307
Paul-Boncour, Joseph 186, 208n
Pennock, Mrs Winthrop 250
Penrose, Boies 98
People's Choice, The (Lazarsfeld *et al*) 209n
Percy, Lord Eustace 177–8
Perkins, Frances 34, 38, 43n, 74, 103, 105, 108, 120, 191
Perlman, Selig 44, 264
Peters, Camille 131, 141n
Peto, G. 71

Philadelphia Gentleman (Baltzell)
  23n, 126n, 207n
Philadelphia Story 145
Pic, Paul 77n
Picture Post 162
Pimlott, Ben 209n
Pinky 279
Platinum Blonde 143
Platt, J. 324, 326, 338n, 339n, 358n
Poincaré, Raymond 189
Point du Jour, Le 282, 296, 335
Poiret, Paul 129, 141n
Polenberg, Richard 229n, 254n
politics, and religion 203
Pourquoi j'ai été exclu . . . (Garmy)
  141n
Pour sauver les classes moyennes
  (Clerc) 57n
Power, Persistence and Change
  (Stacey *et al*) 338n
Power and Privilege (Lenski) 308,
  337n
Précis de droit civil 76n
Précis de droit commercial 77n,
  288n
Précis de législation industrielle 76n
Prédal, René 168, 171n
Prejudice and Promise (Grigg) 97n
Preparez vos mouchoirs 336
Pres. Hoover's Organization for
  Unemployed Relief (POUR) 34,
  72
Priestley, J. B. 198, 217
Problème des classes, Le (Lhomme)
  57n, 58n
professional people 60, 61, 62, 72,
  75, 87, 96, 104, 107–8, 128–9,
  132, 166, 182, 193, 257, 262, 274,
  310
Profession hôtelière, La (Jeanne)
  289n
Professions, The (Carr-Saunders &
  Wilson) 88, 97n
Progress and Disillusionment (Aron)
  337n
Proletarians and Parties . . . (Ben-
  son) 23n
proletariat – *see under* France
Prospero and Ariel (Bridson) 171n
Prost, Antoine 142n
Proud Valley 170

Prouteau, Henri 142n
Psychology of Social Classes, The
  (Centers) 264, 270, 288n
Psychology of the Child (Davis)
  289n
Puaux, Gabriel 208n

Quai des brumes, Le 167
Quatre cents coups, Les 293

Railway Review 96n
Rainwater, Lee 309, 312, 316, 337n
Ransford, E. Edward 358n
Raper, A. 43n
Rathbone, Eleanor 65
Raven, Simon 321, 338n
Rawlins, A. B., Jnr 126n
Raynor, John 15, 23n
Reading, Lady 219
Rees, Goronwy 92–3, 97n
Régime democratique, La (Ripert)
  76n
Règle du jeu, La 167, 171n
Reid, Ivan 338n
Reiss, A. 288n
Reith, Sir John 158, 171n
religion, effects of 28, 203
Rémond, R. 141n, 142n
Renoir, Jean 166, 167, 168–9
*Report of Unemployment Insurance
  . . .* (Min. of Labour) 97n
Resistance in Vichy France (Ked-
  ward) 232–3
Resler, Henrietta 208n
Resnais, Alain 293
Responsibles, The (White) 289n
Réussite sociale en France, La 209n,
  289n
Reuther, Walter 274
Revue politique et parlémentaire
  58n, 209n
Revue socialiste, La 287n
Reynaud, Paul 187–8, 208n
Richardson, H. G. 18, 23n
Richardson, Tom 297
Riesz, Karl 296
Ripert, Georges 76n, 77n
Rippon, Geoffrey 344
Riverdale, Baron 182
Road to Wigan Pier, The 91
Road to 1945 (Addison) 23n

Robinson, Mary V. 40
Rogoff, Natalie 270, 288n
Roosevelt, Mrs E. 39, 105, 108, 120
Roosevelt, Pres. 31, 35, 38, 72–4, 150; and class identity 98–103, 191, 205
Ross, A. A. 23n
Ross, Professor A. S. C. 279
Roth, Andrew 344, 357n
Rouest, André 76n
Rougemont, Denis de 137, 142n
Routh, Guy 289n
Rovere, Richard 289n
Rowse, A. L. 93
Roy, J. 23n
Ruling Class, The (Aaronovitch) 288n
Runciman, W. G. 15, 16, 23n, 89, 176

Sadoul, Georges 303n
Saenger, Gerhart E. 121
Saillaut, Louis 241
Salengro, Roger 168
Samples from English Culture (Bott) 289n
Sarraut, Albert 186
Saturday Night and Sunday Morning 296
Saville, J. 23n
Sayles, G. O. 18, 23n
Scotland, housing in 66, 197; upper class in 363
Seabrook, Jeremy 328, 339n
Second Survey of South Bend, A 209n
Scase, Richard 339n
Schidlow, Joshka 339n
Second World War 63, 162, 213–55, 300, 302
Secret Diary of H. L. Ickes 126n
Seeman, Melvin 358n
Seers, Dudley 289n
Semaines sociales de France XXXI 57n
Semi-detached London . . . (Jackson) 209n
Senator Joe McCarthy (Rovere) 289n
Sennett, Richard 306–7, 337n, 338n

Seydell, Mildred 105, 118, 126n, 127n
Shawcross, Hartley, MP 277
Shipbuilders, The 227
Shipbuilders, The (Blake) 230n
shopworkers 13, 139, 166
Shostack, Arthur B. 303n
Shotwell, Velma 127n
Siegfried, André 142n
Sight and Sound 43n
Silbermann, Charles 354, 358n
Silence de la mer, Le (Vercors) 231, 254n
Sillitoe, Alan 296
Simiand, F. 44–6, 49, 57n
Simon, H. 48, 49
Simon, Sir John 174–5
Simpson, M. A. 209n
Sklar, Robert 304n
Slump, The (Stevenson & Cook) 209n
Smith, H. Llewellyn 58n
Smith, J. D. 342, 357n
Social Analysis (Parkin, ed.) 339n
Social Class Differences . . . (Reid) 338n
social classes (*see also under* class) 19–20, 44–9, 50–3, 62, 203, 256, 266
Social Classes (Laroque) 307
Social Classes in Contemporary France (Ferré) 46, 57n
Social Class in America (Aron) 337n
Social Class in America (Warner, Meeker, Fels) 16, 23n
Social Conditions in Britain 209n
Social Framework, The (Hicks) 58n
Social History of a War-Boom Community (Havighurst & Morgan) 126n, 254n
social legislation – *see under* countries
Social Life of a Modern Community (Warner & Lunt) 57n
Social Mobility in Britain (Moser & Hall) 288n
Social Science . . . (Runciman) 23n
social security (*see also* under countries) 38, 68–70, 72, 216, 221, 268–9

Social Standing in America (Coleman & Rainwater) 337n
Social Trends 319
Social Status of Negroes, The 310
society, classless 18, 91, 252, 310, 329
socio-economic groups 13, 61–2, 104, 202–3, 256
Sociological Review 337n
Sondages 141n
Souvenirs d'en France 335
Speak for England (Bragg) 86, 97n, 209n
Spectator, The 279
'spiralists' 309
Spring Handicap 169
Stacey, Margaret 285–6, 289n, 296, 309, 338n, 360
Stamp, J. 54, 58n
Stanley, Oliver 177
Stanworth, Peter 338n, 357n
Stars Look Down 170
Status Seekers, The (Packard) 297–8, 304n
Status System . . . The (Warner & Lunt) 57n
Steinbeck, J. 153
Sterner, James E. 254n
Stevens, George 280
Stevenson, John 209n
Stimson, Henry L. 192
Stokes, Donald 320, 338n
Stonehaven, Lord 101
Strachey, John 93, 97n
stratification, social 15, 259, 264, 305, 307–8
Strike in the American Novel, The (Blake) 156n
strikes 37, 84, 118, 139–40, 205, 206, 247, 272, 302, 352, 354
Structure and Growth of Residential Neighborhoods 195
Sturgess, Preston 146, 154
Sullivan's Travels 154
Survey of the Social Structure of England and Wales (Carr-Saunders & Jones) 54, 57n, 267, 288n
Swinton, Viscount 208n
Swope, Gerard 191

Taft, Robert 284
Tales of Americans on Trek (Lowry et al) 125, 127n
Tardieu, André 184–5
Tawney, R. H. 54, 57n
Taylor, A. J. P. 11
teachers 62, 68–9, 74, 87, 88, 109, 182
Templewood, Lord 176
Temps, Le 133, 185
Terkel, Studs 315, 338n
Thatcher, Margaret 342, 344–5
Theory of the Labor Movement (Perlman) 44, 264
They Drive by Night 169
Thomas, Hugh 97n
Thomas, J. H. 92, 175
Time 310–11, 338n
Times, The 171n, 224, 230n, 338n, 344, 357n
Tirez sur le pianiste 293
titles, incidence of 30, 329–31
Titmuss, R. M. 209n
Tomlinson, George 85, 91, 92, 96n
Topham, A. J. 289n
Touraine, Alain 334, 339n, 352, 358n
Towards a New Democracy (d'Estaing) 304n
Tradition and Change (Stacey) 289n
Traité élémentaire de legislation . . . (Pic) 77n
Travaux (Navel) 42n
Trenchard, Lord 93
Truffaut, François 293
Truman, Pres. Harry 12, 248, 252, 284
Tully, J. C. 23n

Unemployed Worker, The (Bakke) 52, 57n
unemployment, compensation 38, 64, 67–8, 88, 183, 205; incidence of 34–5, 51–2, 59, 68, 72, 81–3, 117, 183, 205, 206
Unemployment Insurance Acts 68, 69, 183
UNESCO 271
Une ville française (Bettelheim & Frère) 289n

United States, agricultural workers in 33, 61, 73, 75, 274, 291–2, 310, 316, 341; anti-Semitism 245, 279–80; businessmen, and class 192–3, 274; Civil Rights Movement 274, 291, 292; class, and power 190–2, 265, 284; class, and television 317–18; class, and war 241–53; class images in 49–53, 74–5, 98–127, 148, 248, 270, 272–5, 310–18; class mixing in 242–5, 312; class mobility 241, 244; class structure 61–2, 72, 105, 143–56, 242, 259, 270, 285, 291, 306, 310–18; class, and colour 28–9, 32, 62, 75, 123–4, 195–6, 206, 291, 301, 310, 315, 354; Congress (Cttee) of Industrial Organization 31, 34, 52, 116, 206, 244, 249, 253, 302, 347; Democratic Party 99, 203, 314, 345–6, 351; Depression 105, 118, 125, 147, 152, 191–2, 251; domestic workers in 35, 39, 40, 41, 61, 73, 75, 108–9, 119–22, 125–6, 250–1; education in 32, 300; egalitarianism in 259, 300; English accent 143–4, 147, 154; ethnics and race 28–9, 62, 75, 122–6, 150, 152, 195–6, 252–3, 274, 279, 291, 315, 354; Hollywood, and class 143–55, 248, 318; housing in 76, 103–4, 195–6, 242–3; immigrant labor 29, 125, 152, 274; income levels 340–2; industrialization 27, 28, 33, 34, 35–6; industrial relations 37, 116–17, 242, 273; Ivy League 32, 98, 249, 301; Junior Leagues 250–1; Labor, Dept. of 36, 40, 117, 120, 209n, 270, 274, 288n; Labor Relations Act 151; ladies' clubs 99, 103–4, 249–50; language of class 53, 73–4, 98, 116–17, 247–8, 303, 316, 360; legislation 52, 72–6, 108, 109, 151, 192, 250–1, 300; Middle America 292–3, 360; middle classes in 50, 51–3, 56, 106–8, 190–5, 261, 284, 313, 316; National Archives 42n, 43n, 77n, 78n, 120, 126n, 127n, 251; national census 13, 60–2, 310, 338n; pensions 74; politics, and class 99–103, 206, 252, 284, 345, 347, 351; private insurance 115; proletariat 261, 266; religion, and class 28, 203; Republican Party 99, 191, 203, 314; rioting in 354; social registers 98–9, 191, 313; social security 38, 108, 250–2, 310; Social Security Act 74, 75, 102, 109; Social Security Board 74, 75, 78n, 251; trade unions 33–4, 36, 52, 116, 191–2, 206, 244, 247–9, 253, 270, 272–4, 302; unemployment insurance 74; under-class 152–5, 195–6, 292, 316; upper class 30, 50, 51, 53, 98–105, 143–4, 146–7, 149, 150, 151, 153–4, 190–2, 195, 274–5, 284, 312–13; wages 247; Wagner Housing Act 76; Willow Run factory 242–4; working class 50–2, 73, 76, 106–7, 110–11, 113–15, 117, 119–22, 150–2, 191–2, 196, 206, 246–7, 253, 266, 316–17, 361
upper classes (*see also under* countries) 12–13, 172, 199, 346–7, 60
Uses of Literacy, The (Hoggart) 292, 303n

Vansittart, Sir Robert 180
Vaucher, P. 56, 58n
Veblen, T. 44
Vital Majority . . . The 310
Voice of Labour, The 228
Voices from the Middle Class (Deverson & Lindsay) 338n, 358n
Voix de France, La (Bombardier) 339n
Vraie vie des Français (Arbois & Schidlow) 339n

wages 193, 216, 237–8, 247, 341
Wages and Income in the UK (Bowley) 58n
Wagner, Senator Robert 76, 251
Wain, John 303n
Walter, Gerard 238, 254n

Walter P. Reuther (Christmas, ed.)
289n
War and Social Change . . . (Marwick) 229n
War and Society (Bond & Roy, eds)
23n
War and Society (Polemberg) 229n,
254n
War between the Tates, The (Lurie)
338n
Warner, W. Lloyd 16, 18, 23n,
50–1, 57n, 260, 265
Wartime Shipyard (Archibald) 254n
Watch-Maker of St Martin, The 336
Watt, R. J. 43n
wealth, distribution of 341–2
Wealth and Power in America (Kolko) 207n
Weber, Max 15, 18, 44
Weil, Simone 140
Weill-Raynal, Etienne 262–3, 271
Wellman, William 150
Wendel, François de 188, 189–90
Went the Day Well 227
We're in the Money (Bergman) 156n
Werth, Alexander 168
Westergaard, J. 208n
Western Political Quarterly 357n
Whalen, R. J. 126n
What Went Wrong? (Seabrook)
339n
White, Dana F. 127n
White, Helen 127n
White, William 289n
Whitehall Diary (Jones) 208n
Whitelaw, William 344
Who Rules America? (Domhoff)
207n
Wilenski, Harold L. 306, 337n
Wilkinson, Ellen 219
Wilkinson, R. 208n
Williams, Emlyn 169
Williams, Dr Philip 231–2, 254n
Williams, Raymond 23n
Williams, Robert 143
Willow Run . . . (Carr & Sterner)
254n
Wilson, Sir Harold 342
Wilson, Sir Horace 179
Wilson, P. A. 88, 97n
Winant, J. G. 191

*Winchester and the Public School
Elite* (Bishop & Wilkinson) 208n
Winterton, E. 176
Witte, Edwin E. 75, 77n, 78n, 102,
126n
women 99, 103, 228, 285, 311, 345
Women's Voluntary Service 218–19
Wood, David 344, 357n
Wood, Edith E. 126n
Wood, Sir Kingsley 177
Woodin, William H. 191
workers, artisans 31, 45, 47, 48, 64,
66, 81, 104, 128, 132–3, 141, 166,
167, 257, 262, 269; blue-collar
75, 292, 310, 311, 314, 316, 341;
manual 13, 42, 45, 59, 60, 67–9,
80–5, 128, 138, 139–41, 193,
266, 287, 319, 341, 352; semi-
skilled 61, 62; skilled 48, 61, 62,
81, 84, 151, 271, 349; unskilled
62, 63, 81, 115, 340; white-collar
31, 45, 46, 47, 52, 59, 60, 61, 88,
96, 109, 132, 138, 182, 271, 273,
290, 310, 313, 316, 330, 341, 352,
355
Working (Terkel) 338n
Working Class Community (Jackson & Marsden) 327–8, 339n
Working-Class Consciousness, The
(Touraine) 334, 339n
Working classes (*see also under
countries*) 12, 13, 15–16, 29, 46,
48, 49, 96, 194, 199, 213, 346–7,
361, 363; housing for 64–7, 70,
195–8, 269; promotion in 326–7;
power of 347; support from other
classes 216, 218–19
Working Class Home, The (Board
of Trade) 67
Working for Food (Beynon) 339n
*World of the Blue-Collar Worker,
The* (Howe, ed.) 306, 337n
Wrong, Dennis H. 306, 337n
Wynn, Neil A. 229n

Xydias, N. 288n

Yank at Oxford, A 170
You Can't Take it With You 147
Ysmal, C. 358n

Zick, R. 23n